POETS OF
THE MINNESANG

Heinrich von Veldeke: MS. C, fol. 30ʳ

POETS OF
THE MINNESANG

EDITED WITH INTRODUCTION
NOTES AND GLOSSARY

BY

OLIVE SAYCE

Fellow and Tutor of
Somerville College

OXFORD
AT THE CLARENDON PRESS
1967

Oxford University Press, Ely House, London W. 1

GLASGOW NEW YORK TORONTO MELBOURNE WELLINGTON
CAPE TOWN SALISBURY IBADAN NAIROBI LUSAKA ADDIS ABABA
BOMBAY CALCUTTA MADRAS KARACHI LAHORE DACCA
KUALA LUMPUR HONG KONG TOKYO

© *Oxford University Press 1967*

PRINTED IN GREAT BRITAIN

PREFACE

I T is the aim of this edition to provide a representative survey of the lyric poetry written in Germany, Austria, and Switzerland during the period 1150–1400. This is usually known collectively as the *Minnesang*, since it treats predominantly, but not exclusively, themes of *minne*. The mass of extant material and the proliferation of separate editions and critical works makes some such selection desirable as an introduction to the subject. My thanks are due to colleagues with whom I have discussed points of difficulty, in particular Miss R. Harvey and Mr. P. F. Ganz, who has also generously read the proofs; to the Librarian of the Taylorian, Mr. D. M. Sutherland, for his unfailing helpfulness; and to the Leverhulme Trustees for financial assistance. Above all I wish to record my gratitude to my husband for his advice and encouragement.

OLIVE SAYCE

TABLE OF CONTENTS

LIST OF PLATES

INTRODUCTION

THE DEVELOPMENT OF THE LYRIC
1150–1400

THE dating of the most archaic anonymous poems and the earliest named poets is uncertain, but the earliest no doubt go back to at least mid-twelfth century. The evidence of the early Austro-Bavarian poets and the most archaic of the anonymous songs suggests that there was a native tradition of the lyric which was later overlaid with features borrowed from the Romance courtly lyric. (See the section on the conventions.) The pre-courtly survivals in Romance literature, in particular the *cantigas de amigo* of the Galician-Portuguese lyric, which have affinities with the German woman's monologue, also serve to confirm the view that there was an anterior tradition, independent of the courtly one.

Original features of this native tradition appear to have been: the woman's monologue, often in the form of a complaint of desertion, parting or envious rivals, the *Wechsel*, and the dawn song (a type common to many literatures). The relationship between the lovers is an equal one, or the woman is shown in a submissive and suppliant role. Formally these early poems are simple, made up of eight-beat or four-beat lines, rhyming only in couplets, with a high proportion of assonating rhymes, and predominantly monostrophic.

In Anonymous 1–8 there are no traces of features extraneous to this tradition, whereas 9, although it represents an early type of dawn song in a natural setting, without the figure of the watchman, is formally more polished and is already influenced by the idea of the woman's power to command (l. 8). Kürenberc, Dietmar, and to a lesser extent Meinloh are still within the early tradition, but there are new features: in Kürenberc the submissive role of the man in 17 and 19, the mention of *merker* in 11, and *lugenære* in 16, the indication that the poet sang his songs to a musical accompaniment in 12; in Dietmar, the man's submissiveness in 23, the torments and sleeplessness of love in 21, the improving effect of love in 23. These courtly features are considerably increased in Meinloh, in whom there is a discrepancy

between the more archaic *Frauenstrophen* and the more 'modern'
Männerstrophen. Apart from the *merkære*, and the pains of love,
as in **27**, Meinloh introduces the ideas of the lady's supreme perfection and her sovereign power, and for the first time uses the
terms *dienest* and *dienen*. There is no doubt that Meinloh has
heard of the cult of love and its conventions, and it seems as if
distant echoes of it have reached even the two earliest poets, but
in none of them is there anything but the simplest metrical
forms.

Kaiser Heinrich has a mixture of old and new in themes, but
for the first time can be seen the formal influence of the Romance
lyric, in the adoption of a tripartite structure and more complicated rhyme schemes. With the next group of poets from Veldeke
to Reinmar the fashionable cult of courtly love is firmly established, with, however, the occasional persistence of earlier types
such as the *Wechsel*, depicting an equal relationship between the
lovers. In all these poets there are instances of direct borrowings
of substance or form from Romance poets. More important than
individual correspondences, however, is the all-pervasive influence of the new ideas. Once these become widespread in Germany, towards the end of the twelfth century, there is no longer
any need for direct models.

From Reinmar onwards there is a less homogeneous tradition
in the lyric, with new developments towards didacticism, a semblance of greater realism, and a much increased technical virtuosity. Walther is unique in the range which his poetry covers—
religious, didactic, and political themes, as well as those of *minne*.
In the latter he is expert at speaking with different voices, as in
the exposition of the immoderate nature of love which brings
grief in **97**, in the demand for a shared relationship in **98–100**,
or the depiction of idyllic pastoral scenes in **103** and **104**. Critics
have been tempted to see in these different manners the expression of a variety of personal experiences, but they are the product
of creative fertility and not of autobiography. Walther himself
makes it sufficiently clear in **94** and **108.** 7–8, that poetry is a
métier with certain prescribed themes. His great achievement
was to infuse new variety into the treatment of *minne*, and to
widen the bounds of lyric poetry.

Wolfram too is unique in his original treatment of the dawn
song and the freshness of expression and imagery in all his

poems. It is clear that the narrative genre of the dawn song suited his particular talents better than the lyric proper.

With Neidhart there begins what may be called a pseudo-realistic trend, in the depiction of village scenes and festivals. The impression is one of greater precision and particularization, but the picture is highly stylized and selective. Side by side with this new element Neidhart retains many of the conventions of the service of love, often with satiric intent. Poems in Neidhart's manner are found also among the later poets (**134, 136, 164, 166**). The mixture of courtly convention with a greater apparent realism is seen also in Steinmar and Hadlaub, in the former in the incongruous contrast between traditional themes and phraseology and deliberately comic elements in **157–9**, in the latter in the juxtaposition of complaints of hopeless love in the usual manner with more realistic descriptions—of domestic care in **162**, of autumnal delights of food and drink in **165**, and of village festivities in **166**.

Those poets of the later period who still continue to treat the well-worn themes of *minne* after the earlier manner tend to devote increasing importance to technical brilliance—thus in a poet such as Gottfried von Neifen the form outweighs the content, and in Frauenlob the chief preoccupation appears to be with intricacy of expression, ornament, and structure.

TROUBADOURS AND TROUVÈRES

The troubadours are the lyric poets of the south of France, writing in the *langue d'oc* (Old Provençal). They are usually, for linguistic reasons, referred to collectively as Provençal poets although they include poets from Poitou, the Limousin, Auvergne, and Périgord, as well as Provence proper. Guillaume IX, Duke of Aquitaine, Count of Poitiers, 1071–1127, is the first troubadour whose work has survived. In his six extant poems are already found certain of the ideas of the courtly service of love, side by side with other themes. To the first half of the twelfth century belong also Jaufre Rudel and Marcabrun. There is no evidence that these early poets had any direct influence on the *Minnesänger*.

Among the troubadours of the second half of the twelfth century and beginning of the thirteenth century are those who appear

to have influenced certain German poems directly, either in subject matter or form or both: Bernart de Ventadour, Bertran de
Born, Peire Vidal, Gaucelm Faidit, and Folquet de Marseille.

The trouvères are the poets of northern France whose art is
derived from the troubadours. The earliest known trouvère is
probably Chrétien de Troyes, writing about 1160. His work
together with that of Conon de Béthune, Gace Brulé, Guiot de
Provins, and Blondel de Nesle has left specific traces on certain
German poems. As Frank shows, the incidence of trouvère influence is higher than that of the troubadours—thus Friedrich
von Hausen shows direct knowledge of six trouvère poems, but
of only one troubadour poem.

In addition to close textual or formal parallels there is also
a widely diffused general influence of the Romance lyric, as a
result of which its conventions, its commonplaces and images,
and its formal structure became known in Germany.

It is not surprising that direct Romance influence is clearly
seen in those poets geographically most accessible to it—Heinrich von Veldeke in Limburg, Friedrich von Hausen near Worms,
Reinmar in Alsace, and Rudolf von Fenis in western Switzerland. The wide diffusion of the influence, however, is shown by
the fact that Heinrich von Morungen in Thuringia, Albrecht
von Johansdorf in Bavaria, and Hartmann von Aue in Swabia
give clear evidence of it, and there are faint echoes to be heard
even in the earliest Austro-Bavarian poets.

There were many possibilities of contact between French and
German poets at a time when the kingdom of Arles (Provence
and Burgundy) belonged, albeit nominally, to the Holy Roman
Empire, and when the Imperial court frequently resided near
the confines of French territory, at Worms, Mainz, and Maastricht. Poets such as Heinrich von Veldeke and Friedrich von
Hausen had ample opportunity to meet troubadour and trouvère
poets on occasions such as the great festival at Mainz in 1184,
at which, as a chronicler remarks, men of many nations and
tongues were gathered together.

THE CONVENTIONS

The chief conventions of courtly love, as they are found in
troubadours, trouvères, and *Minnesänger* alike, are already

hinted at in the earliest named poets, but are seen most clearly from Meinloh onwards. The relationship between the man and the lady is interpreted in feudal terms as a parallel to that between vassal and lord. The lady is the *frouwe*, as in **64.** 8–9, the lover the *man*, who owes her humble allegiance. This transfer is seen even more clearly in Old Provençal, in which the masculine appellation *midons* ('my lord') may be also used of the lady. Just as in feudal terminology *holt* is used in a double sense referring to the reciprocal relation between vassal and overlord, so too in the lyric it can refer either to the man's submissiveness, as for instance in **31.** 1, or to the lady's gracious condescension as in **127.** 11. The man hopes to win the lady's *hulde* or *genâde*. His devotion to her in the hope of reward is described in terms of a feudal contract, in which service (*dienst*) merits reward (*lôn*). The service of love induces a state of particular exaltation (*hôher muot*), and has an improving effect on the man—both these ideas are combined in **61.** 42. *Hôher muot* is not, however, identical with happiness, and since the lover's hopes are usually unfulfilled, love is the cause of much grief (variously described as *leit*, *sorge*, *trûren*, *kumber*, or *ungemüete*) and is a malady which robs a man of his senses (**47.** 5; **52.** 5 f.; **98.** 27), and of his sleep (**21.** 19 f.).

Apart from the two chief protagonists, the hostile outer world is frequently mentioned, either in the form of envious rivals, as in **5**, **33**, and **36**, or society in general (*liute* **10**, **28**; *welt* **86.** 5), or more particularly *lügenære* or *merkære*. The latter are spies and calumniators who attempt to disrupt the love relationship. Although the original meaning of *merkære* is 'spy', 'watcher', as its use in contexts outside the *Minnesang* makes clear, the close association with *lügenære*, as in **11.** 6 and **16.** 5 in which the two words have the same meaning, and the frequent mention of envy and calumny in connexion with the *merkære* make it virtually certain that the meaning has been influenced by Old Provençal *lauzengier*, Old French *losengeor*. The primary meaning of *lauzengier* is 'liar', 'slanderer', 'calumniator', in keeping with the probable derivation from a Germanic word **lausunga*, 'lie'. Alternative designations for the same figure in Old Provençal are *enveyos* and *gelos*, and in Old French *mesdisant*, 'slanderer'. Although the figure of the hostile critic is no doubt a motif of universal currency, as other literatures testify, the particular specialized form which it takes in the French and German courtly lyric, and the close similarity of meaning and association in the terminology found in both suggest that the figure of the *merkære* has been influenced by its Romance counterpart. Another term used frequently in connexion with the *merkære* is *huote*. The primary meaning is 'guard' or 'watch' and refers to their activity as the custodians of correct behaviour, as in **45.** 7–8, but it can also designate collectively the *merkære* themselves, as in **51.** 25 f. A further meaning of *huote* is the guard the lady imposes on herself, as in **100.** 9 and **139.** 23.

GENRES AND TYPES

Wechsel *and dialogue*

The so-called *Wechsel*, loosely connected strophes spoken by the man and woman respectively, in a kind of echoing exchange, is common, particularly among the early poets. The lovers do not address each other directly, but speak in monologue, or sometimes in address to a messenger. A good example of the simplest type is Kaiser Heinrich **36**. It consists of two monologues, the first spoken by the man, the second by the lady, both expressing joy in shared love. There is no direct link between the strophes, but it is clear that they refer to the same situation, and they are bound into one whole by the metrical form. Nos. **24** and **48** follow a similar pattern. A more complex structure, with two pairs of echoing monologues, is found in **66**, **70**, and **83**. In **10** and **22** the speeches of the man and woman are more closely linked by the address to the messenger.

Dialogue proper is common in the narrative genres such as the dawn song (e.g. Anonymous **9** and Wolfram **116**) and the village scenes of Neidhart and his imitators. A particular type of argumentative dialogue occurs for the first time in Albreht von Johansdorf **61**. This is modelled on a Provençal poem, which is an instance of the type known as the *tenson* or debate, often taking the form of a debate between lovers. Ulrich von Liechtenstein **140** is similar. Walther puts the same form to different use in **109**.

The Woman's Monologue and Complaint

It is characteristic of many of the early poems that they present the woman's point of view. Roughly half of all the poems in the

selection up to and including Kaiser Heinrich are either wholly
or in part monologues spoken by the woman, including those set
in the framework of the *Wechsel* (q.v.). The majority of them are
of the type known as *Frauenklagen*, in which the woman complains of separation, desertion, or envious rivals and ill-wishers.
After the establishment of the conventions of courtly love this
type virtually disappears, except in the dawn song, in which the
woman's complaint at parting is a persistent feature.

After Kaiser Heinrich there are, apart from examples of the
dawn song, only a handful of poems which purport to present
the woman's viewpoint. Two of these are *Wechsel* (**66** and **83**),
and the parallel monologues of man and woman in Veldeke **38**
and **39** are, as it were, an extension of the *Wechsel* into two
separate poems, although the attitude of the woman is now entirely different, showing clearly the new conventions. In **62** the
woman's complaint is given the new form of a lament for the
departing Crusader. In **90** Reinmar uses the monologue, disguised as an address to the messenger, to portray the woman's
conflicting feelings.

The Dawn Song

The type of poem describing lovers' meeting, and parting at
dawn is common to many literatures. The earliest variety, also
attested in the Romance lyric, is that in which the lovers meet
in a natural setting and are awakened by bird song at dawn, as
in **9**. In later examples of the genre it is the watchman who
awakens the lovers. This feature, together with the occurrence
of a refrain in the dawn song or related types, is probably borrowed from France.

There are seven dawn songs proper in the selection (**9**, **115-18**,
150, **163**), all without refrains. In all except **9** and **118**, the watchman occurs, and in **163** the whole poem is spoken by him. Wol-
fram is without doubt the greatest exponent of the genre. There
are in addition other poems which have close affinities with the
dawn song, either in general situation or particular motifs (**1**,
24, **37**, **66**, **70**, **104**). In **66** and **70** these motifs occur in the framework of the *Wechsel*.

In other poems there are allusions to the dawn song, usually
for a particular purpose. Thus in **133** and **146** the poets refer to
the conventions of the dawn song in order to point the contrast

between their own sufferings and the happiness of more fortunate lovers. In **133**, the refrain and the last verse, which is a woman's farewell to the knight at parting, reinforce the allusion. In **119** Wolfram rejects the conventions of the dawn song to praise instead love within marriage. No. **152** refers in a general way to the situation of the dawn song. Finally, **159** is a deliberate parody of the genre.

The Address to the Messenger

A fairly common convention is the address to the messenger. The whole poem may be addressed to or spoken by the messenger, as in **27, 34, 90**. The address to the messenger may also form a link between the speeches in the *Wechsel*, as in **10** and **22**. In other poems reference is made to the convention, as in **19, 88.** 5, and Neidhart **121**. The latter instance makes it clear (in lines 50–51) that it is merely a fiction and a convenient device for the depiction of emotions. In **75** Hartmann speaks of his song as the messenger to the lady.

The Crusading Song

This may treat various themes, either separately or in combination: the exhortation to a Crusade and arguments in favour of undertaking it, as in **58, 62**, and **78** (cf. also **110**); the conflict between worldly love and the Crusader's obligations as in **53, 54, 58, 62**, and **81**. The Crusader's departure provides a new setting for the woman's complaint in **62**. Neidhart gives a characteristically unidealized picture of the hardships of the Crusader's lot in **121**.

THE NATURE INTRODUCTION

The depiction of nature and the seasons is a common introductory topos, of frequent occurrence also in the Romance lyric. Only two seasons are usually mentioned, summer and winter, though a new genre of autumn song originates with the later poets (cf. **165**). The attributes of the seasons are stereotyped and the same general elements occur again and again: *walt, loup, heide, gras, bluomen, vogel*. Greater precision is rare: only *rōse, linde, nahtegal, meie* are fairly common. The mention of *aprille, būken, merelāre* in Veldeke is unusual.

The natural setting and the season have symbolic significance, summer being identical with joy, winter with sadness. This is made particularly clear by instances such as Anonymous **4** and **6**, in which *sumerwunne* is virtually equated with joy in love, or by the identification of winter and grief in Hartmann **73. 3**. The poets express feelings either in harmony or at variance with the season. This correspondence or contrast is either implicitly present or explicitly stated. An example of the simplest type, in which mere juxtaposition points the contrast between the natural setting and the emotions of the speaker is Anonymous **1**. In other poems a connexion is expressly stated as in **6**. 1–5.

The nature introduction is common among the early poets up to and including Veldeke. In the middle period it becomes rare but appears again later. Wolfram makes characteristically original use of it in **114**: syntax and vocabulary are unconventional, and the nature introduction serves not as a mere parallel to the poet's emotions but in order to commend his song: the birds are silenced in winter but he sings unceasingly in praise of the lady. In Neidhart the nature introduction is both an element of realistic description of the setting, and of symbolic significance.

IMAGERY

The most numerous group of images is drawn from natural phenomena. They may take the form of straightforward simile as in **138**:

> Si gelīchet sich der sunnen
> diu den sternen nimt ir schīn . . .

or of metaphor, as in **68**:

> Wā ist nu hin   mīn liehter morgensterne ?
> Wē waz hilfet mich   daz mīn sunne ist ūf gegān ?

A further development is that to symbol, as in **15**, in which the falcon symbolizes the lover.

Images of sun, moon, stars, and fire are frequent, and are a type particularly characteristic of Morungen. Images derived from falconry, bird-snaring, and the chase are also common, as in **5**, **20**, **113**, **134**, **137**, **138**, **148**, and **156**. Traditional or bestiary lore is the source of other animal images as in the central section of **91**, and in **135**. Steinmar uses the similes of pig and dragon in **157** with deliberate humorous intent.

There is an important complex of images associated with the heart. *Herze* is personified and opposed to *līp* as in **53**. It is the lady's servitor (**50.** 17). It is likened to a hermit's cell (**44.** 19, **153.** 1), and a shrine or coffer (**91.** 15–19, **167.** 9), and is locked by a key (**8**). It is the dwelling-place of the loved one (**35.** 17, **116.** 31–32) or of Love (**62.** 17); the lady's image is imprinted upon it (**137.** 26–28). A further development of this idea is the exchange of hearts, as in **150.** 25–27.

A further numerous group of images is that concerned with power, vassalage, and warfare. Success in love is likened to the enjoyment of the highest power (**35.** 8–9; **41.** 15; **69.** 1), or is accounted superior to it (**3**; **35.** 22 f.) The relationship between the man and the lady is expressed in terms of a feudal contract between vassal and overlord, in which service hopes for reward. The lady thus exercises absolute sway over the man's heart:

> Si gebiutet und ist in dem herzen mīn
> Frowe und hērer danne ich selbe sī.   (**64.** 8–9)

The metaphorical use of *krōne*, as in **63.** 12 and of *küneginne*, as in **82.** 27 serve also to express the lady's sovereign power. To the same complex belongs the idea of warfare, as **77** makes clear, in which images of power, feudal tribute, and warfare are combined in one whole. Love takes its victims captive (**62.** 11), imprisoning them in fetters (**144.** 32). The lady or Love inflict wounds (**149.** 14; **151.** 11); Love's darts are shot from the lady's eyes to wound the heart (**147.** 8).

The personification of *Minne* under Romance influence is common from Veldeke onwards. Other instances of personification are largely confined to Walther, for whom it is a characteristic device: *frowe Māze* (**97**), *frō Welt* (**109**), or the personification of abstractions in the image of highway robbery in **91**.

Symbolism is more common in the didactic poems: examples are the symbolic attributes *cirkel, weise, swert, stōle* in **91**, *krōne* in **92**, the overt symbolical interpretation of earthly things in **154**, the symbolic clothing of virtue in **130** and **151**. There is an instance of sustained allegory in **160**, in which both the narrative and the details of the natural setting have a deeper significance.

It is noteworthy that it is in the later poets that there is the highest incidence of metaphor. Stereotyped images such as the wounds of love are more common, as are also original images such as those of Burkhard von Hohenfels and Frauenlob. The conscious search for novelty is seen to disadvantage in Konrad von Würzburg 153, where the result is highly contrived. On the other hand the richly ornamental images of Frauenlob are striking in their deliberate preciosity.

MUSIC

The poems of the *Minnesang* were intended to be sung. The poem was made up of *wort* (text) and *wīse* (melody). The particular formal pattern of a poem, both metrical and musical, is known as the *dōn* (NHG *ton*). However, for the poets up to and including Walther, scarcely any melodies have survived, and these are mostly of a fragmentary nature. The chief manuscripts with musical notation are the following.

Thirteenth century:	M—melodies in staffless neumes, as yet not satisfactorily interpreted.
Fourteenth century:	Z—One complete and three fragmentary Walther melodies.
	J—melodies of Konrad von Würzburg, Der wilde Alexander, Frauenlob, and other later poets.
Fifteenth century:	t—The Colmar MS. of *Meistersang*, containing melodies ascribed to earlier poets such as Walther, but furnished with new texts, and therefore of limited reliability.
	c—Neidhart melodies.

(For further details of these manuscripts see pp. xxiii–xxvi. Extant tunes are referred to in the notes.)

Contrafacta

The term *contrafactum* denotes the use of an already existing melody, and the adaptation to it of a new text. Thus the *Meistersinger* adopt the metrical and musical patterns of earlier poets, and Ulrich von Liechtenstein relates in his *Frauendienst* how his lady sent him a tune unknown in Germany, and bade him compose a new song to it. It has consequently been assumed that where a German poem is modelled in substance and form on a Romance lyric, the melody was also borrowed, though there is no direct evidence to support this. Attempts have been made, particularly by Gennrich, to remedy the paucity of musical material, by adducing *contrafacta* of existing tunes, usually of Romance origin, to fit particular poems, but these hypotheses carry little conviction.

METRE

General Principles

The basic principle is that of stress. This usually coincides with the speech accent. The regular pattern of the metrical foot is a strong stress (*Hebung* ′), followed by an unstressed syllable (*Senkung* ×), as in:

$$
\overset{\times}{\text{In}} \left| \overset{\prime}{\text{ei}}\overset{\times}{\text{nem}} \right| \overset{\prime}{\text{zwī}}\overset{\times}{\text{vel}}\overset{\prime}{\text{lī}}\overset{\times}{\text{chen}} \left| \overset{\times}{\text{wān}} \right| \overset{\prime}{}
$$

The first strong beat of the line may be preceded as here by an unstressed syllable or syllables, the anacrusis or *Auftakt*. Occasionally, particularly in the early poets, there may be two unstressed syllables in the foot, as in:

$$
\overset{\times}{\text{nāh}} \left| \overset{\prime}{\text{mī}}\overset{\times}{\text{me ge}}\overset{\times}{}\overset{\prime}{\text{sel}}\overset{\times}{\text{len}} \right| \overset{\prime}{\text{ist mir}} \left| \overset{\prime}{\text{wē}} \right| \tag{1}
$$

Sometimes a regular dactylic pattern is found, as in **63**:

$$
\overset{\times}{\text{Si}} \left| \overset{\prime}{\text{ist}} \overset{\times}{\text{zal}}\overset{\times}{\text{len}} \right| \overset{\prime}{\text{ēren}} \overset{\times}{\text{ein}} \left| \overset{\prime}{\text{wīp wol}} \overset{\times}{\text{er}}\overset{\times}{} \right| \overset{\prime}{\text{kant.}}
$$

Alternatively the unstressed syllable may be missing altogether, as in the second foot of the following line:

$$
\left| \overset{\prime}{\text{Du}} \overset{\times}{\text{bist}} \right| \overset{\prime}{\text{mīn,}} \left| \overset{\prime}{\text{ich}} \overset{\times}{\text{bin}} \right| \overset{\prime}{\text{dīn}} \tag{8}
$$

The main types of cadence:

(These are distinguished according to Heusler's system. The abbreviations in brackets are those used in the metrical analyses in the notes.)

1. Masculine—*männlich voll (mv)*:

   (*a*) The final beat falls on a stressed syllable not followed by an unstressed syllable: masculine monosyllabic—*einsilbig voll*:

$$\overset{\times}{\text{ich}} \mid \overset{\prime}{\text{sach}}\ \overset{\times}{\text{swaz}} \mid \overset{\prime}{\text{in}}\ \overset{\times}{\text{der}} \mid \overset{\prime}{\text{welte}} \mid \overset{\prime}{\text{was}}$$

(b) The final beat falls on a short stressed syllable followed by
an unstressed syllable: masculine disyllabic—*zweisilbig
voll*:

$$\overset{\times}{\text{wie}} \mid \overset{\prime}{\text{man}}\ \overset{\times}{\text{zer}} \mid \overset{\prime}{\text{welte}}\overset{\times}{} \mid \overset{\prime,\times}{\text{solte}} \mid \overset{\prime}{\text{leben}}\overset{\times}{}$$

2. Feminine—*weiblich voll* (*wv*):

The final beat falls on a long stressed syllable (i.e. one containing (a) a long vowel or diphthong or (b) a short vowel+
double consonant) followed by an unstressed syllable:

$$(a)\ \text{Ich} \mid \text{hān hērn} \mid \text{Otten} \mid \text{triuwe}\ \text{er} \mid \text{welle} \mid \text{mich noch} \mid \text{rīchen}$$

$$(b)\ \text{Ich} \mid \text{wolte hērn} \mid \text{Otten} \mid \text{milte} \mid \text{nāch der} \mid \text{lenge} \mid \text{mezzen}$$

3. Feminine double stress—*klingend* (*k*):

The last beat falls on a final syllable following immediately
after a stressed long syllable. This type is found when the metrical structure demands a certain number of beats, the final one
of which falls on a syllable not bearing the speech accent. It can
be most clearly seen where the cadence alternates, as in Der von
Kürenberc, where the first half of each line (with one exception)
is four-beat, either *männlich voll* or *klingend*. Thus the half line
in **17**

$$\text{die} \mid \text{wīle unz} \mid \text{ich daz} \mid \text{leben} \mid \text{hān} \qquad (4\ mv)$$

is metrically equivalent to that in **19**

$$\text{jō} \mid \text{wurbe ichz} \mid \text{gerne} \mid \text{selbe} \qquad (4\ k)$$

Similarly in **8** where the basic pattern is four-beat, the two central
lines (4 *k*) are equivalent to the two surrounding pairs (4 *mv*).

4. Metrically incomplete—*stumpf* (*s*):

The final foot is missing altogether, and a rest is posited to
take its place. This again can be most clearly seen where cadences
alternate. Thus in Meinloh, where the basic unit is the eight-beat

long line, the second half of each line is usually 4 *mv*. In some cases, however, it is 4 *s* instead. Thus the second half of the third line in **27**

$$\left|\begin{array}{c}\times\\\mathrm{diu}\end{array}\right|\begin{array}{cc}/&\times\\\mathrm{mir}&\mathrm{ist}\end{array}\left|\begin{array}{cc}/&\times\\\mathrm{als}&\mathrm{der}\end{array}\right|\begin{array}{c}/\\\mathrm{l\bar{\imath}p}\end{array}\left|\begin{array}{c}/\\\frown\end{array}\right. \qquad (4\ s)$$

is equivalent to that in **29**

$$\begin{array}{c}\times\\\mathrm{daz}\end{array}\left|\begin{array}{cc}/&\times\\\mathrm{er}&\mathrm{ge}\end{array}\right|\begin{array}{cc}/&\times\\\mathrm{danke}\end{array}\left|\begin{array}{cc}/&\times\\\mathrm{niene}\end{array}\right|\begin{array}{c}/\\\mathrm{h\bar{a}t}\end{array} \qquad (4\ mv)$$

A Survey of Developments

In the early poets, up to and including Meinloh, metrical form is simple. The basic unit is the Germanic eight-beat long line, or the four-beat half line. These occur in rhyming couplets, in groups of six to fourteen lines (cf. **5, 6, 7, 8**), or in the four-line strophe (**1, 2, 9**). Sometimes an extra rhymeless half line (the *Waise*) is inserted, as in **3, 4, 10** and in Meinloh **25–29** and **31–34**. The early poems are monostrophic, apart from Anonymous **9**, Der von Kürenberc **10, 12, 15**, and Dietmar. In most of these, however, the connexion between the strophes is loose, and they represent an early stage in the development towards a more complex structure. There is a gradually ascending proportion of pure rhymes: fourteen pure rhymes beside nineteen assonances in the anonymous poems, but only six assonances against twenty-five pure rhymes in Meinloh. Dietmar **21** has internal rhyme, whereas in **22** the long line with internal rhyme has developed into two short lines with end-rhyme. It is fairly common in the early poets to find two or more unstressed syllables between stresses (as in **1**. 8–10), whereas later a strict alternation between stress and unstressed syllable is the rule.

In the group of poets from Kaiser Heinrich to Heinrich von Morungen, certain older features persist: four- and eight-beat lines in Kaiser Heinrich, predominantly four-beat lines in Heinrich von Veldeke, and assonating rhymes in Friedrich von Hausen. In the main, however, it is the innovations which are more striking, chief among them the introduction of tripartite structure from the Romance lyric. The strophe is made up of two identical groups of lines, the *pedes* or *Stollen*, together forming the *Aufgesang*, followed by a third differing section, the *cauda* or *Abgesang*. The metrical structure is paralleled in the musical accompaniment, the *Stollen* having a repetition of the same melody, the *Abgesang* a new one. The sonnet is a survival of this tripartite form. Greater formal variety results: in length of line and of strophe, and in new rhyme patterns. *Abgesang* is distinguished from *Aufgesang* by the introduction of new rhymes or of a rhymeless line, or by the different arrangement of the same rhymes. Instead of the uniform rhyming couplets of the earlier poets, new combinations of rhyme are frequent, among them alternating rhyme (abab), enclosing rhyme (abba), triple rhyme (aaa). Lines of differing length rhyme, as in **44**. The poems in this group are largely polystrophic, with anything from two to seven strophes. So-called *Responsionen*, by which a rhyme in one strophe is echoed in another, are used as a means to bind the strophes of a poem together: thus in **52**, strophe I is bound to all the others in this way.

In the following period, from Hartmann onwards, there is an even greater increase in metrical variety. It is common for the two *Stollen* to vary in rhyme, as in Wolfram **118**, and for the *Abgesang* similarly to fall into two equal parts, usually differing in rhyme, as in Hartmann **76** and Walther **92–95**. Sometimes the *Aufgesang* is doubled, so that there are two pairs of *Stollen*, as in Hartmann **78**. The *Abgesang* may be placed at the centre of the strophe, surrounded by the two *Stollen*, as in Walther **93–95, 108**.

Particularly in the poets after Walther there is considerable virtuosity in the use of rhyme. Internal rhyme is frequent, as is *Pausenreim*, in which the first word of a line rhymes with the last of a preceding or following line. Another technical device is the so-called *Korn*, when a word rhymes only with one in another verse; thus in Konrad von Würzburg **140**, each line of strophe II rhymes only with the corresponding line in strophe IV. An extreme example of technical skill is **152**, in which each single word or prefix rhymes.

THE MANUSCRIPTS

A The so-called small Heidelberg MS. Universitätsbibliothek, Heidelberg, Cod. pal. germ. 357. End of thirteenth century.

a Additions to A.

Diplomatic edition: F. Pfeiffer, *Die alte Heidelberger Liederhandschrift*, Stuttgart, 1844.

Facsimile: C. von Kraus, *Die kleine Heidelberger Lieder-handschrift in Nachbildung*, Stuttgart, 1932.

B The so-called Weingarten MS. Now Landesbibliothek, Stuttgart, HB XIII, poet. germ. 1. Beginning of the fourteenth century. Twenty-five illustrations.

b A second series of Reinmar in B.
Diplomatic edition: F. Pfeiffer, F. Fellner, *Die Weingartner Liederhandschrift*, Stuttgart, 1843.
Facsimile: K. Löffler, *Die Weingartner Liederhandschrift in Nachbildung*, Stuttgart, 1927.

C The large Heidelberg MS. (the so-called Codex Manesse). Universitätsbibliothek, Heidelberg, Cod. pal. germ. 848. Beginning of the fourteenth century. One hundred and thirty-seven illustrations. Diplomatic edition: F. Pfaff, Heidelberg, 1909, Facsimile: *Faksimile-Ausgabe der Manessischen Liederhandschrift*, Leipzig, 1925–9. See also E. Jammers, *Das Königliche Liederbuch des deutschen Minnesangs*, Heidelberg, 1965.

c Preußische Staatsbibliothek, Berlin, MS. germ. fol. 779, now Universitätsbibliothek, Tübingen. Fifteenth century.

Cᵇ Bayerische Staatsbibliothek, Munich, cgm. 5249, 10. Fourteenth century.

D Universitätsbibliothek, Heidelberg, Cod. pal. germ. 350. Fourteenth century.

d Universitätsbibliothek, Heidelberg, Cod. pal. germ. 696.

E The so-called Würzburg MS. Universitätsbibliothek, Munich, Cod. MS. fol. 731. Before mid-fourteenth century.

e A run of strophes ascribed to Reinmar in E.

F Landesbibliothek, Weimar, Q 564. Beginning of the fifteenth century.

f Preußische Staatsbibliothek, Berlin, MS. germ. quart. 764, now Westdeutsche Bibliothek, Marburg. Fifteenth century.

G MS. of Wolfram's *Parzival*. Bayerische Staatsbibliothek, Munich, cgm. 19. Thirteenth century.

G² (= L/K G) Bayerische Staatsbibliothek, Munich, cgm. 5249/74. Fourteenth century.

i One strophe of Reinmar in the Donaueschingen MS. of the *Parzival* of Claus Wisse and Philipp Colin.

J Universitätsbibliothek, Jena. Fourteenth century. Facsimile: K. K. Müller, Jena, 1896. Diplomatic edition: Holz, Saran, Bernouilli: see p. xxx.

k Universitätsbibliothek, Heidelberg, Cod. pal. germ. 341. Fourteenth century.

L MS. of Ulrich von Liechtenstein's *Frauendienst.* Bayerische Staatsbibliothek, Munich, cgm. 44. Thirteenth century.

M The Codex Buranus, so called because it was formerly in the monastery of Benediktbeuern. Bayerische Staatsbibliothek, Munich, clm. 4660. Facsimile: B. Bischoff: 2 vols., München, 1967. For the dating (early thirteenth century) see: P. Dronke, 'A critical note on Schumann's dating of the Codex Buranus', *Beiträge* (Tübingen), 84 (1962), 173–83.

m Preußische Staatsbibliothek, Berlin, MS. germ. quart. 795, now Westdeutsche Bibliothek, Marburg. Fourteenth century.

n Stadtbibliothek, Leipzig, CCCCXXI, Rep. II fol. 70a. Early fourteenth century.

O Preußische Staatsbibliothek, Berlin, MS. germ. oct. 682, now untraceable. Second half of thirteenth century.

O^2 (= H/W O) Stadt- und Universitätsbibliothek Frankfurt a. M. MS. germ. oct. 18. First half of fourteenth century.

R Preußische Staatsbibliothek, Berlin, MS. germ. fol. 1062, now Universitätsbibliothek, Tübingen. End of thirteenth century or beginning of fourteenth.

s The Royal Library, The Hague, 128 E. 2. Fifteenth century.

s^2 (= Roethe s) Bayerische Staatsbibliothek, Munich, cgm. 351. Fifteenth century.

s^3 (= H/W s) Stadtarchiv, Sterzing (Vipiteno). Late fourteenth or early fifteenth century. Now untraceable.

T Formerly at Tegernsee, now Bayerische Staatsbibliothek, Munich, clm. 19411. Late twelfth century.

t   The Colmar MS. Bayerische Staatsbibliothek, Munich, cgm. 4997. Fifteenth century.

U^x and U^{xx} Landesbibliothek, Wolfenbüttel, 404, 9 Nov. 16 and 16a, now Landeskirchenamt, Brunswick.

w   Preußische Staatsbibliothek, Berlin, MS. germ. fol. 20, now Universitätsbibliothek, Tübingen. Fifteenth century.

w^x Landesbibliothek, Wolfenbüttel, 404, 9 Nov. 21, now Landeskirchenamt, Brunswick. Thirteenth century.

w^{xx} Preußische Staatsbibliothek, Berlin, MS. germ. oct. 462, now untraceable.

Z   The so-called Münster fragment. Staatsarchiv, Münster, MS. VII, 51. Fourteenth century.

THE CONSTITUTION OF THE TEXT

For the purposes of the edition the principal manuscripts have been newly collated. The texts are deliberately conservative, and conform as closely as possible to the manuscript tradition. Significant variants and all emendations adopted in the text are noted, but for reasons of space minor and orthographical variants are not recorded. Editorial additions are given in square brackets. Whenever possible the text follows one manuscript, but where there is a diversified manuscript tradition, in which no single manuscript is decidedly superior to the rest, as for example in much of Walther, a composite text has been preferred, to avoid overloading the footnotes with variants.

At the right of the page are given references to all the manuscripts in which each text occurs, with the numbering customary in the relevant standard editions. This usually indicates either the foliation of the manuscript (e.g. M fol. 60^r), or the number of the strophe under the poet's name in the manuscript (e.g. Der von Kürenberc 1 C). Occasionally, where this is appropriate, the reference indicates the number of both poem and strophe in the manuscript—thus 11, 1 R = poem no. 11, strophe no. 1 in R. For an explanation of the sigla see pp. xxiii–xxvi. After the manuscript reference there is given, in brackets, a reference to the relevant standard edition, using its system of numbering. For an explanation of these abbreviated references see p. xxix.

Each manuscript has its own, frequently inconsistent ortho-graphy, and there are fairly wide divergences between the differ-ent manuscripts. Thus there is not always a distinction between the spirant *z* and *s*, between final *þ* and *b*, and final *c* and *g*, and the diphthongs and modified vowels are indicated in varying fashion. The edition follows usual editorial practice in resolving all abbreviations, distinguishing between *z* and *s*, *þ* and *b*, *c* and *g*, *i* and *j*, in generalizing *æ* for the modified long *ā*, and in marking long vowels.

At the head of each section the names of the poets appear first in their medieval form, secondly, where this is different, in their modern form. In the long lines of early poems, each half-line is numbered separately, as is customary.

BIBLIOGRAPHY

ABBREVIATED REFERENCES

Angermann (see p. xxxiv).

Bartsch = *Die Schweizer Minnesänger* (see p. xxx).

Beiträge = *Beiträge zur Geschichte der deutschen Sprache und Literatur*.

Brinkmann = *Liebeslyrik* (see p. xxx).

CB = *Carmina Burana*, ed. Hilka/Schumann (see p. xxx).

Ettmüller = *Frauenlob*, ed. Ettmüller (see p. xxxi).

Frank (see p. xxx).

Freidank (see p. xxxi).

Gennrich (see p. xxxiv).

Hatto = 'On beauty of numbers . . .' (see p. xxxiv).

Hatto/Taylor = Neidhart, ed. Hatto/Taylor (see p. xxxii).

Heusler = *Deutsche Versgeschichte* (see p. xxxiv).

Holz/Saran/Bernouilli (see p. xxx).

H/W = Neidhart, ed. Haupt/Wießner (see p. xxxii).

KLD = Kraus, *Deutsche Liederdichter* (see p. xxxi).

L/K = Walther von der Vogelweide, ed. Lachmann/Kraus/Kuhn (see p. xxxiii).

Maurer[1] = *Die politischen Lieder* . . . (see p. xxxiii).

Maurer[2] = *Die Lieder Walthers von der Vogelweide* (see p. xxxiii).

MF = *Minnesangs Frühling* (see p. xxxi).

MF[3] = MF, revised Vogt (see p. xxxi).

MF[30] = MF, revised Kraus (see p. xxxi).

MFU = *Minnesangs Frühling, Untersuchungen* (see p. xxxi).

Plenio = 'Bausteine' (see p. xxxiv).

Rathke (see p. xxxi).

Roethe = Reinmar von Zweter, ed. Roethe (see p. xxxiii).

Rohloff (see p. xxxiii).

Schirmer (see p. xxxiii).

Schröder = Konrad von Würzburg, ed. Schröder (see p. xxxii).

Wilmanns/Michel = Walther von der Vogelweide, ed. Wilmanns/Michel (see p. xxxiii).

WU = *Walther von der Vogelweide, Untersuchungen* (see p. xxxiii).

ZfdA = *Zeitschrift für deutsches Altertum*.

SELECT CLASSIFIED BIBLIOGRAPHY

General

Helmut de Boor: *Die höfische Literatur* (Helmut de Boor, Richard Newald, *Geschichte der deutschen Literatur von den Anfängen bis zur Gegenwart*, II), 7. Aufl., München, 1966.

Der deutsche Minnesang, Aufsätze zu seiner Erforschung, herausgegeben von Hans Fromm, Darmstadt, 1963.

Theodor Frings: 'Die Erforschung des Minnesangs', *Forschungen und Fortschritte*, 26 (1950), 9–13, 39–42.

—— *Die Anfänge der europäischen Liebesdichtung im 11. und 12. Jahrhundert*. Sitzungsberichte der Bayerischen Akademie der Wissenschaften, Phil.-hist. Klasse, 1960, Heft 2, München, 1960.

I. Ipsen: 'Strophe und Lied im frühen Minnesang', *Beiträge* 57 (1933), 301–413.

R. Kienast: 'Die deutschsprachige Lyrik des Mittelalters', in *Deutsche Philologie im Aufriß*, herausgegeben von W. Stammler, II, Berlin, 1960, 1–132.

H. Kuhn: *Minnesangs Wende*, Tübingen, 1952.

A. Moret: *Les débuts du lyrisme en Allemagne (des origines à 1350)*, Lille, 1951.

Die deutsche Literatur des Mittelalters, Verfasserlexikon, herausgegeben von W. Stammler und Karl Langosch, 5 vols., Berlin/Leipzig, 1933–55.

Collected Editions

Karl Bartsch: *Die Schweizer Minnesänger*, Frauenfeld, 1886 (= Bartsch). *Deutsche Liederdichter des 12. bis 14. Jahrhunderts*, 8. Auflage besorgt von W. Golther, Berlin, 1928.

Hennig Brinkmann: *Liebeslyrik der deutschen Frühe in zeitlicher Folge*, Düsseldorf, 1952 (= Brinkmann).

István Frank: *Trouvères et Minnesänger: recueil de textes pour servir à l'étude des rapports entre la poésie lyrique romane et le Minnesang au XIIe siècle*, Saarbrücken, 1952 (= Frank) (see also Müller-Blattau under Metre and Music).

F. H. von der Hagen: *Minnesinger. Deutsche Liederdichter des 12., 13. und 14. Jahrhunderts aus allen bekannten Handschriften und früheren Drucken*, 4 vols., Leipzig/Berlin, 1838–56.

Alfons Hilka, Otto Schumann: *Carmina Burana*, mit Benutzung der Vorarbeiten Wilhelm Meyers kritisch herausgegeben. I. Text. 1. Die moralisch-satirischen Dichtungen, Heidelberg, 1930. 2. Die Liebeslieder, herausgegeben von O. Schumann, Heidelberg, 1940. II. Kommentar. 1. Einleitung (Die Handschrift der Carmina Burana). Die moralisch-satirischen Dichtungen, Heidelberg, 1930 (= CB).

Georg Holz, Franz Saran, Eduard Bernouilli: *Die Jenaer Liederhandschrift*,

2 vols., Leipzig, 1901. I Getreuer Abdruck des Textes. II. Übertragung, Rhythmik und Melodik (= Holz/Saran/Bernouilli).

Carl von Kraus: *Deutsche Liederdichter des 13. Jahrhunderts*. I. Text, Tübingen, 1952. II. Kommentar, besorgt von Hugo Kuhn, Tübingen, 1958 (= KLD).

Margarete Lang: *Ostdeutscher Minnesang*. Auswahl und Übertragung von M. Lang. Melodien herausgegeben von Walther Salmen. Lindau/ Konstanz, 1958.

Des Minnesangs Frühling: Mit Bezeichnung der Abweichungen von Lachmann und Haupt und unter Beifügung ihrer Anmerkungen neu bearbeitet von Friedrich Vogt. 3. Ausgabe, Leipzig, 1920 (= MF³), (textually more reliable than the following).

Des Minnesangs Frühling nach Karl Lachmann, Moriz Haupt und Friedrich Vogt, neu bearbeitet von Carl von Kraus. 30. Auflage, Leipzig, 1950 (= MF³⁰).

Des Minnesangs Frühling, Untersuchungen von Carl von Kraus, Leipzig, 1939 (= MFU).

André Moret: *Anthologie du Minnesang*, Paris, 1949 (Bibliothèque de philologie germanique, XIII).

Max Wehrli: *Deutsche Lyrik des Mittelalters*, Zürich, 1955.

Individual Authors

Albreht von Johansdorf: Ulrich Pretzel, 'Die Kreuzzugslieder Albrechts von Johansdorf', in *Festgabe für L. L. Hammerich*, Kopenhagen, 1962, 229–44.

—— R. Bergmann, *Untersuchungen zu den Liedern Albrechts von Johannsdorf*, Diss., Freiburg i. Br., 1963.

Der wilde Alexander: R. Haller, *Der wilde Alexander. Beiträge zur Dichtungsgeschichte des 13. Jahrhunderts*, Würzburg, 1935.

Burkhard von Hohenfels: Max Sydow, *Burkhard von Hohenfels und seine Lieder*, Berlin, 1901.

Dietmar von Aist: Kurt Rathke, *Dietmar von Aist*, Leipzig, 1932 (= Rathke).

Frauenlob: *Heinrichs von Meissen des Frauenlobes Leiche, Sprüche, Streitgedichte und Lieder*, erläutert und herausgegeben von Ludwig Ettmüller, Quedlinburg/Leipzig, 1843 (= Ettmüller).

—— H. Kretschmann, *Der Stil Frauenlobs*, Jena, 1933 (Jenaer Germanistische Forschungen, 23).

Freidank: *Fridankes Bescheidenheit*, von H. E. Bezzenberger, Halle, 1872 (= Freidank).

Friedrich von Hausen: Hennig Brinkmann, *Friedrich von Hausen*, Minden, 1948. F. Maurer, 'Zu den Liedern Friedrichs von Hausen', *Neuphilologische Mitteilungen*, 53 (1952), 149–70. D. G. Mowatt, *The poetry of Friedrich von Hausen*, Ph.D. thesis, London, 1963.

Gottfried von Neifen: Cornelia Maria de Jong, *Gottfried von Neifen*.

Neuausgabe seiner Lieder und literarhistorische Abhandlung über seine Stellung in der mhd. Literatur, Diss., Amsterdam, 1923.

Gottfried von Neifen: *Die Lieder Gottfrieds von Neifen*, herausgegeben von Moriz Haupt, Leipzig, 1851, aufs neue durchgesehen von Edward Schröder, Berlin, 1932.

Gottfried von Straßburg: K. Stackmann, 'Gîte und Gelücke. Über die Spruchstrophen Gotfrids', *Festgabe für Ulrich Pretzel*, herausgegeben von W. Simon, W. Bachofer, und W. Dittmann, Berlin, 1963, 191–204.

Hadlaub: H. Lang, *Johannes Hadlaub*, Berlin, 1959.

—— R. Leppin, *Der Minnesänger Johannes Hadlaub*. Monographie und Textkritik, Diss., Hamburg, 1959–61.

Heinrich von Morungen: F. Michel, *Heinrich von Morungen und die Troubadours*, Straßburg, 1880 (Quellen und Forschungen, 38).

—— C. von Kraus, *Zu den Liedern Heinrichs von Morungen*. Abhandlungen der Gesellschaft der Wissenschaften zu Göttingen, Phil.-hist. Klasse, Neue Folge XVI. 1, Berlin, 1916.

—— Heinrich von Morungen, herausgegeben von C. von Kraus, 2. Aufl., München, 1950.

—— E. J. Morrall, 'Light Imagery in Heinrich von Morungen', *London Medieval Studies*, II (1951), 116–24.

Heinrich von Veldeke: C. von Kraus, *Heinrich von Veldeke und die mhd. Dichtersprache*, Halle, 1899.

—— Th. Frings, G. Schieb, 'Heinrich von Veldeke, die Entwicklung eines Lyrikers', *Festschrift Paul Kluckhohn und Hermann Schneider*, Tübingen, 1948, 101–21.

—— Th. Frings, G. Schieb, *Die Servatiusbruchstücke und die Lieder. Grundlegung einer Veldekekritik*, Halle, 1947.

Konrad von Würzburg: *Kleinere Dichtungen Konrads von Würzburg*, herausgegeben von Edward Schröder, Berlin, 1959. III. Die Klage der Kunst, Leiche, Lieder und Sprüche (= Schröder).

Neidhart: *Neidharts Lieder*, herausgegeben von Moriz Haupt, 2. Auflage, neu bearbeitet von E. Wießner, Leipzig, 1923 (= H/W).

—— *Lieder von Neidhart*, bearbeitet von Wolfgang Schmieder, Revision des Textes von E. Wießner. Mit Reproduktion der Handschriften. Wien, 1930 (Denkmäler der Tonkunst in Österreich, 71).

—— *Die Lieder Neidharts*, herausgegeben von E. Wießner, 2. Aufl. rev. von H. Fischer, Tübingen, 1963 (Altdeutsche Textbibliothek 44).

—— E. Wießner, *Kommentar zu Neidharts Liedern*, Leipzig, 1954.

—— *Vollständiges Wörterbuch zu Neidharts Liedern*, herausgegeben von E. Wießner, Leipzig, 1954.

—— *The Songs of Neidhart von Reuental. Seventeen Summer and Winter Songs set to their original melodies with translations and a musical and metrical canon*, by A. T. Hatto and R. J. Taylor, Manchester University Press, 1958 (= Hatto/Taylor).

Neidhart: Ernst Rohloff, *Neidharts Sangweisen*. I. Kommentarband. II. Melodien und Lieder. Abhandlungen der Sächsischen Akademie der Wissenschaften zu Leipzig, Phil.-hist. Klasse, Bd. 52, Heft 3–4, Berlin, 1962 (= Rohloff).

Reinmar: Carl von Kraus, *Die Lieder Reinmars des Alten*. Abhandlungen der Bayerischen Akademie der Wissenschaften, Phil.-hist. Klasse, XXX. Abh. 4, 6, 7 (= I, II, III), München, 1919.

Reinmar von Zweter: *Die Gedichte Reinmars von Zweter*, herausgegeben von Gustav Roethe, Leipzig, 1887 (= Roethe).

Ulrich von Liechtenstein: Ulrich von Liechtenstein, mit Anmerkungen von K. von Karajan, herausgegeben von K. Lachmann, Berlin, 1841.

—— *Ulrichs von Liechtenstein Frauendienst*, herausgegeben von Reinhold Bechstein, Leipzig, 1888.

—— W. Brecht, 'Ulrich von Liechtenstein als Lyriker', *ZfdA* 49 (1908), 1–122.

Ulrich von Winterstetten: J. Minor, *Die Leiche und Lieder des Schenken Ulrich von Winterstetten*, Wien, 1882.

—— A. Selge, *Studien über Ulrich von Winterstetten*, Berlin, 1929 (German. Studien 71).

Walther von der Vogelweide: *Die Gedichte Walthers von der Vogelweide*. Herausgegeben von Karl Lachmann. 13. auf Grund der 10. von Carl von Kraus bearbeiteten Ausgabe, neu herausgegeben von Hugo Kuhn, Berlin, 1965 (= L/K).

—— *Walther von der Vogelweide, Untersuchungen* von Carl von Kraus, Berlin and Leipzig, 1935 (= WU).

—— Walther von der Vogelweide, herausgegeben und erklärt von Wilhelm Wilmanns. I. Leben und Dichten Walthers von der Vogelweide, 2. Aufl. besorgt von Victor Michels, Halle, 1916. II. Lieder und Sprüche mit erklärenden Anmerkungen, 4. Aufl. besorgt von Victor Michels, Halle, 1924 (= Wilmanns/Michel).

—— Friedrich Maurer, *Die politischen Lieder Walthers von der Vogelweide*, Tübingen, 1954. 2. Aufl. Tübingen, 1964 (= Maurer[1]).

—— *Die Lieder Walthers von der Vogelweide unter Beifügung erhaltener und erschlossener Melodien* neu herausgegeben von Friedrich Maurer. I. Die religiösen und politischen Lieder, 2. Aufl., Tübingen, 1960. II. Die Liebeslieder, 2. Aufl., Tübingen, 1962 (= Maurer[2]).

—— Walther von der Vogelweide, *Gedichte* ausgewählt und übersetzt von Peter Wapnewski, Frankfurt/Hamburg, 1962.

—— *Selected Poems*, ed. M. Richey/H. Sacker, Blackwell, Oxford, 1965.

—— J. A. Huisman, *Neue Wege zur dichterischen und musikalischen Technik Walthers von der Vogelweide*, Utrecht, 1950.

—— Karl-Heinz Schirmer, *Die Strophik Walthers von der Vogelweide*, Halle, 1956 (= Schirmer).

Wolfram von Eschenbach: Wolfram von Eschenbach von Karl Lachmann,

7. Aufl., neu bearbeitet von Eduard Hartl, Berlin, 1952. I. Lieder, Parzival und Titurel.

Wolfram von Eschenbach: A. T. Hatto, 'On beauty of numbers in Wolfram's Dawn Songs', *Mod. Lang. Rev.*, 45 (1950), 2, 181–8 (= Hatto).

—— W. Mohr, 'Wolframs Tagelieder', in *Festschrift P. Kluckhohn und H. Schneider*, Tübingen, 1948, 148–65.

Genres and types

A. Angermann, *Der Wechsel in der mhd. Lyrik*, Diss., Marburg, 1910 (= Angermann).

A. Bielschowsky, *Geschichte der deutschen Dorfpoesie im 13. Jahrhundert*, I, Berlin, 1890.

Heinz Fischer, *Die Frauenmonologe der deutschen höfischen Lyrik*, Diss., Marburg, 1934.

Erika Mergell, *Die Frauenrede im deutschen Minnesang*, Diss., Frankfurt, a. M. 1940.

Th. Frings, 'Frauenstrophe und Frauenlied in der frühen deutschen Lyrik', in *Gestaltung-Umgestaltung, Festschrift für H. A. Korff*, Leipzig, 1957, 13–28.

W. de Gruyter, *Das deutsche Tagelied*, Diss., Leipzig, 1887.

F. Nicklas, *Untersuchung über Stil und Geschichte des deutschen Tageliedes*, Berlin, 1929 (German. Studien 72).

E. Scheunemann, *Texte zur Geschichte des deutschen Tageliedes*, Bern, 1947 (Altd. Übungstexte 6).

A. T. Hatto, 'Das Tagelied in der Weltliteratur', *Deutsche Vierteljahrsschrift für Literaturwissenschaft und Geistesgeschichte*, 36. Jahrgang (1962), 489–506.

A. T. Hatto (ed.), *Eos. An Enquiry into the Theme of Lovers' Meetings and Partings at Dawn in Poetry*, The Hague, 1965.

F. W. Wentzlaff-Eggebert, *Kreuzzugsdichtung des Mittelalters*, Berlin, 1960.

Metre and Music

A. Heusler, *Deutsche Versgeschichte*, 3 vols., Berlin/Leipzig, 1925–9. II. Der altdeutsche Vers (= Heusler).

S. Beyschlag, *Die Metrik der mhd. Blütezeit in Grundzügen*, 5. Aufl., Nürnberg, 1963.

F. Gennrich, 'Liedkontrafaktur in mhd. und ahd. Zeit', *ZfdA* 82 (1948–50), 105–41. Revised version in *Der deutsche Minnesang*: see p. xxx (=Gennrich).

O. Paul/I. Glier. *Deutsche Metrik*, 4. Aufl., München, 1961.

K. Plenio, 'Bausteine zur altdeutschen Strophik', *Beiträge* 42 (1917), 411–502, and 43 (1918), 56–99 (= Plenio).

—— 'Die Überlieferung Waltherscher Melodien', *Beiträge* 42 (1917), 479–90.

C. Bützler, *Untersuchungen zu den Melodien Walthers von der Vogelweide,* Jena, 1940.

W. Müller-Blattau, *Trouvères et Minnesänger,* II. Kritische Ausgabe der Weisen, Saarbrücken, 1956 (cf. I. Frank under Collected Editions).

R. J. Taylor, 'Zur Übertragung der Melodien der Minnesänger', *ZfdA* 87 (1956-7), 132-47.

—— *Die Melodien der weltlichen Lieder des Mittelalters.* I. Darstellungsband. II. Melodienband, Stuttgart, 1964.

B. Kippenberg, *Der Rhythmus im Minnesang. Eine Kritik der literar- und musikhistorischen Forschung,* München, 1962.

E. Jammers, *Ausgewählte Melodien des Minnesangs,* Tübingen, 1963 (Altdeutsche Textbibliothek, Ergänzungsreihe I).

ANONYMOUS

THE anonymous poems preserved in German are of varying date. The most important sources are the *Codex Buranus* (M) and the chief manuscripts of the *Minnesänger*. The *Carmina Burana*, so called because the manuscript was formerly at the monastery of Benedikt-beuern, is a collection of predominantly Latin poems, among which are interspersed some German verses. The manuscript probably dates from the early thirteenth century (see Introduction, p. xxv), but much of the material is of older date, and several of the German poems are very old, notably 1, 2, and 3. In the manuscripts of the *Minnesänger*, the ascription to named poets is often unreliable; thus the ascription of 4–7 to later poets can be disproved on stylistic and other grounds, and these poems shown to be of early date. 8 is preserved in a Latin manuscript of the late twelfth century.

Among the poems here chosen are those whose formal structure indicates an early date (1–5). All have as their basis the four-beat line rhyming in couplets, and are either single strophes (1–4), or larger units with no strophic divisions (5 and 6).

I

I   M fol. 60ᵛ–61ʳ (CB 149)

Floret silva nobilis
floribus et foliis.
ubi est antiquus
meus amicus ?
5 hinc equitavit,
eia, quis me amabit ?

Refl.   Floret silva undique,
nāh mīme gesellen ist mir wē.

II

Gruonet der walt allenthalben:
10 wā ist mīn geselle alsō lange ?
der ist geriten hinnen,
ōwī, wer sol mich minnen ?

---

1. 7 *Refl.* = *Reflecte*, the designation of a refrain in the MS.
10 *also lange*: *alsonlange* M, the *n* probably a scribal error caused by the proximity of *allenthalben*.

2

M fol. 67ᵛ (CB 167 a)

Swaz hie gāt umbe
daz sint allez megede;
die wellent ān man
allen disen sumer gān.

3

M fol. 60ʳ (CB 145 a)

Wære diu werlt alle mīn
von deme mere unze an den Rīn,
des wolt ih mich darben,
daz diu chünegin von Engellant
læge an mīnem arme.

4

Niune 38 A, Alram von Gresten 14 C (MF 3, 17)

Mich dunket niht sō guotes   noch sō lobesam
sō diu liehte rōse   und diu minne mīns man.
5 diu kleinen vogellīn
diu singent in dem walde: dēst menegem herzen liep.
mir enkome mīn holder geselle,   ine hān der sumerwunne niet.

2. 1 *gāt*: cf. *gēt* as a dancing term in **103**. 37.
2 *allez*: *alle* M, with a letter above *e* probably intended to be *z*.
4 *allen*: in M, final *n* appears to have been added later. Some editors prefer the reading *alle*, which would then refer to *megede*.

3. 2 cf. **38**. 11 and **96**. 25.
4 *daz chunich von engellant* M, with a stroke through *chunich*, and above it the correction *diu chünegin* in a later hand.
5 *minen armen* M, corrected from *minem arme* by a later scribe, probably to improve the rhyme. The singular is more usual in this construction in MHG, cf. **24**. 9.

4. Text of A, with *diu* (4) and *sumerwunne* (9) from C.
9 *mir enkome* . . . 'unless my lover returns to me'.

5

Dietmar 12 C (MF 37, 4)

Ez stuont ein frouwe alleine
und warte uber heide
und warte ir liebes,
sō gesach si valken fliegen.
'sō wol dir, valke, daz du bist!
du fliugest swar dir lieb ist:
du erkiusest dir in dem walde
einen boum der dir gevalle.
alsō hān ouch ich getān:
ich erkōs mir selbe einen man,
den erwelton mīniu ougen.
daz nīdent schōne frouwen.
owē wan lānt si mir mīn liep ?
joh engerte ich ir dekeines trūtes niet.'

6

Dietmar 13 C (MF 37, 18)

Sō wol dir, sumerwunne!
daz vogelsanc ist geswunden,
alse ist der linden ir loup.
jārlanc truobent mir ouch
mīniu wol stēnden ougen.
mīn trūt, du solt dich gelouben
anderre wībe;
wan, helt, die solt du mīden.
dō du mich ērste sāhe,
dō dūhte ich dich zewāre
sō rehte minneclīch getān:
des man ich dich, lieber man.

5. 5 Lit. 'well for you, falcon, that which you are' (i.e. *daz* in the double function of demonstrative and relative). 'Happy falcon, how fortunate is your lot'.
11 The full vowel in the ending of *erwelton* is probably archaic.
6. 1 *Sō wol dir* 'farewell'.
2 *dc gevogelsang ist gesvnde* C.
5 *mīniu wol stēnden ougen* 'my bright eyes'.
9 *sāhe: sehe* C. The emendation is required by the assonance.

7

Walther von Mezze 13 A (MF 4, 1)

Diu linde ist an dem ende   nu jārlanc lieht unde blōz.
mich vēhet mīn geselle: nu engilte ich des ich nie genōz.
5   sō vil ist unstæter wībe: die benement ime den sin.
got wizze wol die wārheit,   daz i'me diu holdeste bin.
9   si enkunnen niewan triegen   vil menegen kindeschen man.
owē mir sīner jugende!   diu muoz mir al ze sorgen ergān.

8

T fol. 114ᵛ (MF 3, 1)

Du bist mīn, ich bin dīn:
des solt du gewis sīn.
du bist beslozzen
in mīnem herzen:
5   verlorn ist daz sluzzelīn:
du muost och immer darinne sīn.

9

I   Dietmar 32 C (MF 39, 18)
'Slāfest du, friedel ziere ?
man wecket uns leider schiere:
ein vogellīn sō wol getān
daz ist der linden an daz zwī gegān.'

II   33 C
5   'Ich was vil sanfte entslāfen:
nu rüefestu, kint, wāfen.
liep ane leit mac niht sīn.
swaz du gebiutest, daz leiste ich, friundin mīn.'

III   34 C
Diu frouwe begunde weinen.
10   'du rītest und lāst mich einen.
wenne wilt du wider her zuo mir ?
owē du füerest mīne fröide sant dir.'

7. 4 'now I am punished for that which I never enjoyed'.
6 *benement*: *benenment* A.
10 *kindesch* 'young', cf. 30. 10.

9. 2 *man*: *wan* C (a common Alemannic variant). Some editors take *wan* as a
conjunction and *vogellīn* as the subject of *wecket*, but this is unlikely.
10 *ritest hinnē* C. For *rīten* in this sense cf. 118. 36.

DER VON KÜRENBERC

DER VON KÜRENBERC is the earliest named German lyric poet. His poems are preserved only in manuscript C, where he is grouped among the barons. It has proved impossible to localize or date the poet with any certainty. Similar place-names are common in South Germany and Austria, and the poet no doubt belonged to Bavarian or Austrian stock. He is thought to have been writing round about the mid-twelfth century.

Der von Kürenberc shows the beginning of the development of a more complex lyric structure. The majority of the strophes ascribed to him are still single stanzas, but there are also indisputably three poems made up of two strophes. The question is complicated by the fact that the arrangement of the strophes in the manuscript seems to have been determined by a preconceived principle: that of separating *Frauenstrophen* from *Männerstrophen*. This disposition of the strophes undoubtedly derives from a source considerably anterior to C. There are thus ten *Frauenstrophen*, or what the original compiler took to be such, followed by five *Männerstrophen*. This leaves intact as a unity 15, where both strophes are spoken by a woman, and also strophes 1 and 2 in C, which were probably taken to be separate *Frauenstrophen*, but which more probably represent a dialogue between a man and a woman (see note on 10). The arrangement preserved in the manuscript has disrupted the undoubted unity of strophes 4 and 12 in C, which are here placed together in 12. That such an arrangement could even have been attempted shows that at the time when it was made the predominant type was the single strophe.

The basic metrical unit is the four-beat half-line; the long lines formed of two such halves are combined in rhyming couplets. There are two stanza patterns: the predominant one of four long lines which is the basis of the *Nibelungenstrophe*, and that of 10, where a rhymeless line is inserted as the odd fifth half-line.

IO

I   1 C (MF 7, 1)

Vil lieber friunde scheiden   daz ist schedelīch;
swer sīnen friunt behaltet,   daz ist lobelīch.
5   die site wil ich minnen.
bite in daz er mir holt sī,   als er hie bivor was,
und man in waz wir redeten,   dō ich in ze jungest sach.

II   2 C

10   Wes manst du mich leides,   mīn vil liebe liep ?
unser zweier scheiden   müeze ich geleben niet.
verliuse ich dīne minne,
15   sō lāze ich die liute   [harte] wol entstān,
daz mīn fröide ist der minnist   under allen anderen man.

II

3 C (MF 7, 19)

Leit machet sorge,   vil lieb wunne.
eines hübschen ritters   gewan ich künde:
5   daz mir den benomen hānt   die merker und ir nīt,
des mohte mir mīn herze   nie frō werden sīt.

10. 1 *vil lieber frŭnt* C. This reading is unlikely on grounds of sense and metre. The sense demands a verb parallel to *behaltet* in l. 3, and the vocative is out of place because the lady is not speaking directly to her lover, but to the messenger. All the other first half-lines are four-beat, usually *klingend*, and the metre therefore demands a disyllabic verb. The following verbs have been suggested: *fremeden* (Bartsch), *verliesen* (Sievers), *verkiesen* (Schröder, Kraus), *scheiden* (Joseph, Vogt). Of these the last is the most probable: it is echoed in l. 12, and such verbal echoes are common in strophes which are thematically connected. It could have been omitted by the scribe because of its similarity and proximity to *schedelīch*.

11 *min vil liebe* C. All the other second half-lines of this poem end on a strong stress, as do those of all the other *Männerstrophen*. It is therefore likely that a word has been omitted, most probably a word nearly identical with the preceding one, which the scribe may have thought he had written already.

17 *der minnist*: *der* is probably gen. pl., with the gen. pl. of the noun understood, as in the phrase *aller minnist* for *aller fröiden minnist*.

18 *vñ alle andere man* C. Vogt (MF³) emends *und alle ander verman* ('I spurn all others'), Kraus (MF³⁰) follows Lachmann in preferring the emendation *umb alle andere man* ('with regard to all other men'). This latter emendation rests on the assumption that the strophe is spoken by a woman, which is unlikely. Brinkmann's suggestion *under allen anderen man* is the most satisfactory. The two lines then mean 'that my joy is the least among all other men i.e. that I have the least joy of all men'. It is still not entirely convincing, this probably being an instance where the text is too corrupt to permit of a real approximation to what the poet originally wrote.

11. 1-2 These two propositions balance each other. There are two contrasting pairs

12

I   4 C (MF 8, 1)

Ich stuont mir nehtint spāte   an einer zinne:
dō hōrt ich einen riter   vil wol singen
in Kürenberges wīse   al ūz der menigīn:
er muoz mir diu lant rūmen,   alder ich geniete mich sīn.

II   12 C (MF 9, 29)

Nu brinc mir her vil balde   mīn ros, mīn īsengewant,
wan ich muoz einer frouwen   rūmen diu lant.
diu wil mich des betwingen   daz ich ir holt sī.
si muoz der mīner minne   iemer darbende sīn.

13

6 C (MF 8, 17)

Swenne ich stān aleine   in mīnem hemede,
und ich gedenke an dich,   ritter edele,
sō erbluot sich mīn varwe   als der rōse an dem dorne tuot,
und gewinnet daz herze   vil manigen trūrigen muot.

14

7 C (MF 8, 25)

Ez hāt mir an dem herzen   vil dicke wē getān
daz mich des geluste   des ich niht mohte hān
noch niemer mac gewinnen.   daz ist schedelīch.
jone mein ich golt noch silber: ez ist den liuten gelīch.

of nouns *lieb — leit* and *sorge — wunne*; the first denotes outward good or ill fortune, happiness or unhappiness, particularly in love, the second the corresponding inward states: 'Ill fortune in love brings sorrow in its train, much good fortune joy.' This aphoristic beginning sums up the theme of the whole strophe and is echoed in the last line: the outward misfortune (the interference of ill wishers) has destroyed the lady's inner joy.

12. 1 *mir* is an ethic dative, used in a semi-reflexive way.
   6 'from amidst the assembled throng'.

14. 3–4 'that I desired that which I could not have'. *geluste = gelustete*. The first *des* is the gen. obj. of *geluste*, the second *des* is gen. by attraction to it, or is dependent on *niht*.

15

I   8 C (MF 8, 33)

Ich zōch mir einen valken   mēre danne ein jār.
dō ich in gezamete   als ich in wolte hān
und ich im sīn gevidere   mit golde wol bewant,
er huob sich ūf vil hōhe   und floug in anderiu lant.

II

Sīt sach ich den valken   schōne fliegen:
er fuorte an sīnem fuoze   sīdīne riemen,
und was im sīn gevidere   alrōt guldīn.
got sende si zesamene   die gelieb wellen gerne sīn.

16

10 C (MF 9, 13)

Ez gāt mir vonme herzen   daz ich geweine:
ich und mīn geselle   muozen uns scheiden.
daz machent lugenære.   got der gebe in leit!
der uns zwei versuonde,   vil wol des wære ich gemeit.

17

11 C (MF 9, 21)

Wīp vil schœne,   nu var du sam mir.
lieb und leit   daz teile ich sant dir.
die wīle unz ich daz leben hān   sō bist du mir vil lieb.
wan minnestu einen bœsen,   des engan ich dir niet.

15. 5 Cf. *Wiener Oswald*, ed. Baesecke, ll. 115 ff.
16. 7 The relative clause is used, as often in MHG, in a semi-conditional way,
versuonde is the past subj.: 'if anyone were to reconcile us . . . .'
17. 6–7 Lit. 'for if you love an inferior man, that I do not permit', 'for I do not permit
you to love an inferior man'. The poet is indirectly praising both himself and the
lady.

18

13 C (MF 10, 1)

Der tunkel sterne   der birget sich.
als tuo du, frouwe schône,   sô du sehest mich.
5   sô lā du dīniu ougen gēn   an einen andern man,
sōn weiz doch lützel ieman   wiez under uns zwein ist getān.

19

14 C (MF 10, 9)

Aller wībe wunne   diu gēt noch megetīn.
als ich an si gesende   den lieben boten mīn,
5   jō wurbe ichz gerne selbe,   wær ez ir schade niet.
in weiz wiez ir gevalle: mir wart nie wīb als lieb.

20

15 C (MF 10, 17)

Wīb unde vederspil   die werdent līhte zam:
swer si ze rehte lucket,   sō suochent si den man.
5   als warb ein schœne ritter   umbe eine frouwen guot.
als ich daran gedenke,   sō stēt wol hōhe mīn muot.

18. 1 Schwarz argues convincingly (*Wirkendes Wort*, iii. 3, 129 f.) that *tunkel* is here genitive of the st. f. *tunkel*, 'Morgendämmerung', and that the phrase *der tunkel sterne* thus means 'the morning star'.

19. 2 For this use of *megetīn* denoting an unmarried woman, cf. the similar use of *megede* in 2.

DIETMAR VON EIST
(DIETMAR VON AIST)

THE Aist is a tributary of the Danube in Upper Austria. There is a Dietmar von Eist frequently attested between 1139 and 1170, whose death is recorded in a document of 1171. Under the name of Dietmar, MSS. B and C preserve a collection of strophes differing in amount. Both begin with a common run of eleven strophes. C then inserts the two poems here treated as Anonymous **5** and **6**, and B and C have a further run of five strophes in common. In C there follow five strophes all ascribed to different poets in other manuscripts. C alone has a further seventeen strophes, including the famous dawn song (here Anonymous **9**). C concludes with two strophes ascribed to Lutolt von Seven in A.

The main difficulties in the way of a correct assessment of Dietmar's work have been, on the one hand, the complex manuscript tradition and the widely different strophes ascribed to him, on the other, the early date of the historically attested Dietmar which appears to be incompatible with some, if not all of the poems. These difficulties have been the source of much controversy. The main theories propounded have been: (1) that the poems represent different stages in the work of one poet; (2) that they are the work of two or more poets fortuitously assembled under the name of Dietmar, but containing some genuine Dietmar material.

The most satisfactory view is that of Kraus (MFU, pp. 103–4). He argues that the first eleven strophes common to B and C (with the exception of 9 which is probably an imitation), are homogeneous and represent the basic Dietmar canon. The further additions to this tradition are unlike these early poems both in subject matter and style, and represent a conglomeration of motley character, on whose provenance it is fruitless to speculate.

There remains the further question of the dating of those poems which can with relative certainty be ascribed to Dietmar. Kraus holds that they are not sufficiently archaic to be the work of the Dietmar attested between 1139 and 1170 and therefore attributes them to a slightly later member of the same family (not, however, historically verifiable). Criteria for the dating can be established by an analysis of the formal features of Dietmar's verse, and a comparison of these with Der von Kürenberc, whom Dietmar resembles in many respects.

The archaic features of Dietmar's work are the following: the preference for the Germanic long line, the persistence of assonating rhymes, the loose connexion between related strophes. Compared with Der von

Kürenberc, however, there is a technical advance in the following
respects: the preference for a unit of two or three strophes, by contrast
with the predominantly monostrophic verse of Der von Kürenberc, the
more complex metrical patterns of **21** and **22**, the higher proportion of
pure rhymes.

Thus although Dietmar undoubtedly has archaic features which link
him with Der von Kürenberc, he also shows characteristics which are
a sign of later date. On these grounds it seems likely that Kraus is right
in discounting the historically attested Dietmar, and preferring a slightly
later representative of the same family.

21

I   1 BC, M fol. 81ᵛ (MF 32, 1)

'Waz ist für daz trūren guot,   daz wīp nāch lieben manne hāt ?
gerne daz mīn herze erkande,   wan ez sō betwungen stāt.'
5 alsō redete ein vrowe schœne,   'vil wol ichs an ein ende kœme,
                                      wan diu huote.
selten sīn vergezzen wirt   in mīnem muote.'

II   2 BC

10 'Genuoge jehent daz grōziu stæte   sī der besten vrowen trōst.'
'des enmac ich niht gelouben,   sīt mīn herze ist unerlōst.'
14 alsō redeten zwei geliebe,   dō si von einander schieden.
                        'owē minne,'
'der dīn āne möhte sīn,   daz wæren sinne.'

III   3 BC

19 Sō al diu welt ruowe hat,   sō mac ich eine entslāfen niet.
daz kumet von einer vrowen schœne,   der ich gerne wære liep.
an der al mīn vröide stāt.   wie sol des iemer werden rāt ?
25   joch wæne ich sterben.
wes lie si got mir armen man   ze kāle werden ?

21. Text according to B.
6–7 'I should bring my wishes to a happy conclusion, were it not for the watchers.'

22

I   4 BC (MF 32, 13)

Seneder friundinne bote,   nu sage dem schœnen wībe,
daz mir tuot āne māze wē   daz ich si sō lange mīde.
5 lieber het ich ir minne
danne al der vogellīne singen.
nu muoz ich von ir gescheiden sīn:
trūric ist mir al daz herze mīn.

II   5 BC

9 Nu sage dem ritter edele   daz er sich wol behüete,
und bite in schōne wesen gemeit   und lāzen allez ungemüete.
ich muoz ofte engelten sīn.
vil dicke erkumet daz herze mīn.
15 an sehendes leides hān ich vil,
daz ich ime selbe gerne klagen wil.

III   6 BC

Ez getet nie wīp sō wol   an deheiner slahte dinge,
19 daz al die welt diuhte guot.   des bin ich wol worden inne.
swer sīn liep dar umbe lāt,
daz kumet von swaches herzen rāt.
dem wil ich den sumer und allez guot
widerteilen durch sīnen unstæten muot.

22. Text of B with ll. 3 and 7 according to C.
15 *an sehend* 'visible'.

23

I   7 BC (MF 33, 15)

Ahī nu kumt uns diu zīt   der kleinen vogellīne sanc.
ez gruonet wol diu linde breit,   zergangen ist der winter lanc.
5 nu siht man bluomen wol getān: an der heide üebent sie ir
                                   schīn.
des wirt vil manic herze frō: des selben trœstet sich daz mīn.

II   8 BC, Heinrich von Veltkilchen 8 A

9 Ich bin dir lange holt gewesen,   frouwe biderbe unde guot.
vil wol ich daz bestatet hān,   du hāst getiuret mir den muot.
swaz ich dīn bezzer worden sī,   ze heile müez ez mir ergān.
15 machest du daz ende guot,   sō hāstuz allez wol getān.

24

I   10 BC, Heinrich von Veltkilchen 10 A (MF 34, 3)

Ūf der linden obene   dā sanc ein kleinez vogellīn.
vor dem walde wart ez lūt: dō huop sich aber daz herze mīn
5 an eine stat dā ez ē dā was.   ich sach dā rōsebluomen stān.
die manent mich der gedanke vil   die ich hin zeiner frouwen
                                   hān.

II   11 BC, Veltk. 9 A

9 Ez dunket mich wol tūsent jār   daz ich an liebes arme lac.
sunder alle mīne schulde   frömdet er mich manigen tac.
sīt ich bluomen niht ensach   noch hōrte kleiner vogel sanc,
15 sīt was al mīn fröide kurz   und ouch der jāmer alzelanc.

23. Text according to C.
   11 *bestatet: bestat* C. *bestaten* is a legal term, meaning 'to apply to good use'.
   12 *tiuren* 'to make *tiure*', i.e. 'estimable', 'worthy', in a courtly, rather than a specifically moral sense.
   11–14 'I have derived great profit from that. You have made me more worthy. If I am improved because of my service to you, may it turn out to be propitious for me', i.e. a discreet plea for a reward, because service of the lady has made him more worthy of it.
   15–16 Cf. Freidank 63. 20:
         Ichn schilte niht, swaz ieman tuot,
         machet er daz ende guot.
24. Text according to C.
   11 *alle* with B: *ane* AC.

MEINLOH VON SEVELINGEN

MEINLOH VON SEVELINGEN (now Söflingen near Ulm), belongs to a family attested between 1220 and 1240 as stewards of the counts of Dillingen. Our poet probably lived about 1180. His work marks the beginning of the courtly love lyric, while still containing more archaic features, particularly in the *Frauenstrophen*. The new conception of *minne* as humble service of the lady, and the proliferation of courtly elements in the vocabulary are signs of Romance influence, which has not, however, affected the formal structure.

No satisfactory explanation can be found for the arrangement of the strophes in the manuscripts, which is not, as is customary, according to the *Ton*. Thus although the three gnomic strophes are placed together, the *Frauenstrophen* and *Männerstrophen* are not grouped systematically. Some editors rearrange the strophes according to the *Ton*, and some (e.g. Vogt) believe the manuscript arrangement to be intended to reflect the progression of a love affair, but this is improbable.

25

1 BC (MF 11, 1)

Dō ich dich loben hōrte,   dō het ich dich gerne erkant.
durch dīne tugende manige   fuor ich ie welende, unz ich dich
                                         vant.
5 daz ich dich nu gesehen hān,   daz enwirret dir niet.
er ist vil wol getiuret,   den du wilt, vrowe, haben liep.
9 du bist der besten eine,   des muoz man dir von schulden jehen.
sō wol den dīnen ougen!
die kunnen swen si wellen   an vil güetelīchen sehen.

26

2 BC (MF 15, 1)

Vil schœne unde biderbe,   dar zuo edel unde guot,
sō weiz ich eine vrowen: der zimet wol allez daz si getuot.

25. Text according to B.
    4 *welende*: *wallende* C. Kraus (MF[30]) emends to *sende*.
    6 *niht* BC. *niet* (as e.g. in **34.** 6) is preferable here because of the assonating rhyme with *liep*.
    7 Cf. **23.** 12.
26. Text of B.

5 ich rede ez umbe daz niht,   daz mir got die sælde habe gegeben
   daz ich ie mit ir geredete   oder nāhe bī sī gelegen,
9 wan daz mīniu ougen   sāhen die rehten wārheit.
   si ist edel und ist schœne,   in rehter māze gemeit.
   ich gesach nie eine vrowen   diu ir līp schōner künde hān.
15 durch daz wil ich mich flīzen,
   swaz sie gebiutet,   daz daz allez sī getān.

27

3 BC (MF 11, 14)

Dir enbiutet sīnen dienst   dem du bist, vrowe, als der līp.
er heizet dir sagen zewāre,   du habest ime alliu anderiu wīp
5 benomen ūz sīnem muote,   daz er gedanke niene hāt.
nu tuo ez durch dīne tugende   und enbiut im eteslīchen rāt.
9 du hāst im vil nāch bekēret   beidiu sin unde leben:
er hāt dur dīnen willen
eine ganze vröide   gar umbe ein trūren gegeben.

28

6 BC (MF 12, 14)

Ez mac niht heizen minne,   der lange wirbet umbe ein wīp.
die liute werdent sīn inne,   und wirt zerfüeret dur nīt.
5 unstætiu friuntschaft   machet wankeln muot.
man sol ze liebe gāhen: daz ist für die merkære guot,
9 daz ez iemen werde inne   ē ir wille sī ergān.
sō sol man si triegen.
dā ist gnuogen ane gelungen,   die daz selbe hānt getān.

5–6 *umbe daz niht, daz* 'not for the reason that'.
14 Cf. **29**. 7–8.
27. Text of B, with *niene* (6) from C.
  8 *im: mir* BC.
28. Text of B.
  5 'faithless friends make for inconstancy', i.e. the interference of the *liute* and *merkære* shake the lovers' constancy. There is a similar idea in Heinrich von Morungen: *huote stæten frouwen machet wankelen muot* (MF 137, 7).
  7 *wan* BC. See note on **9**. 2.
  8 *für* 'as a remedy against'.
  9 *iemen* here 'no one'.

29

7 BC (MF 12, 27)

Ich lebe stolzlīche,   in der welt ist niemanne baz.
ich trūre mit gedanken: niemen kan erwenden daz,
5   ez tuo ein edeliu vrowe,   diu mir ist alse der līp.
ich gesach mit mīnen ougen   nie baz gebāren ein wīp.
9   des ist si guot ze lobenne: an ir ist anders wandels niht.
den tac den wil ich ēren
iemer durch ir willen,   sō si mīn ouge ane siht.

30

8 BC (MF 14, 26)

Ich hān vernomen ein mære,   mīn muot sol aber hōhe stān,
wan er ist komen ze lande,   von dem mīn trūren sol zergān.
5   mīnes herzen leide   sī ein urlop gegeben.
mich heizent sīne tugende   daz ich vil stæter minne pflege.
9   ich gelege mir in wol nāhe,   den selben kindeschen man.
sō wol mich sīnes komens!   wie wol er vrowen dienen kan!

31

9 BC (MF 13, 1)

Ich bin holt einer frowen: ich weiz vil wol umbe waz.
sīt ich ir begunde dienen,   si geviel mir ie baz und ie baz.
5   ie lieber und ie lieber   sō ist si zallen zīten mir,
ie schœner und ie schœner: vil wol gevallet si mir.
9   si ist sælic zallen ēren,   der besten tugende pfligt ir līp.
sturbe ich nāch ir minne,
und wurde ich danne lebende,   sō wurbe ich aber umbe daz
                                                         wīp.

29. Text of B. with *gedanken* (3) from C.
    5 'unless a noble lady does so'.
    9 *des* 'on that account'.
30. Text of B.
    10 Cf. note on 7. 10.
31. Text of C.
    11 'if I were to die in pursuit of her love'.

32

10 BC (MF 13, 14)

Sō wē den merkæren!   die habent mīn übel gedāht:
si habent mich āne schulde   in eine grōze rede brāht.
5 si wænent mir in leiden,   sō si sō rūnent under in.
nu wizzen algelīche   daz ich sīn friundinne bin,
9 āne nāhe bī gelegen: des hān ich weizgot niht getān.
stechent si ūz ir ougen,
mir rātent mīne sinne   an deheinen andern man.

33

11 BC (MF 13, 27)

Mir erwelten mīniu ougen   einen kindeschen man.
daz nīdent ander vrowen: ich hān in anders niht getān,
5 wan ob ich hān gedienet   daz ich diu liebeste bin.
dar an wil ich kēren   mīn herze und al den sin.
9 swelhiu sīnen willen   hie bevor hāt getān,
verlōs si in von schulden,
der wil ich nu niht wīzen,   sihe ich si unvrœlīchen stān.

34

12 C (MF 14, 1)

Ich sach boten des sumers: daz wāren bluomen alsō rōt.
weistu, schœne frowe,   waz dir ein ritter enbōt ?
5 verholne sīnen dienest.   im wart liebers nie niet.
im trūret sīn herze   sīt er nu jungest von dir schiet.
9 nu hœhe im sīn gemüete   gegen dirre sumerzīt.
frō enwirt er niemer,
ē er an dīnem arme   sō rehte güetlīche gelīt.

32. Text of C.
2 'they have served me ill'.
7 'now may they all know . . . .'
11 'Even if they pierce their eyes out. . . .' The text is probably corrupt, and is
likely to have contained originally an imprecation similar to that of **161**. 34–35.

33. Text of B.
5 *dienen* has here the general sense of 'deserve', 'merit', rather than the technical
sense of 'to serve' as e.g. in **31**. 3.

34. 11 *enwirt*: *wirt* C.

KEISER HEINRICH
(KAISER HEINRICH)

HEINRICH VI (1165–97), son of Barbarossa, is given the place of honour as the first poet in manuscripts B and C. He was crowned king of Germany in 1169, invested with lands in Germany in 1179, and his coming to knighthood was celebrated at the magnificent Whitsun Festival of 1184. In 1186 he was crowned king of Italy, and in 1191 became Holy Roman Emperor. A famous episode in his career was the retention in captivity of Richard Cœur de Lion, who was only able to procure his release by means of a heavy ransom, and by doing homage to the Emperor for England. Heinrich had an only son, later the Emperor Friedrich II, who was renowned for his cultivation of the arts and who was one of the patrons of Walther von der Vogelweide.

Some editors have doubted the authenticity of the ascription to Heinrich VI, taking the references to power in his poems to be mere poetic comparisons, but the manner of expression leaves little doubt that the author of these poems had real pretensions to the highest power (see note on 35). There is, in fact, no reason to call into question the attribution in the manuscripts. The formal structure of the poems is also appropriate to the approximate date of composition, as it can be deduced from the facts of Heinrich's life (i.e. c. 1180–90).

There is much greater technical virtuosity than in any of the earlier poets. Among the older features, which link Kaiser Heinrich with Der von Kürenberc and Meinloh, are the continued use of the Germanic long line, the loose connexion between the strophes in 36, and the persistence of a variable metrical foot. More advanced, however, is the complex unity of 35, the balance between long line and half-line in 36 and 37, the varied structure of the strophe, achieved by differing length of line and the skilful use of rhyme (the threefold rhyme of 35 and the enclosing rhyme of 37 are not found before this date). The greater formal variety is no doubt a sign of Romance influence.

35

I   1 BC (MF 5, 16)

Ich grüeze mit gesange die süezen
die ich vermīden niht wil noch enmac.
daz ich si von munde rehte mohte grüezen,
ach leides, des ist manic tac.
5   swer nu disiu liet singe vor ir,
der ich sō gar unsenfteclīch enbir,
ez sī wīp oder man, der habe si gegrüezet von mir.

II   2 BC

Mir sint diu rīch und diu lant undertān
swenne ich bī der minneclīchen bin;
10   und swenne ich gescheide von dan,
sō ist mir al mīn gewalt und mīn rīchtuom dāhin,
wan senden kumber den zel ich mir danne ze habe:
sus kan ich an freuden stīgen ūf und ouch abe,
und bringe den wehsel, als ich wæne durch ir liebe ze grabe.

III   3 BC
15   Sīt daz ich si sō herzeclīchen minne
und si āne wenken zallen zīten trage
beide in herze und ouch in sinne,
underwīlent mit vil maniger klage,
waz gīt mir dar umbe diu liebe ze lōne?
20   dā biutet si mirz sō rehte schōne:
ē ich mich ir verzige, ich verzige mich ē der krōne.

IV   4 BC

Er sündet swer des niht geloubet:
ich möhte geleben manigen lieben tac,
ob joch niemer krōne kæme ūf mīn houbet;
25   des ich mich ān si niht vermezzen mac.
verlür ich si, waz hette ich danne?
dā töhte ich ze freuden noch wīben noch manne
und wære mīn bester trōst beide ze āhte und ze banne.

35. Text of C, with some readings from B.
   5 *disiu liet* 'these verses'.
   7 'may he thereby have greeted her on my behalf'.
  12 'I count only longing grief then as my lot'.
  14 'and will, I think, suffer this changing fortune until the grave for her sake'.

36

I   5 BC (MF 4, 17)

Wol hœher danne rīche   bin ich alle die zīt,
sō sō güetlīche   diu guote bī mir līt.
5 si hāt mich mit ir tugende   gemachet leides vrī.
ich kom ir nie sō verre   sīt der jugende,
9 ir enwære mīn stætez herze   ie nāhe bī.

II   6 BC

Ich hān den līp gewendet   an einen ritter guot.
daz ist alsō verendet   daz ich bin wol gemuot.
15 daz nīdent ander frowen   und habent des haz
und sprechent mir ze leide   daz si in wellen schowen.
mir geviel in al der werlte   nie nieman baz.

37

I   7 BC (MF 4, 35)

'Rītest du nu hinnen,   der aller liebeste man ?
du bist in mīnen sinnen   für alle die ich ie gewan.
5 kumest du mir niht schiere,   sō verliuse ich mīnen līp:
den möhte in al der welte
got niemer mir vergelten,'   sprach daz minneclīche wīp.

II   8 BC

10 'Wol dir, geselle guote,   daz ich ie bī dir gelac.
du wonest mir in dem muote   die naht unde ouch den tac.
14 du zierest mīne sinne   und bist mir dar zuo holt:
nu merkent wie ich daz meine:
als edel gesteine,   swā man daz leit in daz golt.'

36. Text of C, with *sō sō* (3) from B: *so also* C.
  1 *danne richer* B. The reading of C is preferable to the emendation *dannez riche*
('than the emperor') usually adopted. 'I am indeed more than powerful. . . .'
  7–8 *ich kom ir nie sit in ivgende* B, *ich kom sit nie so verre ir ivgende* C.

37. Text of B. with a few readings from C.
  1 Cf. **1.** 11.
  7–8 *den mōhte mir in al dē welten. got niemer vergelten* C, *den moht mir got in alle
der welte niemer vergelten* B.

HEINRICH VON VELDEKE

HEINRICH VON VELDEKE was a native of Veldeke, west of Hasselt in Belgian Limburg. Various members of his family are attested between 1195 and 1264, but the poet himself can only be dated approximately by reference to his works. Apart from the lyrics, he composed a life of St. Servatius, patron saint of Maastricht, and the *Eneide*, an epic based on Vergil's *Aeneid* through the intermediary of the Old French *Roman d'Énéas*. The *Servatius* is dedicated to Countess Agnes van Loen, who is last attested in 1175, and it must therefore have been written prior to that date, possibly between 1170 and 1175. The epilogue to the *Eneide* relates that the manuscript was stolen when four-fifths of the poem was already finished and only returned to the poet nine years later in Thuringia, where he finished the work at the court of Landgraf Hermann. In the concluding section of the work the poet also refers to his own participation in the great festival at Mainz in 1184. The work was thus finished after that date, and was probably begun about 1175. The dating of the lyrics is uncertain, but there are definite correspondences between them and the description of the love relation between Eneas and Lavinia in the *Eneide*, which occurs in the second part of the work, but both before and after the break in composition. It is therefore impossible to say more than that the lyrics are roughly contemporaneous with the *Eneide*.

The manuscript tradition of Heinrich von Veldeke's work poses linguistic problems. The Servatius legend is preserved only in Limburg form (mainly no doubt on account of its local interest), the *Eneide* in High German form, and the lyrics in predominantly High German form, but with marked traces of the poet's native dialect in the vocabulary (e.g. *blīde* instead of the High German *frō*), and more particularly in the rhymes. It is usually assumed that the poet wrote the poems in his native dialect, and that they have been imperfectly transposed in the manuscripts into High German form. Frings has attempted a reconstruction of the poems in the Limburg dialect in a form which most editors follow (Frings/Schieb, *Heinrich von Veldeke: Die Servatiusbruchstücke und die Lieder*).

In the illustrations of B. and C (see frontispiece), Heinrich von Veldeke is shown against a natural background suggestive of spring, but in an attitude of pensive melancholy—a clear allusion to the opening lines of **38**.

Heinrich von Veldeke is subject to Romance influences both in content and form. The cult of love, with the lady as the sovereign arbiter of the man's fate, is seen clearly in his work. The tripartite construction, which is found in all the following poems, is of Romance origin. There is great variety and skill in the handling of metrical forms.

38

The texts are given in Frings's reconstruction, except where stated in the notes. For purposes of comparison, the first strophe of 38 is given on the right according to manuscript C.

I	I BC (MF 56, 1)
Het is gūde nouwe māre	Ez sint guotiu niuwe mære
dat dī vogele openbāre	daz die vogel offenbære
singen dā men blūmen sīt.	singent dā man die bluomen siet.
tūt den tīden in den jāre	ze den zīten in dem jære
5 stūnde't dat men blīde wāre:	stüende wol daz man frō wære:
leider des ne bin ich nīt.	leider des enbin ich niet.
mīn dumbe herte mich verrīt,	mīn tumbez herze mīn verriet
dat ich mūt unsachte ende	daz [ich] muoz unsanfte und
swāre	swære
dragen leit dat mich geschīt.	tragen daz leit daz mir beschiet.

II	2 BC
10 Dī scōneste ende dī beste vrouwe	
tuschen Roden ende der Souwen	
gaf mich blītscap hī bevoren.	
dat is mich komen al te rouwen	
dore dumpheit, nīwet van untrouwen,	
15 dat ich here hulde hebbe verloren	
dī ich ter bester hadde erkoren	
ofte in der werelt īman scouwe.	
noch dan vorchte ich heren toren.	

38. 4 *in den jāre*: acc. and dat. fall together in this dialect; cf. also **38**. 9, 12, 23, 25, and **39**. 5, 9, 27, 28.
  5 'it would be fitting to rejoice'.
  9 *tragen* BC. Frings emends to *dougen*, 'suffer'.
  11 'Between the Rhône and the Save'. Such geographical formulas are common; cf. **3**. 2 and **96**. 25.
  17 *ofte* = HG *oder*; 'or (the best) anyone can see anywhere'.
  18 *noch dan* 'moreover': *noch sere* BC.

III 3 BC

Al te hōge gerende minne
brachte mich al ūt den sinne.
dū ich here ougen ende munt
sach sō wale stān ende here kinne,
dū wart mich dat herte binnen
van sō sūter dumpheit wunt,
dat mich wīsheit wart unkunt.
des bin ich wale worden inne
bit scaden sint te maneger stunt.

IV 4 BC

Dat quāde wort het sī verwāten
dat ich nīne kunde lāten,
dū mich bedrouch mīn dumbe wān.
der ich was gerende ūter māten,
ich bat here in der caritāten
dat si mich mūste al umbevān.
sō vele ne hadde ich nīt gedān
dat si ein wēnech ūter strāten
dore mich te unrechte wolde stān.

39

I 13 A (MF 57, 10)

'Ich bin blīde, sint dī dage
līchten ende werden lanc,'
sprac ein vrouwe al sunder clage
vrīlīke ende āne al gedwanc.
'des segge ich mīnen gelucke danc
dat ich ein sulic herte drage
dat ich dore negeinen bōsen cranc
ane mīner blītscap nīne verzage.

27 *bit* = HG *mit*.
28 *quāde*: *ùbel* BC. Frings emends to *quāt* as the appropriate form in the Limburg dialect.
33 *mūste* 'might'.
34 f. According to Frings, Middle Dutch *so vele doen dat* = 'bring sth. about'. 'I was not able to prevail upon her to agree for my sake to deviate a little from the straight path of rectitude.'
39. 1 Frings emends *fro* A to *blīde* in keeping with *blītscap* of l. 8.
5–8 'I thank my good fortune that I am so disposed as never to be shaken in my happiness by any wrong done to me.'

II   14 A, 5 BC

Mich hadde wīlen te einen stunden
10   wale gedīnet ouch ein man,
sō dat ich heme vele gūdes unde;
des ich heme nū nīwet an,
sint dat hē den mūt gewan
dat'er eischen mich begunde
15   dat ich heme bat entseggen kan
dan hē't ane mich gewerven kunde.

III   15 A

Het quam van dumbes herten rāde,
het is te dumpheit ouch ergān.
ich warnde heme es al te spāde
20   dat'er hedde ane mich misdān.
wi mochte ich dat in gūde verstān
dat hē mich dorperlīke bāde
dat ich heme mūste al umbevān ?
[het sal heme noch ergān te quāde.]

IV   16 A, 6 BC

25   Ich wānde dat'er hovesch wāre:
des was ich heme van herten holt.
dat segge ich ūch al openbāre:
des is er van mich āne scolt.
des drage ich mich ein gūt gedolt:
30   mich is sīn scade vele unmāre.
hē īsch mich al te rīken solt:
des ich vele wale van heme entbāre.

9 *te einen stunden* (with the pl. of the indefinite article), 'at one time'.
11 *unde*, 12 *an*. The MSS. have *gunde* and *gan* which obscure the rhyme.
15–16 'that which I am better able to refuse him, than he to gain from me'.
18 *is: zal* A.
21 *in gûde verstān* 'take in good part'.
24 'it will have further ill consequences for him'.
28 *des ist er von mir vnverscholt* BC. This line is probably corrupt. In the form adopted here it would mean 'in respect of that (i.e. that I should be favourably disposed to him) he is without reason', 'he has no reason to expect it from me'.
29 'I am unmoved by that'.

V   17 A, 7 BC

Hē īsch mich al te lōse minne,
dī ne vant'er ane mich nīt.
35 dat quam van sīnen cranken sinne,
want et heme sīn dumpheit rīt.
wat of heme scade dār ave geschīt ?
des brenge ich heme vele wale in inne
dat hē sīn spil te unrechte ersīt
dē't breket ēre hē't gewinne.'

40

                                1 A, 10 BC (MF 58, 35)

Tristrant mūste āne sīnen danc
stāde sīn der koninginnen,
want poisūn heme dār tū dwanc
mēre dan dī cracht der minnen.
5 des sal mich dī gūde danc
weten dat ich nīne gedranc
sulic pīment ende ich sī minne
bat dan hē, ende mach dat sīn.
wale gedāne, valsches āne,
10 lāt mich wesen dīn
ende wis dū mīn.

41

I   12 B, 13 C (MF 59, 23)

In den tīden van den jāre
dat dī dage werden lanc
ende dat weder weder clāre,
sō ernouwen openbāre
5 merelāre heren sanc,

38–40 'I will indeed make it plain to him that he misunderstands the game who breaks off before winning it.'

40. 6–7 *das ich sólhen (solkē C) trank. nie genam* BC.
      dc ich niene gedranc alsvlhen pin A.
Bartsch's emendation to *pĭment* 'spiced wine', 'love potion' is usually adopted.
      10 *lāt: la* ABC.

41. 2 *werden: sint* BC.

di uns brengen līve māre.
gode mach her's weten danc
dē hevet rechte minne
sunder rouwe ende āne wanc.

II   14 BC

10   Ich bin blīde dore here ēre
dī mich hevet dat gedān
dat ich van den rouwen kēre,
dē mich wīlen irde sēre.
dat is mich nū alsō ergān:
15   ich bin rīke ende grōte hēre
sint ich mūste al umbevān
dī mich gaf rechte minne
sunder wīc ende āne wān.

III   13 B, 12 C

Dī mich drumbe willen nīden
20   dat mich līves īt geschīt,
dat mach ich vele sachte līden
noch mīne blītscap nīwet mīden,
ende ne wille drumbe nīt
nā gevolgen den unblīden,
25   sint dat sī mich gerne sīt
dī mich dore rechte minne
lange pīne dolen līt.

10 *dore here ēre*: Frings translates 'zu ihrem eigenen Ruhm, wofür sie gepriesen sei'.

13 *irde* 'tormented'.

15 Frings points out that *hēre* must here be a noun, because in Veldeke's dialect the adjective would be *gehēre*: 'I am rich and a great lord. . . .'

16 *mūste* 'was permitted to'.

18 *wīc* corresponds to the HG form *wīch*, and is virtually identical in meaning with *wanc* of l. 9: 'without wavering or vain hope'.

25 *sint dat*: *da nach das* BC.

27 *dolen*. Frings emends to *dougen* here as the form appropriate to Veldeke's dialect, but this seems unnecessary as *dolen* is found also in Veldeke's *Servatius* fragments, written in his native dialect. It is probably a case where he is influenced by HG.

42

I   21 BC (MF 61, 33)

Sō wē der minnen is sō vrūt
dat hē der minnen dīnen kan,
ende hē dore minne pīne dūt,
wale heme, dē is ein sālech man.
5   van minnen komet allet gūt,
dī minne maket reinen mūt,
wat solde ich āne minne dan ?

II   22 BC

Dī scōne minne ich āne wanc,
ich weit wale here minne is clār.
10   of mīne minne is valsche ende cranc,
sō ne wirt ouch nimmer minne wār.
ich segge here mīner minnen danc,
bī here minnen steit mīn sanc.
hē is dump deme minne dunket swār.

43

I   28 B, 26 C (MF 62, 25)

In den aprillen   sō dī blūmen springen,
sō louven dī linden   ende grūnen dī būken,
5   sō heven bit willen   dī vogele here singen,
sint sī minne vinden   al dā sī sī sūken
9   ane heren genōt,   want here blītscap is grōt
der mich nīne verdrōt,   want sī swegen al den winter stille.

42. 1 'whoever has an aptitude for love'.
3 *pīne dūt* 'takes pains'.
4 *wol im derst ein selig man* C, missing B. Frings emends to *dē is ein vele minne-sālech man*, because of the repetition of *minne* in every other line, and the use of the compound *minnesālech* in Veldeke's *Eneide*, l. 10023. The reading adopted here is that of Brinkmann.
8 *āne wanc: svnder dank* BC.
10 *ob miniv minne ist kranc* C, *obe mine minne mit velsche sin* B. Frings adopts the unconvincing emendation of Vogt: *of mīne minne īt velsche ein cranc*, translating it as 'Wenn man meint, meine Minne trübe ein Makel ....' The MSS. readings are no doubt corrupt, and even the emendation of Brinkmann adopted here can only be regarded as an approximation.

43. 5–6 'The birds begin to sing with a will.' *so singēt die vogele ōn heben iren willen* B, *so haben ir wellen. da die vogel singen* C. The form *heben* in B probably indicates that the original verb was *heven* and that the phrase is parallel to that in l. 19.
7 *sint: wan* BC.

II   25 BC

Dū si ane den rīsen   dī blūmen gesāgen
15 bī den bladen springen,   dū wāren sī rīke
here manechfalder wīsen   der sī wīlen plāgen.
19 sī huven here singen   lūde ende vrōlīke,
nedere ende hō.   mīn mūt steit ouch alsō
dat ich wille wesen vrō.   recht is dat ich mīn gelucke prīse.

III   26 B, 27 C

25 Mochte ich erwerven   mīner vrouwen hulde!
kunde ich dī gesūken   als't here getāme!
29 ich sal noch verderven   al dore mīne sculde,
sī ne wolde gerūken   dat sī van mich nāme
būte āne dōt   up genāde ende dore nōt,
35 want et got nīne gebōt   dat negein man gerne solde sterven.

24 *gelucke* 'lot', 'fate'.
28 The form first suggested by Frings is adopted here (*als es ir gezeme* BC). In his most recent edition of the text he prints *als here wale getāme* after the pattern of similar examples in the *Eneide*.
31 f. 'unless she would deign to accept from me a penance other than death in exchange for her favour, for it must be so, since God never decreed that any man should be willing to die.'

FRIDERICH VON HŪSEN

(FRIEDRICH VON HAUSEN)

THE poet appears in the illustrations of both manuscripts as a Crusader in a small boat. He was probably born about 1155, in the neighbourhood of Worms. He is attested between 1171 and 1190 in the immediate entourage of Friedrich I (Barbarossa), and his son Heinrich VI (see 35–37). He was in Italy in 1175, 1186, and 1187. He was no doubt present at the great Whitsun Festival at Mainz in 1184, where he perhaps met Guiot de Provins, who is known to have been there, and possibly also Conon de Béthune. He was present at the meeting between Barbarossa and the French king Philippe Auguste at Meuzon in 1187. Friedrich von Hausen took part in the Third Crusade and perished at the battle of Philomelium in Asia Minor in 1190.

His poetry is subject to considerable Romance influence, both in content and form. Most strophes have a tripartite construction. There is great skill in the disposition of rhymes and the use of *Responsionen*. There are still a considerable number of assonating rhymes, as in the early poets.

There have been several attempts to determine the chronological order of the poems, but the evidence is insufficient. Those poems dealing solely with the theme of *minne* are here placed together, and the two which introduce the new theme of the conflict between the service of God and the service of the lady are at the end of the selection. It is, however, impossible to tell when each poem was actually written, and the Crusading poems need not necessarily be any later than the others.

44

I   1 BC (MF 42, 1)

Ich muoz von schulden sīn unfrō,
sīt si jach dō ich bī ir was,
ich möhte heizen Ēnēas,
und solte aber des wol sicher sīn,   si wurde niemer mīn Tīdō.
6 wie sprach sī dō?

44. Text according to C.

3–6 'even if I were called Aeneas, I could be very sure she would never be my Dido'. Virgil's epic was known in France through the *Roman d'Énéas* on which Heinrich von Veldeke based his *Eneide*. The poet may have known either the French or the German version.

aleine frömdet mich ir līp,
si hāt iedoch des herzen mich   beroubet gar für elliu wīp.

II   2 BC

10 Mit gedanken muoz ich die zīt
vertrīben als ich beste kan,
und lernen des ich nie began:
trūren unde sorgen pflegen;   des was vil ungewent mīn līp.
15 durch elliu wīp
wānde ich niemer sīn bekomen
in sō rehte kumberlīche nōt,   als ich von einer hān genomen.

III   3 BC

Mīn herze muoz ir klūse sīn
20 al die wīle ich habe den līp;
sō muozen iemer elliu wīp
vil ungedrungen drinne wesen,   swie līhte si sich getrœste mīn,
nu werde schīn
25 ob rehte stæte iht müge gefromen.
der wil ich iemer gegen ir pflegen;   diu ist mir von ir güete
komen.

45

I   5 C (MF 43, 28)

An der genāden al min fröide stāt,
dā enmac mir gewerren weder huote noch nīt.
mich enhilfet dienst noch mīner friunde rāt,
und daz si mir ist liep alsam mīn selbes līp.

7–8 'it is she alone who is cold to me, yet she before all (other) women has completely robbed me of my heart', i.e. it is the reverse of the Aeneas–Dido situation, in which Dido remains faithful, whereas Aeneas deserts her.
19 'my heart must be her hermit's cell'—there is the twofold idea that the lady is enclosed in his heart, and that she is enshrined there alone.
21–23 Lit.: 'therefore all (other) women will never be jostled in it by me, however easily she can dispense with me'. These lines are not entirely satisfactory, but the sense seems to be: 'I will never trouble other women with my attentions, however little she cares for me.'
45. 1 'All my happiness depends on her favour.'
2 *hŏte noch kip* C. MS. C frequently makes changes to improve the rhyme, and this is no doubt an instance.

5   mir erwendet ir hulde nieman wan si selbe;
     si tuot mir alleine den kumber den ich muoz tragen.
     warumbe solte ich danne von den merkæren klagen,
     nu ich ir huote alsō lützel engelde?

          II   6 C

     Mangen herzen ist von der huote wē,
10   und jehent ez sī in ein angstlīchiu nōt;
     sō engerte daz mīne aller rīchheit niht mē
     wan müese ez si līden unz an mīnen tōt.
     wer möhte hān grōze fröide āne kumber?
     nach solher swære sō rang ich alle zīt:
15   dōne maht ich leider niht komen in den nīt.
     des hat gelücke vil getān an mir tumber.

          III   7 C

     Einer grōzen swære muoz ich leider ænic sīn,
     die doch erfürhtet vil manic sælic man:
     unbetwungen von huote sō ist daz herze mīn;
20   mir ist leit daz ich von ir den fride ie gewan,
     wande ich die nōt wolde iemer güetlich līden,
     het ich von schulden verdient den haz.
     nīt umbe ir minne daz tæte mir baz
     danne ich si beide sus muoz mīden.

46

          I   11 C (MF 45, 1)

     Gelebt ich noch die lieben zīt
       daz ich daz lant solte beschouwen,
     dar inne al mīn fröide līt
       nu lange an einer schœnen frouwen,

---

5 *wan ir melde* C. See note on l. 2.
10 *angeslichiu* C.
16 *gelücke* 'fortune', 'fate' (not specialized in a good sense).
20 *mir ist leit vō ir dc ich den fride ie gewan* C.
23 *tæte: tet* C.

5   sō gesæhe mīnen līp
       niemer weder man noch wīp
       getrūren noch gewinnen rouwen.
       mich dūhte nu vil manigez guot,
       dā von ie swære was mīn muot.

       II   12 C
10   Ich wānde ir ē vil verre sīn
       dā ich nu vil nāhe wære.
       alrērste hat daz herze mīn
       von der frömde grōze swære.
       ez tuot wol sīn triuwe schīn.
15   wær ich iender umb den Rīn,
       sō friesche ich līhte ein ander mære,
       des ich doch leider nie vernam
       sīt daz ich über die berge kam.

                        47
       I   15 C (MF 52, 37)
       Wāfenā, wie hāt mich Minne gelāzen!
       diu mich betwanc daz ich lie mīn gemüete
       an solhen wān der mich wol mac verwāzen,
       ez ensī daz ich genieze ir güete,
5   von der ich bin   alsō dicke āne sin.
       mich dūhte ein gewin,   und wolte diu guote
       wizzen die nōt diu wont in mīnem muote.
       II   16 C
       Wāfenā, waz habe ich getān sō ze unēren
       daz mir diu guote ir gruozes niht engunde?
10   sus kan si mir wol daz herze verkēren.
       daz ich in der werlte bezzer wīp iender funde,
       seht dēst mīn wān,   dā für sō wil ichz hān,
       und wil dienen   mit triuwen der guoten,
       diu mich dā bliuwet vil sēre āne ruoten.

46. 5 *min lip* C.
  7 *rouwen* cf. **49**. 21.
47. 3 *verwāzen* 'destroy'.
  10 *verkēren*, lit. 'change, pervert, lead astray': 'ensnare my heart'; cf. **27**. 9.
  11 *iender*, here 'nowhere'.
  12 *dā für*, etc. 'I will consider it to be so.'
  13 The metrical pattern of the corresponding lines suggests that a word is missing
after *dienen*. Vogt (MF³) and Kraus (MF³⁰), following Schröder, add *nochdan*,
Brinkmann *so ich kan*.

III 43 B, 45 C

15 Waz mac daz sīn daz diu werlt heizet minne,
und ez mir tuot sō wē zaller stunde
und ez mir nimet sō vil mīner sinne?
ich wānde niht daz ez ieman erfunde.
getorste ich ez jehen   daz ich ez hete gesehen
20 dā von mir ist geschehen   alsō vil herzesēre,
sō wolte ich dar an gelouben iemer mēre.

IV 44 B, 46 C

Minne, got müeze mich an dir rechen!
wie vil du mīnem herzen der fröiden wendest!
und möhte ich dir dīn krumbez ouge ūz gestechen,
25 des het ich reht, wan du vil lützel endest
an mir solhe nōt   sō mir dīn līp gebōt.
und wærest du tōt,   sō dūhte ich mich rīche.
sus muoz ich von dir leben betwungenlīche.

48

I 30 B, 32 C (MF 48, 32)

Dō ich von der guoten schiet
und ich zir niht ensprach
als mir wære liep,
des līde ich ungemach.
5 daz liez ich durch die valschen diet
von der mir nie liep geschach.
ich wünsche ir anders niet,
wan der die helle brach,
der füege ir wē unt ach.

II 31 B, 33 C

10 'Si wænent hüeten mīn
die sīn doch niht bestāt,
und tuont ir nīden schīn,
daz wenic si vervāt.

---

18 *ez . . . erfunde* 'could find it out' (i.e. the nature of love).
24 *krump*: 'squinting', because Love has looked askance at him.
48. Text of C, with l. 3 according to B.
11 'those whom it concerns not at all'.

15

si möhten ē den Rīn
gekēren in den Pfāt,
ē ich mich iemer sīn
getrōste, swiez ergāt,
der mir gedienet hāt.'

49

I   32 B, 34 C (MF 49, 13)

Mir ist daz herze wunt
und siech gewesen nu vil lange
— daz ist reht, wan ez ist tump —
sīt ez eine vrowen ērst bekande.

5

der keiser ist in allen landen,
kuste er si ze einer stunt
an ir vil rōten munt,
er jæhe ez wære im wol ergangen.

II   33 B, 35 C

Sīt ich daz herze hān

10

verlāzen an der besten eine,
des sol ich lōn enpfān
von der selben die ich dā meine,
swie selten ich ez ir bescheine,
sō bin ich ez doch der man

15

der ir baz heiles gan
danne in der welte lebe deheine.

III   34 B, 36 C

Wer möhte mir den muot
getrœsten, wan ein schœne vrowe,
diu mīnem herzen tuot

20

leit diu nieman kan beschouwen?
dur nōt sō līde ich den rouwen,
wan ez sich ze hōhe huop.
wirt mir diu Minne unguot,
sō sol ir niemer man volle trouwen.

49. Text of B.
    21 *roúwen*: *rúwen* BC, 'grief'. It is clear from the rhyme that the poet must have
written *rouwen*, the form in his native Rhenish-Franconian dialect. cf. **46. 7.**
    22 'because it (my heart) aspired too high'.
    24 *troúwen*: *trúwen* BC.

50

I   35 B, 37 C (MF 49, 37)

Ich sihe wol daz got wunder kan
von schœne würken ūz wībe.
daz ist an ir wol schīn getān,
wan er vergaz niht an ir lībe.
5   den kumber den ich [des] līde,
den wil ich [iemer] gerne hān,
zediu daz ich mit ir belībe
und al mīn wille sül ergān.
mīn vrowe sehe waz si des tuo:
10   dā stāt dehein scheiden zuo.

II   36 B, 38 C

Si gedenke niht daz ich sī der man
der si ze kurzen wīlen minne.
ich hān von kinde an si verlān
daz herze mīn und al die sinne.
15   ich wart an ir nie valsches inne,
sīt ich si sō liep gewan.
mīn herze ist ir ingesinde,
und wil ouch stæte an ir bestān.
mīn vrowe sehe waz si des tuo:
20   dā stāt dehein scheiden zuo.

51

I   37 B, 39 C (MF 50, 19)

Ich lobe got der sīner güete,
daz er mir ie verlēch die sinne
daz ich si nam in mīn gemüete,
wan si ist wol wert daz man si minne.
5   noch bezzer ist daz man ir hüete
dan iegelīcher sīnen willen
spræche, daz si ungerne hōrte
und mir die vröide gar zerstōrte.

II   38 B, 40 C

Noch bezzer ist daz ich si mīde
10   danne si āne huote wære
und ir deheiner mir ze nīde
spræche des ich vil gerne enbære.

50, 51. Text of B, with a few readings from C.

ich hān si erkorn ūz allen wīben,
sō lāze ich niht durch die merkære;
vrömede ich si mit den ougen,
si minnet iedoch mīn herze tougen.

III   39 B, 41 C
Mīn līp was ie unbetwungen
und ungemuot von allen wīben:
alrēst hān ich rehte befunden
waz man nāch liebem wībe līde.
des muoz ich ze manigen stunden
der besten vrowen eine mīden,
des ist mīn herze dicke swære,
als ez mit vröiden gerne wære.

IV   40 B, 42 C
Swie dicke ich lobe die huote,
dēswār ez wart doch nie mīn wille
daz ich in iemer in dem muote
wurde holt, die dar die sinne
gewendet hānt daz si der guoten
entpfrömden wellent stæte minne.
dēswār, tuon ich in niht mēre,
ich gefreische doch gerne alle ir unēre.

52

I   6 B, 20 C (MF 45, 37)
Si darf mich des zīhen niet,
ich enhete si von herzen liep.
des möhte si die wārheit an mir sehen,
und wil si es jehen.
ich kom sīn dicke in sō grōze nōt,
daz ich den liuten guoten morgen bōt
gegen der naht.
ich was sō verre an si verdāht
daz ich mich underwīlent niht versan,
und swer mich gruozte daz ich sīn niht verstān.

51. 18 *und ungemuot: und doch gemůt* BC.
      28 *die so gar die sinne* BC.
52. Text of B.
      1 *niht* BC. The usually accepted emendation to *niet* is rendered probable by the
impure rhyme with *liep*.

II   7 B, 21 C

Mīn herze unsanfte sīnen strīt
lāt den ez nu mange zīt
hāt wider daz alrebeste wīp,
der ie mīn līp
15   muoz dienen swar ich iemer var.
ich bin ir holt: swenne ich vor gote getar,
sō gedenke ich ir.
daz geruoch ouch er vergeben mir:
ob ich des sünde süle hān,
20   wie geschuof er si sō rehte wol getān?

III   8 B, 22 C

Mit grozen sorgen hat mīn līp
gerungen alle sīne zīt.
ich hete liep daz mir vil nāhe gie;
daz verlie mich nie,
25   an wīsheit kērte ich mīnen muot.
daz was diu minne, diu noch manigem tuot
die selben klage.
nu wil ich mich an got gehaben:
der kan den liuten helfen ūz der nōt.
30   nieman weiz wie nāhe im ist der tōt.

IV   9 B, 23 C

Mīner vrowen was ich undertān,
diu āne lōn mīnen dienst nam.
von der sprich ich niht wan allez guot,
wan daz ir muot
35   wider mich ze unmilte ist gewesen.
vor aller nōt dō wānde ich sīn genesen,
dō sich verlie
mīn herze ūf genāde an sie,
der ich dā leider funden niene hān.
40   nu wil ich dienen dem der lōnen kan.

16 *vor* with C: *von* B.
24–25 Kraus (MF³⁰) emends to *dazn lie mich nie an wīsheit kēren mīnen muot.*
32 *nam*: *nan* BC.

V   28 B, 24 C
Ich kom von minne in kumber grōz,
des ich doch selten ie genōz.
swaz schaden ich dā von gewunnen hān,
sō friesch nie man
45   daz ich ir iht spræche wan guot,
noch mīn munt von vrowen niemer getuot.
doch klage ich daz
daz ich sō lange gotes vergaz:
den wil ich iemer vor in allen haben,
50   und in dā nāch ein holdez herze tragen.

53

I   10 B, 25 C (MF 47, 9)
Mīn herze und mīn lip die wellent scheiden,
diu mit ein ander wāren nu manige zīt.
der līp wil gerne vehten an die heiden:
sō hāt iedoch daz herze erwelt ein wīp
5   vor al der welt. daz müet mich iemer sīt,
daz si ein ander niht volgent beide.
mir habent diu ougen vil getān ze leide.
got eine müeze scheiden noch den strīt.

II   24 B, 27 C
Ich wānde ledic sīn von solher swære,
10   dō ich daz kriuze in gotes ēre nam.
ez wære ouch reht daz ez alsō wære,
wan daz mīn stætekeit mir sīn verban.
ich solte sīn ze rehte ein lebendic man,
ob ez den tumben willen sīn verbære.
15   nu sihe ich wol daz im ist gar unmære
wie ez mir an dem ende süle ergān.

III   11 B, 26 C
Sīt ich dich, herze, niht wol mac erwenden,
dune wellest mich vil trūreclīchen lān,
sō bite ich got daz er dich geruoche senden
20   an eine stat dā man dich welle enpfān.

53. Text of B, with a few readings from C.
12 'but that my constancy forbade me that'. Most editors emend *mīn* to *sīn*,
referring it to *herze*.
16 *wie es mir sūle (svle C) an dem ende ergan* BC.
20 *welle enpfān: wol enpfan* B, *wol welle enpfan* C.

owē wie sol ez armen dir ergān!
wie getorstest du eine an solhe nōt ernenden?
wer sol dir dīne sorge helfen enden
mit [solhen] triuwen als ich hān getān?

ALBREHT VON JOHANSDORF

NOTHING certain is known of the poet's life and the date at which he lived. He belongs to a Bavarian family attested as *ministeriales* of the bishops of Bamberg and Passau between the years 1172 and 1253. The identification of the poet is made difficult by the fact that different generations of the family bear the same name; thus for instance a Passau charter of *c.* 1180 is witnessed by 'Alberto de Janestorf et filio suo Adalberto' (both variant forms of the name whose German form is Albreht). It is usually thought that the poet is the Albreht attested between 1180 or 1185 and 1209. If this is correct, he appears in 1201 and 1204 as witness to two deeds of Bishop Wolfger of Passau, the patron of Walther von der Vogelweide. His poems appear to suggest his participation in a Crusade, possibly that of 1189–90.

Halbach has tried to show that Albreht is a follower of Walther and Morungen, and that his work is later than is usually thought. (*Walther von der Vogelweide und die Dichter von Minnesangs Frühling*, Stuttgart, 1927, pp. 28–44.) His arguments are, however, unconvincing, as the supposed influence is nothing more than the use of common formulas which are the stock-in-trade of all the poets alike. Another argument advanced in favour of a later dating is the poem *Ich vant āne huote* (**61**) which seems more 'modern' than the rest of Albreht's work and appears to contain reminiscences of Reinmar and Walther. As this poem is, however, only preserved in C, it is insufficient evidence upon which to base a late dating. Indeed it is possible, as has been suggested, that this poem is the work of a later poet—there is a stricter logical connexion between the strophes, a greater number of strophes making up the poem, and a higher degree of technical skill than in his other work. There have been attempts to arrange his poems in chronological order, but the evidence is too slight.

All the strophes are tripartite in structure. There is considerable use of varying length of lines (much more frequent than in Friedrich von Hausen). The *Abgesang* is clearly contrasted from the *Aufgesang* in every poem by this variation in length of lines and by the introduction in every instance of new rhymes. There is very little use of impure rhymes (an instance is *hān: kan* of **58**), and there are none of the consonantal assonances found in Friedrich von Hausen.

54

I   4 B, 5 C, Niune 48 A (MF 87, 29)

Ich und ein wīp, wir haben gestriten
nu vil menege zīt.
ich hān vil leides von ir zorne erliten.
noch heldet si den strīt.
5   nu wænet si dur daz ich var
daz ich si lāze vrī.
got vor der helle niemer mich bewar,
obe daz mīn wille sī.
swie vil daz mer unde ouch die starken ünde toben,
10   ich enwil si niemer tac verloben.
der donreslege mohte aber līhte sīn
dā si mich dur lieze.
nu sprechent wes si wider mich genieze.
si kumet mir niemer tac ūz den gedanken mīn.

II   20 C, Niune 49 A

15   Ob ich si iemer mēre gesehe,
des enweiz ich niht für wār.
dā bī geloube mir, swes ich ir jehe,
ez gēt von herzen gar.
ich minne si vür alliu wīp
20   und swer ir des bī gote.
alle mīne sinne und ouch der līp
daz stēt in ir gebote.
ine erwache niemer ez ensī mīn ērste segen
daz got ir ēren müeze phlegen
25   und lāze ir līp mit lobe hie gestēn.
darnāch ēweclīche
nu gip ir, herre, vröide in dīme rīche,
daz ir geschehe alsō, als müeze ouch mir ergēn.

---

54. Text mainly according to A, with lines 15–18, 20 (missing A), and a few other readings from C.

3 *leides von ir zorne vil* A, *von ir zorne laides* (*leides* C) BC.

11 *līhte* is here used substantivally, meaning 'a small amount': 'it would, however, need but few thunderclaps for her to leave me'.

13 'Now say what advantage she can claim over me.'

17 *dā bī* refers back to 15–16· 'on that account let her believe what I say . . .'.

55

6 B, 7 C, Niune 50 A (MF 88, 19)

Swie verre ich var, sō jāmert mich
wiez noch hie gestē.
ich weiz wol, ez verkēret allez sich,
diu sorge tuot mir wē.
5   die ich hie lāze wol gesunt,
der envind ich leider niht.
der leben sol, dem wirt menic wunder kunt,
daz alle tage geschiht.
wir haben in eime jāre der liute vil verlorn.
10   dā bī sō merkent gotes zorn
und erkenne sich ein ieglichez herze guot.
diu werlt ist unstæte.
ich meine die dā minnent valsche ræte:
den wirt ze jungest schīn wiez an dem ende tuot.

56

5 B, 6 C (MF 88, 33)

Swer minne minneclīche treit
gar āne valschen muot,
des sünde wirt vor gote niht geseit.
si tiuret unde ist guot.
5   man sol mīden bœsen kranc
und minnen reiniu wīp.
tuot erz mit triuwen, sō habe iemer danc
sīn tugentlīcher līp.
kunden si ze rehte beidiu sich bewarn,
10   für die wil ich ze helle varn.
die aber mit [valschen] listen wellent sīn,
für die wil ich niht vallen.
ich meine die dā minnent āne gallen,
als ich mit triuwen tuon die lieben frowen mīn.

55. Text of A, with *ez* (3) from BC (*er* A).
56. Text of C.
   9 *sich bewarn* 'guard against false behaviour', 'act fittingly'. *beidiu* 'both men and women'.

57

I   7 B, 8 C (MF 89, 9)

Swaz ich nu gesinge,
daz ist allez umbe niht: mir weiz sīn niemen danc;
ez wiget allez ringe.
dar ich hān gedienet, dā ist mīn lōn vil kranc.
5   ez ist hiure an gnāden unnæher danne vert
und wirt über ein jār vil līhte kleines lōnes wert.

II   8 B, 9 C

Wie der einez tæte,
des frāge ich, ob ez mit fuoge muge geschehen,
wær ez niht unstæte,
10   der zwein wīben wolte sich für eigen jehen,
beidiu tougenlīche? sprechent, herre, wurre ez iht?
'man solz den man erlouben unde den vrowen niht.'

58

I   9 B, 10 C (MF 89, 21)

Die hinnen varn, die sagen durch got
daz Jerusalēm der reinen stat und ouch dem lande
helfe noch nie nœter wart.
diu klage wirt der tumben spot.
5   die sprechent alle 'wær ez unserm herren ande,
er ræche ez ān ir aller vart'.
nu mugen si denken daz er leit den grimmen tōt.
der grōzen marter was ime ouch vil gar unnōt,
10   wan daz in erbarmet unser val.
swen nu sīn criuze und sīn grap niht wil erbarmen,
daz sint von ime die sælden armen.

---

57. Text of B.
  10 *jehen: geben* BC.
58. Text of B, with *tumben* (4), *herren* (5), *si* (7) according to C.
  7 *mugent* BC.
  11 'they will receive little blessing from Him'.

II   10 B, 11 C

Nu waz gelouben wil der hān,
und wer sol im ze helfe komen an sīnem ende,
der gote wol hulfe und tuot ez niht?
15   als ich mich versinnen kan,
ez ensī vil gar ein ēhaft nōt diu in des wende,
ich wæne er ez übel übersiht.
nu lāt daz grap und ouch daz criuze geruowet ligen:
die heiden wellent einer rede an uns gesigen,
20   daz gotes muoter niht sī ein maget.
swem disiu rede niht nāhe an sīn herze vellet,
owē war hāt sich der gesellet!

III   11 B, 12 C

Mich habent die sorge ūf daz brāht
daz ich vil gerne kranken muot von mir vertrībe;
25   des was mīn herze her niht frī.
ich gedenke alsō vil manige naht
'waz sol ich wider got nu tuon, ob ich belībe,
daz er mir genædic sī'?
sō weiz ich niht vil grōze schulde die ich habe,
30   niuwan eine, der kume ich niemer abe;
alle sünde liez ich wol wan die:
ich minne ein wīp vor al der welte in mīnem muote.
got herre, daz vervāch ze guote.

59

I   12 B, 13 C (MF 90, 16)

Ich wil gesehen die ich von kinde
her geminnet hān für elliu wīp.
und ist daz ich genāde vinde,
sō gesach ich nie sō guoten līp.
5   obe aber ich ir wære
vil gar unmære,
sō ist si doch diu tugende nie verlie.
fröide und sumer ist noch allez hie.

16 *ein ēhaft nōt* is a legal phrase: 'unless it be a valid reason which prevents him,
I think he does ill to neglect it.'
18 'Now assume that the sepulchre and the cross are not threatened', i.e. even
apart from this, there is a further argument.
27 *belībe* 'remain behind at home'.
59. Text of C.

II 13 B, 14 C

Ich hān alsō her gerungen
10   daz vil trūreclīche stuont mīn leben.
dicke hān ich 'wē' gesungen,
dem wil ich vil schiere ein ende geben.
'wol mich' singe ich gerne,
swenne ichz gelerne.
15   des ist zīt, wan ich gesanc sō nie.
fröide und sumer ist noch allez hie.

60

I 21 C (MF 91, 22)

Wie sich minne hebt daz weiz ich wol;
wie si ende nimt des weiz ich niht.
ist daz ichs inne werden sol
wie dem [herzen] herzeliep geschiht,
5   sō bewar mich vor dem scheiden got,
daz wæn bitter ist.
disen kumber fürhte ich āne spot.

II 22 C

Swā zwei herzeliep gefriundent sich
und ir beider minne ein triuwe wirt,
10   die sol niemen scheiden, dunket mich,
al die wīle unz si der tōt verbirt.
wær diu rede mīn, ich tæte alsō:
verlüre ich mīnen friunt,
seht, sō wurde ich niemer mēre frō.

III 16 B, 17 C

Dā gehœret manic stunde zuo
15   ē daz sich gesamne ir zweier muot.
dā daz ende [denne] unsanfte tuo,
ich wæne wol, daz sī niht guot.
lange sī ez mir [vil] unbekant.
20   und werde ich iemen liep,
der sī sīner triuwe an mir gemant.

60. Text of C.
  4 *geschiht*: *beschiht* C.
  5 *scheiden*: *bescheidē* C.
  6 *wæn* = *wæn ich* 'I think'.
  12 *rede* here 'concern', 'affair': 'If I were in this position . . .'.

IV   17 B, 18 C

Der ich diene und iemer dienen wil,
diu sol mīne rede vil wol verstān.
spræche ich mēre, des wurde alze vil.
25   ich wil ez allez an ir güete lān.
ir genāden der bedarf ich wol.
und wil si, ich bin frō;
und wil si, sō ist mīn herze leides vol.

61

I   29 C (MF 93, 12)

Ich vant āne huote
die vil minneclīchen eine stān.
jā dō sprach diu guote
'waz welt ir sō eine her gegān'?
5   'frouwe, ez ist alsō geschehen.'
'saget, war umbe sīt ir her ? des sult ir mir verjehen.'

II   30 C

'Mīnen senden kumber
klage ich [iu vil] liebe frouwe mīn.'
'wē, waz saget ir tumber ?
10   ir muget iuwer klage wol lāzen sīn.'
'frouwe, ich enmac ir niht enbern.'
'sō wil ich in tūsent jāren niemer iuch gewern.'

III   31 C

'Neinā, küniginne!
daz mīn dienest sō iht sī verlorn!'
15   'ir sīt āne sinne,
daz ir bringet mich in solhen zorn.'
'frouwe, iuwer haz tuot mir den tōt.'
'wer hāt iuch, vil lieber man, betwungen ūf die nōt?'

IV   32 C

'Daz hāt iuwer schœne
20   die ir hāt, vil minneclīchez wīp.'
'iuwer süezen dœne
wolten krenken mīnen stæten līp.'
'frouwe, niene welle got.'
'werte ich iuch, des hetet ir ēre; sō wǣre mīn der spot.'

61. 1 *vant si* C.
22 'were intended to shake my constancy'.

V   33 C
25   'Lāt mich noch geniezen
        daz ich iu von herzen ie was holt.'
        'iuch mac wol verdriezen
        daz ir iuwer wortel gegen mir bolt.'
        'dunket iu mīn rede niht guot?'
30   'jā si hāt beswæret dicke mīnen stæten muot.'

VI   34 C
        'Ich bin ouch vil stæte,
        ob ir ruochet mir der wārheit jehen.'
        'volget miner ræte,
        lāt die bete diu niemer mac geschehen.'
35   'sol ich alsō sīn gewert?'
        'got der wer iuch anderswā des ir an mich dā gert.'

VII   35 C
        'Sol mich dan mīn singen
        und mīn dienest gegen iu niht vervān?'
        'iu sol wol gelingen:
40   āne lōn sō sult ir niht bestān.'
        'wie meinet ir daz, frouwe guot?'
        'daz ir deste werder sīt und dā bī hōchgemuot.'

62

I   36 C, Gedrut 20 A (MF 94, 15)
        Guote liute, holt
        die gābe die got unser herre selbe gīt.
        der al der welte hāt gewalt.
        dienent sīnen solt,
5   der den vil sældehaften dort behalten līt
        mit vröiden iemer manecvalt.
        līdet eine wīle willeclīchen nōt
        vür den iemer mēre wernden tōt.
        got hāt iu beide sēle und līp gegeben:
10   gebt ime des lībes tōt;   daz wirt der sēle ein iemer leben.

25 *So lant* C.
27 'you may well grow weary of aiming your words at me'.
62. Text of A with *iu* (9), *bī* (14), *daz* (32), *hie* (36), *stille* (37), and *der* (39) from C.
5 *līt*, contracted form of *liget*; 'which is stored up there for the blessed'.
8 *vür* 'in exchange for'.
10 *dem libe ein iemᵉ leben* A; *der sele dort ein ewig lebē* C.

II   37 C, Gedrut 21 A
Lā mich, Minne, vrī.
du solt mich eine wīle sunder liebe lān.
du hāst mir gar den sin benomen.
komest du wider bī

15   als ich die reinen gotes vart volendet hān,
sō wis mir aber willekomen.
wilt aber du ūz mīnem herzen scheiden niht,
daz vil līhte unwendic doch geschiht,
vüer ich dich danne mit mir in gotes lant,

20   sō sī er der guoten hie   umbe halben lōn gemant.

III   38 C, Gedrut 22 A
'Owē' sprach ein wīp,
'wie vil mir doch von liebe leides ist beschert!
waz mir diu liebe leides tuot!
vröideloser līp,

25   wie wil du dich gebāren, swenne er hinnen vert,
dur den du wære ie hōchgemuot?
wie sol ich der werlde und mīner klage geleben?
dā bedorft ich rātes zuo gegeben.
kund ich mich beidenthalben nu bewarn,

30   des wart mir nie so nōt.   ez nāhet, er wil hinnen varn.'

IV   39 C, Rubin v. Rͮdigēr C², Gedrut 23 A
Wol si sælic wīp
diu mit ir wības güete daz gemachen kan
daz man si vüeret über sē.
ir vil guoten līp

35   den sol er loben, swer ie herzeliep gewan,
wande ir hie heime tuot alsō wē,
swenne si gedenket stille an sīne nōt.
'lebt mīn herzeliep, oder ist er tōt',
sprichet si, 'sō müeze sīn der pflegen

40   dur den er süezer līp   sich dirre welte hāt bewegen.'

20 *so si er vmbe halben lon der gͦten hie gemant.* A.
so si er der gͦtē dort vmb halben lon gemāt. C.
The reading adopted places *hie* at the end of the first half-line, because in all the other strophes the word in this position is echoed elsewhere, e.g. *tōt* of l. 10 rhymes with *nōt*: *tōt* in I and IV and *nōt* in l. 30. *hie* echoes *vrī*: *bī* (an impure dialect rhyme).
'then may He (God) be exhorted to grant half the reward to the lady in this life'.
Cf. Hartmann von Aue **78**. 45 f.
29 'If I were now able to act fittingly in both respects . . .' (refers to l. 27).

HEINRICH VON MORUNGEN

HEINRICH VON MORUNGEN was a native of northern Thuringia, in the neighbourhood of Sangerhausen. Nothing is known of his date of birth. He is attested in two charters of 1217 and 1218, in the service of Margrave Dietrich of Meissen, who was also a patron of Walther. The document of 1217 relates how Heinrich von Morungen made over to the Thomaskloster in Leipzig the yearly pension granted him by Dietrich as 'miles emeritus'. He may have accompanied Dietrich on the Crusade of 1197. He is reputed to have died in Leipzig in 1222. The poet is celebrated in a late medieval ballad (Uhland, *Volkslieder* V, 298) which relates how he returns after a seven-year absence on a pilgrimage in time to interrupt the marriage of his wife to a knight named von Neifen, presumably the poet Gottfried von Neifen. It is undoubtedly an entirely fictional account.

His poetry is a striking blend of the commonplaces of courtly love, which betray a close familiarity with the Romance lyric, with fresh visual images, which give new life to traditional metaphors. Morungen shows great mastery of poetic technique in his use of varying length of lines, the differentiation of structure in *Aufgesang* and *Abgesang*, and the exact adaptation of syntax to metrical form.

63

I   1 BC (MF 122, 1)

Si ist zallen ēren ein wīp wol erkant,
schōner gebērde, mit zühten gemeit,
sō daz ir lop in dem rīche umbe gēt.
alse der māne vil verre über lant
5 liuhtet des nahtes wol lieht unde breit
sō daz ir schīn al die welt umbe vēt,
alse ist mit güete umbevangen diu schōne,
des man ir jēt,
si ist aller wībe ein krōne.

63. Text of C, with *alse* (4, 7,) as in B.

3 *gēt*, 6 *vēt*, 8 *jēt*: BC has forms with *a* in the first two verbs and *giht* in the last instance, thus obscuring the rhyme.

4 *wol verre* BC.

II   2 BC

10   Diz lop beginnet vil frouwen versmān,
        daz ich die mīne für alle andriu wīp
        hān zeiner krōne gesetzet sō hō,
        unde ich der deheine ūz genomen hān.
        des ist vil lūter vor valsche ir der līp,
15   smal wol ze māze, vil fier unde frō.
        des müez ich in ir genāden belīben,
        gebiutet si sō,
        mīn liebeste vor allen wīben.

III   4 BC

        Ir tugent reine ist der sunnen gelīch,
20   diu trüebiu wolken tuot liehte gevar,
        swenne in dem meien ir schīn ist sō klār.
        des wirde ich stēter fröide vil rīch,
        daz überliuhtet ir lop alsō gar
        wīp unde frouwen die besten für wār,
25   die man benennet in tiutschem lande.
        verre oder nār
        sō ist si ez diu baz erkande.

64

I   8 A, 9 B, 17 C (MF 126, 8)

        Von den elben wirt entsēn vil manic man:
        sō bin ich von grōzer liebe entsēn
        von der besten die ie man ze vriunt gewan.
        wil si aber mich dar umbe vēn,
5   und ze unstaten stēn,   mac si danne rechen sich
        und tuo des ich si bite: sō vreut si sō sēre mich,
        daz mīn līp vor wunnen muoz zergēn.

16 *mvs* BC.
20 *trûben wolken tônt* BC.
22–23 *des . . . daz* 'for that reason . . . because'.
26 *nahe* B *nach* C, which obscure the rhyme.

64. Text of A.
    entsēn (1, 2), *vēn* (4), *sēn* (23), *geschēn* (28): it is clear that these words rhyming
with *stēn* (5 and 26) and *zergēn* (7 and 25) must have contracted forms. The MSS.
have some syncopated spellings but in some cases they have restored the full forms
(e.g. *vehen* ABC).
    3 *ie dehein man* ABC.
    4 *aber si* ABC.

II   9 A, 20 C

Si gebiutet und ist in dem herzen mīn
frowe und hērer danne ich selbe sī.
10   hei wan müeste ich ir alsō gewaltic sīn
daz si mir mit triuwen wēre bī
ganzer tage drī   und eteslīche naht!
sō verlür ich niht den līp und al die maht.
jā ist si leider vor mir al ze vrī.

III   10 A, 11 B, 19 C

15   Mich enzündet ir vil liehter ougen schīn
same daz viur den dürren zunder tuot,
und ir fremeden krenket mir daz herze mīn
same daz wazzer die vil heize gluot;
und ir hōher muot,   ir schōne, ir werdecheit,
20   und daz wunder daz man von ir tugenden seit,
daz wirt mir vil übel oder līhte guot.

IV   11 A, 10 B, 18 C

Swenne ir liehten ougen sō verkērent sich
daz si mir al dur mīn herze sēn,
swer dā entzwischen danne gēt und irret mich,
25   dem müeze al sīn wunne gar zergēn.
ich muoz vor ir stēn   und warten der frouwen mīn
rehte alsō des tages diu kleinen vogellīn:
wenne sol mir iemer liep geschēn?

65

I   24 A, 21 C (MF 127, 1)

Wist ich obe ez möhte wol verswigen sīn,
ich lieze iuch sehen   mīne lieben frouwen.
der enzwei gebrēche mir daz herze mīn,
der möhte sie   schōne drinne schouwen.
5   si kam her   dur diu ganzen ougen
sunder tür gegangen:
ōwē, solte ich von ir reinen minne sīn
alsō werdeclīche enphangen!

19 ABC have *und* before *schōne* and before the final noun (*edelkeit* BC).
26 *waren* A, *warte* BC. *frouwen* with BC, *der vreuden min* A.
65. Composite AC text (ll. 13–20 missing A).
3 *gebrēche*: *breche* AC.
5 *min* after *ougen* AC.

II

Der sō vil geriefe in einen touben walt,
10 ez antwürt ime   dar ūz eteswenne.
nu ist der schal dicke vor ir manicvalt
von mīner nōt,   swie sis niht erkenne.
doch klaget ir   maniger mīnen kumber
vil dicke mit gesange:
15 ōwē jā hāt si geslāfen allez her
alder geswigen al ze lange.

III

Wēr ein sitich ader ein star, die möhten sīt
gelernet hān   daz si sprēchen 'minne'.
ich hān ir gedienet her vil lange zīt:
20 mac si sich doch   mīner rede versinnen?
nein si, niht,   got enwelle ein wunder
vil verre an ir erzeigen.
jā möhte ich baz einen boum mit mīner bete
sunder wāfen nider geneigen.

66

I

Ich hān si für alliu wīp
mir ze vrowen und ze liebe erkorn.
minneclīch ist ir der līp.
seht, durch daz sō hab ich des gesworn,
5 daz mir in der welte niht
niemer solde lieber sīn:
als aber si mīn ouge an siht,
sō tagt ez in dem herzen mīn.

II

'Owē des scheidens des er tete
10 von mir, dō er mich vil senende lie.
wol aber mich der lieben bete
und des weinens des er dō begie,

---

12 *swie sis niht erkenne* C, *wil si die bekennen* A.
18 *minne: minnen* C, no doubt a scribal correction to 'improve' the rhyme. The rhyme indicates a dialect pronunciation of *versinnen* without the final *n*.
66. 5–6 *das mir in der welt niemen lieb' sin* B.

dō er mich trūren lāzen bat
und hiez mich in fröiden sīn.
15　von sīnen trehenen wart ich nat
unde erkuolte iedoch daz herze mīn.'

III　　　　　　　　　　　　　　14 B, 36 C

Der durch sīne unsēlikeit
iemer arges iht von ir gesage,
dem müeze allez wesen leit,
20　swaz er minne und daz im wol behage.
ich fluoche in und schadet in niht,
dur die ich ir muoz frömde sīn:
als aber si mīn ouge an siht,
sō tagt ez in dem herzen mīn.

IV　　　　　　　　　　　　　　15 B, 37 C

25　'Owē waz wīzent si einem man
der nie frouwen leit noch arc gesprach
und in aller ēren gan?
durch daz müet mich sīn ungemach,
daz si in sō schōne gruozent wal
30　unde zuo im redende gānt
unde in doch als einen bal
mit bōsen worten umbe slānt.'

<h1 style="text-align:center">67</h1>

I　　　　　　　　　　12 A, 23 B, 44 C (MF 132, 27)

Ist ir liep mīn leit und ungemach,
wie solte ich danne iemer mēre rehte werden vrō?
sine getrūrte nie, swaz mir geschach:
klaget ich ir mīn jāmer, sō stuont ir daz herze hō.
5　sist noch hiute vor den ougen mīn alse si was dō
dō si minneclīche mir zuo sprach
und ich si ane sach.
owē, solte ich iemer stēn alsō.

15 *nat*: *nas* BC, but the rhyme demands the dialect form.
16 *iedoch* with B, *ē doch* C.
20 *wal*: *wol* B, *vber al* C.
67. Text of A, but with *klaget* (4), *und* (10), *nāch ir* (10) as in BC.
1 *min* before *ungemach* ABC.

II   13 A, 24 B, 43 C

Si hāt liep ein kleine vogellīn
10   daz ir singet und ein lützel nāch ir sprechen kan:
müest ich dem gelīch ir heimlich sīn,
sō swüere ich des wol daz nie frowe selchen vogel gewan.
für die nahtegal wolte ich hōhe singen dan:
'owē, liebe schōne frowe mīn,
15   nu bin ich doch dīn:
mahtu trōsten mich vil senenden man?'

III   14 A, 25 B, 45 C

Sist mit tugenden und mit werdecheit
sō behuot vor aller slahte unvrowelīcher tāt,
wan des einen daz si mir verseit
20   ir gnāde und mīnen dienest sō verderben lāt.
wol mich des daz si mīn herze sō besezzen hāt
daz der stat dā nieman wirt bereit
als ein hār sō breit,
swenne ir rehtiu liebe mich bestāt.

68

I   51 C (MF 134, 14)

Ez tuot vil wē,   swer herzeclīche minnet
an sō hōher stat   dā sīn dienest gar versmāht.
sīn tumber wān   vil lützel dran gewinnet,
swer sō vil geklaget   dā'z ze herzen niht engāt.
5   er ist vil wīs   swer sich sō wol versinnet
daz er dienet dā   dā man dienest wol enpfāt
und sich dar lāt   dā man sīn genāde hāt.

II   52 C

Ich bedarf vil wol   daz ich genāde vinde,
wan ich habe ein wīp   ob der sunnen mir erkorn.
10   daz ist ein nōt   die ich niemer überwinde,
[sine] gesehe mich ane   als si tete hie bevorn.

13 *für* 'better than'.
21 f. 'Fortunate am I that she has so occupied my heart that there is no room, not
even a hair's breadth, for anyone else, when true love for her takes possession of me.'
68. 10 *daz ist*: *dest* C.

si ist mir liep   gewest dā her von kinde,
wan ich wart durch si   und durch anders niht geborn:
ist ir daz zorn,   weiz got, sō bin ich verlorn.

III   53 C

15 Wā ist nu hin   mīn liehter morgensterne?
wē waz hilfet mich   daz mīn sunne ist ūf gegān?
si ist mir ze hōch   und ouch ein teil ze verne
gegen mittem tage   unde wil dā lange stān.
ich gelebte noch   den lieben ābent gerne,
20 daz si sich her nider   mir ze trōste wolte lān,
wand ich mich hān   gar verkapfet ūf ir wān.

69

I   87 C, M fol. 61ʳ (MF 142, 19)

Ich bin keiser āne krōne,
sunder lant: daz meine ich an den muot;
dern gestuont mir nie sō schōne:
wol ir lībe, diu mir sanfte tuot.
5 daz schaffet mir ein frowe fruot.
dur die sō wil ich stēte sīn,
wan in gesach nie wīp sō rehte guot.

II   88 C

'Gerne sol ein riter ziehen
sich ze guoten wīben: dēst mīn rāt.
10 bœsiu wīp die sol man fliehen:
er ist tump swer sich an si verlāt;
wan sine gebent niht hōhen muot.
iedoch sō weiz ich einen man,
den ouch die selben frowen dunkent guot.

14 *weiz got: das weis got* C.
21 *ūf ir wān* 'in expectation of her'. 'For I have wearied my dazzled sight. awaiting her coming'.

69. 2 *daz meine ich an dem muot* M: *das meinet mir der mv̊t* C.
3 *dern: der* C, *ern* M.
4 *danc ir liebes* C.

III   89 C

15 Mirst daz herze worden swēre,
seht, daz schaffet mir ein sende nōt.
ich bin worden dem unmēre
der mir dicke sīnen dienest bōt.
owē war umbe tuot er daz?
20 und wil er sichs erlouben niht,
sō muoz ich im von schulden sīn gehaz.'

70

I   93 C (MF 143, 22)

Owē,   sol aber mir iemer mē
geliuhten dur die naht
noch wīzer danne ein snē
ir līp vil wol geslaht?
5 der trouc diu ougen mīn:
ich wānde, ez solde sīn
des liehten mānen schīn,
dō taget ez.

II   94 C

'Owē,   sol aber er iemer mē
10 den morgen hie betagen?
als uns diu naht engē,
daz wir niht durfen klagen:
"owē, nu ist ez tac",
als er mit klage pflac,
15 dō er jungest bī mir lac.
dō taget ez.'

III   95 C

Owē,   si kuste āne zal
in dem slāfe mich:
dō vielen hin ze tal
20 ir trehene nider sich.

20 'and if he will not renounce it . . .'.

70. 8 MS. C has *tagt* here and *tagte* in the other instances; *taget*, here preferred for reasons of euphony, is the past form with final *e* elided.

12 'so that we do not need to complain'.

iedoch getrōste ich sie,
daz si ir weinen lie
und mich al umbevie.
dō taget ez.

IV   96 C

25 'Owē,   daz er sō dicke sich
bī mir ersehen hāt!
als er endahte mich,
sō wolte er sunder wāt
mīn arme schouwen blōz.
30 ez was ein wunder grōz
daz in des nie verdrōz.
dō taget ez.

71

I   100 C, her reymar 364 e (MF 145, 1)

Mir ist geschehen als einem kindelīne,
daz sīn schœnez bilde in einem glase gesach
unde greif dar nāch sīn selbes schīne
sō vil biz daz ez den spiegel gar zerbrach.
5 dō wart al sīn wunne ein leitlich ungemach.
alsō dāhte ich iemēr frō ze sīne,
dō ich gesach die lieben frouwen mīne,
von der mir bī liebe leides vil geschach.

II   365 e

Minne, diu der werlde ir frōide mēret,
10 seht, diu brāhte in troumes wīs die frouwen mīn
dā mīn līp an slāfen was gekēret
und ersach sich an der besten wunne sīn.
dō sach ich ir werden tugende, ir liehten schīn,
schōne und für alle wīp gehēret;
15 niwan daz ein lützel was versēret
ir vil frōiden rīchez [rōtez] mündelīn.

---

29 *mīn arme*: Kraus (MF³⁰) here emends to *mich armen*, but this is out of keeping
with the atmosphere and style of the poem.

71. 11 *slāfen: slaffe* e.
   12 *an der: an die* e.
   13 *ir liehten tugenden, ir werden schin* e.
   14 *schōne und für alle wīp gehēret: schone unde auch für* e.

III   366 e

Grōze angest hān ich des gewunnen,
daz verblīchen süle ir mündelīn sō rōt.

20   des hān ich nu niuwer klage begunnen,
          sīt mīn herze sich ze solcher swēre bōt,
          daz ich durch mīn ouge schouwe solche nōt,
          sam ein kint daz wīsheit unversunnen
          sīnen schaten ersach in einem brunnen
          und den minnen muose unz an sīnen tōt.

IV   367 e

25   Hōher wīp von tugenden und von sinne,
          die enkan der himel niender ummevān,
          sō die guoten die ich vor ungewinne
          vremden muoz und immer doch an ir bestān.
          ōwē leider, jō wānde ichs ein ende hān,
30   ir vil wunneclīchen werden minne:
          nu bin ich vil kūme an dem beginne:
          des ist hin mīn wunne und ouch mīn gerender wān.

72

                                              104 C (MF 147, 4)

Vil süeziu senftiu tōterinne,
war umbe welt ir tōten mir den līp,
und ich iuch sō herzeclīchen minne,
zewāre, frouwe, für elliu wīp?
5   wēnet ir ob ir mich tōtet,
          daz ich iuch niemer mē beschouwe?
          nein, iuwer minne hāt mich des ernōtet
          daz iuwer sēle ist mīner sēle frouwe.

18 *mündelīn: munt* e.
24 *muose: mŭz* e.
25 *sinne: sinnen* e.
27 *ungewinne: vngewinnē* e.
72. 1, 2 *tŏterinne, tŏten* C. the rhyme *tōtet: ernōtet* shows that the original forms must
have been unmodified.
4 *zewāre: zwar* C.
6 *niemer: iemer* C.
7 'Love of you has compelled me to submit to your soul as mistress of mine.'

sol mir hie niht guot geschehen
10 von iuwerm werden lībe,
sō muoz mīn sēle iu des verjehen
dazs iuwerre sēle dienet dort   als einem reinen wībe.

9 *hie* . . . 12 *dort*: 'in this life . . . in the next'.

HARTMAN VON OUWE
(HARTMANN VON AUE)

HARTMANN VON AUE is not attested in any documents, and nothing certain is known of his life. He describes himself in *Der Arme Heinrich* as *dienestman ze Ouwe*. *Ouwe* ('stream', 'water meadow', 'island') is a very common element in place-names. From the language of his works it is clear that his dialect was Alemannic. The possible places suggested within the Alemannic dialect area have been: Obernau near Rottenburg on the Neckar, Au near Freiburg, the island Reichenau in Lake Constance, Eglisau in the Canton of Thurgau. According to *Der Arme Heinrich* (ll. 31 and 49) *Ouwe* appears to be situated in *Swāben*, but the medieval duchy of Swabia extended over a wide area including parts of present-day Switzerland. The illustrations of manuscripts B and C show Hartmann with the arms (three eagles' heads) attested as those of a family resident in the neighbourhood of Eglisau, but this is not necessarily proof conclusive, as the manuscripts were not compiled until roughly a hundred years after the poet was writing, and it may be an arbitrary attribution.

Hartmann is praised by Gottfried in *Tristan* (*c.* 1210) and his death is lamented by Heinrich von dem Türlin in *Diu Crône* (*c.* 1220–30). He appears to have taken part in a Crusade, probably that of 1189–90 (see note on **81**). He was probably born between 1160 and 1170. He is well known for his other works, the courtly epics *Erec* and *Iwein*, the so-called *Büchlein*—a debate between *herze* and *līp* on the theme of love, and the two moral tales *Gregorius* and *Der Arme Heinrich*.

Hartmann's poems show great formal skill. He seems to have a strong preference for the masculine line ending; thus four of the poems here included have it exclusively, and in **76** there are 72 instances of this type of cadence. Two poems have a fourfold repetition of the same masculine rhyme in the *Abgesang*. There are also instances of a new variation in the basic tripartite structure: thus **78** has four equal *Stollen* instead of two, and in **76** the *Abgesang* is also divided into two equal halves. No. **76** shows a very skilful use of echoing rhymes.

There have been various attempts to arrange Hartmann's poems chronologically, none of them convincing. Nor is the theory convincing that **81** marks a turning away from the worldly *Minnesang* and the conclusion of his lyric poetry.

73

1 BC (MF 205, 1)

I

Sīt ich den sumer truoc riuwe unde klagen
sō ist ze fröiden mīn trōst niht sō guot,
mīn sanc ensüle des winters wāpen tragen:
daz selbe tuot ouch mīn senender muot.
wie lützel mir mīn stæte liebes tuot!
wan ich vil gar an ir versūmet hān
die zīt, den dienst, dar zuo den langen wān.
ich wil ir anders ungefluochet lān
wan alsō, si hāt niht wol ze mir getān.

II

2 BC

Wolte ich den hazzen der mir leide tuot,
sō möht ich wol mīn selbes vīent sīn.
vil wandels hāt mīn līp und ouch der muot:
daz ist an mīnem ungelücke worden schīn.
mīn frowe gert mīn niht: die schulde ist mīn.
sīt sinne machent sældehaften man
und unsin stæte sælde nie gewan,
ob ich mit sinnen niht gedienen kan,
dā bin ich alterseine schuldic an.

III

11 C

Dō ir mīn dienest niht ze herzen gie,
dō dūhte mich an ir bescheidenlich
daz si ir werden lībes mich erlie:
dar an bedāhte si vil rehte sich.
zürne ich, daz ist ir spot und altet mich.
grōz was mīn wandel: dō si den entsāz,
dō meit si mich, vil wol geloube ich daz,
mēre dur ir ēre danne ūf mīnen haz:
si wænet des, ir lop stē deste baz.

---

73. Text of C with *leide* (10) and *mīn līp* (12) from B.
    3 *ensule*: *súle* C.
    12 *wandel* 'fault', 'imperfection'.
    15 *sældehaften*: *schadehaften* BC.
    15 Cf. **82.** 10–11.
    24 *entsāz* 'feared'.
    26 Cf. Reinmar, MF 186, 25.

IV   4 C

Si hāt mich nāch wāne unrehte erkant,
dō si mich ir von ērste dienen liez:
30   dur daz si mich sō wandelbæren vant,
mīn wandel und ir wīsheit mich verstiez.
si hāt geleistet swaz si mir gehiez;
swaz si mir solde, des bin ich gewert.
er ist ein tump man, der iht anders gert.
35   si lōnde mir als ich si dūhte wert:
michn sleht niht anders wan mīn selbes swert.

74

3 C (MF 206, 10)

Ich hān des reht daz mīn līp trūric sī
wan mich twinget ein vil sendiu nōt.
swaz fröiden mir von kinde wonte bī,
die sint verzinset als ez got gebōt.
5   mich hāt beswæret mīnes herren tōt;
dar zuo sō trüebet mich ein varende leit:
mir hāt ein wīp genāde widerseit,
der ich gedienet hān mit stætekeit
sīt der stunde daz ich ūf mīme stabe [reit].

75

I   4 A, 12 B, 14 C (MF 206, 19

Swes vröide an guoten wīben stāt,
der sol in sprechen wol
und wesen undertān.
daz ist mīn site und ist mīn rāt,
5   alse ez mit triuwen sol.
daz kan mich niht vervān

28 *nāch wāne* 'in her expectations of me'.
36 *michn*: *min* C.

74. 4 *verzinset* 'paid in tribute'; cf. **77.** 18, **78.** 13.
6 *varende* 'transient', 'earthly'.

75. Text of A, with lines 3 and 8 according to C, and *mich* (9), *iemer* (10) and *dā* (22)
as in BC.
I ff. cf. Reinmar **89.** 20.

an einer stat
dar ich noch ie genāden bat.
swaz si mir tuot, ich hān mich ir gegeben
10   und wil ir iemer leben.

II   5 A, 11 B, 15 C
Möht ich der schœnen mīnen muot
nāch mīnem willen sagen,
sō liez ich mīnen sanc.
nū ist mīn sælde niht sō guot:
15   dā von muoz ich ir klagen
mit sange daz mich twanc.
swie verre ich sī,
sō sende ich ir den boten bī
den si wol hœret unde niene siht:
20   der enmeldet mīn dā niht.

III   6 A, 10 B, 16 C
Ez ist ein klage und niht ein sanc
dā ich der guoten mite
erniuwe mīniu leit.
die swæren tage sint alze lanc
25   die ich si genāden bite
und si mir doch verseit.
swer selchen strīt,
der kumber āne vröide gīt,
verlāzen kunde, des ich niene kan,
30   der wære ein sælic man.

76

I   7 A, 4 B, 6 C (MF 207, 11)
Ich sprach, ich wolte ir iemer leben:
des liez ich wīte mære komen.
mīn herze hete ich ir gegeben:
daz hān ich nu von ir genomen.

19 *niene*: *eine* A, *niht* C, missing B.
20 'he will not betray me there'.
76. Text of VI according to A, I–V from B with *ē* (23), *manic jār* (38), *heiles* (45)
from C; *sō* (12), *engerte* (53), *der* (56), *liep* (57), *deiz* (59) from A.

1 Cf. **75.** 10.
2 *des*: *daz* ABC.

5 swer tumben antheiz trage,
der lāze in ē der tage
ē in der strīt
beroube sīner jāre gar.
alsō hān ich getān.
10 der kriec sī ir verlān;
für dise zīt
sō wil ich dienen anderswar.

II   5 B, 7 C

Ich was untriuwen ie gehaz:
und wolte ich ungetriuwe sīn,
15 mir tæte untriuwe verre baz
denne daz mich diu triuwe mīn
von ir niht scheiden liez
diu mich ir dienen hiez.
nu tuot mir wē,
20 si wil mir ungelōnet lān.
ich sprich ir niuwan guot:
ē ich beswære ir den muot,
sō wil ich ē
die schulde zuo dem schaden hān.

III   3 B, 5 C

25 Waz solte ich arges von ir sagen
der ich ie wol gesprochen hān?
ich mac wol mīnen kumber klagen
und si darunder ungevelschet lān.
si nimet von mir für wār
30 mīnen dienst manic jār.
ich hān gegert
ir minne und vinde ir haz.
daz mir dā nie gelanc,
des habe ich selbe undanc:
35 dūhte ich sis wert,
si hete mir gelōnet baz.

5 *antheiz*, a legal term meaning 'promise', 'oath'.
28 'and meanwhile not accuse her of falsehood'.
34 'I am myself to blame'.
35 *sis*: *si sin* BC. Cf. **73.** 35.

IV   8 A, 6 B, 9 C

Sīt ich ir lōnes muoz enbern,
der ich manic jār gedienet hān,
sō geruoche mich got eines wern,
40   daz ez der schœnen müeze ergān
nāch ēren unde wol.
sīt ich mich rechen sol,
dēswār daz sī,
und doch niht anders wan alsō
45   daz ich ir heiles gan
baz danne ein ander man,
und bin dā bī
ir leides gram, ir liebes frō.

V   9 A, 9 B, 10 C

Mir sint diu jār vil unverlorn
50   diu ich an si gewendet hān:
hāt mich ir minne lōn verborn,
doch trœstet mich ein lieber wān.
ich engerte nihtes mē,
wan müese ich ir als ē
55   ze vrowen jehen.
manic man der nimt sīn ende alsō
daz ime niemer liep geschiht,
wan daz er sich versiht
deiz süle geschehen,
60   und tuot in der gedinge vrō.

VI   10 A, 8 C

Der ich dā her gedienet hān,
dur die wil ich mit vröiden sīn,
doch ez mich wēnic hāt vervān.
ich weiz wol daz diu frowe mīn
65   [niwan] nāch ēren lebet.
swer von der sīner strebet,

51 'if the reward for loving her has not been granted to me'.
56 'many a man reaches the end of his life without happiness falling to his lot'.
66–68 'a curse on him who seeks to abandon his lady. His life will be very weari-
some.' *betrāgen* is intended as a contrast to *mit vröiden sīn*.

der habe ime daz.
in beträget sīner jāre vil.
swer alsō minnen kan,
70 der ist ein valscher man.
mīn muot stēt baz:
von ir ich niemer komen wil.

77

I   7 B, 12 C (MF 209, 5)

Mīn dienst der ist alze lanc
bī ungewissem wāne:
nāch der ie mīn herze ranc,
diu lāt mich trōstes āne.
5 ich möhte ir klagen   und wunder sagen
von maniger swæren zīt.
sīt ich erkande ir strīt,
sīt ist mir gewesen für wār
ein stunde ein tac, ein tac ein woche, ein woche ein
    ganzes jār.

II   8 B, 13 C

10 Owē waz tæte si einem man
dem si doch vīent wære,
sīt si sō wol verderben kan
ir friunt mit maniger swære?
mir tæte baz   des rīchez haz:
15 joch möhte ich eteswar
entwīchen sīner schar;
diz leit wont mir alles bī
und nimt von minen vröiden zins alse ich sīn eigen sī.

77. Text of B.
    5 *in* BC: Vogt's emendation to *ir* (MF³) is generally accepted.
    7 'since I first experienced the struggle she is waging against me'.
    14–16 probably refers to banishment: *schar*, more usually *harmschar*, 'punish-ment'.
    18 'and exacts tribute from my joy, as if I were its thrall'.

78

I   13 B, 17 C (MF 209, 25)

Dem kriuze zimt wol reiner muot
und kiusche site:
sō mac man sælde und allez guot
erwerben dā mite.
5   ouch ist ez niht ein kleiner haft
dem tumben man
der sīme lībe meisterschaft
niht halten kan.
ez wil niht daz man sī
10   der werke darunder frī:
waz touc ez ūf der wāt,
der sīn an dem herzen niene hāt?

II   14 B, 18 C

Nū zinsent, ritter, iuwer leben
und ouch den muot
15   durch in der iu dā hāt gegeben
beide līp unde guot.
swes schilt ie was zer werlte bereit
ūf hōhen prīs,
ob er den gote nū verseit,
20   der ist niht wīs.
wan swem daz ist beschert
daz er dā wol gevert,
daz giltet beidiu teil,
der werlte lop, der sēle heil.

III   15 B, 19 C

25   Diu werlt mich lachet triegend an
und winket mir.
nū hān ich als ein tumber man
gevolget ir.

---

78. Text of C.
5–8 'it is no small support to the foolish man who lacks self-mastery'.
10 *der werke . . . frī* 'dispensed from works'.
11 *touc: tȫget* B, *tȫgt* C.
18 'to win renown'.
25 *lachet mich* BC.
25–28 after 29–32 BC.

30 der hacchen hān ich manigen tac
geloufen nāch:
dā niemen stæte vinden mac,
dar was mir gāch.
nu hilf mir, herre Krist,
der mīn dā vārende ist,
35 daz ich mich dem entsage
mit dīnem zeichen daz ich hie trage.

IV   16 B, 20 C

Sīt mich der tōt beroubet hāt
des herren mīn,
swie nū diu werlt nāch im gestāt,
40 daz lāze ich sīn.
der fröide mīn den besten teil
hāt er dā hin,
[und] schüefe ich nū der sēle heil,
daz wær ein sin.
45 mac im ze helfe komen
mīn vart die ich hān genomen,
ich wil ime ir halber jehen:
vor gote müeze ich in gesehen.

79

I   23 B, 27 C (MF 211, 27)

Der mit gelücke trūric ist,
der wirt mit ungelücke selten gemellīche frō.
für trūren hān ich einen list,
swaz mir geschiht ze leide, sō gedenke ich iemer sō:
5 'nu lā varn, ez solte dir geschehen:
schiere kumt   daz dir gefrumt.'
sus sol ein man des besten sich versehen.

39 *nāch im* 'after his death'.
45 The MSS. have *ich* after *mac*.
47 'I will grant him half of it', i.e. 'half the reward shall be his'.
79. Text of C.
3 *für* 'as a remedy against'.

II   24 B, 28 C

Swer anders giht, der misseseit,
wan daz man stætiu wīp mit stætekeit erwerben muoz.
10   des hāt mir mīn unstætekeit
ein stætez wīp verlorn. diu bōt mir alsō schœnen gruoz,
daz si mir ougte lieben wān.
dō si erkōs   mich stætelōs,
dō muose ouch diu genāde ein ende hān.

III   25 B, 29 C

15   Ez ist mir iemer mēre guot
daz mīn unstæte an [stæten] fröiden mich versūmet hāt:
nu kēre ich mich an stæten muot,
und muoz mit heile mīnes ungelückes werden rāt.
ich bin einer stæten undertān:
20   an der wirt schīn   diu stæte mīn
und daz ich an stæte meister nie gewan.

80

I   52 C (MF 216, 29)

Maniger grüezet mich alsō
(der gruoz tuot mich ze māze frō),
'Hartman, gēn wir schouwen
ritterlīche frouwen.'
5   mac er mich mit gemache lān
und īle er zuo den frowen gān!
bī frowen triuwe ich niht vervān,
wan daz ich müede vor in stān.

II   53 C

Ze frowen habe ich einen sin:
10   als si mir sint als bin ich in;
wand ich mac baz vertrīben
die zīt mit armen wīben.

19 The impure rhyme *undertān: gewan* is unique in Hartmann. Some editors
therefore emend *undertān* with Lachmann to *dienestman*.
80. 2 *ze māze* 'moderately', i.e. ironical for 'not at all'.
7–8 'I expect to gain nothing but weariness from ladies.'

swar ich kum dā ist ir vil,
dā vinde ich die diu mich dā wil;
15   diu ist ouch mīnes herzen spil:
waz touc mir ein ze hōhez zil?

III   54 C

In mīner tōrheit mir geschach
daz ich zuo zeiner frowen sprach
'frowe, ich hān mīne sinne
20   gewant an iuwer minne.'
dō wart ich twerhes an gesehen;
des wil ich, des sī iu bejehen,
mir wīp in solher māze spehen
diu mir des niht enlānt geschehen.

81

I   58 C (MF 218, 5)

Ich var mit iuwern hulden, herren unde māge:
liut unde lant die müezen sælic sīn.
ez ist unnōt daz ieman mīner verte vrāge:
ich sage wol für wār die reise [mīn].
5   mich vienc diu Minne und lie mich varn ūf mīne sicherheit.
nu hāt si mir enboten bī ir liebe daz ich var.
ez ist unwendic: ich muoz endelīchen dar:
wie kūme ich bræche mīne triuwe und mīnen eit!

II   59 C

Sich rüemet maniger waz er dur die Minne tæte:
10   wā sint die werc? die rede hœre ich wol.
doch sæhe ich gern daz si ir eteslīchen bæte
daz er ir diente als ich ir dienen sol.

17, 24 *beschach, beschehen* C.
23 *in solher māze* 'of such a kind'.
81. 1–2 'By your leave I depart, lords and kinsmen: a blessing on land and people.'
5 *sicherheit*: the oath of submission exacted from a vanquished opponent.
6 *bī ir liebe* 'by the love I owe her'.

ez ist geminnet, der sich dur die Minne ellenden muoz.
nū seht wie si mich ūz mīner zungen ziuhet über mer.

15 und lebte mīn her, Salatin und al sīn her
dien bræhten mich von Vranken niemer einen fuoz.

III   60 C

Ir minnesinger, iu muoz ofte misselingen:
daz iu den schaden tuot, daz ist der wān.
ich wil mich rüemen, ich mac wol von minne singen,
20 sīt mich diu Minne hāt und ich si hān.
daz ich dā wil, seht daz wil alse gerne haben mich;
sō müezt aber ir verliesen underwīlent wānes vil:
ir ringent umbe liep daz iuwer niht enwil:
wan müget ir armen minnen solhe minne als ich?

13 'that is love indeed, if a man must be an exile for love's sake'.
14 *zunge* ('tongue', 'language') is here used meaning 'nation' as in Walther **91**. 41.
16 *Vranken*, literally Franconia, but probably here meaning Germany in a general way, as a parallel to *zunge* above.
19 *minne*: *mīnē* C.

REINMAR

REINMAR DER ALTE, so named in MS. C to distinguish him from
Reinmar von Zweter and Reinmar der Fiedler, is attested in no documents and no certain dates are known for his life. Only one of his poems
can be approximately dated, an elegy on the death of Leopold V of
Austria, no doubt his patron, who died in 1194. Reinmar is usually
identified with the 'nightingale' of Hagenouwe (probably Hagenau in
Alsace), whom Gottfried celebrates as leader of the choir of lyric poets,
and whose death he laments. Since the *Tristan* is thought to have been
written during the first decade of the thirteenth century, Reinmar must
have died before 1210. He was thus probably born between about 1150
and 1160. Walther too laments the loss of Reinmar as a poet but not as
a man (cf. **106**). This fact points to the rivalry between them, reflected
in certain of Walther's poems which parody Reinmar. The two poets
were probably at the Viennese court together.

Reinmar's poetry is distinguished above all by its subtle analysis of
hopeless service in all its aspects. His favourite themes are uncondi-
tional praise of the lady, uncomplaining devotion in spite of adversity,
and fortitude in the acceptance of suffering, but he can also, on occasion, write of the fulfilment of love. Many of his poems are conceived as
replies to his detractors and are clearly set against the background of
courtly society. Reinmar is a master of veiled expression, which conveys
emotion indirectly.

Kraus has attempted to group the poems in order (cf. *Die Lieder
Reinmars des Alten*, II). He believes that with the exception of three
youthful poems (**82** and **83** and the above-mentioned elegy), all Reinmar's poems form a coherent cycle, depicting the progress of an imagi-
nary love-relationship. It is true that there are definite links in subject-
matter and phraseology between separate poems, but this is inevitable
in a poetry based on a limited range of motifs and diction. The evidence
is too slender for the arrangement and the relative chronology which
Kraus bases on it.

82

I   44 A, 1 BC (MF 150, 1)

Ein liep ich mir vil nāhe trage,
des ich ze guote nie vergaz.
des ēre singe ich unde sage:
mit rehten triuwen tuon ich daz.

82. 2 'which I never omitted to praise'.

Reinmar: MS. C, fol. 98ʳ

5   si sol mir iemer sīn vor allen wīben:
    an dem muote wil ich manigiu jār belīben.
    waz bedarf ich leides mēre,
    wan swenn eht ich si mīden sol?
    daz klage ich unde müet mich dicke sēre.

II   43 A, 2 C, Husen 15 B

10 Ez wirt ein man der sinne hāt
    vil līhte sælic unde wert,
    der mit den liuten umbe gāt,
    des herze niht wan ēren gert.
    diu vröide wendet im sīn ungemüete.
15 sich sol ein ritter vlīzen maniger güete:
    ist ieman der daz nīde,
    daz ist ein sō gevüeger schade,
    den ich vür al die werlt gerne līde.

III   45 A, 3 C, Husen 16 B

    Ez ist ein nīt der niene kan
20 verhelen an den liuten sich.
    war umbe sprichet manic man
    'wes tœrt sich der?' und meinet mich?
    daz kunde ich im gesagen, obe ich wolde.
    ich enwānde niht daz des ieman frāgen solde
25 der pflæge schœner sinne;
    wan nieman in der werlte lebt,
    er envinde sīnes herzen küneginne.

83

I   2 B, 4 C (MF 151, 1)

    'Si koment underwīlent her
    die baz dā heime möhten sīn.
    ein ritter des ich lange ger,
    bedæhte er baz den willen mīn,

---

11 *wert* 'accounted worthy', 'esteemed'.

12 *liute*, here in the sense of 'courtly society'.

18 'which I bear in preference to all others'; *vür al die werlt* is used here in an intensifying sense.

19 *niene*: *niemā* A, *niht kan* B, *niht enkan* C.

83. Text of C, with line 8 as in B.

5
sō wære er zallen zīten hie,
als ich in gerne sæhe.
owē, waz suochent die
die nīdent daz, ob iemen guot geschæhe?'

II   4 B, 6 C
Genāde suochet an ein wīp
10
mīn dienst nu vil manigen tac.
durch einen alsō guoten līp
die nōt ich gerne līden mac.
ich weiz wol daz si mich geniezen lāt
mīner grōzen stæte.
15
wā næme si sō bœsen rāt
daz si an mir missetæte?

III   5 B, 7 C
'Genāden ich gedenken sol
an ime der mīnen willen tuot.
sīt daz er mir getriuwet wol,
20
sō wil ich hœhen sīnen muot.
wese er mit rehter stæte frō,
ich sage im liebiu mære,
daz ich in gelege alsō,
mich diuhte es vil, ob ez der keiser wære.'

IV   3 B, 5 C
25
Mir ist geschehen daz ich niht bin
langer frō wan unz ich lebe.
si wundert wer mir schœnen sin
und daz hōchgemüete gebe
daz ich ze der werlte niht getar
30
ze rehte alsō gebāren.
nie genam ich frowen war,
ich wære in holt die mir ze māze wāren.

8 *ieman gûter lieb geschehe* C.
16 Appears to be defective: Kraus adds *alsō harte* before *missetæte* (MF30).
24 'in such a way that I would consider myself to be granting a great deal, even if it were the emperor.'
29–30 'that I do not dare to behave before others truly in accordance with that joy' (i.e. because it would arouse suspicion and envy).
31 'I never beheld women but I was well disposed to those who were suited to me.'

84

I   15 A, 21 B, 31 C, 305 E (MF 158, 1)

Wol im, daz er ie wart geborn,
dem disiu zīt genædeclīchen hine gāt
ān aller slahte senden zorn,
und doch ein teil dar under sīnes willen hāt.
5   wie deme nāhet manic wünneclīcher tac!
wie lützel er mir, sælic man,   gelouben mac!
wan ich nāch fröide bin verdāht,
und kan doch niemer werden frō.
mich hāt ein liep in trūren brāht.
10   daz ist unwendic: nu sī alsō.

II   16 A, 32 C, 302 E

Daz ich mīn leit nu lange klage,
des spottent die den ir gemüete hōhe stāt.
waz ist in liep daz ich in sage?
waz sprichet der von fröiden, der dekeine hāt?
15   wil ich liegen, sō ist mir wunders vil geschehen:
sō trüge aber ich mich āne nōt,   wolt ich des jehen.
wan lānt si mich erwerben daz
dar nāch ich ie mit triuwen ranc?
zeme ieman danne ein lachen baz,
20   daz gelte ein ouge, und habe er doch danc.

III   17 A, 22 B, 33 C, 304 E

Ich wil von ir niht ledic sīn,
die wīle ich iemer gernden muot zer werlte hān.
daz beste gelt der fröiden mīn
daz līt an ir, und aller miner sælden wān.
25   swenne ich den verliuse, sō enhān ich niht
und enruoche ouch für den selben tac   waz mir geschiht.

84. 3 'without any kind of dissension in love'.
19–20 'If laughter then befits anyone more, let an eye be the price, and I will still
be grateful to him.' Two ideas are here combined: if his wishes are granted (*a*) it
would be impossible for anyone to be happier, (*b*) he would willingly make a sacrifice
in exchange. The offer of an eye has thus a double sense, firstly as something impossible of fulfilment, secondly as a willing sacrifice.
26 *für den selben tac* 'from that day forward'.

ich muoz wol sorgen umbe ir leben:
stirbet si, sō bin ich tōt.
hāt si mir anders niht gegeben,
30   sō erkenne ich doch nu senede nōt.

IV   18 A, 23 B, 34 C, 303 E
Genāde ist endelīche dā:
diu erzeige sich als ez an mīnem heile sī.
die ensuoche ich niender anderswā:
von ir gebote wil ich niemer werden frī.
35   daz si dā sprechent von verlorner arebeit,
sol daz der mīner einiu sīn,   daz ist mir leit.
ich enwānde niht, dō ich es began,
ich engelebte an ir noch lieben tac:
ist mir dā misselungen an,
40   doch gab ichz wol als ez dā lac.

85

I   6 A, 1 b, 35 C, 297 E (MF 159, 1)
Ich wirbe umb allez daz ein man
ze wereltlīchen fröiden iemer haben sol.
daz ist ein wīp der ich enkan
nāch ir vil grōzen werdekeit gesprechen wol.
5   lob ich si sō man ander frowen tuot,
daz ennimet eht si von mir niht für guot.
doch swer ich des, sist an der stat
daz ūzer wīplīchen tugenden nie fuoz getrat.
daz ist in mat.

28 Walther parodies this line as *stirbe aber ich, sō ist si tōt* (L/K 73, 16).

31 *endelīche* is here used not in a temporal sense but for purposes of emphasis: 'it is indisputable (i.e. "final") that favour is to be found there'.

32 'let it show itself as my fortune dictates'.

36 *mīner einiu*, literally 'one of mine', referring to *arebeit*: 'if that is intended to refer to my pains'.

37–38 'I did not think . . . but that I would yet experience a day of happiness at her hands'.

40 'I acted well, according to the circumstances.'

85. 8 Cf. **38. 35–36**.

9 *in* as in E; *diu* bC, *iv* A.

mat 'checkmate': the terminology of chess, which was a popular pastime in the Middle Ages, is frequently used figuratively as here.

II   7 A, 4 b, 38 C, 298 E

10 Si ist mir liep, und dunket mich
    daz ich ir volleclīche gar unmære sī.
    nu waz dar umbe? daz līde ich,
    und bin ir doch mit triuwen stæteclīchen bī.
    waz obe ein wunder līhte an mir geschiht,
15 daz si mich eteswenne gerne siht?
    sā denne lāze ich āne haz,
    swer giht daz ime an fröiden sī gelungen baz:
    der habe im daz.

III   8 A, 2 b, 36 C, 299 E

    Als eteswenne mir der līp
20 dur sīne bœse unstæte rātet daz ich var
    und mir gefriunde ein ander wīp,
    sō wil iedoch daz herze niender wan dar.
    sō wol ime daz ez sō reine weln kan
    und mir der süezen arebeite gan.
25 des hān ich mir ein liep erkorn
    dem ich ze dienste, und wære ez al der werlte zorn,
    muoz sīn geborn.

IV   5 Ab, 39 C, 300 E

    Swaz jāre ich noch ze lebenne hān,
    swie vil der wære, ir enwurde ir niemer tac genomen.
30 sō gar bin ich ir undertān
    daz ich unsanfte ūz ir genāden möhte komen.
    ich fröwe mich des daz ich ir dienen sol.
    si gelōnet mir mit līhten dingen wol:
    geloube eht mir, swenne ich ir sage
35 die nōt die ich an dem herzen von ir schulden trage
    dicke an dem tage.

V   9 A, 3 b, 37 C, 301 E

    Und ist daz mirs mīn sælde gan
    daz ich von ir redendem munde ein küssen mac versteln,
40 gīt got daz ich ez bringe dan,
    sō wil ichz tougenlīche tragen und iemer heln.

18 Lit. 'let him keep it', 'that is a matter of indifference to me'; cf. **76**. 67.
33 'She will perhaps give me some slight reward'.
34 *sage*: *clage* A.

ist aber daz si ez für groze swære hāt
und vēhet mich dur mīne missetāt,
waz tuon ich danne, unsælic man?
dā heb i'z ūf und lege ez hin wider, als ich wol kan,
45   dā ich ez dā nam.

86

I   19 A, 12 b, 47 C, 326 E (162, 7)
Ein wīser man sol niht ze vil
sīn wīp versuochen noch gezīhen, dēst mīn rāt,
von der er sich niht scheiden wil
und er der wāren schulde doch keine hāt.
5   swer wil al der welte lüge   an ein ende komen,
der hāt im āne nōt   ein vil herzeclīchez leit genomen.
man sol bœser rede gedagen;
und frāge ouch nieman lange des
daz er ungerne hœre sagen.

II   20 A, 46 C, 328 E, 6
10   War umbe vüeget diu mir leit
von der ich hōhe solte tragen den muot?
jō wirb ich niht mit kündekeit
noch dur versuochen, alsam vil meneger tuot.
ich enwart nie rehte vrō   wan sō ich si sach;
15   sō gie von herzen gar   swaz mīn munt wider si gesprach.
sol nu diu triuwe sīn verlorn,
sō endarf ez nieman wunder nemen,
hān ich underwīlen einen kleinen zorn.

III   21 A, 13 b, 48 C, 327 E
Si jehent daz stæte sī ein tugent,
20   der andern frowe. sō wol im der si habe!
si hāt mir fröide in mīner jugent
mit ir wol schœner zuht gebrochen abe,

£6. I–III according to A, with *und* (8) from BC, and *diu mir* (10) from C; IV–VI
from C with *gāt* (29) from b.

2 All the MSS. agree in having *sīn wīp*, and the trouvère poem which probably
served as a model (see note on subject-matter) also has *sa feme*. Kraus (MF[30]) omits
sīn wīp altogether for metrical reasons, whereas Brinkmann emends to *ein wīp*.

4 *schulde* 'grounds of accusation'. C has *si* instead of *er*; *schulde* would then refer
to the lady and mean 'guilt'.

19–20 'They say that constancy is a virtue, above all others', lit. 'mistress of all others'.

daz ich unz an mīnen tōt   niemer si gelobe.
ich sihe wol swer nu   vert wüetende als er tobe,
25 daz den diu wīp sō minnent ē
danne einen man der des niht kan.
ich ensprach in nie sō nāhe mē.

IV   11 b, 45 C, 331 E
Ich weiz den wec nu lange wol
der von der liebe gāt unz an daz leit.
30 der ander der mich wīsen sol
ūz leide in liebe, der ist mir noch unbereit.
daz mir von gedanken ist   als unmāzen wē,
des überhœre ich vil   und tuon als ich des niht verstē.
gīt minne niht wan ungemach,
35 sō müeze minne unsælic sīn:
die selben ich noch ie in bleicher varwe sach.

V   60 C, 330 E
Des einen und dekeines mē
wil ich ein meister sīn al die wīle ich lebe;
daz lop wil ich daz mir bestē
40 und mir die kunst diu werlt gemeine gebe,
daz nieman sīn leit   sō schōne kan getragen.
des begēt ein wīp an mir   daz ich naht noch tac niht kan
                                gedagen,
nu hān eht ich sō senften muot
daz ich ir haz ze fröiden nime.
45 owē wie rehte unsanfte daz mir doch tuot!

VI   61 C, 329 E
Ez tuot ein leit nach liebe wē,
sō tuot ouch līhte ein liep nach leide wol.
swer welle daz er frō bestē,
daz eine er dur daz ander līden sol
50 mit bescheidenlīcher klage   und gar ān arge site.
zer welte ist niht sō guot   daz ich ie gesach sō guot gebite.

---

27 'My words have never yet affected them so closely' (i.e. as those of the unworthy suitor of l. 24).
31 *unbereit* 'inaccessible'.
36 *in bleicher varwe* 'in the colours of sadness'.
51 'Nothing that I have ever seen in this life is as good as patient waiting.'

swer die gedulteclīchen hāt,
der kam des ie mit frœiden hin.
alsō dinge ich daz mīn noch werde rāt.

87

I   34 A, 32 B, 56 C, 306 E (MF 165, 10)

Waz ich nu niuwer mære sage
des endarf mich nieman frāgen: ich enbin niht vrō.
die friunt verdriuzet mīner klage.
des man ze vil gehœret, dem ist allem sō.
5   nu hān ich es beidiu schaden unde spot.
waz mir doch leides unverdienet, daz erkenne got,
und āne schult geschiht!
ich engelige herzeliebe bī,
sōne hāt an mīner vröide nieman niht.

II   36 A, 33 B, 57 C, 307 E

10   Die hōchgemuoten zīhent mich,
ich minne niht sō sēre, als ich gebāre, ein wīp.
si liegent unde unērent sich:
si was mir ie gelīcher māze sō der līp.
nie getrōste si darunder mir den muot.
15   der ungenāden muoz ich, und des si mir noch tuot,
erbeiten als ich mac.
mir ist eteswenne wol gewesen:
gewinne aber ich nu niemer guoten tac?

III   35 A, 34 B, 58 C, 308 E

Sō wol dir, wīp, wie reine ein nam!
20   wie sanfte er doch z'erkennen und ze nennen ist!
ez wart nie niht sō lobesam,
swā duz an rehte güete kērest, sō du bist.

---

87. 2 *endarf* 'has no need'.
4 'It is always thus with anything of which too much is heard.'
8 *ich engelige* 'unless I lie . . .'.
9 'No one will have any profit from my joy', i.e. through his songs.
11 'I do not love a woman as much as my behaviour suggests'.
19 *nam: name* ABCE.
21–22 'Nothing was ever so praiseworthy, if you apply yourself to true goodness,
such as is your nature'.
ez kēren is a set phrase, in which *ez* does not refer to a particular object.

dīn lop mit rede nieman volenden kan.
swes du mit triuwen phligest, wol im, der ist ein sælic man
25 und mac vil gerne leben.
du gīst al der welte hōhen muot:
wanne maht och mir ein wenic frōide geben?

IV   37 A, 35 B, 59 C, 309 E
Zwei dinc hān ich mir für geleit,
die strītent mit gedanken in dem herzen mīn.
30 obe ich ir hōhen werdekeit
mit mīnem willen wolte lāzen minre sīn,
oder obe ich daz welle daz si grœzer sī
und si vil sælic wīp stē mīn und aller manne vrī.
diu tuont mir beidiu wē:
35 ich enwirde ir lasters niemer vrō;
vergēt si mich, daz klage ich iemer mē.

V   310 E
Ob ich nu tuon und hān getān
daz ich von rehte in ir hulden solte sīn,
und si vor aller werlde hān,
40 waz mac ich des, vergizzet si darunder mīn?
swer nu giht daz ich ze spotte künne klagen,
der lāze im mīne rede beide singen unde sagen
.   .   .   .   .   .
und merke wā ich ie spreche ein wort,
45 ezn lige ē i'z gespreche herzen bī.

88
I   38 A, 20 b, 62 C, 291 E (MF 166, 16)
Der lange süeze kumber mīn
an mīner herzelieben vrowen, der ist erniuwet.
wie möhte ein wunder grœzer sīn,
daz mīn verlorner dienest mich so selten riuwet,

---

28 *Ich han ein dinc* ABC.
35 'I will never rejoice at her discredit'.
42 *beide min rede* E.

5   wan ich noch nie den boten gesach
    der mir ie bræhte trōst von ir,   wan leit und ungemach.
    wie sol ich iemer dise unsælde erwenden?
    unmære ich ir, daz ist mir leit,
    si enwart mir nie sō liep, kund i'z volenden.

II   39 A, 21 b, 63 C, 293 E

10   Wā nu getriuwer friunde rāt?
    waz tuon ich, daz mir liebet daz mir leiden solte?
    mīn dienest spot erworben hāt
    und anders niht: obe ich ez [niht] gelouben wolte,
    joch wæn ich ez nu gelouben muoz.

15   des wirt och niemer leides mir   unz an mīn ende buoz,
    sīt si mich hazzet die ich von herzen minne.
    mir enkunde ez nieman gesagen:
    nu bin ich es vil unsanfte worden inne.

III   40 A, 22 b, 64 C, 294 E

    Daz si mich alse unwerden habe

20   alse si mir vor gebāret, daz geloube ich niemer;
    nu lāze ein teil ir zornes abe,
    wan endeclīchen ir genāden beite ich iemer.
    von ir enmac ich noch ensol.
    sō sich genuoge ir liebes fröwent,   sōst mir mit leide wol,

25   und enkan ich anders niht an ir gewinnen,
    ē daz ich āne ir hulde sī,
    ich wil ir güete und ir gebærde minnen.

IV   24 b, 65 C, 295 E, Walther 10 m

    Owē daz alle die nu lebent
    wol hānt erfunden wie mir ist nāch einem wībe

30   und si mir niht den rāt engebent
    daz ich getrœstet würde noch bī lebendem lībe.

88. 8 'if she is indifferent to me'.
    11 'What shall I do, so that that which was intended to grieve me makes me happy?'
    12 *spot* probably has a double meaning here, designating both the scorn of the lady and the mockery of others.
    13 None of the MSS. has *niht*, which the sense seems to require. MSS. b and C have *noch* before *gelouben*, which may be a corruption of an original *niht*.
    17 This line probably refers not to what immediately precedes (the fact that the lady does not love him) but to the questions in ll. 10–11.

jō klage ich niht mīn ungemach,
wan daz den ungetriuwen ie   baz danne mir geschach,
die nie gewunnen leit von senender swære.
35 wolte got, erkanden guotiu wīp
ir sumelīcher werben, wie dem wære!

V   42 A, 66 C, 296 E, Walther 11 m
Ein rede der liute tuot mir wē:
dā enkan ich niht gedulteclīchen zuo gebāren.
nu tuont siz alle deste mē:
40 si frāgent mich ze vil von mīner frowen jāren,
und sprechent, welher tage si sī,
dur daz ich ir sō lange bin   gewesen mit triuwen bī.
si sprechent daz ez möhte mich verdriezen.
nu lā daz aller beste wīp
45 ir zühteloser vrāge mich geniezen.

VI   41 A, 67 C, 292 E
Mac si mich doch lāzen sehen
ob ich ir wære liep, wie si mich haben wolte.
sīt mir niht anders mac geschehen,
sō tuo gelīche deme als ez doch wesen solte,
50 und lege mich ir nāhe bī
und biete ez eine wīle mir   als ez von herzen sī:
gevalle ez danne uns beiden, sō sī stæte;
verliese aber ich ir hulde dā,
sō sī verborn als obe siz nie getæte.

89

I   39 b, 82 C (MF 170, 36)
Nieman sender suoche an mich deheinen rāt:
ich mac mīn selbes leit erwenden niht.
nun wæne ieman grœzer ungelücke hāt,
und man mich doch sō frō dar under siht.
5 dā merkent doch ein wunder an.
ich solde iu klagen die meisten nōt,
niwan daz ich von wīben niht übel reden kan.

36 *wie dem wære* 'how it was with regard to that'. For the same construction cf. **87.** 4.
44–45 'May the best of women permit me to profit by their discourteous question.'
54 *verborn* 'nullified'; *verlorn* E, *verborgen* AC.
89. Text of C.
3 *ungelücke* 'misfortune'.

II   40 b, 83 C
Spræche ich nu des ich si selten hān gewent,
dar an begienge ich grōze unstætekeit.
10   ich hān lange wīle unsanfte mich gesent
und bin doch in der selben arebeit.
bezzer ist ein herzesēre
danne ich von wīben misserede.
ich tuon sīn niht: si sint von allem rehte hēre.

III   41 b, 84 C
15   In ist liep daz man si stæteclīche bite,
und tuot in doch sō wol daz si versagent.
hey wie manigen muot und wunderlīche site
si tougenlīche in ir herzen tragent!
swer ir hulde welle hān,
20   der wese in bī und spreche in wol.
daz tet ich ie: nu kan ez mich leider niht vervān.

IV   42 b, 85 C
Dā ist doch mīn schulde entriuwen niht sō grōz
als reht unsælic ich ze lōne bin.
ich stān aller fröiden reht als ein hant blōz
25   und gāt mīn dienst wunderlīche hin.
daz geschach nie manne mē.
volende ich eine senende nōt,
si getuot mir niemer, mag ichz behüeten, wol noch wē.

V   43 b, 86 C
Ich bin tump daz ich sō grōzen kumber klage
30   und ir des wil deheine schulde geben.
sīt ich si āne ir danc in mīnem herzen trage,
waz mac si des, wil ich unsanfte leben?
daz wirt ir doch vil līhte leit.
nu muoz ichz doch alsō lāzen sīn.
35   mir machet nieman schaden wan mīn stætekeit.

22–23 'My fault is not so great as my unfortunate lack of reward.'
24 *als ein hant blōz*: most editors emend to *hendeblōz*.
27 *eine* is not altogether satisfactory. Vogt emends to *mīne* (MF³), Kraus (MF³⁰)
to *einest*. The meaning of 27–28 is obscure, no doubt because the text is corrupt. *si*
of 28 could refer to the lady, or more probably to *senende nōt*: 'If I ever attain fulfilment of my longing desires, they shall no longer cause me happiness or sorrow, if
I can prevent it.' Kraus translates l. 27 as 'wenn ich einst am Ende meiner Liebesnot
bin' (MFU, p. 364), and takes the lines to mean that only death can end his longing,
but this does not explain *mag ichz behüeten*, and is generally unconvincing.

90

I   75 b, 118 C, 229 E, van Nyphen 1 m (MF 178, 1)

'Lieber bote, nu wirbe alsō,
sihe in schiere und sage im daz:
vert er wol und ist er frō,
ich lebe iemer deste baz.
5   sage im durch den willen mīn
daz er iemer solhes iht getuo
dā von wir gescheiden sīn.

II   230 E, Nyphen 2 m

Frāge er wie ich mich gehabe
gihe daz ich mit fröiden lebe.
10   swā du mügest, dā leit in abe
daz er mich der rede vergebe.
ich bin im von herzen holt
und sæhe in gerner denne den tac:
daz aber du verswīgen solt.

III   77 b, 120 C

15   Ē daz du iemer im verjehest
daz ich im holdez herze trage,
sō sich daz du alrērst besehest
und vernim waz ich dir sage:
meine er wol mit triuwen mich,
20   swaz im danne müge ze fröiden komen,
daz mīn ēre sī, daz sprich.

IV   121 C, 231 E, Nyphen 3 m

Spreche er daz er welle her,
daz ichs iemer lōne dir,
sō bite in daz er verber
25   die rede die er jungest sprach ze mir:
sō mac ich in an gesehen.
wes wil er dā mit beswæren mich
daz doch niemer mac geschehen?

90. 6 *iemer* has here a negative meaning: 'that he should never do anything of such
a kind as to separate us'.
10–11 'Whenever you can, distract him, so that I may be spared his plea'.
13 *denne dē liehten tac* E.
17 'See to it that you are first of all prudent. ....'
21 *daz mīn ēre sī* (missing C): 'compatible with my good repute'.

V   76 b, 119 C, 232 E, Nyphen 5 m

Des er gert daz ist der tōt
30   und verderbet manigen līp;
bleich und eteswenne rōt
alsō verwet ez diu wīp.
minne heizent ez die man,
und möhte baz unminne sīn.
35   wē im ders alrērst began.

VI   235 E, Nyphen 4 m

Daz ich alsō vil dā von
hān geredet, daz ist mir leit,
wande ich was vil ungewon
sō getāner arebeit
40   alse ich tougenlīchen trage;
dune solt im nimmer niht verjehen
alles des ich dir gesage.'

31 Changes of colour are frequently mentioned as a symptom of love. Here the chief emphasis is on *bleich* as a sign of the sadness of love; cf. Heinrich von Morungen **71**. 18 and Reinmar **86**. 36.

WALTHER VON DER VOGELWEIDE

T H E R E is only one piece of documentary evidence relating to Walther's life, an entry in the accounts of Bishop Wolfger of Passau in November 1203, noting a sum given to the poet for the purchase of a fur coat. Neither his family nor place of birth are attested, but it is usually assumed that his home was Austria. He himself states that it was there that he learnt his art—'ze Ōsterrīche lernte ich singen unde sagen'—and it was there that he became the rival of Reinmar, a relationship indicated by the candid comments of **106**, and the parodies of Reinmar among his work (cf. notes on Reinmar **84.** 28 and **85**). One of Walther's earliest political poems indicates that he left the Viennese court after the death of his patron, Duke Frederick of Austria, in 1198. He is given the title *her* in the manuscripts and probably belonged to the rank of *ministerialis*. In **108** he claims the right to be accounted among the members of courtly society, whatever the outward circumstances of his life. His poems leave no doubt that he led a wandering life, and was dependent on the bounty of patrons (cf. **94**).

There are references to the political events of his times in his poetry which permit at least an approximate dating of his life. The first events to which he refers are those of 1198–1201 (in **91**), the last those of 1227 in **110**. He declares in **108** that he has sung for forty years or more. He was probably born about 1170, and died soon after 1227. From 1198 onwards he was in the service of Philip of Swabia and an ardent supporter of the Hohenstaufen cause against the Pope (**91** and **92**). After the death of Philip in 1208, Walther supported Philip's rival Otto of Brunswick, as the divinely appointed ruler, but he clearly gained little reward from Otto, and he castigates his meanness in no uncertain terms (**93**). Walther's support of Otto seems to have been at best half-hearted, and **93** shows him on the point of transferring his allegiance to Friedrich II. The *lēhen* of **95** was possibly in the neighbourhood of Würzburg, since there is a tradition that Walther is buried there.

The references to political events permit a fairly accurate dating of the poems in which they occur. No. **110** is usually thought to be Walther's last poem. In addition **108** and probably **109** seem to have been written towards the end of the poet's life. Otherwise there is nothing which permits the dating of his other poems, in spite of the considerable ingenuity which has been expended on this problem. It is significant that every critic who has examined the question has arrived at a different chronology. The arguments put forward are vitiated by certain basic assumptions, chiefly that the different types of poems, e.g. the so-called *Mädchenlieder* such as **103** and **104**, correspond to a definite period in Walther's life. There is, however, no reason to assume that Walther could not write in differing manners at one and the same time.

Walther's poems display a much greater variety than those of any other *Minnesänger*. He is the heir to a threefold tradition, that of *Minnesang*, that of religious poetry, and that of didactic poetry into which he infuses a new political content. The poems are here arranged in groups according to subject-matter: **91–95** political, **96–105** concerned with *minne* or the praise of women, including the lament for the decay of courtly poetry, and **106–10**, those with a more philosophical or religious theme.

91

I   43 A, 18 B, 1 C (L/K 8, 4)

Ich saz ūf eime steine,
und dahte bein mit beine;
dar ūf satzte ich den ellenbogen,
ich hete in mīne hant gesmogen
5   daz kinne und ein mīn wange.
dō dāht ich mir vil ange
wie man zer welte solte leben.
dekeinen rāt konde ich gegeben,
wie man driu dinc erwurbe,
10   der deheinez niht verdurbe.
diu zwei sint ēre und varnde guot,
daz dicke ein ander schaden tuot;
daz dritte ist gotes hulde,
der zweier übergulde.
15   die wolte ich gerne in einen schrīn:
jā leider des enmac niht sīn,
daz guot und weltlich ēre
und gotes hulde mēre
zesamene in ein herze komen:
20   stīge und wege sint in benomen,

91. 2 *dahte*, pret. of *decken*.
6 *ange*, lit. 'narrowly': 'earnestly'.
11 *varnde guot*, literally 'movable property': 'worldly possessions'.
19 *zesamene*: *zesame* A, missing BC.
20 ff. The image is that of highway robbery.

untriuwe ist in der sāze,
gewalt vert ūf der strāze,
fride und reht sint sēre wunt.
diu driu enhabent geleites niht, diu
               zwei enwerden ē gesunt.

    II   44 A, 20 B, 3 C (L/K 8, 28)

25   Ich hōrte ein wazzer diezen
und sach die vische vliezen;
ich sach swaz in der welte was,
velt, walt, loup, rōr unde gras.
swaz kriuchet unde vliuget
30   und bein zer erde biuget,
daz sach ich, unde sage iu daz:
der dekeinez lebet āne haz.
daz wilt und daz gewürme
die strītent starke stürme;
35   same tuont die vogel under in,
wan daz si habent einen sin:
si dūhten sich ze nihte,
si enschüefen starc gerihte.
si kiesent künege unde reht,
40   si setzent hērren unde kneht.
sō wē dir, tiuschiu zunge,
wie stēt dīn ordenunge,
daz nū diu mugge ir künec hāt,
und daz din ēre alsō zergāt!
45   bekērā dich, bekēre,
die cirkel sint ze hēre,

24 'these three will have no safe conduct, unless these two (*fride und reht*) are first restored'.

33 *wilt* corresponds to l. 30, *gewürme* (33) and *vogel* (35) to l. 29.

37–38 *endvhten* A, *si weren anders zenihte* BC.

    schvfen A, *schaffent* BC.

A negative particle seems to be required before the second verb: 'They would consider themselves undone if they did not establish a firm rule.'

41 *zunge*, here used meaning 'nation'; cf. **81**. 14.

Other instances in this poem of a part or attribute for the whole are *cirkel, weise, swert*, and *stôle*.

46 *cirkel*, either circlets worn by princes, here = 'princes', or the coronets of *die armen künege*.

die armen künege dringent dich:
Philippe setze den weisen ūf, und heiz si treten hinder sich.

III   45 A, 19 B, 2 C (L/K 9, 16)

Ich sach mit mīnen ougen
50   man unde wīp tougen,
dā ich gehōrte und gesach
swaz iemen tet, swaz iemen sprach.
ze Rōme hōrte ich liegen
und zwēne künege triegen.
55   dā von huop sich der meiste strīt
der ē was oder iemer sīt,
dō sich begunden zweien
die pfaffen unde leien.
daz was ein nōt vor aller nōt,
60   līp unde sēle lac dā tōt.
die pfaffen striten sēre,
doch wart der leien mēre.
diu swert diu leiten si dernider,
und griffen zuo der stōle wider.
65   si bienen die si wolten
und niht den si solten.
dō stōrte man diu gotes hūs.
ich hōrte verre in einer klūs
vil michel ungebære;
70   dā weinte ein klōsenære,
er klagete gote sīniu leit:
'Owē der babest ist ze junc; hilf, hērre, dīner kristenheit.'

47 *armen künege*: 'lesser kings', 'vassal kings', i.e. those who should owe homage to the Emperor. *arm* is frequently used to designate a vassal, and it is also in deliberate contrast to *rīch* which is the usual adjective applied to *künec*.
48 *weise* = the imperial crown, so called after a gem of singular beauty, the *lapis orphanus*, which adorned it.
49–52 missing A.
49–50 This is the reading of both the MSS.: 'I observed . . . men and women secretly.' Lachmann construed *tougen* as a noun and emended to the gen. pl. *manne unde wībe*: 'the secrets of men and women'.
51 *dā*: Lachmann and with him most editors emend to *daz*, 'so that'.
54 The two kings are Friedrich and Philip.
56 'that ever has been or ever will be'.
64 *stōle* 'stole', as an emblem of ecclesiastical office.
67 *stōrte* 'destroyed', cf. *Rolandslied* 203.

92

109 B, 291 C (L/K 18, 29)

Diu krōne ist elter danne der künic Philippes sī,
dā mugent ir alle schouwen wol ein wunder bī,
wie si ime der smit sō ebene habe gemachet.
5 sīn keiserlīchez houbet zimt ir alsō wol,
daz si ze rehte nieman guoter scheiden sol:
ir deweders dā daz ander niht enswachet.
si liuhtent beide ein ander an,
daz edel gesteine wider den jungen süezen man:
die ougenweide sehent die fürsten gerne.
10 swer nu des rīches irre gē,
der schouwe wem der weise ob sīme nacke stē:
der stein ist aller fürsten leitesterne.

93

I 75 A, 308 C, 3 wʰ (L/K 26, 23)

Ich hān hērn Otten triuwe, er welle mich noch rīchen:
wie genam aber er mīn dienest ie sō trügelīchen?
waz bestēt ze lōne des den künic Friderīchen?
mīn forderunge ist ūf in kleiner danne ein bōne,
5 ez ensī sō vil, obe er der alten sprüche wære frō.
ein vater lērte wīlent sīnen sun alsō:
'sun, diene manne bœstem, daz dir manne beste lōne.'

92. 3 *ebene* 'a perfect fit'.
6 'neither detracts from the other'.
7 *liuhtent*: *lachēt* C.
10 Lit. 'whoever goes astray with regard to the Emperor' (the literal meaning is taken up by *leitesterne*): 'whoever is uncertain as to the rightful emperor'.
11 *nacke* 'back of the neck'; Walther seems to suggest, in keeping with one tradition, that the *weise* (cf. **91.** 48) is at the back of the crown. It is, however, more probable that it was the most important central jewel at the front which has since been replaced by another which does not fit the setting.

93. I *triuwe* 'promise'.
3 'What obligation has Friedrich to reward me for it?'
4–5 'I have the smallest possible claim on him, unless in as far as he were willing to recognize the old saying': *spruch* can in both singular and plural mean 'saying' and probably refers to l. 7.
7 *bœse* here has the double meaning of 'bad' and 'mean'; cf. **95.** 3. There is a type of didactic poetry, in which proverbial wisdom is couched in the form of advice from father to son, e.g. *Winsbecke*.

Hēr Otte, ich binz der sun, ir sīt der bœste man,
wand ich sō rehte bœsen hērren nie gewan:
10   hēr künic, sīt irz der beste, sīt iu got des lōnes gan.

II   309 C

Ich wolte hērn Otten milte nāch der lenge mezzen,
dō hāt ich mich an der māze ein teil vergezzen:
wær er sō milt als lanc, er hete tugende vil besezzen.
vil schiere maz ich abe den līp nach sīner ēre,
15   dō wart er vil gar ze kurz als ein verschrōten werc,
miltes muotes minre vil danne ein getwerc,
und ist doch von den jāren daz er niht wahset mēre.
dō ich dem künege brāhte daz mez, wie er ūf schōz!
sīn junger līp wart beide michel unde grōz.
20   nū seht waz er noch wahse: erst ieze über in wol risen genōz.

94

76 A, 30 B, 319 C, 2 wˣˣ, 23 Z (L/K 28, 1)

Von Rōme voget, von Pülle künec, lāt iuch erbarmen
daz man mich bī rīcher kunst lāt alsus armen.
gerne wolte ich, möhte ez sīn, bī eigenem viure erwarmen.
zāhiu wie ich danne sunge von den vogellīnen,
5   von der heide und von den bluomen, als ich wīlent sanc!
swelch schœne wīp mir danne gæbe ir habedanc,
der liez ich liljen unde rōsen ūz ir wengel schīnen.
sus kume ich spāte und rīte fruo: 'gast, wē dir, wē!'
sō mac der wirt baz singen von dem grüenen klē.
10   die nōt bedenkent, milter künec, daz iuwer nōt zergē.

10 *lōn,* here 'the wherewithal to reward'.
13 *als lanc: so lange* C.
15 *verschrōten* 'spoil by cutting', 'cut too small'.
20 *genōz: gros* C.
94. 1 *Pülle,* Apulia (Ital. Puglia).
2 This is the reading of C except that C has *mich* before *lāt.*
8 This is the reading of AC with the addition of *sus* from B: *sus rite ich fruo und*
kume niht hain gast, etc., B.
sus 'as it is'.
9 *sō* 'whereas'.

95

314 C (L/K 28, 31)

Ich hān mīn lēhen, al die werlt, ich han mīn lēhen:
nu enfürhte ich niht den hornunc an die zēhen,
und wil alle bœse hērren dester minre vlēhen.
der edel künic, der milte künic hāt mich berāten,
5   daz ich den sumer luft und in dem winter hitze hān.
mīne nāhgebūren dunke ich verre baz getān,
si sehent mich niht mēr an in butzen wīs als si wīlent tāten.
ich bin ze lange arm gewesen āne mīnen danc,
ich was sō volle scheltens daz mīn ātem stanc:
10   daz hat der künic gemachet reine, und dar zuo mīnen sanc.

96

I   57 A, 196 C, 101 E, 54ᵉ L, 7 Uˣˣ (L/K 56, 14)

Ir sult sprechen willekomen:
der iu mære bringet, daz bin ich.
allez daz ir habt vernomen,
daz ist gar ein wint: nū vrāget mich.
5   ich wil aber miete:
wirt mīn lōn iht guot,
ich sage iu vil līhte daz iu sanfte tuot.
seht waz man mir ēren biete.

II   58 A, 197 C, 102 F, 8 Uˣˣ

Ich wil tiuschen vrowen sagen
10   solhiu mære daz si deste baz
al der werlte suln behagen:
āne grōze miete tuon ich daz.
waz wolde ich ze lōne?
si sint mir ze hēr:
15   sō bin ich gevüege und bite si nihtes mēr
wan daz si mich grüezen schōne.

---

95. 6–7 'I seem much handsomer to my neighbours; they do not look at me as if I
were a scarecrow, as they formerly did.'
   8 *arm*: *arn* C.
   9 *ātem*: *aten* C.
96. 7 *sage iu* as in ELU (*iu* missing AC); *vil* with A.
   13 ff. Cf. **101.** 53 f.

III   59 A, 199 C, 105 E

Ich hān lande vil gesehen
unde nam der besten gerne war.
übel müeze mir geschehen,
20   kunde ich ie mīn herze bringen dar,
daz im wol gevallen
wolde fremeder site.
waz hulfe mich, ob ich unrehte strite?
tiuschiu zuht gāt vor in allen.

IV   60 A, 200 C, 103 E, 9 U^{xx}

25   Von der Elbe unz an den Rīn
und her wider unz an Ungerlant
mugen wol die besten sīn,
die ich in der werlte hān erkant.
kan ich rehte schouwen
30   guot gelāz und līp,
sem mir got, sō swüere ich wol daz hie diu wīp
bezzer sint dan ander frouwen.

V   61 A, 198 C, 104 E

Tiusche man sint wol gezogen,
rehte als engel sint diu wīp getān.
35   swer si schildet, derst betrogen:
ich enkan sīn anders niht verstān.
tugent und reine minne,
swer die suochen wil,
der sol komen in unser lant: dā ist wünne vil:
40   lange müeze ich leben dar inne!

21 AC have *wolte* before *wol*.
23 'Of what advantage would it be to me if my contention were false ?'
31 *sem mir got* for *sam mir got helfe*, 'so help me God', missing in A.
31–32 It is not clear whether Walther is here using *wīp* and *frouwe* synonymously, or whether he intends a distinction as in 101. 40 f.

97

I   4 A, 69 B, 157 C, 184 E, 16 F (L/K 46, 32)

Aller werdekeit ein vüegerinne,
daz sīt ir zewāre, frowe Māze:
er sǣlic man, der iuwer lēre hāt!
der endarf sich iuwer niender inne
5 weder ze hove schamen noch an der strāze.
dur daz sō suoche ich, frowe, iuwern rāt,
daz ir mich ebene werben lēret.
wirb ich nidere, wirb ich hōhe, ich bin versēret.
ich was vil nāch ze nidere tōt,
10 nū bin ich aber ze hōhe siech: unmāze enlāt mich āne nōt.

II   5 A, 70 B, 158 C, 185 E, 17 F

Nideriu minne heizet diu sō swachet
daz der muot nāch kranker liebe ringet:
diu minne tuot unlobelīche wē.
hōhiu minne reizet unde machet
15 daz der muot nāch hōher wirde ūf swinget:
diu winket mir nū, daz ich mit ir gē.
mich wundert wes diu māze beitet.
kumpt diu herzeliebe, ich bin iedoch verleitet.
mīn ougen hānt ein wīp ersehen,
20 swie minneclīch ir rede sī, mir mac doch schade von ir geschehen.

98

I   13 A, 241 C, 157 E, 45 F, 29 s (L/K 69, 1)

Saget mir ieman, waz ist minne?
weiz ich des ein teil, sō wist ichs gerne mē.
der sich baz denn ich versinne,
der berihte mich durch waz si tuot sō wē.
5   minne ist minne, tuot si wol:

97. Text of A, with *sō* (6) from BC.
1 *vüegerinne* 'author', 'bestower'.
3 'fortunate is the man who is guided by you'.
7 *ebene*, i.e. in accordance with *māze*.
10 *unmāze*, etc., 'lack of moderation will not spare me distress'.
11 *nideriu*: *nidere* A.
12 *muot* A, *lip* other MSS.
14 *hōhiu*: *hohe* A.
15 *wirde*: *wurde* A, *werder liebe* BCF, *daz der mût so hohe stiget* E.

tuot si wē, sō enheizet si niht rehte minne.
sus enweiz ich wie si danne heizen sol.

II   12 A, 242 C, 158 E, 46 F, 13 O
Obe ich rehte rāten künne
waz diu minne sī, sō sprechet denne jā.
10   minne ist zweier herzen wünne:
teilent si gelīche, sost diu minne dā:
sol aber ungeteilet sīn,
sō enkan si ein herze alleine niht enthalten.
owē woldest du mir helfen, frowe mīn!

III   10 A, 243 C, 159 E, 47 F, 14 O
15   Frowe, ich trage ein teil ze swære:
wellest du mir helfen, sō hilf an der zīt.
sī aber ich dir gar unmære,
daz sprich endelīche: sō lāz ich den strīt,
unde wirde ein ledic man.
20   du solt aber einez rehte wizzen, [frouwe,]
daz dich lützel ieman baz geloben kan.

IV   11 A, 240 C, 161 E, 49 F, 16 O
Kan mīn frouwe süeze siuren?
wænet si daz ich ir liep gebe umbe leit?
sol ich si dar umbe tiuren,
25   daz si ez wider kēre an mīne unwerdekeit?
sō kund ich unrehte spehen.
wē waz sprich ich ōrenlōser ougen āne?
den diu minne blendet, wie mac der gesehen?

99

I   121 A, 166 C, 58 E, 4 G², 18 O (L/K 49, 25)
Herzeliebez vrowelīn,
got gebe dir hiute und iemer guot.
kund ich baz gedenken dīn,
des het ich willeclīchen muot.
5   waz mac ich dir sagen mē,
wan daz dir nieman holder ist? owē, dā von ist mir vil wē.

98. 6 Cf. Reinmar 86. 34–35.
   7 *sus* 'in that case'.
99. 3 'Could I wish anything better for you. . . .'

II   122 A, 167 C, 59 E, 5 G², 20 O

Si verwīzent mir daz ich
sō nidere wende mīnen sanc.
daz si niht versinnent sich
10 waz liebe sī, des haben undanc!
sie getraf diu liebe nie,
die nāch dem guote und nāch der schœne minnent; wē wie
    minnent die?

III   123 A, 169 C, 60 E, 6 G², 21 O

Bī der schœne ist dicke haz:
zer schœne niemen sī ze gāch.
15 liebe tuot dem herzen baz:
der liebe gēt diu schœne nāch.
liebe machet schœne wīp:
des enmac diu schœne niht getuon, si ne machet niemer lieben
    līp.

IV   124 A, 168 C, 61 E, 7 G², 19 O

Ich vertrage als ich vertruoc
20 und als ich iemer wil vertragen.
du bist schœne und hāst genuoc:
waz mugen si mir dā von gesagen?
swaz si sagen, ich bin dir holt,
und nim dīn glesīn vingerlīn für einer küneginne golt.

V   125 A, 170 C, 62 E, 8 G², 22 O

25 Hāst du triuwe und stætekeit,
sō bin ich des ān angest gar
daz mir iemer herzeleit
mit dīnem willen widervar.
hāst aber du der zweier niht,
30 sōne müezest du mīn niemer werden. owē danne, ob daz geschiht!

---

8 *sō* as in CG²; *tzo* O, *zů* E, missing A.
9–10 'A curse on those who do not understand what love is.'
13 *haz*, here the opposite of *liebe* in 15–17, therefore 'hateful, disagreeable qualities'.
15–17 *liebe* is the quality of being *liep* as l. 18 makes clear. It therefore means 'lovableness', 'charm', '*Liebenswürdigkeit*'.
16 'beauty is inferior to charm'.
24 *für* 'in preference to'.

100

I   86 B, 171 C, 63 E (L/K 50, 19)

Bin ich dir unmære,
des enweiz ich niht: ich minne dich.
einez ist mir swære,
du sihest bī mir hin und über mich.
5   daz solt du vermīden.
ine mac niht erlīden
selhe liebe āne grōzen schaden:
hilf mir tragen, ich bin ze vil geladen.

II   172 C, 65 E, 41² s

Sol daz sīn dīn huote,
10   daz dīn ouge mich sō selten siht?
tuost dū daz ze guote,
sōne wīze ich dir dar umbe niht.
sō mīt mir daz houbet,
daz sī dir erloubet,
15   und sich nider an mīnen fuoz,
sō du baz enmügest: daz sī dīn gruoz.

III   173 C, 41¹ s

Swanne ichs alle schouwe,
die mir suln von schulden wol behagen,
sō bist duz mīn frowe,
20   daz mac ich wol āne rüemen sagen.
edel unde rīche
sint si sumelīche,
dar zuo tragent si hōhen muot:
līhte sint si bezzer, du bist guot.

100. Text of C, with *ensī* (28), *sō gemeine* (31) from B.
  1 *unmære* 'an object of indifference'.
  4 'you look past me and ignore me'.
  9–12 'Is that intended to be the guard which you place on yourself that you look at me so seldom? If you do it for a good reason, I will not reproach you for it.'
  16 'when you can do nothing else'.
  24 There is a play on the double meaning of *guot* as (1) morally good, (2) socially acceptable; *bezzer* refers to the latter, *guot* to the former meaning.

IV   85 B, 174 C, 64 E, 41³ s

25 Frowe, du versinne
dich ob ich dir zihte mære sī.
eines friundes minne
diu ist niht guot, dā ensī ein ander bī.
minne entouc niht eine,
30 si sol sīn gemeine,
sō gemeine daz si gē
dur zwei herze und dur dekeinez mē.

IOI

I   164 C her reymar 356 e, (L/K 47, 36)

Zwō fuoge hān ich doch, swie ungefüege ich sī,
der hān ich mich von kinde her vereinet.
ich bin den frōn bescheidenlīcher fröide bī,
und lache ungerne swā man bī mir weinet.
5 durch die liute bin ich frō,
durch die liute wil ich sorgen.
ist mir anders danne alsō,
waz dar umbe? ich wil doch borgen.
swie si sint, sō wil ich sīn,
10 daz si niht verdrieze mīn.
manigem ist unmære
swaz einem anderen werre:
der sī ouch bī den liuten swære.

II   85 A, 72 B, 161 C, 355 e

Hie vor, dō man sō rehte minneclīchen warp,
15 dō wāren mīne sprüche fröiden rīche:
sīt daz diu minneclīche minne alsō verdarp,
sīt sanc ouch ich ein teil unminneclīche.

IOI. 1–2 'I have two seemly rules of conduct, however unseemly I may be otherwise;
I resolved on them from childhood on.' *fuoge* means what is fitting in a courtly sense,
as the contrast between *unfuoge* and *höfesch* in 20–21 makes clear.
   3–4 Cf. Rom. xii. 15 and Freidank 117. 20: *man sol bi fröuden wesen frō, bi*
trūren trūren, kumt ez sō.
   8 *borgen*, i.e. borrow from the emotions of others.
   13 'let him be sad in society'.

iemer als ez danne stāt,
alsō sol man danne singen.
20 swenne unfuoge nū zergāt,
sō singe aber von höfschen dingen.
noch kumpt fröide und sanges tac:
wol im, ders erbeiten mac!
derz gelouben wolte,
25 sō erkande ich wol die fuoge,
wenne und wie man singen solte.

III   87 A, 73 B, 162 C, 357 e

Ich sage iu waz uns den gemeinen schaden tuot:
diu wīp gelīchent uns ein teil ze sēre.
daz wir in alsō liep sīn übel alse guot,
30 seht, daz gelīchen nimet uns fröide und ēre.
schieden uns diu wīp als ē,
daz si sich ouch liezen scheiden,
daz gefrumt uns iemer mē,
mannen unde wīben beiden.
35 waz stēt übel, waz stēt wol,
sīt man uns niht scheiden sol?
edeliu wīp gedenket
daz ouch die man waz kunnen:
gelīchents iuch, ir sīt gekrenket.

IV   88 A, 163 C, 358 e, III 17 n

40 Wīp muoz iemer sīn der wībe hōhste name,
und tiuret baz danne frowe, als ichz erkenne.
swā nū deheiniu sī diu sich ir wīpheit schame,
diu merke disen sanc und kiese denne.
under frowen sint unwīp,
45 under wīben sint si tiure.
wībes name und wībes līp
die sint beide vil gehiure.

---

21 *singe*, 1st pers. singular present indicative, with pronoun omitted.
24 *derz*, etc., 'if anyone were willing to believe it . . . '.
39 *gelīchents = gelīchent si.*
45 *tiure* 'rare'.

swiez umb alle frowen var,
wîp sint alle frowen gar.
zwîvellop daz hœnet,
als under wîlen frowe:
wîp daz ist ein name der si alle krœnet.

50

V   86 A, 165 C, 359 e

Ich sanc hie vor den frowen umbe ir blôzen gruoz:
den nam ich wider mîme lobe ze lône.
swâ ich des geltes nû vergebene warten muoz.
dâ lobe ein ander, den si grüezen schône.
swâ ich niht verdienen kan
einen gruoz mit mîme sange,
dar kêre ich vil hêrscher man
mînen nac oder ein mîn wange.
daz kît 'mir ist umbe dich
rehte als dir ist umbe mich.'
ich wil mîn lop kêren
an wîp die kunnen danken:
waz hân ich von den überhêren?

55

60

65

102

1   442 C, 21 F, 41 O (L/K 65, 33)

In einem zwîvellîchen wân
was ich gesezzen und gedâhte,
ich wolte von ir dienste gân,
wan daz ein trôst mich wider brâhte.
trôst mac ez niht geheizen, owê des!
ez ist vil kûme ein kleinez trœstelîn;
sô kleine, swenne ichz iu gesage, ir spottet mîn.
doch fröwet sich lützel ieman, er enwizze wes.

5

48–49 'However it may be with ladies, (true) women are all ladies.' Kraus (L/K)
emends *sint* to *sîn* and interprets as 'let all ladies be (true) women' (WU, p. 164).
61 *kît*, 3rd pers. singular of *keden, queden*: 'that means'.
102. 1–2 'I sat, lost in doubting thoughts . . .'.
5 *owê des* with FO (missing C).
8 'yet no one ever rejoices, unless he has some cause'.

II   102 B, 234, 443 C, 22 F, 42 O

Mich hāt ein halm gemachet vrō:

10   er giht, ich sül genāde vinden.
ich maz daz selbe kleine strō,
als ich hie vor gesach von kinden.
nū hœret unde merket ob siz denne tuo.
'si tuot, si entuot, si tuot, si entuot, si tuot.'

15   swie dicke ich alsō maz, sō was ie daz ende guot.
daz trœstet mich: dā hœret ouch geloube zuo.

103

I   134 A, 262 C, 51 E (L/K 74, 20)

'Nemt, frowe, disen kranz':
alsō sprach ich zeiner wol getānen maget,
'sō zieret ir den tanz,
mit den schœnen bluomen, als irs ūffe traget.

5   het ich vil edele gesteine,
daz müest ūf iuwer houbet,
obe ir mirs geloubet.
sēt mīne triuwe, daz ich ez meine.'

II   136 A, 264 C, 53 E

Si nam daz ich ir bōt,

10   einem kinde vil gelīch daz ēre hāt.
ir wangen wurden rōt,
same diu rōse, dā si bī der liljen stāt.
des erschampten sich ir liehten ougen:
doch neic si mir vil schōne.

15   daz wart mir ze lōne:
wirt mirs iht mēr, daz trage ich tougen.

III   135 A, 263 C, 52 E

'Ir sīt sō wol getān
daz ich iu mīn schapel gerne geben wil,
daz aller beste daz ich hān.

20   wīzer unde rōter bluomen weiz ich vil,

---

103. 4 *irs = ir si.*
10 *daz ēre hāt* 'who receives an honour'.
17 *Frowe ir sīt* all MSS., but *frowe* is usually omitted in the interests of the metre.

die stēnt sō verre in jener heide.
dā si schōne entspringent
und die vogele singent,
dā suln wir si brechen beide.'

IV   138 A, 373 C

25 Mich dūhte daz mir nie
lieber wurde, danne mir ze muote was.
die bluomen vielen ie
von dem boume bī uns nider an daz gras.
seht, dō muoste ich von fröiden lachen.
30 dō ich sō wünnecliche
was in troume rīche,
dō taget ez und muose ich wachen.

V   137 A, 372 C, 54 E

Mir ist von ir geschehen,
daz ich disen sumer allen meiden muoz
35 vaste under diu ougen sehen:
līhte wirt mir einiu, sō ist mir sorgen buoz.
waz obe si gēt an disem tanze?
frowe, dur iuwer güete
rucket ūf die hüete,
40 owē gesæhe ichs under kranze!

104

I   42 B, 128 C (L/K 39, 11)

Under der linden   an der heide,
dā unser zweier bette was,
dā muget ir vinden   schōne beide
gebrochen bluomen unde gras.
5 vor dem walde in einem tal,
tandaradei,
schōne sanc diu nahtegal.

22 *entsprungen* AC.
23 *sungen* AC.
25 *nie: ie* AC.
37 *gēt* 'is participating in this dance'.
40 *ichs = ich si.*
104. Text of C with l. 12 and *nu enwelle* (23) as in B.

II   43 B, 129 C
Ich kam gegangen   zuo der ouwe,
dō was min friedel komen ē.
10   dā wart ich enpfangen,   hēre frouwe,
daz ich bin sælic iemer mē.
kust er mich? wol tūsentstunt,
tandaradei,
seht wie rōt mir ist der munt.

III   44 B, 130 C
15   Dō hāt er gemachet   alsō rīche
von bluomen eine bettestat.
des wirt noch gelachet   inneclīche,
kumt iemen an daz selbe pfat.
bī den rōsen er wol mac,
20   tandaradei,
merken wā mirz houbet lac.

IV   45 B, 131 C
Daz er bī mir læge,   wessez iemen
(nu enwelle got!), sō schamt ich mich.
wes er mit mir pflæge,   niemer niemen
25   bevinde daz, wan er und ich,
und ein kleinez vogellīn,
tandaradei,
daz mac wol getriuwe sīn.

105

I   112 C (L/K 64, 31)
Owē, hovelīchez singen,
daz dich ungefüege dœne
solten ie ze hove verdringen!
daz die schiere got gehœne!
5   owē daz dīn wirde alsō geliget!
des sint alle dīne friunde unfrō.
daz muoz eht alsō sīn: nū sī alsō:
frō Unfuoge, ir habt gesiget.

9 *friedel* is a word not usually found in courtly poetry; cf. **9**. 1.
10 *hēre frouwe* has been differently interpreted as (1) 'like a high-born lady';
(2) 'with the greeting "noble lady"'; (3) an apostrophe to the Virgin, used as an
interjection: 'Blessed Lady'.
105. 4 *die: dich* C.

II 113 C

Der uns fröide wider bræhte,
10 diu reht und gefüege wære,
hei wie wol man des gedæhte
swā man von im seite mære!
ez wære ein vil hovelîcher muot,
des ich iemer gerne wünschen sol:
15 frowen unde hērren zæme ez wol:
owē daz ez nieman tuot!

III 114 C

Die daz rehte singen stœrent,
der ist ungelîche mēre
danne die ez gerne hœrent:
20 doch volge ich der alten lēre:
ich enwil niht werben zuo der mül,
dā der stein sō riuschent umbe gāt
und daz rat sō mange unwîse hāt.
merkent wer dā harpfen sül.

IV 115 C

25 Die sō frevellîchen schallent,
der muoz ich vor zorne lachen,
daz si in selben wol gevallent
mit alsō ungefüegen sachen.
die tuont sam die frösche in eime sē,
30 den ir schrîen alsō wol behaget,
daz diu nahtegal dā von verzaget,
sō si gerne sunge mē.

V 101 B, 116 C

Swer unfuoge swîgen hieze,
waz man noch von fröiden sunge
35 und si abe den bürgen stieze,
daz si dā die frōn niht twunge.

21 ff. a proverbial saying found also in Freidank (126. 27–28):
  mich dunket niht, daz ieman sül   ze lange harpfen in der mül.
30 *alsō: so* C.
33 *vngefûge* B, *vngefûge* C.
36 *das si da von niht twnge* B, *dc vnfûge da verswûde* C.

> wurden ir die grōzen höve benomen,
> daz wær allez nāch dem willen mīn.
> bī den gebūren liez ich si wol sīn:
40 dannen ist si her bekomen.

106

> Owē daz wīsheit und jugent,
> des mannes schœne noch sīn tugent,
> niht erben sol, sō ie der līp erstirbet!
> daz mac wol klagen ein wīser man,
5 der sich des schaden versinnen kan,
> Reimār waz guoter kunst an dir verdirbet.
> du solt von schulden iemer des geniezen,
> daz dich des tages nie wolte verdriezen,
> dun spræches ie den vrowen wol . . .
10 des sün si iemer danken dīner zungen,
> hetest anders niht wan eine rede gesungen:
> 'sō wol dir wīp, wie reine ein nam!', du hetest alse gestriten
> an ir lop daz elliu wīp dir genāden solten biten.

> Dēswār, Reimār, du riuwes mich
15 michels harter danne ich dich,
> ob du lebtes und ich wære erstorben.
> Ich wilz bī mīnen triuwen sagen,

106. 3 *niht erben sol* 'cannot be handed down'.

8 Lachmann and with him most editors transposes the MS. order to *wolte nie*.

8–9 'that you never at any time grew weary of speaking well of ladies'.

9 Some final phrase, probably ending in *siten* on account of the rhyme, is missing in the MS.

10 For *zunge* as the instrument of poetic skill, see Gottfried's *Tristan* 4705, 4783 (referring to Reinmar), 4790, 4828, 4854, 4887.

11 *hetest*: *vn hettist* a.

Reinmar himself designates his praise of women as *rede* (cf. **87.** 23).

12 *ein*: *din* a.

12 Cf. **87.** 19.

12–13 *dv hettest an ir lob alse gi stritin daz ellu wib dir iemir ginadin soltin bittin* a.

'. . . you would have so striven in the cause of their praise that all women should pray for mercy for you (i.e. on your soul).' Some editors take *an ir lop gestriten* to mean 'striven to win their praise', but this is less likely.

14 *du riuwes mich* 'I regret your loss'.

15 *michel* a.

dich selben wolt ich lützel klagen,
ich klage dīn edel kunst, daz si ist verdorben.
20   du kundest al der werlte fröide mēren,
sō duz ze guoten dingen woltes kēren.
mich riuwet dīn wol redender munt und dīn vil süezer sanc,
daz die verdorben sint bī mīnen zīten.
daz du niht eine wīle mohtest bīten!
25   sō leiste ich dir geselleschaft: mīn singen ist niht lanc.
dīn sēle müeze wol gevarn, und habe dīn zunge danc.

107

I   MSS. C and k (L/K 4, 2)

Maget und muoter, schouwe   der kristenheite nōt,
dū blüende gert Aarōnes,   ūf gēnder morgenrōt,
Ezechīeles porte,   diu nie wart ūf getān,
dur die der künec hērlīche   wart ūz und in gelān.
5   alsō diu sunne schīnet   durch ganz geworhtez glas,
alsō gebar diu reine Krist,   diu magt und muoter was.

II
Ein bosch der bran,   dā nie niht an
besenget noch verbrennet wart.
breit unde ganz   beleip sīn glanz
10   vor fiures flamme unverschart.
daz was diu reine   magt alleine
diu mit magetlīcher art

18 *wolt*: *wil* a.
20 This is a common description of the poet's task.
21 Cf. **87**. 22.
25 Probably means: 'as it is, I shall join you: my singing will soon be over'. Wilmanns–Michel take *leiste* to be a contraction for *leistete*. The meaning would then be: 'then I would have joined you', but this is unlikely, as the other verb in the line is clearly future.

107. 2 *dū blüende gert Aarōnes*: the budding of Aaron's rod was divine confirmation of his authority (Num. xvii. 1–8).
    ūf gēnder morgenrōt: *quæ est ista, quæ progreditur quasi aurora consurgens? . . .* (Cant. Cant. vi. 9). Among the allegorical interpretations of the Song of Songs common in the Middle Ages was that referring it to Mary.
3 Ezek. xliv. 2 f.: *Et dixit Dominus ad me: Porta hæc clausa erit: non aperietur, et vir non transibit per eam: quoniam Dominus Deus Israel ingressus est per eam, eritque clausa.*
5 The image of the sun shining through glass is frequently used in illustration of the Virgin Birth.
    ganz geworht 'fashioned in one piece': the idea is no doubt that of something remaining whole and perfect.
7 Exod. iii. 2.

III

Kindes muoter worden ist
ān aller manne mitewist,
15   [und] wider menneschlīchen list
den wāren Krist
gebar, der uns bedāhte.
wol ir, daz si den ie getruoc,
der unsern tōt ze tōde sluoc!
20   mit sīnem bluote er ab uns twuoc
den ungefuoc
den Even schulde uns brāhte.

IV

Salomōnes   hōhes trōnes
bist du, frowe, ein selde hēre und ouch gebieterinne.
25   balsamīte,   margarīte
ob allen megden bist dū, maget, ein magt, ein küneginne.
gotes lambe   was dīn wambe
ein palas kleine,   dā ez reine   lac beslozzen inne.

108

I   101 A, 103 B, 235 C, 2 **w**   (L/K 66, 21)

Ir reinen wīp, ir werden man,
ez stēt alsō daz man mir muoz
ēre und minneclīchen gruoz
noch volleclīcher bieten an.

14 'without human paticipation'; cf. Luke i. 34: *Quomodo fiet istud, quoniam virum non cognosco?*
    15 The line is missing in C.
       'and in defiance of earthly wisdom'.
    17 *bedāhte* 'provided for us'.
    19 Cf. 1 Cor. xv. 26, and Freidank 9. 25: *daz Kristes tōt tōt unsern tōt.*
    20 Cf. Rev. i. 5; 1 John i. 7.
    25 *balsamīte*, cf. the praise of wisdom in Eccles. xxiv. 15: *Sicut cinnamomum et balsamum aromatizans odorem dedi*, which is customarily applied to Mary.
        margarīte 'pearl': the designation of Mary as a jewel (*gimme*), or more particularly as diamond or pearl, is common.
    27–28 *Gotes lambe. was din wamme ein palas reine. da er eine lag beslossen inne.* C.
        was: ez was k.
    28 *daz daz reine. lamp aleine.* k.
    28 *kleine* 'precious'.
    108. 1 *rein* is a stereotyped courtly attribute meaning 'perfect', 'excellent'.

5   des   habet ir von schulden grœzer reht dan ē:
         welt ir vernemen, ich sage iu wes.
         wol   vierzec jār hab ich gesungen oder mē
         von minnen und als ieman sol.
         dō was ichs mit den andern geil:
10   nu enwirt mirs niht, ez wirt iu gar.
         mīn minnesanc der diene iu dar,
         und iuwer hulde sī mīn teil.

         II   102 A, 104 B, 236 C, 3 w^x

         Lāt mich an eime stabe gān
         und werben umbe werdekeit
15   mit unverzageter arebeit,
         als ich von kinde hān getān,
         sō   bin ich doch, swie nider ich sī, der werden ein,
         genuoc in mīner māze hō.
         daz   müet die nideren. ob mich daz iht swache? nein.
20   die biderben hānt mich deste baz.
         der werden wirde diu ist sō guot,
         daz man in daz hœhste lop sol geben.
         ez enwart nie lobelīcher leben,
         swer sō dem ende rehte tuot.

5 *reht* has the double meaning of 'right' and 'obligation' as here.

9 f. 'Then I rejoiced in it (my song) with others. Now I derive no profit from it, it accrues entirely to you.'

11 *dar*, here used predominantly in a temporal sense: 'further, in future'.

13 *Lāt mich* introduces a hypothetical condition: 'Even supposing I were to walk with a staff....' The staff is the emblem of poverty and old age. The thought is as follows: 'Even if I were reduced to penury, I would still be counted among the worthy members of society.'

19 *mv̊t dc die nideren* A, *hassent dc die nidern* BC. *Daz müet* is necessary because the first word must rhyme with *baz* in l. 20 (see note on metrical form).

19–20 'That irks the inferior members of society. Does that detract from my position at all ? No, the worthy prize me the more highly.'

21 *der werden* with A; *dû werde* BC. Kraus (L/K) emends to *diu wernde wirde*, but this is unnecessary.

22 *in daz* with A; *irs* C, *ir das* B. Lines 21–22 thus mean 'The repute of the worthy is so great that they should be accorded the highest praise.'

24 *Denne swa man dem ende rehte tv̊t* BC, *swer so dem ende tv̊t* A.

23–24 'There never was a more praiseworthy manner of life, if a man acts in saccordance with the end', i.e. here int houghts of death and the next life; cf. Eccles. vii. 36.

III   103 A, 105 B, 237 C, 6 wˣ

25   Welt, ich hān dīnen lōn ersehen:
     swaz du mir gīst, daz nimest du mir.
     wir scheiden alle blōz von dir.
     schame dich, sol mir alsō geschehen.
     ich   hān līp und sēle (des was gar ze vil)
30   gewāget tūsentstunt dur dich:
     nū   bin ich alt und hāst mit mir dīn gampelspil;
     ist mir daz zorn, sō lachest dū.
     nū lache uns eine wīle noch:
     dīn jāmertac wil schiere komen,
35   und nimet dir swaz du uns hāst benomen,
     und brennet dich dar umbe iedoch.

IV   100 A, 107 B, 239 C, 5 wˣ

     Ich hāt ein schœnez bilde erkorn:
     owē daz ich ez ie gesach
     alder ie sō vil zuo zime gesprach!
40   ez hāt schœne unde rede verlorn.
     dā   wonte ein wunder inne: daz vuor ine weiz war,
     dā von gesweic daz bilde iesā.
     sīn   liljerōsevarwe wart sō karkelvar,
     daz ez verlōs smac unde schīn.
45   mīn bilde, ob ich bekerkelt bin
     in dir, sō lā mich ūz alsō
     daz wir ein ander vinden vrō:
     wan ich muoz aber wider in.

25 *der werlt lōn* is a common phrase describing the illusory rewards of the world.
27 Cf. Job i. 21, and 1 Tim. vi. 7.
30 *gewāget* 'imperilled'.
36 For the idea that the world will be destroyed by fire, see 2 Pet. iii 10 and the
OHG *Muspilli*.
37 *erkorn* 'perceived'.
41 *ine weiz*, a frequent poetic formula expressing doubt or ignorance.
44 *smac unde schīn* 'fragrance and beauty'.
45–48 'My image, if I am imprisoned in you, then set me free, so that we may find
each other again rejoicing, for I must return to you again'. The idea of the body as
the prison of the spirit is a common one; ll. 45–46 are a plea to be set free from the
tyranny of the body, doomed to decay, whereas ll. 47–48 refer to the reunion of body
and soul at the resurrection.

V   99 A, 106 B, 238 C, 4 wˣ

Mīn sēle müeze wol gevarn!
50   ich hān zer welte manegen līp
     gemachet vrō, man unde wīp:
     künde ich dar under mich bewarn!
     lobe   ich des lībes minne, daz ist der sēle leit:
     si giht, ez sī ein lüge, ich tobe.
55   der   wāren minne giht si ganzer stætekeit,
     wie guot si sī, wie si iemer wer.
     līp, lā die minne diu dich lāt,
     und habe die stæten minne wert:
     mich dunket der du hāst gegert,
60   diu sī niht visch unz an den grāt.

109

I   133 A, 105 C, 7 wˣ (L/K 100, 24)

Frō Welt, ir sult dem wirte sagen
daz ich im gar vergolten habe.
mīn grœste gülte ist abe geslagen,
daz er mich von dem briefe schabe.
5   swer im iht sol, der mac wol sorgen.
    ē ich im lange schuldic wære, ich wolt ē zeinem juden borgen.
    er swīget unz an einen tac:
    sō wil er danne ein wette hān, sō jener niht vergelten mac.

---

52 'Could I but preserve myself from harm meanwhile', i.e. without forfeit of the soul.

55 'She ascribes to true love perfect constancy'.

60 is a proverbial phrase, meaning literally 'not solid fish to the bone', 'lacking in substance'.

109. Text of C.

1 *wirt*: the range of meanings in MHG is as follows: (1) master of the house, host (opposed *gast*) as in **94.** 9; (2) lord, ruler, e.g. *der wirt des landes, der helle wirt* (the devil); (3) husband; (4) innkeeper. See note on contents of poem.

2–4 'that I have paid my debt in full. My greatest debt is paid off; let him erase me from the bond': *brief* is the bond or promissory note exacted from the debtor by the creditor.

5 *sol* 'owes'.

6 *e ich des leides wolte phlegen. ich solte e . . .* A.
  ich wolt ē: ich wolt es C.

8 *wette* 'pledge', 'payment', i.e. the soul.

II   106 C

'Walther, du zürnest āne nōt,
10 du solt bī mir belīben hie.
gedenke waz ich dir ēren bōt,
waz ich dir dīnes willen lie,
als du mich dicke sēre bæte.
mir was vil innȩclīche leit daz duz sō selten tæte.
15 bedenke dich, dīn leben ist guot.
sō du mir rehte widersagest, sōn wirst du niemer wol gemuot.'

III   107 C

Frō Welt, ich hān ze vil gesogen,
ich wil entwonen, des ist zīt.
dīn zart hat mich vil nāch betrogen,
20 wand er vil süezer fröiden gīt.
dō ich dich gesach reht under ougen,
dō was dīn schouwen wunderlīch al sunder lougen.
doch was der schanden alse vil,
dō ich dīn hinden wart gewar, daz ich dich iemer schelten wil.

IV   108 C

25 'Sīt ich dich niht erwenden mac,
sō tuo doch ein dinc des ich ger.
gedenke an mangen liehten tac,
und sich doch underwīlent her,
niuwan sō dich der zīt betrāge.'
30 daz tæt ich wunderlīchen gerne, wan daz ich fürhte dīne lāge,
vor der sich nieman kan bewarn.
got gebe iu, frowe, guote naht, ich wil ze herberge varn.

110

I   439 C, 212 E (L/K 124, 1)

Owē war sint verswunden alliu mīniu jār!
ist mir mīn leben getroumet, oder ist ez wār?

---

14 The line is metrically defective. Most editors emend to *daz du daz ie* for this
reason.
17 'I have sucked at your breasts too long'.
28–29 'come here sometimes, only if time hangs heavy on your hands'.
32 *herberge*: probably means here a safe haven, away from the snares of the world.
110. 2 *min leben mir* C.

daz ich ie wānde daz iht wǣre, waz daz iht?
dar nāch hān ich geslāfen, und enweiz es niht.
5   nū bin ich erwachet und ist mir unbekant
daz mir hie vor was kündic als mīn ander hant.
liute und lant dar innen ich von kinde bin erzogen,
die sint mir frömde worden, reht als ob ez sī gelogen.
die mīne gespilen wāren, die sint trǣge unde alt.
10   bereitet ist daz velt, verhouwen ist der walt.
wan daz daz wazzer fliuzet als ez wīlent flōz,
für wār ich wānde mīn ungelücke wurde grōz.
mich grüezet maniger trāge, der mich bekande ē wol.
diu welt ist allenthalben ungenāden vol.
15   als ich gedenke an manigen wünneclīchen tac,
die mir sint enpfallen als in daz mer ein slac,
iemer mēre owē.

II   440 C
Owē wie jæmerlīche junge liute tuont,
den vil unriuweclīche ir gemüete stuont!
20   die kunnen niuwan sorgen, owē wie tuont si sō?
swar ich zer werlte kēre, dā ist nieman vrō.
tanzen, [lachen], singen zergāt mit sorgen gar:
nie kristen man gesach sō jæmerlīche jār.
nū merkent wie den frouwen ir gebende stāt,
25   die stolzen ritter tragent dörpellīche wāt.
uns sint unsenfte brieve her von Rōme komen,
uns ist erloubet trūren und fröide gar benomen.

---

3 Lit. 'that which I took to be something, was it anything?': 'did that which I
believed real in fact exist?'

4 *dar nāch*: Kraus (WU, p. 467) takes it as causal and translates as *dem gemäß*;
Wilmanns-Michel suggest that it is both temporal ('since then') and causal ('if that
is so, then . . .').

6 *mīn ander hant*, either 'one of my two hands', or probably simply 'my own
hand', with *ander* used emphatically as in French *nous autres*.

7 *dar innen*: *dannā* C. *erzogen*: *geborn* CE.

8 *gelogen*: *gelegen* C.

10 *bereitet* is the MS. reading and would mean 'prepared for cultivation', 'tilled'.
It has been variously emended to *vereitet*, *gebreitet*, and *bebouwen*.

12 'I would indeed consider my misfortune to be great.'

16 A common proverbial phrase; cf. NHG *ein Schlag ins Wasser*.

19 *nv vil núweklíche* C: Paul's emendation to *vil unriuweclīche* is accepted here
as that nearest to the MS. The other principal emendations are: *e vil wünnecliche(n)*,
e vil hoveliche(n), *unvil riuwecliche*.

daz müet mich inneclīchen sēre, wir lebten ie vil wol,
daz ich nū für mīn lachen weinen kiesen sol.

30 die wilden vogel betrüebet unser klage:
waz wunders ist ob ich dā von verzage?
waz spriche ich tumber man durch mīnen bœsen zorn?
swer dirre wunne volget, der hāt jene dort verlorn,
iemer mēre owē.

III   441 C, 1 wˣ

35 Owē wie uns mit süezen dingen ist vergeben!
ich sihe die bittern gallen mitten in dem honige sweben.
diu welt ist ūzen schœne, wīz, grüen unde rōt,
und innān swarzer varwe, vinster sam der tōt.
swen si nū habe verleitet, der schouwe sīnen trōst,

40 er wirt mit swacher buoze grozer sünde erlōst.
dar an gedenkent, ritter, ez ist iuwer dinc.
ir tragent die liehten helme und manigen herten rinc,
dar zuo die vesten schilte und diu gewīhten swert.
wolte got, wær ich der sigenünfte wert,

45 sō wolte ich nōtic man verdienen rīchen solt:
joch meine ich niht die huoben noch der hērren golt.
ich wolte selbe krōne eweclīchen tragen,
die möhte ein soldener mit sīme sper bejagen.
möhte ich die lieben reise gevarn über sē,

50 sō wolte ich denne singen wol und niemer mēr owē,
niemer mēr owē.

33 *dirre* 'of this world'; *jene* 'of the next'.
35 'How are we poisoned with sweetness.'
39 *verleitet habe* C.
44 *sigenünfte: segenunge* wˣ.
47 *selbe* is frequently emended to *sælden*.
50–51 The refrain is not repeated in C, but the repetition is likely.

GÖTFRIT VON STRASBURG
(GOTTFRIED VON STRASSBURG)

THERE is no documentary evidence of Gottfried's life. In MS. C he is given the title *meister* which indicates that he was a member of the middle class. From his *Tristan* can be gleaned certain indications of the date at which he wrote. In his famous review of the literature of his day (*Tristan* 4620 ff.), he speaks of Veldeke and Reinmar as already dead and mentions among living poets Hartmann and Walther. He also attacks a certain obscure and extravagant style of writing in a passage which has been interpreted as a criticism of Wolfram's *Parzival*. All these facts permit the inference that the *Tristan* was completed in its present form, without a conclusion, by *c.* 1210 and that Gottfried was thus writing in the first decade of the thirteenth century. There is no reason to doubt the testimony of later authors that death prevented Gottfried from finishing the epic.

The manuscripts ascribe to Gottfried one *Minnelied*, a poem in praise of the Virgin, and several didactic strophes couched in the form of advice from father to son. None of these attributions can be considered authentic. On the other hand MS. C preserves two strophes under the name of Ulrich von Liechtenstein, which can with relative certainty be ascribed to Gottfried. The second one is quoted almost verbatim by Rudolf von Ems, an imitator of Gottfried, prefaced by the phrase: *der wîse meister Gotfrit sprach* (*Alexander*, ed. Junk, 20621 ff.). Both strophes also contain links in style, vocabulary, and theme with *Tristan* (cf. R. Heinzel, *Kleine Schriften*, Heidelberg, 1907, pp. 58 ff., and K. Stackmann in *Festgabe für Ulrich Pretzel*, Berlin, 1963, pp. 191 ff.).

III
Uolrich von Liechtenstein, 307 C (KLD 16, I)

Liute unde lant diu möhten mit genāden sīn
wan zwei vil kleiniu wortelīn 'mīn' unde 'dīn',
diu briuwent michel wunder ūf der erde.
wie gānt si früetende unde wüetende über al

111. 2 Cf. Freidank 31. 6: *zer werlde mac niht bezzer sīn, dan ein wort, daz heizet mīn.*

3 *briuwent*: cf. *Tristan* 13023.

4 'how they proceed everywhere, causing both good and ill', i.e. the profit of *mīn* is to the disadvantage of *dīn*.

5   und trībent al die welt umbe als einen bal:
       ich wæne ir krieges iemer ende werde.
       diu vertāne gīte
       diu wahset allez umbe sich dā her sīt Ēven zīte
       und irret elliu herze und elliu rīche.
10   weder hant noch zunge
       die meinent noch minnent niht wan valsch und anderunge;
       lēre unde volge liegent offenlīche.

112

Uolrich von Liechtenstein 308 C (KLD 16, II)

       Gelücke daz gēt wunderlīchen an unde abe:
       man vindet ez vil līhter danne manz behabe;
       ez wenket dā man ez niht wol besorget.
       swen ez beswæren wil, dem gīt ez ē der zīt
5   und nimt ouch ē der zīt wider swaz ez gegīt.
       ez tumbet den swem ez ze vil geborget.
       fröide gīt den smerzen:
       ē daz wir āne swære sīn des lībes und des herzen,
       man vindet ē daz glesīn gelücke.
10   daz hāt kranke veste:
       swenne ez uns under diu ougen spilt und schīnet aller beste,
       sō brichet ez vil līhte in kleine stücke.

5 Cf. **66.** 31–32 and *Tristan* 1027 and 11362.
6 *ir krieges* 'the conflict between them'; *iemer* here = *niemer*.
7 'evil covetousness'.
10 *weder*: *dewede*[s] C.
12 'Moral teaching and practice clearly lie'. *lēre* is frequent in the sense of 'moral teaching', and *volge* is used in association with it, meaning 'observation in practice', as in Reinmar von Zweter, ed. Roethe, 57, 3:

sī valscher volge vrī, sī guoter lēre willic unde vrō.

112. 1 *an unde abe* 'up and down'.
5 Cf. Walther **108.** 25–26.
6 *tumbet* 'renders foolish'.
7 *den smerzen*, weak masculine singular. The line is probably corrupt. It appears to mean: 'joy brings pain', i.e. there can be no unalloyed joy.
8–9 'We cannot be without pain of either body or heart; instead we find brittle fortune'. For *glesīn* see note on subject-matter.
10 'that has no permanence'.

WOLFRAM VON ESCHENBACH

WOLFRAM's home appears to have been Eschenbach (now Wolframs-Eschenbach) near Ansbach in Bavaria, formerly in the duchy of Franconia, a place which lies at the centre of the topographical names mentioned in his works. He is given the title *her* in MS. C and was no doubt a member of the *ministerialis* class. There is no documentary evidence to permit the dating of his life, but he refers in his works to events of the first decade of the thirteenth century (for example, in *Willehalm* 393. 30, to the coronation of Otto IV as emperor in 1209). It is usually thought that *Parzival* was written in the first decade of the thirteenth century, and *Willehalm* and *Titurel* after 1210. It is not possible to date his lyrics or to place them in chronological order. He probably lived from *c.* 1170 to 1220 and was thus roughly contemporary with Walther whom he no doubt met at the court of Hermann of Thuringia who is mentioned by both poets as their patron.

Certain details can be gleaned from his works. He asserts in *Parzival* that he is above all a knight—*schildes ambet ist mîn art* (115. 11)—and would prefer to win love by feats of arms rather than by his poetry. In a much-discussed passage he disclaims all pretension to learning—*ichne kan deheinen buochstap* (115. 27). In fact his works are full of miscellaneous knowledge, and this statement is probably only an instance of the customary modesty-formula combined with a dig at a poet such as Hartmann who is at pains to stress that he is *gelêret*—skilled in book-learning (*Der Arme Heinrich* 1, *Iwein* 21). With humorous feeling Wolfram speaks of his own poverty in *Parzival* (185. 1):

> dâ heime in mîn selbes hûs,
> dâ wirt gevröut vil selten mûs.

The seven poems given here are the only surviving authentic lyric poems. Only two are *Minnelieder* proper, and the other five are variations on the dawn song. All the poems, like his other works, bear the stamp of an original mind. They are distinguished by unusual images (for instance those of **113** and the opening lines of **116**) and unconventional vocabulary, including technical terms drawn from different spheres (e.g. the language of falconry in **113**). There are marked idiosyncrasies of style: a preference for nouns to express verbal ideas, as in **114**, the extreme concentration of elliptical constructions such as the opening lines of **119**, the departure from normal word-order, often for purposes of emphasis, as in the closing lines of **116** and **117**.

There is a great variety of metrical form, ranging from the simplicity and regularity of **113** to the extreme virtuosity and complication of **118**. In all but **114** there are instances of a deliberate disharmony between syntactical and metrical divisions. Thus the first strophe of **117** and the last strophe of **118** are marked off from the rest by the syntactical fusion of *Aufgesang* and *Abgesang*. In **115** the first *Stollen* is syntactically distinct, but the second merges into the *Abgesang* in each of the three strophes. In **119** the climax is marked by the only instance in the whole poem of a correspondence between syntax and metre. The disregard of convention to deliberate effect is thus seen in vocabulary, style, and metre. The poems are here arranged according to type.

113

I   1 BC (KLD 69, III)

Ein wīp mac wol erlouben mir
daz ich ir neme mit triuwen war.
ich ger (mir wart ouch nie diu gir
verhabet): mīn ougen swingen dar.
5   wie bin ich sus iuwelenslaht?
si siht mīn herze in vinster naht.

II   2 BC

Si treit den helfelīchen gruoz,
der mich an fröiden rīchen mac,
dar ūf ich iemer dienen muoz.
10   vil līhte erschīnet noch der tac
daz man mir muoz fröiden jehen.
noch grœzer wunder ist geschehen.

113. 3 *gern* (Engl. bate) is a technical term of falconry, designating the falcon's eagerness to mount in pursuit of prey.

die gir verhaben 'restrain a bird of prey by hooding it'. This has precise significance here because it refers to the poet's eyes which are not 'hooded'. For the metaphorical use of hood and bate as applied to love, cf. *Romeo and Juliet*, III. ii. 14.

4 *swingen* with BC. KLD emends to *swingent*, but the subjunctive form can be explained as the formulation of a wish dependent on *gern*: 'may my eyes soar thither'.

5 'How am I thus owl like? My heart perceives her amid dark night.' Cf. Freidank **145. 19**: *Mich dunket er sī iulenslaht | swer für den tac nimt die naht.*

9 *dar ūf* 'in pursuit of which'.

12 Cf. Reinmar **85. 14–15**.

III   3 BC

Nu seht waz ein storch sæten schade:
noch minre schaden habent mīn diu wīp.
15   ir haz ich ungerne ūf mich lade.
diu nū den schuldehaften līp
gegen mir treit, daz lāze ich sīn:
ich wil nu pflegen der zühte mīn.

114

I   9 C (KLD 69, VI)

Ursprinc bluomen, loup ūz dringen
und der luft des meigen urbort vogel ir alten dōn:
eteswenne ich kan niuwez singen,
sō der rīfe liget, guot wīp, noch allez an dīn lōn.
5   die waltsinger und ir sanc
nāch halben sumers teile in niemannes ōre enklanc.

II   10 C

Der bliclīchen bluomen glesten
sō des touwes anehanc erliuternt, swā si sint;
vogel die hellen und die besten,
10   al des meigen zīt si wegent mit gesange ir kint.
dō slief niht diu nahtegal:
nu wache aber ich und singe ūf berge und in dem tal.

13–14 'Now see what damage a stork does to crops (i.e. none); women suffer even less injury from me'.

16–18 'I make no complaint against her who has now incurred a debt of obligation towards me. I will now show my good-breeding.'

114. 1 *bluomen* is a genitive dependent on *ursprinc*, whereas *loup* and *ūz dringen* are merely juxtaposed: 'the springing up of flowers, foliage thrusting forth. . .'.

2 *urbor* is a piece of land bringing in revenue, *urborn* 'to produce or exact revenue'; thus 'exacts from the birds the tribute of their former song'.

3–6 'On occasion I can sing a new song when frost lies on the ground . . ., all in hope of your reward, (whereas) the singers of the forest and their song resounded in no one's ears after half the summer was over.'

6–7 This is the reading of the MS. in which *sō*, as is frequent, stands for a relative pronoun: 'The splendour of brilliant flowers, which brighten the dew, wherever they are.' This loose construction would be a parallel to l. 1 and not uncharacteristic of Wolfram. KLD emends *sō* to *sol* and *erliuternt* to *erliutern*. Neither the MS. reading nor the emendation is entirely satisfactory.

III   11 C
Mīn sanc wil genāde suochen
an dich, güetlich wīp: nu hilf, sīt helfe ist worden nōt.
15   mīn lōn dienstes sol geruochen,
daz ich iemer bitte und biute unz an mīnen tōt.
lāze mich von dir nemen den trōst
daz ich ūz mīnen langen klagen werde erlōst.

IV   12 C
Guot wīp, mac mīn dienst ervinden
20   ob dīn helflīch gebot mich fröiden welle wern,
daz mīn trūren müeze swinden
und ein liebez ende an dir bejagen mīn langez gern?
dīn güetlīch gelāz mich twanc
daz ich dir beide guot singe al kurz oder wiltu lanc.

V   13 C
25   Werdez wīp, dīn süeze güete
und dīn minneclīcher zorn hāt mir vil fröide erwert.
maht du trœsten mīn gemüete?
wan ein helflīchez wort von dir mich sanfte ernert.
mache wendic mir mīn klagen,
30   sō daz ich werde grōz gemuot bī mīnen tagen.

115

I   1 G (KLD 69, I)
Den morgenblic bī wahtæres sange erkōs
ein frouwe, dā si tougen
an ir werden friundes arme lac;
dā von si ... fröiden vil verlōs.

15–16 'My reward should take account of my service, since I shall always request
(your favour) and offer (my service) until my death.'
20 *dīn helflīch gebot* 'your kindly command over me'.
24 *kurz und lanc* appear to be technical terms whose exact meaning is obscure.
A similar example occurs in the criticism of Walther in *Der Welsche Gast* 11219:
ich wæn daz allez sīn gesanc, beide kurz unde lanc, sī got niht wol gevallen. It probably means here 'in whatever metrical form you choose'.
29 *wendic*: *ein wendig* C. Cf. *Parzival* 795. 14: *dā mite ist wendec al mīn klage.*
115. 1–3 The opening lines are similar to a dawn song by Walther (L/K 88, 11):
Friuntlīchen lac | ein riter vil gemeit | an einer frowen arme.
4 A stroke in the MS. before *fröiden* indicates that a word is missing. KLD supplies
hōher.

5   des muosen liehtiu ougen
    aver nazzen. si sprach 'owē tac,
    wilde und zam daz frewet sich dīn
    und siht dich gerne, wan ich eine.
    wie sol ez mir ergēn!
10   nu enmac niht langer hie bī mir bestēn
    mīn vriunt: den jaget von mir dīn schīn.'

    II   2 G
    Der tac mit kraft al durch diu venster dranc.
    vil slōze si besluzzen:
    daz half niht, des wart in sorge kunt.
15   diu friundīn den vriunt vast an sich dwanc:
    ir ougen diu beguzzen
    ir beider wangel. sus sprach zim ir munt
    'zwei herze und einen līp hān wir:
    gar ungescheiden unser triuwe
20   mit einander vert.
    der grōzen liebe der bin ich vil gar verhert,
    wan sō du kumest und ich zuo dir.'

    III   3 G
    Der trūric man nam urloup balde alsus:
    ir liehten vel diu slehten
25   kōmen nāher. sus der tac erschein:
    weindiu ougen, süezer frouwen kus;
    sus kunden si dō vlehten
    ir munde, ir brüste, ir arm, ir blankiu bein:
    swelh schiltær entwurfe daz
30   geselleclīche als si lāgen,
    des wære ouch dem genuoc.
    ir beider liebe doch vil sorgen truoc.
    si phlāgen minne ān allen haz.

7 *wilde und zam*, lit. 'wild and tame animals'—a formal phrase for 'all creatures'.
18 *zwei*: the word in the MS. beginning with *z* is illegible.
einen: *ein* G.
25–26 The syntax and punctuation of these lines is difficult. Some editors have
taken *erschein* as a poetic use of an intransitive verb with the same function as a
transitive verb such as *beschein*: 'shone upon'. Thus Brinkman punctuates *sus der tac
erschein | weindiu ougen, süezer frouwen kus*. It is preferable to take the lines as
loosely connected as is not uncommon in Wolfram. The compression of line 26, with
nouns instead of verbs, is also frequent.
31 Lit. 'that would satisfy even him', i.e. could he paint them as they really were:
'he would indeed be equal to his task'.

116

I   4 G (KLD 69, II)

'Sīne klāwen   durh die wolken sint geslagen,
er stīget ūf mit grōzer kraft,
ich sih in grāwen   tägelīch als er wil tagen,
den tac, der im geselleschaft
5   erwenden wil, dem werden man,
den ich mit sorgen īn bi naht verliez.
ich bringe in hinnen, ob ich kan.
sīn vil manigiu tugent mich daz leisten hiez.'

II   5 G

'Wahtær, du singest   daz mir manige fröide nimt
10   unde mēret mīne klage.
mære du bringest,   der mich leider niht gezimt,
immer morgens gegen dem tage.
diu solt du mir verswīgen gar.
daz gebiut ich den triuwen dīn:
15   des lōn ich dir als ich getar.
sō belībet hie der geselle mīn.'

III   6 G

'Er muoz et hinnen   balde und āne sūmen sich:
nu gip im urloup, süezez wīp.
lāze in minnen   her nāch sō verholne dich,
20   daz er behalte ēre und den līp.
er gap sich mīner triuwe alsō,
daz ich in bræhte ouch wider dan.
ez ist nu tac; naht was ez, dō
mit drucken an die brust dīn kus mir in an gewan.'

IV   7 G

25   'Swaz dir gevalle,   wahtær sinc, und lā den hie,
der minne brāhte und minne enphienc.
von dīnem schalle   ist er und ich erschrocken ie:
sō ninder der morgenstern ūf gienc

116. Strophes I–IV are spoken alternately by the watchman and the lady.
3 *tägelīch* 'day-like'.
11 *mære*, neut. pl., *der* gen. pl. agreeing with it: 'you bring tidings which ill
suit me'.
20 Cf. **117.** 7; *līp und ēre* is a formal phrase: 'life and good repute'.
23–24 'when with embrace and kiss you received him from my keeping'.

ūf in, der her nāch minne ist komen,
30 noch ninder lūhte tages lieht,
du hāst in dicke mir benomen
von blanken armen, und ūz herzen nieht.'

V   8 G
Von den blicken,   die der tac tet durh diu glas,
und dō [der] wahtære warnen sanc,
35 si muose erschricken   durch den der dā bī ir was.
ir brüstelīn an brust si dwanc
der riter ellens niht vergaz
(des wold in wenden wahtærs dōn):
urloup nāhe und nāher baz
40 mit kusse und anders gab in minne lōn.

117

I   6 BC (KLD 69, V)
'Von der zinnen
wil ich gēn, in tagewīse   sanc verbern.
die sich minnen
tougenlīche, und obe si prīse   ir minne wern,
5 sō gedenken sēre
an sīne lēre
dem līp und ēre
ergeben sīn.
der mich des bæte,
10 deswār ich tæte
ime guote ræte
und helfe schīn.
ritter, wache, hüete dīn.

---

29 *ūf in*, lit. 'directed at him', 'with intent to warn him'.
30 *lūhte: luhtet* G.
32 *nieht: niht* G.
39–40 'The reward of love sealed their parting, in ever closer embrace, **with kiss**
and more besides'; for *urloup geben* cf. l. 18 and **117**. 39.

117. Text as B with *daz* (23), *meldes* (21), and ll. 16–17 and 26 according **to C.**
2 *in tagewīse*, etc., 'omit to sing a dawn song'.
4 Lit. 'and if they dedicate their love to good repute'.
5 *gedenken: gedenke* BC.

II   7 BC
Niht verkrenken
15   wil ich aller wahtere triuwe   an werden man.
niht gedenken
solt du, vrowe, an scheidens riuwe   ūf kunfte wān.
ez wære unwæge,
swer minne pflæge,
20   daz ūf ime læge
meldes last.
ein sumer bringet
daz mīn munt singet:
durh wolken dringet
25   ein tagender glast.
hüete dīn, wache, süezer gast.'

III   8 BC
Er muose eht dannen
30   der si klagen ungerne hōrte.   dō sprach sīn munt
'allen mannen
trūren nie sō gar zerstōrte   ir vröiden funt.'
swie bald ez tagete,
der unverzagete
35   an ir bejagete
daz sorge in flōch:
unvrömedez rucken,
gar heinlīch smucken,
ir brüstel drucken
und mē dannoch
urlop gap, des prīs was hōch.

14 *verkrenken* 'violate'.
18–21 'It should be unfitting for the burden of betrayal to weigh on him who
devotes himself to love' (refers back to 14–15).
30 *vröiden funt*: cf. *Parzival* 752. 4.
39 *des prīs was hōch* refers back to *mē dannoch*: 'and more besides, whose worth
was great, bade him farewell'.

118

I   1 A, 14 C (KLD 69, VII)

'Ez ist nu tac,   daz ich wol mac   mit wārheit jehen,
ich wil niht langer sīn.
diu vinster naht   hāt uns nu brāht   ze leide mir
den morgenlīchen schīn.
5   sol er von mir scheiden nuo,
mīn friunt, diu sorge ist mir ze vruo:
ich weiz vil wol, daz ist ouch ime,
den ich in mīnen ougen gerne burge,
möht ich in alsō behalten.
10   mīn kumber wil sich breiten.
owē des, wie kumt ers hin ?
der hōhste fride müeze in noch
an mīnen arm geleiten.'

II   2 A, 15 C

Daz guote wīp   ir friundes līp   vaste umbevie:
15   der was entslāfen dō.
dō daz geschach   daz er ersach   den grāwen tac,
dō muost er sīn unfrō.
an sīne brüste druhte er sie,
und sprach 'jō erkande ich nie
20   kein trūric scheiden alsō snel.
uns ist diu naht von hinnen alze balde:
wer hāt si sō kurz gemezzen ?
der tac wil niht erwinden.
hāt minne an sælden teil,
25   diu helfe mir daz ich dich noch
mit fröiden müeze vinden.'

118. Text according to C, except where noted.
1 Some editors take 1–4 as spoken by the watchman, but it is more likely that they form part of the lady's complaint, particularly on account of the words *ze leide mir* (3).
4 *den morgē schin* C.
6 Some editors refer *mīn friunt* to the watchman, taking the whole speech as addressed to him. It is more satisfactory to regard it as an apposition to *er* in l. 5.
10 *breiten: bereiten* AC.
11 'Alas how will he achieve it ?' i.e. his safe escape and return; cf. **86**. 53.
12 *der hōhste fride*, 'God's protection'; cf. KLD II, 695.
18 *er si druhte* AC.
21 *uns: vñ* AC.
23 'The day will not desist.'

III   3 A, 16 C

Si beide luste   daz er kuste   si genuoc:
gevluochet wart dem tage.
urlop er nam,   daz dā wol zam; nu merket wie:
30   dā ergie ein schimpf bī klage.
si hāten beide sich bewegen,
ez enwart sō nāhe nie gelegen,
des noch diu minne hāt den prīs:
ob der sunnen drī mit blicke wæren,
35   sine möhten zwischen si geliuhten.
er sprach 'nu wil ich rīten.
dīn wīplich güete neme mīn war,
und sī mīn schilt hiute hin und her
und zallen zīten.'

IV   4 A, 17 C

40   Ir ougen naz   dō wurden baz,   ouch twanc in klage:
er muoste [dan] von ir.
si sprach hin zime   'urlop ich nime   ze den fröiden mīn:
diu wil nu gar von mir,
sīt [daz] ich vermīden muoz
45   dīnen munt, der manigen gruoz
mir bōt und ouch dīn kus,
alse in dīn ūzerwelte güete lērte,
und diu geselle dīn, diu triuwe.'
si sprach 'weme wilt du mich lāzen?
50   nu kum schiere wider ūf rehten trōst.
owē dur daz enmac ich strenge sorge niht gemāzen.'

32 *nie*: *nien* C.
34 'If there were three suns shining, they could not have shone in the space between them.'
35 *möhten*: *mŏhte* C.
39 *und* with A: *noch* C.
42 *er sprach hin zir* A.
43 *diu wil*: such singulars after abstract nouns in the plural (*fröiden*) are common.
nu missing C.
44 AC have *muoz* before *vermīden*, but it is the rhyme word.
48 *diu geselle dīn*: *din geselle din* AC.
51 *enmac*: *mac* A. *mag* C. *gemāzen*: *gelazen* A, *gelasse* C. This long line (representing two orginal lines) is corrupt. Brinkman places a caesura after *strenge*,
which is unsatisfactory. KLD emends to:

> owē dur daz enmac ich doch
> mich sorge niht gemāzen.

119

I   4 BC (KLD 69, IV

Der helden minne ir klage
du sunge ie gen dem tage,
daz sūre nāch dem süezen,
swer minne und wīplich grüezen
5   alsō enpfienc,
daz si sich muosen scheiden:
swaz du dō riete in beiden,
dō ūf gienc
der morgensterne, wahtære, swīc,
10   dā von niht [langer] sinc.

II   5 BC

Swer pfliget oder ie gepflac
daz er bi lieben wībe lac
den merkern unverborgen,
der darf niht durh den morgen
15   dannen streben,
er mac des tages erbeiten:
man darf in niht ūz leiten
ūf sin leben.
ein offen süeze wirtes wīp
20   kan solhe minne geben.

119. 1 *helden* for *helenden*, pres. part. of *helen* 'conceal': 'secret'.
klage here 'cause for lament'; cf. **116. 10.**
1–6 'You ever sang at daybreak a cause of lament to secret love, the bitter after
the sweet, so that whoever received love and a woman's greeting thus (i.e. in secret),
(those lovers) had to part.'
6 *muosen*: *můzent* C, *můssent* B.
7 Cf. **117. 10–11.**
8 *gienc*: *gie* BC.
9 Cf. **116. 28.**
14, 17 *darf niht* 'has no need'.
18 'at the risk of his life'.
19 *offenů* BC, *sůzů* C.
wirt 'master of the house', 'husband'.

NĪTHART
(NEIDHART VON REUENTAL)

THERE is no documentary evidence of the poet's life. He is referred to in the manuscripts and by Wolfram as *her Nīthart* which perhaps indicates his knightly origin. The final strophes of many of his poems introduce the place-name *Riuwental*, the poet referring to himself as *von Riuwental* or *einen ritter von Riuwental*, hence the customary modern designation. It has proved impossible to localize a place of like name with any certainty, and it has even been suggested that the name is only a poetic fiction since Neidhart frequently plays on its allegorical meaning ('vale of grief'), as in the lines:

> Swie Riuwental mīn eigen sī,
> ich bin disen sumer aller sorgen frī . . . (H/W 5, 32).

The poet's original home is thought to have been in Bavaria, but the evidence for this is slight. The only Bavarian place-name he mentions is *ze Landeshuote* (H/W 14, 1), and a verse of doubtful authenticity, interpolated in **127** by MS. c only, contains the lines:

> des hān ich ze Beiern lāzen allez, daz ich ie gewan (H/W 75, 1).

It is clear from **127** that he was given a home in Austria, no doubt by Duke Frederick II who succeeded his father in 1230. He mentions various places in the neighbourhood of Melk and Vienna, particularly in the region known as the Tullnerfeld.

He probably lived between about 1180 and 1250. He is mentioned by Wolfram in *Willehalm* (after 1210) as still alive, but in the *Meier Helmbreht* (*c.* 1260) as already dead. The Crusading expedition to which he refers was no doubt that of 1217.

The poems are of two types: the summer songs such as **120–5** and winter songs such as **126–8**. All begin with a nature introduction of one to three strophes. Neidhart still makes considerable use of the conventions of the *Minnesang*, but he introduces the new theme of peasant festivities, and there is often a deliberate pointed contrast between the courtly phraseology and the village setting. The earlier *Minnesang*, although depicting a personal relationship, is essentially idealized and generalized. Neidhart introduces a semblance of greater realism by the inclusion of particular details: place and proper names, descriptions of clothing, images drawn from everyday life, colloquial words and phrases. The latter often serve a particular purpose as part of the incongruous contrast between courtly and non-courtly elements—thus in **122** the contrast between *zieren* and *zāfen* is a means of characterizing the speakers.

The summer songs are particularly distinguished by the use of dialogue, whereas a usual feature of the winter songs is a description in the past tense of a peasant brawl at the dance. It is particularly in the winter songs that the poet mocks at upstart peasants, though the same element occurs also in **124**. The juxtaposition of contrasting spheres is a means of satirizing both the conventions of courtly love and the peasant world. In three of the poems Neidhart turns at the end to his own affairs with the intention, whether explicit or disguised, of pleading for support.

The metrical forms of the winter songs are tripartite, but the summer songs are predominantly bipartite. There is no great display of technical virtuosity, as for instance in Wolfram, but the metrical patterns are highly accomplished in their deliberate plainness.

120

I   11, 1 R; 75, 1 c (H/W 10, 22)

'Diu zīt ist hie:
ichn gesach vor mangem jāre ein schœner nie.
ende hāt der winter kalt;
des vreut sich manc herze, daz sīn sēre enkalt.
5   aber geloubet stāt der walt.

II   11, 2 R; 75, 2 c

Des meien zil
bringet vogele sanc und schœner bluomen vil.
wartet wie diu heide stāt
schōne in liehter varwe und wünneclīcher wāt.
10   leides si vergezzen hāt.

III   11, 3 R; 75, 3 c

Wol dan mit mir
zuo der linden, trūtgespil! dā vinde wir
alles, des dīn herze gert.
jā weist du vil wol, war ich dich sande vert.
15   disiu reise ist goldes wert.'

120. 2 *vor mangem jāre* 'for many a year'.
    9 *varwe*: *waete* R *farbe* c.

IV   11, 4 R; 75, 4 c
'Nu balde hin
nach der wæte, sît ichs in dem willen bin,
daz ich leiste mîne vart.
nune sage ez niemen, liebiu Irmegart:
20   wol mich sîner künfte wart.'

V   11, 5 R; 75, 5 c
Sâ dô zehant
brâhte man der mägde ir sûberlîch gewant.
schiere het siz an geleit.
'zuo der grüenen linden mich mîn wille treit:
25   ende habent mîniu leit.'

121

I   12, 1 R; 26 C; M fol. 68[r]; 26, 1 c (H/W 11, 8)
Ez gruonet wol diu heide,
mit grüenem loube stât der walt:
der winder kalt
twanc si sêre beide.
5   diu zît hât sich verwandelôt.
mîn sendiu nôt
mant mich an die guoten, von der ich unsanfte scheide.

II   12, 2 R; 27 C; 26, 2 c
Gegen der wandelunge
wol singent elliu vogelîn
10   den vriunden mîn,
den ich gerne sunge,
des si mir alle sagten danc.
ûf mînen sanc
ahtent hie die Walhen niht: sô wol dir, diutschiu zunge!

16 *nu da hin* R, *nün pald dahin* c.
19 *nune sage: nu sag* Rc.
20 'his coming is fortunate for me'. The acc. *mich* is retained after *werden* by
analogy with the common interjection *wol mich*.
21 *sa zehant* R, *so so zu handt* c.
121. 5 *verwandelôt*: this archaic form, with full final vowel, survives in rhyme; cf.
Heinrich von Rugge: *diu zît hat sich verwandelôt* (rhyming with *rôt*), MF 107, 13.
14 *sô wol dir, diutschiu zunge* is perhaps an ironic reminiscence of Walther **91.** 41,
but Neidhart uses *zunge* in a more usual sense.

III   12, 3 R; 28 C; 26, 3 c

15 Wie gerne ich nu sande
der lieben einen boten dar,
(nu nemt des war)
der daz dorf erkande,
dā ich die seneden inne lie:
20 jā meine ich die,
von der ich den muot mit stæter liebe nie gewande.

IV   12, 4 R; 31 C; 26, 4 c

Bote, nu var bereite
ze lieben vriunden über sē!
mir tuot vil wē
25 sendiu arebeite.
du solt in allen von uns sagen,
in kurzen tagen
sæhens uns mit vröuden dort, wan durch des wāges breite.

V   12, 5 R; 32 C; 26, 5 c

Sage der meisterinne
30 den willeclīchen dienest mīn!
si sol diu sīn,
die ich von herzen minne
vür alle vrouwen hinne vür.
ē ich si verkür
35 ē wold ich verkiesen der ich nimmer teil gewinne.

VI   12, 6 R; 33 C; 26, 6 c

Vriunden unde māgen
sage daz ich mich wol gehabe!
vil lieber knabe,
ob si dich des vrāgen
40 wiez umbe uns pilgerīne stē,
sō sage wie wē
uns die Walhen haben getān: des muoz uns hie betrāgen.

27–28 'within a short time they would see us there rejoicing, were it not for the breadth of the ocean.'
     29 *meisterinne*: this word is not found as a designation of the lady before Neidhart.
     34–35 'Rather than give her up I would give up those (i.e. *alle vrouwen*) to whom I shall never win a claim.'

VII   12, 8 R; 26, 8 c

Wirp ez endelīchen,
mit triuwen lā dir wesen gāch!
45   ich kum dar nāch
schiere sicherlīchen,
sō ich aller baldist immer mac.
den lieben tac
lāze uns got geleben, daz wir hin heim ze lande strīchen!

VIII   12, 7 R; 29 C; 26, 9 c

50   Ob sich der bote nu sūme,
sō wil ich selbe bote sīn
ze den vriunden mīn:
wir leben alle kūme,
daz her ist mēr dan halbez mort.
55   hey, wære ich dort!
bī der wolgetānen læge ich gerne an mīnem rūme.

IX   12, 9 R; 30 C; 26, 10 c

Solt ich mit ir nu alten,
ich het noch eteslīchen dōn
ūf minne lōn
60   her mit mir behalten,
des tūsent herze wurden geil.
gewinne ich heil
gegen der wolgetānen, mīn gewerft sol heiles walten.

X   12, 10 R; 26, 7 c

Si reien oder tanzen,
65   si tuon vil manegen wīten schrit,
ich allez mit.
ē wir heime geswanzen,
ich sage iz bī den triuwen mīn,
wir solden sīn
70   ze Oesterrīche: vor dem snite sō setzet man die phlanzen.

59 *minne*: *minnē* R, *minen* C, *meinem* c.
62–63 'If I experience good fortune at the fair one's hands, then my art too will be fortunate.'
64 This refers to different types of dancing, *reie* being a round dance.
70 The sense of the proverbial phrase ('plants must be put in before the harvest') is: 'one thing at a time'.

XI   12, 11 R; 26, 11 c

Er dünket mich ein narre,
swer disen ougest hie bestāt.
ez wær mīn rāt,
lieze er sīn geharre
75 und vüer hin wider über sē:
daz tuot niht wē;
nindert wære ein man baz dan dā heime in sīner pharre.

122

I   15, 1 R; 146 C; 21, 1 c; 16, 1 f (H/W 15, 21)

Ine gesach die heide
nie baz gestalt,
in liehter ougenweide
den grüenen walt:
5 bī den beiden kiese wir den meien.
ir mägde, ir sult iuch zweien,
gein dirre liehten sumerzīt   in hōhem muote reien.

II   15, 2 R; 147 C; 21, 2 c; 16, 2 f

Lop von mangen zungen
der meie hāt.
10 die bluomen sint entsprungen
an manger stat,
dā man ē deheine kunde vinden,
geloubet stāt diu linde:
dā hebt sich, als ich hān vernomen,   ein tanz von höfschen
kinden.

III   15, 3 R; 148 C; 21, 3 c; 16, 3 f

15 Die sint sorgen āne
und vröuden rīch.
ir mägede wolgetāne
und minneclīch,
zieret iuch wol, daz iu die Beier danken,
20 die Swābe und die Vranken!
ir brīset iuwer hemde wīz   mit sīden wol zen lanken!

73 *rāt: tot* R, *rate* c.
74 *sīn: sich* R, *sein* c. Wiessner takes *sich* as a spelling variant of *siech* and reads
siech geharre.
122. 14 This is the reading of c. *sich hebt als ir wol habt vernomen* R.

IV   15, 4 R; 149 C; 21, 4 c; 16, 4 f
'Gein wem solt ich mich zāfen?'
sō redete ein maget.
'die tumben sint entslāfen;
25   ich bin verzaget.
vreude und ēre ist al der werlde unmære.
die man sint wandelbære:
deheiner wirbet umbe ein wīp,   der er getiuwert wære.'

V   15, 5 R; 150 C; 21, 5 c; 16, 5 f
'Die rede soltu behalten',
30   sprach ir gespil.
'mit vröuden sul wir alten:
der manne ist vil,
die noch gerne dienent guoten wīben.
lāt solhe rede belīben!
35   ez wirbet einer umbe mich,   der trūren kan vertrīben.'

VI   15, 6 R; 21, 6 c; 16, 6
'Den soltu mir zeigen,
wie er mir behage.
der gürtel sī dīn eigen,
den umbe ich trage!
40   sage mir sīnen namen, der dich minne
sō tougenlīcher sinne!
mir ist getroumet hīnt von dir,   dīn muot der stē von hinne.'

VII   15, 7 R; 21, 7 c; 16, 7 f
'Den si alle nennent
von Riuwental
45   und sīnen sanc erkennent
wol über al,
der ist mir holt, mit guote ich im des lōne:
durch sīnen willen schöne
sō wil ich brīsen mīnen līp.   wol dan, man liutet nōne!

24 *die tumben* refers to *man* of 27.
28 *getiuwert*: this verb frequently denotes the elevating influence of love in the
courtly lyric, e.g. Walther: *si lāze in iemer ungewert | ez tiuret doch wol sīnen līp*
(L/K 93, 9–10).
42 'I dreamt last night that you have a mind to be gone from here.'
49 *nōne*: the ninth hour, reckoned from 6 a.m.

123

I   51, 1 R; 110 C; 22, 1 c (H/W 24, 13)

'Nu ist der küele winder gar zergangen,
diu naht ist kurz, der tac beginnet langen,
sich hebet ein wünneclichiu zīt,
diu al der werlde vreude gīt;
5   baz gesungen die vogele ē noch sīt.

II   51, 2 R; 109 C; 22, 2 c

Komen ist uns ein liehtiu ougenweide:
man siht der rōsen wunder ūf der heide,
die bluomen dringent durch daz gras.
wie schōne ein wise getouwet was,
10   dā mir mīn geselle zeinem kranze las.

III   51, 3 R; 111 C; 22, 4 c

Der walt hāt sīner grīse gar vergezzen,
der meie ist ūf ein grüenez zwī gesezzen:
er hāt gewunnen loubes vil.
bint dir balde, trūtgespil!
15   du weist wol, daz ich mit einem ritter wil.'

IV   51, 4 R; 112 C; 22, 5 c

Daz gehōrte der mägde muoter tougen;
si sprach: 'behalte hinne vür dīn lougen!
dīn wankelmuot ist offenbār.
wint ein hüetel umb dīn hār!
20   du muost āne dīne wāt, wilt an die schar.'

V   51, 5 R; 113 C; 22, 6 c

'Muoter mīn, wer gap iu daz ze lēhen,
daz ich iuch mīner wæte solde vlēhen,

---

123. 5 *ē noch sīt*: cf. Walther **91**. 56.
   10 For the offer of a garland, cf. Walther **103**.
   14 *bint dir balde: pindt den har auff* c. The reference is to the *gebende* which designates either (1) female headdress in general, particularly as worn for the dance, as here; (2) the headdress of married women. The second meaning permits the mother's taunt in 19, which is an aspersion on the girl's virginity.
   17 'keep your denials to yourself in future'.
   21 *iu* according to C: *dir* R. The girl addresses her mother as *ir*, except in the imperious command of 25. 'Who authorized you to compel me to ask you for my clothes ?'

dern gespunnet ir nie vadem?
lāzet ruowen solhen kradem!
25   wā nu slüzzel? sliuz ūf balde mir daz gadem!'

VI   51, 6 R; 115 C; 22, 7 c
Diu wāt diu was in einem schrīne versperret:
daz wart bī einem staffel ūf gezerret.
diu alte ir leider nie gesach:
dō daz kint ir kisten brach,
30   dō gesweic ir zunge, daz si niht ensprach.

VII   51, 7 R; 116 C; 22, 8 c
Dar ūz nam si daz röckel alsō balde,
daz was gelegen in maneger kleinen valde.
ir gürtel was ein rieme smal.
in des hant von Riuwental
35   warf diu stolze magt ir gickelvēhen bal.

124

I   58, 1 R; 70, 2 c (H/W 28, 36)
Vreude und wünne hebt sich aber wīten.
ir gevrieschet sīt künc Karels zīten
nie vogele schal,
die baz sungen über al:
5   gar verborgen
sint aber alle ir sorgen.

II   58, 2 R; 70, 5 c
'Vrō sint [nu] diu vogelīn geschreiet,
nū belībe ich aber ungereiet',
sprach Wendelmuot;
10   'golzen, rīsen unde huot
hāt mīn eide
verspart mir vor ze leide.'

28 *leider* is the comparative of the adverb *leide*: 'The mother never saw anything which distressed her more.'
34–35 Throwing the ball is a mark of favour; cf. **124**.
124. 2 'Since the time of Charlemagne'.
5 *verborgen*: here 'vanished'.
7 *geschreiet*, from the causative verb *schreien*, lit. 'to cause to shout'.

III 58, 3 R; 70, 6 c

'Nu sage mir, waz sint die dīnen schulde?'
'ich enweiz, Rīchilt, sam mir gotes hulde,
15 wes ich enkalt,
wan daz ich ein vrīheistalt
hān versprochen:
daz ist an mir gerochen.

IV 58, 4 R; 70, 7 c

Der kom dā her: dō bat er mīn ze wībe.
20 dō zugen si mir daz röckel ab dem lībe.
jā muoz er mīn
weizgot gar versūmet sīn,
er gebūwer!
jā nams mich gar untūwer.

V 58, 5 R; 70, 8 c

25 Swanne er wānte, daz ich dā heime læge
unde ime sines dingelīnes phlæge,
würf ich den bal
in des hant von Riuwental
an der strāze:
30 der kumt mir wol ze māze.'

125

I 54, 1 R; 59, 1 c (H/W 29, 27)

Nu ist vil gar zergangen
der winder kalt,
mit loube wol bevangen
der grüene walt.

14 *sam mir gotes hulde*: a conventional abbreviated imprecation, cf. **96. 31**.

16 *vrīheistalt*: *vreiheit stalt* R, *hailstat* c. This word, corrupt in the MSS., is probably from *vrī-hagestalt*, the second element meaning 'bachelor'. The whole word probably means 'unmarried free peasant'.

22 *versūmen* here means 'to do without'.

24 'I didn't care about it at all.'

25–29 The verbs are subjunctives of unreal condition; therefore in 27 *würf* (*wurff* c) seems preferable to *warf* in R: 'When he thought that I would be shut up at home looking after his household affairs, I should be throwing the ball . . .'.

30 'He suits me well.'

5   wünneclīch
        in süezer stimme lobelīch
        vrō singent aber die vogele, lobent den meien:
        sam tuo wir den reien!

II   54, 2 R; 59, 3 c; der junge Spervogel 34 A; her Alram
                                                von Gresten 5 C

        Al der werlde hōhe
10   ir gemüete stāt.
        bluomen in dem lōhe
        mīn ouge hāt
        an gesehen.
        ich mac leider niht gejehen,
15   daz mir mīn tougen senediu sorge swinde:
        diu ist mīn ingesinde.

III   54, 3 R; 59, 4 c; der junge Spervogel 35 A; her Alram von
                                                Gresten 6 C

        Zwō gespilen mære
        begunden sagen,
        herzensenede swære
20   besunder klagen.
        einiu sprach:
        'trūren, leit und ungemach
        hāt mir verderbet līp und al die sinne:
        dā ist niht vreuden inne.'

IV   54, 4 R; 59, 5 c; der junge Spervogel 37 A; her Alram
                                                von Gresten 8 C

25   'Leit und ungemüete
        ist mir bekant:
        liebes vriundes güete
        mich beider mant.
        mir ist ein man
30   vremde, der hāt mir getān,
        dā von mir lange senediu sorge mēret
        unt mīn herze sēret.

125. 15 *daz mir min ovge senediv sorge swinde* R, *daz mir min sorgen (sorge* C) *iht da von verswinde* AC. Wiessner plausibly suggests that *ovge* is a scribal error for *tougen.*
    16 *ingesinde* is a feudal term meaning 'retinue', 'servant'; cf. **50.** 17.
    17 *mære* is the object of *sagen.*

V   54, 5 R; 59, 6 c; der junge Spervogel 36 A; her Alram
von Gresten 7 C

Sage bī dīnen triuwen,
waz wirret dir ?
35 lebst in senenden riuwen,
sō volge mir:
habe gedult!
sīz von liebes mannes schult,
daz hil mit allen dīnen sinnen tougen!
40 gerne ich vür dich lougen.'

VI   54, 6 R; 59, 7 c
'Du hœrst eteswenne
ze einem māl
einen ritter nennen
von Riuwental.
45 der sīne sanc
mīn gemüete sēre twanc.
nu phlege sīn, der des himmels immer walte.
daz er mirn behalte!'

VII   54, 7 R; 59, 8 c
Unt hān ich indert heime,
50 wā sol daz sīn ?
ein swalwe klent von leime
ein hiuselīn,
dā si inne ist
sumers ein vil kurze vrist.
55 got vüege mir ein hūs mit obedache
bī dem Lengebache!

126

I   27, 1 R; 139 C; 106, 1 c (H/W 38, 9)

Kint, bereitet iuch der sliten ūf daz īs!
uns kumt der leide winter kalt.
der hāt uns der wünneclīchen bluomen vil benomen.
manger grüenen linden stēnt ir tolden grīs;

38 *sīz = sī ez* 'if it be'.
45 *od' sinen sanch* R, *sein gesanck* c.
56 Probably the village Altlengbach, in the valley of the Lengbach, SW. of Vienna.
126. 4 *stēnt: stet* R, *ist* C, *sind* c.
grīs cf. **123.** 11.

5   unbesungen ist der walt:
daz ist allez von des rīfen ungenāden komen.
mugt ir schouwen, wie er hāt die heide erzogen?
diu ist von sīnen schulden val.
dar zuo sint die nahtigal
10   alle ir wec gevlogen.

II   27, 2 R; 141 C; 106, 2 c

Wol bedörfte ich mīner wīsen vriunde rāt
umbe ein dinc, als ich iu sage,
daz si rieten, wā diu kint ir vreuden solten phlegen.
Megenwart der wīten stuben eine hāt:
15   ob ez iu allen wol behage,
dar sul wir den gofenanz des vīretages legen.
ez ist sīner tohter wille, kom wir dar.
ir sultz alle ein ander sagen.
einen tanz alumbe den schragen
20   den brüevet Engelmār.

III   27, 3 R; 142 C; 106, 3 c

Wer nāch Künegunde gē, des wert enein!
der was ie nāch tanze wē;
ez wirt uns verwizzen, ist daz man ir niht enseit.
Gīsel, ginc nāch Jiuten hin und sage in zwein,
25   sprich, daz Elle mit in gē.
ez ist zwischen mir und in ein starkiu sicherheit.
kint, vergiz durch niemen Hädewīgen dā,
bit si balde mit in gān.
einen site si sulen lān:
30   daz binden ūf die brā.

IV   27, 4 R (and repeated at bottom of page); 143 C; 106, 4 c

Got gebiete den jungen wīben über al,
die der māze wellen sīn,
daz si hōchgemuoten mannen holdez herze tragen,
ruckenz vorne hōher, hinden hin ze tal,

---

7 *erzogen*: here 'maltreated'.
21 'Agree who is to fetch Künegunde'.
26 'We have given each other a firm promise'.
30 ff. The poet criticizes the prevailing fashion for headdresses which cover the brow; they should be worn further back to cover the neck instead: of what use is a helmet without a neck-piece to protect the neck?

35   decken baz daz näckelīn!
        war zuo sol ein tehtier āne ein collier umbe den kragen?
        wīp sint sicher umbe daz houbet her gewesen,
        daz et in daz niemen brach.
        swaz in anderswā geschach,
40   des sint si ouch genesen.

V   27, 5 R; 145 C; 106, 6 c

    Eppe der zuht Geppen Gumpen ab der hant;
        des half im sīn drischelstap:
        doch geschiet ez mit der riutel meister Adelber.
        daz was allez umbe ein ei, daz Ruopreht vant
45   (jā, wæn, imz der tievel gap):
        dā mit drōte er im ze werfen allez jenenther.
        Eppe der was beidiu zornic unde kal;
        übellīchen sprach er: 'tratz!'
        Ruopreht warf imz an den glatz,
50   daz ez ran ze tal.

VI   27, 6 R; 140 C; 106, 7 c

    Hie envor dō stuont sō schōne mir mīn hār,
        umbe und umbe gie der spān.
        des vergaz ich, sīt man mich ein hūs besorgen hiez:
        salz und korn muoz ich koufen durch daz jār.
55   wē, waz het ich im getān,
        der mich tumben ie von ērste in disen kumber stiez?
        mīne schulde waren kleine wider in.
        mīne vlüeche sint niht smal,
        swanne ich dā ze Riuwental
60   unberāten bin.

127

I   2, 1 R; 1, 13 C^b; 80, 1 c; 16, 1 d; 1 s³; 51 A (Niune) (H/W 73, 24)

    Sumer, dīner süezen weter müezen wir uns ānen:
        dirre kalte winder trūren unde senen gīt.
        ich bin ungetrœstet von der lieben wolgetānen.
        wie sol ich vertrīben dise langen swæren zīt,

---

41 'Eppe snatched Geppe (girl) away from Gumpe'.
43 *geschiet* from *gescheiden* 'settle a dispute'.
52 'I had curls all round.'

5 diu die heide velwet unde mange bluomen wolgetān?
  alsō sint die vogele in dem walde des betwungen, daz si ir singen
  müezen lān.

II   2, 2 R; 1, 14 Cᵇ; 80, 2 c; 16, 2 d; 2 s³; 52 A (Niune)

Alsō hāt diu vrouwe mīn daz herze mir betwungen,
daz ich āne vröude muoz verswenden mīne tage.
ez vervæhet niht, swaz ich ir lange hān gesungen;
10 mir ist alsō mære, daz ich mēre stille dage.
ich geloube niht, daz si den mannen immer werde holt:
wir verliesen, swaz wir dar gesingen unde gerūnen, ich und jener
  Hildebolt.

III   2, 3 R; 80, 3 c; 16, 3 d; 3 s³; 53 A (Niune)

Der ist nū der tumbist under geilen getelingen,
er und einer, nennet man den jungen Willegēr:
15 den enkunde ich disen sumer nie von ir gedringen,
sō der tanz gein abent an der strāze gie entwer.
mangen twerhen blic den wurfen si mich mit den ougen an,
daz ich sunder mīnes guoten willen vor in beiden ie ze sweime
  muose gān.

IV   2, 4 R; 80, 4 c; 16, 4 d; 4 s³; 54 A (Niune)

Wē, daz mich sō manger hāt von lieber stat gedrungen
20 beidiu von der guoten unde ouch wīlent anderswā!
œdelīchen wart von in ūf mīnen tratz gesprungen.
ir gewaltes bin ich vor in mīnem schophe grā.
iedoch sō neic diu guote mir ein lützel über schildes rant.
gerne mugt ir hœren, wie die dörper sint gekleidet: üppiclīch ist
  ir gewant.

127. 10 'I may as well continue to be silent in future.'
    12 Wiessner points out that *gesingen* refers to the poet, *gerūnen* to Hildebolt.
    14 All the MSS. have *hildeger*, but at line 30 all except R have *willeger* or variants
of the same name.
    18 *ze sweime gān* means literally 'wander', 'roam': 'that against my will I had to
make myself scarce on account of them both'.
    21 *ūf mīnen tratz* 'to spite me'; *gesprungen* 'danced'.
    22 *vor* 'in front'. Reinmar says of his lady: *ir gewaltes wirde ich grā* (MF 172, 15),
but here *ir* must refer to the peasant rivals.
    23 *über schildes rant* 'cursorily', 'by the way'.

V   2, 5 R; 80, 5 c; 16, 5 d; 5 s³; 55 A (Niune)

25 Enge röcke tragent si und schmale schaperūne,
rōte hüete, rinkelohte schuohe, swarze hosen.
Engelmār getet mir nie sō leide an Vriderūne,
sam die zwēne tuont. ich nīde ir phellerīne phosen,
die si tragent: dā līt inne ein wurze, heizet ingewer.
30 der gap Hildebolt der guoten eine bī dem tanze; die gezuhte ir
     Willegēr.

VI   2, 6 R; 80, 7 c; 16, 6 d; 6 s³; 56 A (Niune)

Sagte ich nū diu mære, wie siz mit ein ander schuofen,
des enweiz ich niht: ich schiet von danne sā zehant.
manneglīch begunde sīnen vriunden vaste ruofen;
einer der schrē lūte: 'hilf gevater Weregant!'
35 er was līhte in grōzen nœten, dō er sō nach helfe schrē.
Hildeboldes swester hōrte ich eines lūte schrīen: 'wē mir mīnes
     bruoder, wē!'

VII   2, 7 R; 80, 12 c; 9 s³; 57 A (Niune)

Wā von sol man mīn geplätze hinne vür erkennen?
hie envor dō kande man iz wol bī Riuwental.
40 dā von solde man mich noch von allem rehte nennen:
eigen unde lēhen sint mir dā gemezzen smal.
kint, ir heizet iu den singen, der sīn nū gewaltic sī!
ich bin sīn verstōzen āne schulde: mīne vriunde, lāzet mich des
     namen vrī.

VIII   2, 8 R; 80, 14 c; 10 s³

Mīner vīnde wille ist niht ze wol an mir ergangen:
45 wolde ez got, sīn mähte noch vil līhte werden rāt.
in dem lande ze Oesterrīche wart ich wol enphangen
von dem edeln vürsten, der mich nū behüset hāt.

27 Engelmar's theft of a mirror from Vriderūn is referred to in several poems, e.g.
128.
38 *geplätze* 'idle chatter', a contemptuous expression for his songs.
39 refers to his custom of mentioning his name in a final verse.
44 'My enemies' intentions against me have not succeeded too well.'
45 *sīn* must refer in a general way to his distress, without a particular antecedent:
'God willing, there may yet be a remedy for my ills.'

hie ze Medelicke bin ich immer āne ir aller danc.
mir ist leit, daz ich von Eppen und von Gumpen ie ze Riuwental
 sō vil gesanc.

128

I   6, 1 R; 2, 4 C^b; 1, O²; 92, 1 c (H/W 79, 36)

Mir ist von herzen leide,
daz der küele winder
verderbet schœner bluomen vil:
sō verderbet mich ein senelīchiu arebeit.
5 dise sorge beide
dringent mich hin hinder
ze ende an mīner vreuden zil.
owē, daz diu guote mit ir willen daz vertreit,
sīt si wol geringen mac
10 alle mīne swære!
owē, gelebte ich noch den tac,
daz si genædic wære!

II   6, 2 R; 3 A; 92, 2 c

Swenne ich mich vereine
unde an si gedenke,
15 wær inder wībes güete dā,
diune hæte sich sō lange bī ir niht verholn.
sīt si lōnet kleine
mīner niuwen klenke,
wan mag ich dienen anderswā?
20 nein, ich wil mit willen disen kumber langer doln.
waz ob noch ein sælic wīp
gar den muot verkēret?
vreu mīn herze und trœste den līp!
diu zwei diu sint gesēret.

---

48 *Medelicke*: Melk.
49 *mir ist leit* is the reading of R and s³, whereas MS. c has *mir ist nicht laid*; cf.
126. 41.
128. 5–7 'These two sorrows finally repulse me from my goal of joy.'
 18 *klenke*: like *geplätze* in **127**, a derogatory word for his songs.
 23 The reading of A which is metrically more satisfactory than that of R, adopted
by H/W (*vñ vreut min hertz vñ ovch den lip*), since there is not usually anacrusis in
other lines.

III   6, 3 R; 2, 6 C^b; 92, 3 c

25 Zuo dem ungemache,
    den ich von ir līde,
    sō twinget mich ein ander leit,
    daz vor allem leide mich sō sēre nie betwanc,
    swie ich dar umbe lache
30 und gebāre blīde:
    mir hāt ein dörper widerseit
    umbe anders niht wan umbe den mīnen üppeclīchen sanc.
    der ist geheizen Adeltir,
    bürtic her von Ense.
35 zallen zīten drōt er mir
    als einer veizten gense.

IV   6, 4 R; 2, 7 C^b; 2, O²; 92, 4 c
    Hiwer an einem tanze
    gie er umbe und umbe.
    den wehsel het er al den tac:
40 glanziu schapel gap er umb ir niuwen krenzelīn.
    Etzel unde Lanze,
    zwēne knappen tumbe,
    die phlāgen ouch des jener phlac.
    Lanze der beswæret ein vil stolzez magedīn;
45 eine kleine rīsen guot
    zarte er ab ir houbet,
    dar zuo einen bluomenhuot:
    wer het im daz erloubet?

V   6, 5 R; 2, 9 C^b; 3, O²; 92, 5 c
    Owē einer hende!
50 daz si sīn verwāzen!
    die vinger müezen werden vlorn,
    dā mit er gezerret hāt den schedelīchen zar!
    hiete er ir gebende
    ungezerret lāzen,
55 daz kränzel hiete ouch si verkorn.
    er ist ungevüeger, danne wīlen Engelmār,

27–30 For a similar motif, cf. Reinmar **89.** 3–4.
34 *Ens* = Enns.
39 *wehsel* refers to the exchange of garlands in the next line.
53–55 'Had he not disarranged her headdress, she too (like the others) would have
sacrificed the garland.'

der gewalticlīchen nam
den spiegel Vriderūne.
des bin ich dem dörper gram,
60   dem selben Walberūne.

VI   6, 6 R; 2, 5 C^b; 92, 6 c

Dise alten schulde
wecket mir diu niuwe:
ez hāt jener getelinc
hiuwer an mir erwecket, swaz mir leides ie geschach.
65   ē ichz langer dulde,
sēt des mīne triuwe,
gespringe ich zuo zim in den rinc,
er bestāt sīn buoze, daz er ir ze vrouwen jach,
der ich lange gedienet hān
70   her mit ganzer stæte!
wolde er si geruowet lān,
wie rehte er danne tæte!

VII   6, 7 R; 2, 8 C^b; 92, 7 c

Wē, waz hāt er muochen!
si kumt im niht ze māze.
75   zwiu sol sīn pīneclīch gebrech?
im enmac gehelfen niht sīn hovelīch gewant.
er sol im eine suochen,
diu in werben lāze.
diu sīnen rōten buosemblech
80   diu sint ir ungenæme gar, dar zuo sīn hiufelbant.

60 *Walberūn*: the etymology of this word is obscure, but it is clear from the context that it is a derogatory designation for peasant.

61–64 'This new offence (Lanze's rough theft of the garland) reawakens the old one (Engelmar's). That boor (Lanze) has aroused in me this year the memory of all the wrongs I have ever suffered' (i.e. at the hands of upstart peasants).

63 *jener*: *ein* R, *ein geiler* C^b, *derselb* c.

67 *rinc*: the circle of dancers.

73 *muochen*: this word has not been satisfactorily explained, but it clearly means something like 'fantastic notions'.

74 Cf. **124.** 30.

75 *gebrech*: Wiessner points out that this word, elsewhere unattested, probably has the same meaning as *zar* in l. 52, i.e. 'tearing off' (of the garland).

enge ermel treit er lanc,
die sint vor gebræmet,
innen swarz und ūzen blanc.
mit sīner rede er vlæmet.

84 'He speaks after the Flemish fashion.' The knighthood of Flanders was held in high repute, and words were borrowed in Low German form; e.g. *dörper, blīde, ors, wāpen.* For an example of a peasant aping Flemish speech, cf. *Meier Helmbreht* 717 and 763–8.

REINMAR VON ZWETER

THE poet's name is given as Reinmar (or Reimar) von Zweter in MS. C. He was probably born *c.* 1200 and died *c.* 1260. His first datable poem refers to the excommunication of the Emperor Frederick II in 1227, the last to events of 1246–8. It has not proved possible to identify his birth-place although he provides certain biographical details:

Von Rīne sō bin ich geborn,
in Ōsterrīche erwahsen,   Bēheim hān ich mir erkorn
mēre durch den hērren   dan durch daz lant: doch beide sint si guot.

(Roethe 150)

The *hērre* referred to is Wenceslas I (1230–53). Reinmar's poetry is didactic, whether religious, moral, political, or concerned with the theme of *minne*. The poems are for the most part monostrophic, and apart from a *Leich*, all those whose authenticity is certain are in the so-called *Frauen-Ehren-Ton*.

129

31 D; 128 C; 1, 1 n; 47, 1 s² (Roethe 31)

Alle schuole sint gar ein wint
wan diu schuole al eine,   dā der Minne junger sint:
diu ist sō künsterīche,   daz man ir muoz der meisterschefte
                             jehen.
ir besem zamt sō wilden man,
5 daz er nie gehōrte   noch gesach, daz er daz kan:
wā hāt ieman mēre   sō hōher schuole gehœret oder gesehen?
diu Minne lērt die vrouwen schōne grüezen,
die Minne lēret manegen spruch vil süezen,
diu Minne lēret grōze milte,
10 diu Minne lēret grōze tugent,
diu Minne lēret, daz diu jugent
kan ritterlīch   gebāren under schilte.

129. 3 *künsterīche* 'knowledgeable', 'skilled'.
   5 'in such a way that he never before heard or saw that he was capable of it.'

130

41 D; 18 C; 48, 2 s² (Roethe 41)

Waz kleider vrouwen wol an stê,
daz wil ich iuch bescheiden: ein hemede wîz alsam ein snê,
daz ist daz si got minne   unt habe in liep, dêst wol ein rîchez
kleit.
dar obe sol sîn ein roc gesniten,
5 sô daz si liep unt leit   sol tragen mit vil kiuschen siten;
ir gürtel sî diu minne,   ir vürspan daz si tugende sî bereit;
diu êre ir mantel, daz der an ir decke,
ob iht des sî, daz wandel an ir blecke;
ir rîse daz sol sîn diu triuwe,
10 dar ob ein schapel von der art,
daz si vor valsche sî bewart:
si sælic wîp,   der lop ist iemer niuwe!

131

171 D, 69 C (Roethe 170)

Diu werlt gelîchet sich dem mer,
daz iemer tobet und ündet   über mâze und âne wer:
alsô tobet und ündet   der werlte leben mit gelîcher geselleschaft.
der ungetouften sî geswigen!
5 ich klage, daz die getouften   in den kumber sint gedigen,
des si wol mugen verderben,   ez enwende diu starke gotes
kraft.
belîbent si die lenge in dirre vreise,
sô werden wir kielbrüstic ûf der reise:
wir sweben in der sünden ünden:
10 prîmâten mit ir krumben steben
die vischent niht wan nâch den geben
und lânt dâ bî   die sêle in grôzen sünden.

---

130. 6 *tugende* gen. pl. (Wackernagel's emendation) is preferable to *tugenden* DC.
  8 *wandel*: *wandels* DC.
  9 *diu*: *ir* DC.
131. 2 *âne wer* 'unimpeded'.
  3 *mit gelîcher geselleschaft* 'in the same fashion'.
  6 *ez enwende* . . , 'unless the strong might of God prevents it'.

UOLRICH VON SINGENBERG, DER TRUHSÆZE VON SANT GALLEN

(ULRICH VON SINGENBERG)

THE poet belongs to a *ministerialis* family of the canton of Thurgau. He, his father, and his son are all attested as *dapifer* (*truhsæze*) *sancti Galli*, holding a fief from the Abbey. The poet appears in charters between 1209 and 1228. He is particularly influenced by Reinmar and Walther.

132

I   1 A, 20 C (Bartsch II, 4)

Daz frō mīn muot von herzen sī,
des müeze diu vil werde sæliclīche leben,
diu mich von maniger sorge vrī
gemachet hat und ouch vil līhten trōst gegeben,
5 daz lieber trōst nie manne von sō reinem wībe kam,
dō si mir alle unfröide mit sō stæter fröide nam.
ich sage iu, wære ez als ich hān gesaget,
sō möhte nū mīn endelōsiu clage wol sīn verdaget.

II   2 A, 21 C

Der werden wirde wirdet mich,
10 ūf die si sich mit allen guoten dingen wiget.
waz lobe ich ? si lobet selbe sich
dā mit daz si sō stæteclīche ir güete phliget.
ir sælde sældet līp und ēre swem si wil;
diu selbe [sælde] vreut ein teil mich mēre danne vil.
15 ich sage iu, wære ez als ich hān gesaget,
sō möhte nū mīn endelōsiu clage wol sīn verdaget.

III   3 A, 22 C

'Ir sprāchet ie den frowen wol:
hab ich des iht genozzen, daz vergelte iu got.
vil gerne ouch ichz gedienen sol,
20 wan sō daz ich dar umbe niht ensī der werlte spot.

132. Text according to C with *sō* (12) and *inneclīche* (22) from A.
 10 'to which she applies herself . . .'.

ich gewan noch nie gegen iu dekeinen muot;
mir ist anders inneclîche liep, swer iu iht ze liebe tuot.
ich sage iu, [ist ez] als ich hân gesaget,
sô endarf noch iuwer endelosiu clage niht sîn verdaget.'

133

I   21 A, 33 C (Bartsch II, 9)

Wie hôhes muotes ist ein man,
der sich zuo herzeclîchen liebes schœnem lîbe hât geleit!
zer vreude ich niht gelîchen kan:
mir ist elliu vreude gar en niht gegen dirre, swaz mir ieman seit.
5 swer sich sô wünneclicher wünne wol für wâr gevreuwen mac,
der hât die naht niht angest wan daz in vertrîben sol der tac.

II   22 A, 34 C

Geselliclîcher umbevanc
mit blanken armen sunder wân tuot senede herze hôhgemuot.
dâ wirt daz ungemüete kranc,
10 swâ minneclîcher minne kus sô lieplich liep ân ander tuot.
swer sich sô wünneclicher wünne wol für wâr gevreuwen mac,
der hât die naht niht angest wan daz in vertrîben sol der tac.

III   23 A, 35 C

Der tac mich leider hât betaget
sô selten nâch der êren sige, daz ich niht vreude mac verjehen.
15 vil sælic man, der des niht claget
und ime sîn herze mac gesagen, waz ime ze liebe ist geschehen!
swer sich sô wünneclicher wünne wol für war gevreuwen mac,
der hât die naht niht angest wan daz in vertrîben sol der tac.

21 *muot* 'inclination'.
22 *anders* 'apart from that'.
133. Text according to A unless noted.
   1 *Wie* with C: *swie* A.
   2 *herzeclîchen liebes*: *hͤzeclichem* (*hͤzeclichē* C) *liebe* AC.
   10 *ân ander* 'apart from all else'.
   13–14 'The day bringing the conquest of honour has alas so seldom dawned for me . . .'.
   16 *gesagen* with C; *sagen* A. *ze liebe*: *ze leide* AC.

IV   24 A, 36 C

Der süeze wehsel under zwein
20 den werdiu minne vüegen kan, wie rucket der daz herze enbor!
diu beide ir muotes sint al ein:
ich kan nāch wunsch erdenken niht zer welte sælde dirre vor.
swer sich sō wünneclicher wünne wol für wār gevreuwen mac,
der hāt die naht niht angest wan daz in vertrīben sol der tac.

V   25 A, 37 C

25 'Der tac wil scheiden, ritter wert,
von liebe liep; ez muoz eht sin. wol ūf, lāz ir daz herze hie,
diu dīn ze friunde hāt gegert:
si wil och dir ir herze lān, diu triuwen dir gewankte nie.
die leist och ir, als ez dīn werder lip vil wol geleisten mac,
30 mit schiere komenne. ez mac niht langer hie gesīn: ich sihe den
tac.'

22 *sælde* is gen. dependent on *niht*: 'I can imagine no happiness in the world
superior to this in perfection.'
28 *triuwen*, gen. pl.

BURKART VON HOHENVELS
(BURKHARD VON HOHENFELS)

THE poet's home was the castle of Hohenvels, near Überlingen on
Lake Constance. He is attested frequently between 1212 and 1242 and
is designated as *ministerialis*. He appears once in the entourage of the
Emperor Frederick II and frequently in that of King Henry VII, and
church dignitaries of Au, Weingarten, Überlingen, and Constance.

His poetry is chiefly remarkable for the varied and striking use of
metaphor, drawn from different spheres, but chiefly from those of
hunting and bird-snaring. There are traces of Wolfram's influence in
the phraseology. The verse forms are polished and skilful, in particular
the dancing rhythm of 134 and the great virtuosity in the rhyme scheme
of 135.

134

I   1 C (KLD 6, 1)

Wir sun den winder   in stuben enpfāhen,
wol ūf ir kinder,   ze tanze sun wir gāhen!
volgent ir mir,
sō sun wir smieren   und zwinken und zwieren   nāch lieplīcher
gier.

II   2 C

5 Schōne umbeslīfen   und doch mit gedrange.
breste uns der pfīfen,   sō vāhen ze sange,
respen den swanz:
sō sun wir rucken   und zocken und zucken,   daz ēret den
tanz.

III   3 C

Nieman verliese   sīner fröiden gewinne,
10 ie der man kiese   sīn trūt daz er minne:
sanfte daz tuot.
swie si dā wenke,   sō trefs anz gelenke,   daz kützelt den
muot.

134. 1 *in: die* C.
  12 *trefs = tref si: trefes* C.

IV
                                                    4 C

Nieman sol stœren   die minne ūz dem muote:
er wil si tœren: si wehset von huote.
15 liep āne wanc,
swie si doch smucket,   si lüedert, si lucket   ir friundes
                                                                 gedanc.

V
                                                    5 C

Fröide uns behüete   vor sorclīchen dingen:
slīchendem gemüete   daz gevider lānt swingen.
nieman sol toben:
20 wenket si dicke   die smierenden blicke,   daz reizet zem
                                                                 kloben.

135

I   6 C (KLD 6, II)

Nāch des arn site ir ēre
hōhe sweimet und ir muot.
schande wenket von ir sēre,
sam vor valken lerche tuot.
5   swer   ir gruoz nimt, derst vor schanden
banden   vrī, sist sælden wer.

II   7 C

Der wilde visch in dem bēre
nie genam sō manigen wanc
als mīn herze in jāmers lēre
10   nāch ir; dest mīn fröide kranc.
wan   mīn vrīheit sich vür eigen
neigen   der vil lieben kan.

16 'although she eludes him, she baits and entices the lover's thoughts'.
18 *lant slichen zegemvte. dc gevider zerswingē* C. The MS. reading is corrupt. No
other line begins with anacrusis, and there is no verb *zerswingen* attested. The
emendation adopted here means: 'let earth-bound mood soar on wings'.
20 *zem: den* C; *klobe* is a cleft piece of wood for catching birds.
135. 6 *sælden wer* 'the source of bliss'.
7–8 'The wild fish never struggled so much in the net . . .' .
9 *jāmers lēre*: probably an instance of Wolfram's influence; cf., e.g. *Parzival*
28. 19.
10 *dest = des ist.*

III   8 C

Swie der affe sī gar wilde,
doch sō vāhet in sīn schīn,
15   sō'r in dem spiegel siht sīn bilde.
sus nimt mir diu frowe mīn
sin   līp herze muot und ougen
tougen,   dest mīn ungewin.

IV   9 C

Einen fürsten hānt [die] bīen,
20   swar der vert, si volgent nāch.
mīnen gedenken den vrīen
ist sus nāch der lieben gāch.
ir   vil vröidenfrühtic lachen
machen   kan wol fröide mir.

V   10 C

25   Der einhürn in megede schōze
gīt dur kiusche sīnen līp.
dem wild ich mich wol genōze,
sīt ein reine sælic wīp
mich   verderbet: an den triuwen,
30   riuwen   mac si der gerich.

136

I   27 C (KLD 6, VII)

'Ich wil reigen',
sprach ein wunneclīchiu magt.
'disen meigen
wart mir fröide gar versagt.
5   nu hāt mīn jār ein ende,

---

19 In a literary tradition common from Virgil onwards the leader of the bees was
held to be a king; cf. note on subject-matter of **91**. II.
23 *vröidenfrühtic*: *vröidē flühtig* C. The emendation is in keeping with *fröiden
frühte* and *tugentfrühtic* in other poems by the same author (KLD 6, XI and XIV).
26 *dur kiusche*: 'on account of her purity'.
29–30 'she may repent of her vengeance upon faithfulness'.
136. 5 *jār* 'year of service'.

des bin ich vrō.
nieman mich fröiden wende,
mīn muot stet hō.
mir ist von strōwe ein schapel und mīn vrīer muot
10   lieber danne ein rōsenkranz, sō ich bin behuot.'

II   28 C
'Lāz erbarmen
dich', sprach ir gespil zehant,
'daz mich armen
niht geschuof diu gotes hant,
15   wan si geschuof mich rīchen.
hī wær ich arn,
sō wolt ich mit dir strīchen,
ze fröiden varn.
mir ist von strōwe ein schapel und mīn vrīer muot
20   lieber danne ein rōsenkranz, sō ich bin behuot.

III   29 C
Ez ist verdrozzen
hie sīt daz mīn müemel hāt
vor beslozzen
mir die mīne liehten wāt.
25   trūre ich, si giht ich gewinne
von liebe nōt:
fröwe ich mich, daz tuot minne.
wē wan wær si tōt!
mir ist von strōwe ein schapel und mīn vrīer muot
30   lieber danne ein rōsenkranz, sō ich bin behuot.'

IV   30 C
'Wilt du sorgen,
waz sol dir dīn schœner līp?
du solt morgen
sant mir, trūren von dir trīp.

10 *behuot* 'guarded', 'watched'.
11 *Lāz*: *das* C.
16-18 *arn*: *varn*: a dialect rhyme.
23-24 *beslossē mir vor* C.
25 *gewinne*: *habe* C.
27 *tuot*: *tŭnt* C.
33-34 'You shall go with me tomorrow, banish sorrow from you.'

35 ich wil dich lēren snīden,
    wis vröiden vol.
    tuot daz wē, wir sonz mīden,
    uns wirt sus wol.
    mir ist von strōwe ein schapel und mīn vrīer muot
40 lieber danne ein rōsenkranz, sō ich bin behuot.'

    V   31 C
    'Ich hān schiere
    mir gedāht einen gerich:
    wan ich zwiere,
    swā man zwinket wider mich.
45 si enlāt mich niender lachen
    gegen werdekeit:
    sō nim ich einen swachen,
    daz ist ir leit.
    mir ist von strōwe ein schapel und mīn vrīer muot
50 lieber danne ein rōsenkranz, sō ich bin behuot.'

137

    I   37 C (KLD 6, IX)
    Mīn herze hāt mīnen sin
    wilt ze jagen ūz gesant.
    der vert nāch mit mīnem muote.
    vil gedanke vert vor in.
5 den ist daz vil wol bekant,
    daz daz wilt stēt in der huote
    bī der, der ich dienstes bin bereit.
    ir sin, ir muot, ir gedenken
    kan vor in mit kunste wenken:
10 wol bedorft ich fuhses kündekeit.

---

37 *sonz*: *son* is a variant of *sun* (**134**. 1) < *suln*.
137. 3 *vert nāch* 'is in pursuit'.
    4 *vert vor in* 'leads the chase'.
    6 *huote* 'cover'.
    9 'can skilfully elude them'.

II   38 C

Wie wirt mir daz stolze wilt?
daz ist snel, wīse und starc.
snel gedenken vert vor winde,
wīser sin bī menschen spilt,
15   sterke in leuwen sich ie barc:
der gelīch ir muot ich vinde
ir snelheit mir wenket hōhe enbor,
ir wīsheit mich überwindet,
mit ir sterke si mich bindet.
20   sus ir schœne tōrte mich hie vor.

III   39 C

Trūren mit gewalte hāt
gankert in mīnes herzen grunt;
dā von hōher muot mir wildet.
fröiden segel von mir gāt,
25   werder trōst ist mir niht kunt,
sist mir in dem muot gebildet,
wol versigelt und beslozzen dā,
sam der schīn ist in der sunnen.
diu bant hānt die kraft gewunnen,
30   daz siu bræche niht des grīfen klā.

IV   40 C

Ir vil liehten ougen blic
wirfet hōher fröiden vil,
ir gruoz der gīt sælde und ēre.
ir schœne diu leit den stric
35   der gedanke vāhen wil;
des gīt ir gedanke lēre

13 'Swift thought outstrips the wind.' The idea of *wint* as a hunting term meaning 'scent' is also present.
22 Cf. *Parzival* 461. 16: *waz ankers wær diu vröude mīn? | diu sinket durch der riuwe grunt.*
23 *wildet* 'is strange to me'. There is the additional play on the word *'wilt'* in the first two verses and the adjective in l. 41.
26 Cf. the so-called II. *Büchlein* ascribed to Hartmann, 726: *Ez muoz diu guote | Versigelt in mīnem herzen sīn, | Sam in der sunnen der schīn.*
32 The image is that of casting the lure (*luoder*).

mit zuht, daz irz nieman wīzen sol.
swes gedenken gegen ir swinget,
minne den sō gar betwinget,
40   daz er gīt gevangen fröiden zol.

V   41 C

Minne vert vil wilden strich
unde suochet triuwen spor:
zuo der wirte wil si pflihten.
wunderlīch si liebet sich:
45   si spilt im mit fröiden vor,
wunsches wils in gar berihten,
mit gedanken si im entwerfen kan
wünneclīch in sīme sinne
herzeliep: von dem gewinne
50   scheiden muoz, swer triuwe nie gewan.

138

I   42 C (KLD 6, X)

Si gelīchet sich der sunnen
diu den sternen nimt ir schīn,
die dā vor sō liehte brunnen.
alsus nimt diu frowe mīn
5   allen wīben gar ir glast,
si sint doch dest unschœner niht.
ēre ist ir, si ist niht ir gast.
alle tugent si gar zündet,
daz der werlte vröide kündet.
10   dā von man ir prīses giht.

---

38 *swingen*: cf. **134**. 18 and **138**. 19 and 30.

40 *fröiden zol*: cf. *fröiden zins* **77**. 18 and *Parzival* 185. 12: *dā gap diu diet von vröuden zol.*

40 'that he, a captive, pays tribute of joy'.

43 *der wirte*: this is the reading of the MS. which can stand in spite of the various attempts to amend it; *der* is gen. pl. referring to *triuwen* and dependent on *wirt*, thus 'its guardian'; cf. Frauenlob: *mīnes herzen wirt* (Ettmüller, *Lieder* I, 1).

45 'she shows him visions of joy'.

138. 6 'yet they are none the less beautiful'.

7 'Honour is hers, it is not a stranger to her'; cf. *Parzival* 219. 22: *mir ist vröude gestīn, hōchgemuot gast.*

8–9 'She kindles every virtue, so as to make men glad.'

II　　　　　　　　　　　　　　　　43 C

Dō mīn wilder muot vil tougen
streich nāch fröide in elliu lant,
dō lūhten ir liehten ougen:
er vuor dar; dā von si in bant
15　　mit ir stæten wībes zuht.
ich viel mit im in den stric.
wir hān von ir keine fluht,
wir hān aber den gedingen,
daz ir spilnden ougen swingen
20　　und uns werfen einen blic.

III　　　　　　　　　　　　　　　44 C

Dō mīn muot sīt wolde vliegen
als ein valke in fröiden gir,
sō moht er si niht betriegen,
er müese aber wider zir,
25　　von der er verstolne floug:
er forhte si næme es war,
ob er si mit wandel troug
und er anders wolde denken.
dō dūhte in, si solde wenken,
30　　alsō swanc er wider dar.

16 *mit im*: *mit ir* C, but it can only refer to *wilder muot*.
22 *gir*: see note on Wolfram **113**. 3.
29 *solde* 'was about to'.

UOLRICH VON LIEHTENSTEIN
(ULRICH VON LIECHTENSTEIN)

THE poet, a member of a Styrian family, was probably born about 1198. He is attested very frequently between 1227 and 1274 and died in 1275 or 1276. In 1241 he appears as *dapifer Stirie* (*truhsæze*) and in 1272 as marshal. He was active in the political events of his day, taking part in the wars against Hungary and fighting in the battle of 1246, at which Duke Frederick II, the last of the Babenberger, was killed. He was later in the service of Ottokar of Bohemia who became Duke of Styria in 1261.

His chief work, the so-called *Frauendienst*, is a narrative in stanza form, interspersed with numerous lyrics, from which the following are taken. The work purports to be autobiographical, but there is probably a large admixture of fiction. The poet relates how he became the page of a noble lady at the age of twelve and later served the margrave of Istria. He became a knight in Vienna on the occasion of the marriage of the daughter of Duke Leopold VI. He performed fantastic exploits in the service of his first mistress and another lady, including the celebrated expedition as *vrowe Vēnus*, when, dressed in womanly attire, with two long plaits, he rose from the sea near Venice, proceeding through Friuli, Carinthia, Styria, and Austria as far as the Bohemian border, challenging all comers.

His poetry enshrines the classic conventions of the service of love and shows considerable technical virtuosity in the use of rhyme.

139

I   83 C, L fol. 92ᵛ (KLD 58, XVIII)

Er tōre vil tumber, des līp sī gehaz
den merkæren durch ir kargez spehen.
ir merken, ir hüeten, daz trœstet noch baz
danne an den tumben daz toube übersehen.
5 swer guoten wīben ir güetelīchen muot
wol kan gemerken, des merken ist guot.
swer des niht merket, der ist toub und unfruot.

---

139. 1–2 'A stupid fool is he who hates the watchers on account of their shrewd spying.'

2 *kargez* with L: *arges* C.

II 84 C

Unvalschlīchez merken, seht daz ist ein prīs,
mannen und wīben der vil hōhe stāt.
von güetlīchem merken wirt man ēren wīs.
unwerdez merken, daz in nīde ergāt,
und huote in nīde, den zwein trage ich haz.
von rehtem hüeten wil ich sprechen daz,
daz al der werlde zimt niht dinges baz.

III 85 C

Diu huote an den wīben diu tuot mich sō vrō,
daz ich in wünsche daz si eht sīn behuot,
mit huote beslozzen vil sēre und alsō
daz in diu huote behüete den muot
mit rehter güete vor valschlīchem sit,
daz si niender wenken von güete einen trit.
der huote in allen ich wünsche und bit.

IV 86 C

Mīn frouwe kan hüeten ir ēren sō wol
daz si in ir huote sō werlīchen stāt,
si wert sich unprīses ze rehte als si sol;
niuwan des einen des si an mir begāt.
si enwil niht merken daz ich von ir trage
leitlīche swære nu vil manige tage
und daz ich ringe mit wē tuonder klage.

V 87 C

Unde kunde si merken, si müese mir jehen
daz ir mīn dienest ist stæte āne wanc.
nu mac si des tougen in mīn herze sehen,
wie gegen ir hulden spilt al mīn gedanc.
si mac dā schouwen, ob siz merken wil,
süezen gedingen, dā bī jāmers vil.
der zweier schanze ich gegen ir hulden spil.

35 'I stake these two in hope of her favour.'

140

I   159 C, L fol. 98ᵛ (KLD 58, XXXIII)

Wizzet, frouwe wol getān,
daz ich ūf genāde hān
herze und līp an iuch verlān.
daz riet mir ein lieber wān:
5   durch des rāt hān ichz getān
und wil es niht abe gestān.
daz lāt mir ze guot ergān.

II   160 C

'Sīt ir dienstes mir bereit,
tuot ir daz ūf lōnes reht,
10   sō lāt mich erkennen daz,
wie der dienest sī gestalt,
den ich mich sol nemen an,
wie der lōn geheizen sī,
der iu von mir sol geschehen.'

III   161 C

Frouwe, ich wil in mīnen tagen
15   sō nāch iuwern hulden jagen,
daz ez iu muoz wol behagen,
den muot durch iuch hōhe tragen
und an fröiden niht verzagen,
iuwer lop der werlde sagen,
20   und des lōnes noch gedagen.

IV   162 C

'Sīt ir frō, dar zuo gemeit,
mir ze dienest als ir jeht,
ez gefrumt iuch selben baz
danne mich wol tūsentvalt.
25   tuot daz schamelop hin dan:
mir ist der spiegel swære bī,
dar inne ich mīn leit sol sehen.'

140. 9 *ūf lōnes reht* 'with a claim to reward'.
27–28 'The mirror is unwelcome, in which I see my own disgrace', i.e. the discrepancy between praise and reality.

V   163 C

30   Iuwer lop die wirde hāt,
        daz ez wol ze hove gāt,
        baz danne aller künege wāt
        āne scham al dā bestāt.
        'lieber herre, sælic man,
        ir sīt spotes alze frī.
35   daz ist unprīs, tar ichs gejehen.'

141

I   184 C, L fol. 101ᵛ (KLD 58, XXXVIII)

Ēren gernde ritter, lāt iuch schouwen
under helme dienen werden frouwen.
welt ir die zīt vertrīben
ritterlīch,   ēren rīch
5   wert ir von guoten wīben.

II   185 C

Ir sült hōchgemuot sīn under schilde,
wol gezogen, küene, blīde, milde.
tuot ritterschaft mit sinnen
und sīt frō,   minnet hō:
10   sō mügt ir lop gewinnen.

III   186 C

Denket an der werden wībe grüezen,
wie sich daz kan guoten friunden süezen.
swen frouwen munt wol grüezet,
der ist gewert   swes er gert:
15   sīn fröide ist im gesüezet.

IV   187 C

Swer mit schilde sich decken wil vor schanden,
der sol ez dem lībe wol enplanden.
des schildes ampt gīt ēre.
im ist bereit   werdekeit:
20   si muoz aber kosten sēre.

141. 5 *wert = werdet.*
17 'he should make a strenuous effort'.

V   188 C

    Manlīch herze vindet man bī schilde:
    zeglīch muot muoz sīn dem schilde wilde.
    gegen wīben valsch der blecket,
    swer in hāt,   an der stat
25   dā man mit schilden decket.

VI   189 C

    Tuo her schilt: man sol mich hiute schouwen
    dienen mīner herzelieben frouwen.
    ich muoz ir minne erwerben
    unde ir gruoz,   oder ich muoz
30   gar in ir dienst verderben.

VII   190 C

    Ich wil si mit dienste bringen inne
    daz ich si baz danne mich selben minne.
    ūf mir muoz sper erkrachen.
    nū tuo her   sperā sper!
35   des twinget mich ir lachen:
    daz kan si süeze machen.

22 *dem schilde wilde* 'foreign to the shield'.
23–25 'it is a sign of falsehood to women, if a man has it in his breast.'
34 *sperā*: *ā* is an interjection attached to other words, cf. *wāfenā*.

GÖTFRIT VON NÎFEN
(GOTTFRIED VON NEIFEN)

THE poet belongs to a Swabian family of Nîfen, now Hohenneuffen near Urach. The poet's father appears in the entourage of the Emperor Friedrich II, taking part in his Crusading expedition of 1228. The poet is attested between 1234 and 1255, at first at the court of King Heinrich VII (d. 1242), the son of the Emperor. Both Gottfried and his brother were taken prisoner in the fighting of 1235, when Heinrich rebelled against his father.

MS. C attributes to him 190 strophes, some of them of doubtful authenticity. The poems here chosen illustrate his usual manner: the varied reformulation of a certain number of recurrent motifs in metrical forms of a dazzling virtuosity.

142

I   21 C (KLD 15, V)

Walt   heide anger vogel singen
sint verdorben von des kalten winters zît.
dā man bluomen sach ūf dringen,
dā ist ez blōz: nu schouwet wie diu heide lît.
5   daz klage ich: sō klage ich mīne swære,
daz ich der unmære
der ich gerne liep in herzen wære.
frowe Minne, daz ist allez dīn gewalt.

II   22 C

Bar   mīn herze in bernder wunne,
10   daz was swenne ich sach ir wunneclīchen schīn
unde ir ougen sam der sunne
dur mīn ougen lūhten in daz herze mīn.
dar nāch wart mir leit in kurzen stunden.
owē Minne wunden!
wie hāst du dich sus mīn underwunden
daz ich sender siecher bin noch fröiden bar!

142. 6 *bin* after *unmære* C.

III   23 C

Bant · diu Minne mich der süezen
und lāt die vil lieben sunder trūren gān,
Minne, wie wilt duz gebüezen ?
20   Minne, ich hānz dā für, ez sī niht guot getān.
Minne, hilf enzīt: ich muoz verderben
unde an fröiden sterben.
sol ich niht den rōten kus erwerben,
sō ist mir fröiden strāze in riuwen pfat gebant.

IV   24 C

25   Lōs   in rehter wībes güete
sach ich zeinem māle ir kiuschen wībes līp.
dā von fröit sich mīn gemüete,
daz ich dāchte 'jā du reine sælic wīp,
du maht mir wol mīnen kumber wenden
30   unde helfe senden.'
frouwe Minne, trœstet mich vil senden,
wan ich stān von iuweren schulden fröidelōs.

V   25 C

Wer   kan mich nu frō gemachen ?
nieman dan ir minneclīcher rōter munt.
35   wil mir der von herzen lachen,
dā von wirde ich sender siecher wol gesunt.
guoten wīp, nu wünschet daz diu hēre
mich die strāze lēre
wā ich ūzer leide in liebe kēre.
40   Minne, hilf daz mich diu liebe ir liebe wer!

143

I   49 C (KLD 15, XII)

Waz vervāhet   mich des wunnenclīchen meigen zīt,
der uns nāhet   unde manigem herzen fröide gīt?
bluomen unde vogelsanc,
der beider   trōst ist leider   mīnen fröiden alze kranc.

20 'I consider it ill done.'
33 f. Cf. Reinmar **86.** 28–31.

II   51 C

5   Jā verkēret   mir ein wīp die besten frōide mīn,
     der ich geēret   von ir reinen tugenden solde sīn.
     diu hāt sō betwungen mir
     die sinne   mit ir minne   daz ich trūren muoz nāch ir.

III   50 C

     Mīn gemüete   hāt betwungen ir vil süezer līp.
10   sō mit güete,   sō mit schœne wart nie bezzer wīp.
     als mir mīn herze seit.
     daz wunder   hāt besunder   got mit flīze an si geleit.

IV   52 C

     Ich wil singen   gegen dem meigen minneclīchen sanc.
     swære ringen   kan si nāch der ie mīn herze ranc.
15   trōste mich diu frowe mīn,
     diu guote   wol gemuote,   seht sō wolt ich frœlīch sīn.

V   53 C

     Mit ir gruoze   möhte si mir wenden swæren pīn,
     der sō suoze   fröite mir daz sende herze mīn.
     rœselehter rōter munt,
20   scheit den strīt   und hilf enzīt,   sō bin ich wol gesunt.

144

I   130 C (KLD 15, XXXII)

     Sumer, nū wil dīn   gewalt
     walt   den anger und die heide
     beide   kleiden: dast dien kleinen vogelīn nōt.
     man siht bluomen manicvalt,
5   valt   an maniger stolzen meide:
     reide   löcke tragents unde mündel rōt.

---

143. 12 The idea of the lady's perfection as an example of divine workmanship is common; cf. **50.** 1–4.
   14 *ie* after *herze* C.
   20 *mir* before *sō* C, here omitted for metrical reasons.
144. 3 *dien* = *den.*
   5 *valt* 'pleat', i.e. 'pleated dress'.
   6 *tragents* = *tragent si.*

seht, der fröide was vil nāch zergangen.
ach mīs herzen! jā muoz mich belangen
nāch dem triutelehten lībe. owē wan wær er mīn!

II   131 C

10   Wil si daz mich leit   verber,
ber   mir fröide von ir munde.
wunde   von der minne wirt vil schiere heil.
daz ir güete mich gewer,
wer   ist der mir des verbunde?
15   kunde   ich fluochen, dem wunschte ich daz im unheil
wære bī vil lange unz an sīn ende.
süeziu Minne, süeze helfe sende.
des ist nōt, sīt ich von dīnen schulden sorge ie leit.

III   132 C

Ach wie ist si gar   liep guot.
20   guot   næme ich niht für die ich meine.
seine   trœstet mich, daz ist der Minne haz,
ir munt rōter danne ein bluot.
bluot   des meigen fröit mich kleine.
reine   sælic wīp, nū trœstet baz.
25   tuot irs niht, sō muoz ich gar verderben.
sol ich niht den rōten kus erwerben
und den triutelehten līp, sō wirde ich fröiden bar.

IV   133 C

Rātet wie ich daz   ervar
var   ich umbe in allem lande?
30   rande   ich tūsent mīle, ez wær bewendet wol,
ob ich des genæme war
war   ich kērte ūz minne bande.
brande   si mich niht, sō hete ich senften dol:

7 *der* gen. pl. referring to *si* of the preceding line.
8 *mīs* = *mīnes.*
14 'who grudges me that?'
19 *si*: *so* C.
21 *seine trœstet*: *si eine trôste* C. The emendation of KLD is preferable syntactically and metrically, in particular for the rhyme. *seine* adv. = slowly, not at all:
'her mouth is slow to comfort me; that is due to the enmity of Love'.
23 *bluot* st. m. 'blossom'.
25 *tuot irs niht*: *beschiht niht* C.
30 *rande*, pret. subj. *rennen*, meaning here 'to ride swiftly'.
31 *ob*: *wie* C.

sus hāt mich diu minneclīche entzündet.
ich enweiz wes si sich an mir sündet:
laschte si mich mit ir minne, mir wurde deste baz.

V   134 C

Minne, ich diene dir :   du solt
solt   mir geben minneclīchen.
rīchen   maht du mich an fröiden, des ist zīt.
ob mir daz dīn helfe erholt,
holt   bin ich dir inneclīchen;
wīchen   muoz von mir leit daz mir nāhe līt.
minneclīchiu Minne, ich was gebunden
dir von kinde ie. wiltu mich nu wunden,
was tougt danne stætiu triuwe ? Minne, daz verbir.

WAHSMUOT VON KUNZICH

DATE and localization of the poet are uncertain. His place of origin
has been variously identified as Künzing in Bavaria, Kuntzig in Lor-
raine, and Küntzig in Luxembourg. The latter is most likely on grounds
of dialect and the similarity of the armorial bearings attributed to the
poet by MS. C and those of the Luxembourg family von Kuntzich. He
was probably writing *c.* 1250.

His poetry is considerably influenced by Reinmar and Walther, but
he is no mere imitator. The conventions of courtly love are expressed
in well-turned phrases, in metrical forms of great fluency and polish.

145

I   10 C (KLD 60, III)

Sol mir iemer sīn ein wīp vor allen wīben
unde ich ir doch niht vor einem man,
wer sol danne sende swære mir vertrīben,
ob ich des erwerben niene kan
5 und ich doch von ir, der guoten, niht enscheide
weder herze noch den sin:
liebet si mir dā von daz ich ir sō leide,
sō weiz ich daz ich ir tōre bin.

II   11 C

Ich muoz dur die übeln valschen merekære
10 mīner besten ougenweide enbern;
herre got, du vüege in laster unde swære,
durch dīn ēre solt du mich gewern
daz si mīn vergezzen mit ir selber leide
und der lieben frowen mīn.
15 daz si got von sælden und von ēren scheide
die unrehter huote vlīzic sīn!

---

145. 2 'and I no dearer to her than any other man'.
    7 'If she is so dear to me because I am unpleasing to her'; cf. also l. 18.
    8 Cf. Reinmar MF 157, 39: *nu tuo si durch den willen mīn | und lāze mich ir tōre sīn.*

III

Herre got, durch dīner lieben muoter ēre
leide si mir alder liebe ir mich:
in gesach sō herzeliebes nie niht mēre;
20   dā von bin ich maniger sorgen rīch.
wære si mir in der māze als ich ir wære,
sō möht es wol werden rāt.
ez enhāt nieman sō herzeclīche swære
sō der herzeleit bī liebe hāt.

146

I   5 A, 15 C, Chuonze von Rosenhein 3 C (KLD 60, V)

Wē warumbe trūrent si
die bī liebe habent gelegen?
jō vröiwe ich mich und ich doch nie
liep gewan noch solhen segen
5   den liep nāch liebe tuot mit seneden sorgen,
sō si scheident sich:
sō slāf aber ich unz an den morgen,
daz nieman sprichet 'vriunt, got segen dich!'

II   6 A, 16 C, Ch. v. R. 4 C

Frowen diene ich unverzaget:
10   owē torst ich lōnes gern!
jā vürht ich, obe si mir versaget,
daz ich müeze ir hulde enbern.
ir vriuntschaft wil ich gerne alsō behalten
danne ich hete ir haz.
15   des muoz ich jæmerlīchen alten:
ei jā endiene ich in niht umbe daz.

III   7 A, 17 C, Ch. v. R. 5 C

Waz hilfet daz ich kriege dar
unde krenke mīnen līp?
si nimt mīn alze kleine war,
20   diu mir ist vür alliu wīp.

19 *gesach*: *gelas* C.
146. 3–4 Cf. Reinmar 89. 3–4.
     5 *liebe* with C²: *leide* AC.
     13 *gerne* here 'rather'.
     15 Cf. Reinmar MF 157, 15: *Ich wirde jæmerlīchen alt.*
     20 Cf. 145. 1.

meinet [mich] mīn frowe alse ich si meine,
sō wirt mīn guot rāt:
mīn dienest dunket si ze kleine:
dā setze ich guoten willen gein der tāt.

147

I   8 A, 18 C (KLD 60, VI)

Waz hāt mich diu liebe zīt vervangen
daz der sumer sō schœne was?
der ist āne vröide mir zergangen:
owē bluomen unde gras!
5   wenne wiltu trœsten mich,
unde ein wīp nāch der mich muoz erlangen?
owē, wie daz lenget sich!

II   9 A, 19 C

Ūz ir ougen vliegent strālen sēre
mitten in daz herze mīn,
10   swelches endes ich der welte kēre.
sol daz iemer alsō sīn,
sō wære ich ze tōde wunt.
alle meister geheilent niemer mēre
mich, ez entuo ir rōter munt.

21–22 Cf. **145.** 21–22.
24 Cf. Walther, L/K 100, 22: *Mīn wille ist guot und klage diu werc | gēt mir an den iht abe.*

147. 13–14 Cf. Walther L/K 74, 14: *mīnes herzen tiefiu wunde | diu muoz iemer offen stēn, si enküsse mich mit friundes munde,* and Gottfried von Neifen **142.** 34–36 and **143.** 19–20.

UOLRICH VON WINTERSTETTEN
(ULRICH VON WINTERSTETTEN)

THE poet was a member of the Swabian family of Winterstetten, near Waldsee in Württemberg. His maternal grandfather was tutor to Heinrich VII and counsellor to Konrad IV. The poet is attested between 1241 and 1280, appearing as canon of Augsburg in 1258. MS. C gives him the title *Schenk*, 'cup-bearer'.

His output is varied, comprising *Leiche*, songs, and *Tagelieder*. His poetry shows great formal virtuosity, akin to that of Gottfried von Neifen. The majority of his lyrics have a refrain.

148

I   62 C (KLD 59, XVI)

Sumer ouget sīne wunne,
daz ist an der zīt:
prüeve er wol swer tihten kunne
waz materje līt
5   an dem walde und ūf der heide breit.
man mac schouwen   wie die ouwen   stānt bekleit,
waz der anger liehter bluomen treit.
est ein alt gesprochen wort,
swā dīn herze wont, dā līt dīn hort.

II   63 C

10   Ich hab endelīchen funden
einen schœnen hort.
den kōs ich mir zeinen stunden:
nūst mīn herze dort
bī dem horde der mir füeget pīn.
15   diu vil reine   wandels eine   muoz mir sīn
hort in dem vil senden herzen mīn.
est ein alt gesprochen wort,
swā dīn herze wont, dā līt dīn hort.

148. 8–9 cf. Matt. vi. 21.

III   64 C
Mīn hort kan wol tugende horden
20   unde hōhen muot.
diu mir ist ze horde worden,
dest mīn frowe guot,
in der güete lōse wol gestalt.
ir gebāren   an den jāren   mich tuot alt,
25   swie ir tugende doch sīn manicvalt.
est ein alt gesprochen wort,
swā dīn herze wont, dā līt dīn hort.

IV   65 C
Maniger der hāt hort verborgen
des er trœstet sich:
30   mīn hort gīt mir niht wan sorgen
unde smēhet mich.
mīn vil lieber hort ist mir alsō
gar unnütze.   minne schütze   Cupīdō
traf mīn herze, sīt bin ich unfrō.
35   est ein alt gesprochen wort,
swā dīn herze wont, dā līt dīn hort.

V   66 C
Minne diu ist gewalteclīchen
allen dingen obe.
ir kan niht ūf erde entwīchen,
40   ez gevāhe ir klobe.
wīsheit hort diu beide nīgent ir.
Minne süeze,   kumber büeze   nach der gir,
twinge mīnen hort gelīche mir.
est ein alt gesprochen wort,
45   swā dīn herze wont, dā līt dīn hort.

149

I   81 C (KLD 59, XXI)
Ich wil allen liuten   betiuten   mīs herzen klage
und wie grōzen kumber   ich tumber   nu trage,
wie mich sorge twinget   und singet   doch mir der līp:
seht daz muoz ich līden   durh mīden   ein wīp.

23 *in dˢ gûte lôse* C. Kraus emends with Bartsch to *in ir getelœse*, 'in her capriciousness', but this is unnecessary. *lôs* is common in the sense of 'charming' in the later poets; cf. **142**. 25 and **153**. 3.
40 Cf. **134**. 20.

5 des muoz ich dem jāmerschricke leider undertænic sīn.
ich lige in ir minnen stricke, daz ist an mir worden schīn.
si kan senden smerzen ūz herzen vertrīben wol.
rōse ob allen wīben man si nennen sol.

II   82 C

Wā ist nu diu schœne? ich dœne und nīge ir gar.
10 ich wil aber grüezen die süezen (nement war!)
schōne mit gesange. swie lange ich ir frömde sī,
doch sō hāt ir jugende vil tugende, dā bī
hāt si güete ein michel wunder in dem herzen zaller stunt,
und si doch vor ūz besunder mir daz herze hāt verwunt.
15 si kan senden smerzen ūz herzen vertrīben wol.
rōse ob allen wīben man si nennen sol.

III   83 C

Wenne sun ir ougen mir tougen ze blicke varn?
und diu süeze junge mir swunge den arn
und mich umbevienge, sō gienge mir sorge hin.
20 seht, sō wolt ich scheiden von leiden den sin.
wāfenā der lieben stunde, wenne sol ich die geleben,
daz ich von ir rōten munde solte ein lieplich küssen nemen?
si kan senden smerzen ūz herzen vertrīben wol.
rōse ob allen wīben man si nennen sol.

150

I   107 C (KLD 59, XXVIII)

Bī liebe lac ein ritter tougenlīche
die naht bis an den tac.
der minne enpflac mit im diu minneclīche.
die minne er widerwac,
5 bis daz der wahter sanc 'ez tagt'.
daz von in beiden wart geklagt.
'ach herzeliebiu frowe mīn',
sō sprach der ritter wolgemuot,
'ich wæne ez müeze ein scheiden sīn.'

149. 10–11 Cf. **35.** 1.
 18 *arn = arm.*
 und here has the meaning 'and if'.
 22 On account of the rhyme with *geleben*, KLD emends to: *daz si von ir rōtem munde wolte ein lieplich küssen geben.*

II   108 C

10 Ez wart niht lanc   daz dā mit nāhem smucke
    ergie ein umbevanc
    mit armen blanc   und herzeclīchem drucke,
    der liep gen liebe twanc.
    diu frowe sprach 'mīn sender līp
15 und ich vil siufteberndez wīp
    bin iemer mē an fröiden vrī,
    sol ich dir, herre, niemer mē
    geligen alsō nāhe bī.'

III   109 C

    Owē und ach!   der jāmerbæren scheiden
20 ir beider herze brach,
    daz [dā] geschach   von den gelieben beiden:
    daz schuof in ungemach.
    der ritter sprach 'gehabe dich wol!
    dīn līp ist maniger tugende vol:
25 mīn herze dir belībet hie.'
    si sprach 'sō füere mīn herze hin.'
    der wehsel dā mit kus ergie.

150. 10–12 Cf. Wolfram 117. 36–37 and 116. 32.
    15 *siuftebernd*, 19 *jāmerbære*: such compounds, although not found in his dawn
songs, are in Wolfram's manner.
    22 *in*: *im* C.

KUONRÂT VON WIRZEBURC
(KONRAD VON WÜRZBURG)

THE poet, a member of the middle class, was born *c.* 1225 and died
in 1287. He lived in Strassburg and Basle, and mentions in his works
several patrons who enabled him to produce a substantial body of
poetry: saints' lives, chivalric narratives, didactic tales, an ornate poem
in praise of the Virgin (the so-called *Goldene Schmiede*), as well as
numerous lyrics and didactic poems. He was highly prized in his day
and was one of the twelve masters of the *Meistersinger*. His poetry is
characterized by great facility and supreme technical skill, and is above
all noteworthy for its formal qualities.

151

I   78 C (Schröder 28)

Mînen muot
hât diu minne   sêre enzunt:
als ein gluot
ich enbrinne   zaller stunt.
5 ungewinne
sint mir inne   worden kunt.
küniginne,
mîne sinne   tuo gesunt!
hôher fröiden funt
10 sende in mînes herzen grunt;
ich bin in den tôt verwunt:
daz tet mir dîn rôter munt.

II   79 C

Frowe mîn,
du verkêre   mîniu leit!
15 lâ mir sîn
fröiden lêre   vil bereit!
prîs und êre
dir, vil hêre,   sî geseit
iemer mêre;
20 dîn lop sêre   werde breit,

151. 9 Cf. Wolfram 117. 30.

sīt dīn name treit
hōher wībe werdekeit;
āne wandels gunterfeit
zieret dich der tugende kleit.

152

83 C (Schröder 30)

Swā tac er- schīnen sol zwein liuten,
die ver- borgen inne liebe stunde müezen tragen,
dā mac ver- swīnen wol ein triuten:
nie der morgen minne- diebe kunde büezen klagen.
5 er lēret ougen weinen trīben;
sinnen wil er wunne selten borgen.
swer mēret tougen reinen wīben
minnen spil, der kunne schelten morgen.

153

99 C (Schröder 32, 106)

Ūf erde nie kein man gesach sō tougenlīche klōsen,
sō wībes herze in dem diu minne lūzet āne kōsen:
si kan mit ir lōsen
gebærde ir friunt beschāchen wol.
5 ahī wie sæleclīchen der mit fröiden wirt gerīchet,
der si vil reinen winkeldiupen vāhet unde erslīchet,
diu der strāze entwīchet
dur lāge in gar ein engez hol!
ūf den si den roup muoz lān, den si verborgenlīchen hilt,
10 swaz si ir friunden abe gestilt,
daz si ze loche tücket,
daz wirt herwider ūz von in gehelset und gedrücket,

152. 3 *verswīnen*: *vᵉswindē* C.
  4 'The morning could never remedy the complaints of those who steal love.'
  5 *er lēret*: *ert* C.
  'He teaches eyes to weep.'
  6 *sinnen*: *sinen sinnē* C.

153. 9 follows on after *vāhet unde erslīchet*: 'so that she has to give up the booty which she is secretly hiding.'
  10–13 'that which she steals from her friends, and which she snatches into her hiding place, is drawn out again by them and clasped in embraces; she repays kiss for kiss to him from whom she has secretly stolen . . .'.

si giltet kus mit kusse dem si tougen hāt gezücket,
swā sich liep gesmücket
15   zuo liebe als ez von rehte sol.

154

109 C; 7 J; n fol. 96; t fol. 533; w fol. 99 (Schröder 32, 256)

Mir ist als ich niht lebende sī, swenne ich entnücke sēre:
dā von den tōt betiutet mir der slāf mit sīner lēre.
bī der sunnen kēre
bezeichent mir der schate mīn,
5   daz im gelīch zergāt mīn leben; ouch wirde ich bī der hitze
der helle ermant, swenne ich in einer badestuben gesitze.
bī der bluomen glitze
spür ich unstæter wunnen schīn.
in dem spiegel ich erkenne daz ich asche bin als er:
10   sō kan mir der kerenter
mit dem gebeine künden,
daz mich die würme nagende werdent mit unreinen münden.
wil ich dā bī niht hüeten mich vor allen houbetsünden,
in der helle gründen
15   muoz ich ān ende quelnde sīn.

155

110 C; 8 J; n fol. 96; t fol. 532 (Schröder 32, 271)

Sō wē mir tumber daz mich iemer langer tage verdriuzet,
und mīner jāre vrist enwec sō rehte balde schiuzet,
daz ein bach niht fliuzet
sō drāte ūz velse noch ūz hage!
5   ich wünsche dicke daz diu stunde werde mir gekürzet,
und ist si doch ūf einen gæhen louf alsō geschürzet,
daz darinne erstürzet
geswinde sich mīn lebetage.
jā klag ich mīn gelt daz ich verzer, unde klage niht mīne zīt,
10   die mir nieman wider gīt,

154. 8 *wunnen* with Jnw: *blůmen* C.
   10 *kerenter* ('charnel house' < Lat. *carnarium*) with Jn: *gerner* C (a variant form from *carnarium*).
155. 4 *hac*: here 'enclosure'.

swenne ich si gar verliure.
vertet ich verne guot, ich mag gewinnen anderz hiure,
verswende ich aber mīniu jār, diu sint mir iemer tiure:
von dekeiner stiure
15   verlorne zīt ich wider bejage.

13 'but if I waste the years of my life, they will never return'.
15 *verlorne* with Jnt: *v^stanú* C.

STEINMAR

THE poet is most probably Berthold Steinmar of Clingenouwe (Kling-
nau in Canton Thurgau), who is frequently attested between 1251 and
1288. He held a fief from Walther von Klingen, himself a poet. From a
reference in one of Steinmar's poems, it appears that he took part in
Rudolf of Habsburg's siege of Vienna in 1276. He can write in the
traditional vein, as in 156, but also introduces elements of parody. The
metrical forms are simple, with a predominance of the four-beat line;
in 156 and 157, where all the lines are four-beat, the insertion of a rhymeless line prevents monotony.

156

I   6 C (Bartsch XIX, 2)

Swenne ich komen wil von swære,
sō gedenke ich an ein wīp:
diu ist schœne und ērebærè,
daz ir tugentlīcher līp
5   hœhet mīnen senden muot,
als einen edelen valken wilde
sīn gevider in lüften tuot.

II   7 C

Süezer wunsch bī allen wīben,
dīn hānt ēre tiutschiu lant.
10   du kanst herzeleit vertrīben
und enbinden sorgen bant.
dīn sint gēret elliu wīp:
alsō hēre und alsō reine
ist dīn fröidebernder līp.

III   8 C

15   Ich wānde, ūz dem himelrīche
mich ein engel lachet an,
dō ich si sach sō minneclīche:
gar von aller swære ich kan.

156. 7 *in lüften*: *in dē lúfte* C.
     18 *kan = kam.*

ich wart aller fröiden vol,
20   als ein sēle von der wīze,
diu ze himelrīche sol.

157

I   12 C (Bartsch XIX, 4)
Wer sol mich ze fröiden stiuren
gēn den wünneclīchen tagen?
sol mir hōhgemüete tiuren,
daz wil ich dien guoten klagen.
5   ich weiz wol, ez ist in leit:
ich was ie den fröide gernden
mīnes dienstes vil bereit
und wær ouch noch vil gern.
mirst mīn lōn gēn der vil süezen
10   hiure unnāher danne vern.

II   13 C

Sælderīche sumerwunne,
du solt haben mīnen gruoz.
swie [si] fröide mir erbunne,
doch wirt mangem herzen buoz
15   von dir grōzer swære vil:
dā von ich dich, süezer sumer,
willeclīche grüezen wil
unde muoz doch fröide enbern,
wan mīn lōn ist gēn der süezen
20   hiure unnāher danne vern.

III   14 C

Ich mac wol mīn herze strāfen,
daz ichs gegen ir began,
ūf mīn ougen schrīen wāfen,
diu von ērst si sāhen an.
25   ach, dō was sō schœn ir schīn,
daz er kam dur ganziu ougen
in daz sende herze mīn.
daz muoz iemer nāch ir gern,
swie mīn lōn ist gēn der süezen
30   hiure unnāher danne vern.

157. 4 *dien = den.*

IV   15 C

Als ein swīn in einem sacke
vert mīn herze hin und dar.
wildeclīcher danne ein tracke
viht ez von mir zuo zir gar.

35   ez wil ūz durch ganze brust
von mir zuo der sælden rīchen:
alsō starc ist sīn gelust.
wē, wie lange sol daz wern,
sīt mīn lōn ist gēn der süezen
40   hiure unnāher danne vern!

V   16 C

'Nu hāt si doch schœne und ēre
Steimār, swazs an dir begāt,
ganzer tugende michels mēre,
aller sælden vollen rāt:
45   an ir līt der wunsch vil gar.'
wünschent alle, guoten liute,
daz ich wol gēn ir gevar.
ez gāt mir dur ganzen kern
daz mīn lōn ist gēn der süezen
50   hiure unnāher danne vern.

158

I   24 C (Bartsch XIX, 7)

Sumerzīt, ich fröwe mich dīn
daz ich mac beschouwen
eine süeze selderīn,
mīnes herzen frouwen.
5   eine dirne diu nāch krūte
gāt, die hān ich zeinem trūte
mir erkorn:
ich bin ir ze dienst erborn.
wart umbe dich,
10   swer verholne minne, der hüete sich.

41 *nv si hat* C.
42 *swazs = swaz si: swe* C.
48 'It pierces me to the marrow'.
158. 3 *selderīn* 'peasant', a derivative of *selde* 'peasant cottage'.

II 25 C

Si was mir den winter lanc
vor versperret leider:
nu nimt si ūf die heide ir ganc,
in des meien kleider,
15 dā si bluomen zeinem kranze
brichet, den si zuo dem tanze
tragen wil:
dā gekōse ich mit ir vil.
wart umbe dich,
20 swer verholne minne, der hüete sich.

III 26 C

Ich fröwe mich der lieben stunt
sō si gāt zem garten
und ir rōserōter munt
mich ir heizet warten:
25 sō wirt hōhe mir ze muote,
wan si ist ūz ir muoter huote
danne wol,
vor der ich mich hüeten sol.
wart umbe dich,
30 swer verholne minne, der hüete sich.

IV 27 C

Sīt daz ich mich hüeten sol
vor ir muoter lāge,
herzeliep, du tuo sō wol,
balde ez mit mir wāge.
35 brich den truz und al die huote,
wan mir ist des wol ze muote,
sol ich leben,
dir sī līp und guot gegeben.
wart umbe dich,
40 swer verholne minne, der hüete sich.

14 'on the flower-bedecked carpet of May'.
37 *vñ sol ich leben* C.

V   28 C

Steimār, hœhe dīnen muot
wirt dir diu vil hēre,
si ist sō hübesch und sō guot,
du hāst ir iemer ēre.
45 du bist an dem besten teile
der zer werlte fröiden heile
hœren sol:
des wirstu gewert dā wol.
wart umbe dich,
50 swer verholne minne, der hüete sich.

159

I   29 C (Bartsch XIX, 8)

Ein kneht der lac verborgen
bī einer dirne er slief
unz ūf den liehten morgen:
der hirte lūte rief
5 'wol ūf, lāz ūz die hert!'
des erschrac diu dirne   und ir geselle wert.

II   30 C

Daz strou daz muost er rūmen
und von der lieben varn.
er torste sich niht sūmen,
10 er nam si an den arn.
daz höi daz ob im lac
daz ersach diu reine   ūf fliegen in den tac.

III   31 C

Dā von si muoste erlachen,
ir sigen diu ougen zuo.
15 sō suoze kunde er machen
in dem morgen fruo
mit ir daz bettespil;
wer sach ān geræte   ie fröiden mē sō vil!

DER WILDE ALEXANDER

THE poet is given in MS. C the title *Der wilde Alexander*, in which the adjective *wild* probably means 'unsettled', 'wandering'. This, together with the title *meister* ascribed to him in MS. J, indicates that the poet was a wandering singer. Nothing is known of his life, but on linguistic and other grounds he is usually thought to have been writing in the last decades of the thirteenth century. His dialect is Alemannic. Apart from **160**, his best-known poem, he wrote didactic and religious verses, and poems on themes of *minne*, including a *Leich*.

160

I   30 J (KLD 1, V)

Hie bevorn dō wir kinder wāren
und diu zīt was in den jāren
daz wir liefen ūf die wisen
von jenen her wider ze disen,
5   dā wir under stunden
fīol vunden,
dā siht man nu rinder bisen.

II   31 J

Ich gedenke wol daz wir sāzen
in den bluomen unde māzen
10   welch diu schœneste möhte sīn.
dā schein unser kintlich schīn
mit dem niuwen kranze
zuo dem tanze.
alsus gēt diu zīt von hin.

III   32 J

15   Seht, dō liefe wir ertberen suochen
von der tannen zuo der buochen
über stoc unde über stein
der wīle daz diu sunne schein.
dō rief ein waltwīser
20   durch diu rīser
'wol dan, kinder, unde gēt hein!'

IV   33 J

Wir entfiengen alle māsen
gestern, dō wir ertberen lāsen;
daz was uns ein kintlich spil.
25   dō erhōrte wir so vil
unsern hirten ruofen
unde wuofen
'kinder, hie gēt slangen vil.'

V   34 J

Ez gienc ein kint in dem krūte
30   daz erschrac und rief vil lūte
'kinder, hie lief ein slang īn,
der beiz unser gfeterlīn;
daz ne heilet nimmer,
ez muoz immer
35   sūren unde unsælic sīn.'

VI   35 J

'Wol dan, gēt hin ūz dem walde!
unde enīlet ir niht balde,
iu geschiht als ich iu sage:
erwerbet ir niht bī dem tage
40   daz ir den walt rūmet,
ir versūmet
iuch und wirt iuwer vreuden klage.

VII   36 J

Wizzent ir daz vünf juncvrouwen
sich versūmten in den ouwen
45   unz der künic den sal beslōz?
ir klage unde ir schade was grōz;
wante die stocwarten
von in zarten
daz si stuonden kleider blōz.'

160. 22 'we were all covered with red spots. . .'.
32 *gfeterlīn* (Kraus): *pherierlin* J.
43 Cf. Matt. xxv. 1–13.
47 *stoc* = (1) 'stocks', (2) 'prison'. *stocwarte* probably here refers to the custodians of hell.

JOHANS HADLOUB
(HADLAUB)

THE poet, a citizen of Zürich, was probably born about 1280 and died before 1340. He is attested in 1302 when he bought a house in Zürich. He mentions in his poetry various patrons, including the Manesse family who made large collections of poems constituting *liederbuoch*, which probably formed part of the basis for MS. C, formerly loosely designated as the *Manessische Handschrift*.

He is the most prolific of the Swiss *Minnesänger*, 240 strophes being preserved in C. His poetry is a mixture of traditional themes and a more realistic vein, frequently combined in the same poem, as in **162**, **165**, and **166**. The poems in praise of autumn (already anticipated by Steinmar) and of harvest were to become a popular type. The poems show great metrical skill, particularly in the handling of internal rhyme.

161

I   24 C (Bartsch XXVII, 3)

Waz man wunnen hœrte und sach, dō voglīn schal
sō suoze hal   den sumer clār!
des man schœne frowen sach sich dicke ergān,
des werde man   gerne nāmen war.
5 wan swæriu kleit diu leiten si dō hin,
des man sach, wie wīplich wol si sint gestalt,
und manicvalt   ir lichten schīn:

II   25 C

Wan si burgen niht ir wunne in süezer zīt.
der winter gīt   kalt winde und snē,
10 dess ir antlüt nekil kelen bergent sint.
an hiuten lint   tuot winter wē.
ir hende wīz ouch dicke bergent si
und sint in dien stuben, des mans selten sicht:
wen tæte daz nicht   vil fröiden frī?

---

161. 10 *dess* = *des si*: *des* C.
'so that they cover their faces and necks and throats.'

III   26 C

15 Nieman mac die sumerzīt verklagen wol
wan der der sol   sīn liep umbvān:
dem ist winter liep, dur daz diu nacht ist lanc,
vür voglīn sanc,   vür schœnen plān.
mir wære ouch sō, tæte si gnāde mir:
20 noch tuot si recht als daz niemer sül irgān.
ūf lieben wān   diene ich doch ir.

IV   27 C

Ich kume in dem sinne selten icht vür si
daz ich ir frī   muge sanfte sīn.
merker und diu huote diu verderbent mich,
25 dur diu mīde ich   die frowen mīn.
ir wort diu snīdent, si gent scharpfen slac.
doch sende ich ir mīn herze und mīn triuwe gar,
swenne ich nit dar   selb komen mac.

V   28 C

Waz ich dur die merker und durch huote lān,
30 daz ich nit gān   sō dicke vür si!
daz si sīn verfluocht! ir zungen sint sō lanc,
ir hæler ganc   ist tugende frī.
si sehent umb sam diu katze nāch der mūs.
daz der tievel müeze ir aller pfleger sīn
35 und brechen in   ir ougen ūz!

162

I   39 C (Bartsch XXVII, 7)

Er muoz sīn ein wol berāten ēlich man
der hūs sol hān,   er müeze in sorgen stēn.
nōtic lidic man fröit sich doch mangen tac,
er sprichet 'ich mac   mich einen sanft begēn.'
5 ach, nōtic man, kumst du zer ē,
wan du kūme gewinnen macht muos unde brōt,
du kumst in nōt: hūssorge tuot sō wē.

22 *icht*: *nicht* C.

162. 1–2 'The married man with a household must be well provided, if he is not to be
in difficulties.'
4 'He says: "I can easily feed myself alone".'
5–7 'Alas, needy man, if you enter upon marriage, you will be plunged into distress, for you can only with difficulty acquire food and bread.'

II 40 C

Sō dich kint anvallent, sō gedenkest du
'war sol ich nū?   mīn nōt was ē sō grōz':
10 wan diu frāgent dicke wā brōt und kæse sī,
sō sitzt dā bī   diu muoter rātes blōz.
sō sprichet si 'meister, gib uns rāt':
sō gīst in dan Riuwental und Siuftenhein
und Sorgenrein   als der nicht anders hāt.

III 41 C

15 Sō spricht si dan 'ach daz ich ie kan zuo dir!
jān haben wir   den witte noch daz smalz,
noch daz fleisch, noch vische, pfeffer noch den wīn:
waz wolte ich dīn?   sōn hān wir niender salz.'
sō riuwetz ir: dā sint fröide ūz,
20 dā vāt frost und turst den hunger in daz hār
und zihent gar   oft in al dur daz hūs.

IV 42 C

Mich dunket daz hūssorge tüeje wē:
doch klage ich mē   daz mir mīn frowe tuot.
swenne ich für si gēn dur daz si grüeze mich,
25 sō kērt si sich   von mir, daz reine guot.
sō warte ich jæmerlīchen dar
unde stēn verdāht als ein ellender man,
der nicht enkan   und des nieman nimt war.

V 43 C

Daz si mich versēret hāt sō manic jār,
30 daz wolt ich gar   lieplīch vergeben ir,
gruozte si mich als man friunde grüezen sol:
sō tæte si wol.   si sündet sich an mir,
wan ir mīn triuwe wonet bī:
dā von solte si mich grüezen āne haz.
35 wan tuot si daz?   daz si iemer sælic sī!

13–14 *Riuwental* 'Vale of Grief'; *Siuftenhein* 'House of Sighs'; *Sorgenrein* 'Enclosure of Sorrows'. These allegorical names are reminiscent of Neidhart's punning
allusions to *Riuwental*; cf. the last verse of 126, in which he similarly complains of
household cares.
15 *kan = kam.*
20 'then frost and drought contend with hunger . . .'.
21 *zihent = ziehent.*

163

I　　　　　　　　　　　　　　　59 C (Bartsch XXVII, 14)

Ich wil ein warnen singen,
daz liep von liebe bringen
nū mac, die māze kunnen hān.
sus rāte ich dien ein scheiden,
5　　der ich nū hüete beiden:
der tac der wil sō schiere ūf gān.
des ich wunder sorgen hān,
wie ez uns noch irgange:
ir nāhen umbevange
10　　die wellent si sō kūme lān.

II　　　　　　　　　　　　　　　　　　　　60 C

In gibe dem herren die schulde;
ich weiz ir ungedulde
sō wol, si lāt in kūme varn.
er sol si lāzen weinen:
15　　der nacht ist noch sō kleinen,
er sol ez langer nicht ensparn.
nū bin ich aller fröiden arn:
ich vürchte mir sō sēre.
ez stāt umb līp und ēre:
20　　in kan ir [leider] nicht bewarn,

III　　　　　　　　　　　　　　　　　　61 C

Sin volgen mīnem rāte
und tuont si daz ze spāte,
owē ich bin mit in verlorn.
nū hœrent si doch wol mīn warnen:
25　　muoz ich ir minne erarnen
noch mē, daz ist mir leit und zorn.
owē daz ich wart erkorn,
daz ich wart ir wahtære.
noch wendent unser swære:
30　　den tac man kündet dur diu horn.

163. 11 *herren*: *herzen* C.
14 *er*: *d^s h^s re* C.
21 *danne* after *volgen* C.

164

I   62 C (Bartsch XXVII, 15)

Ich was dā ich sach
in ir swert zwēn dörper grīfen junge:
Ruodolf dā bigonde in zorne stetschen.
Chuonze dar zuo sprach
5 'nieman ist dem an mir ie gelunge:
ich hān dīnen zorn nit wan vür getschen.'
Ruodolf sprach 'du hāst Ellen gemeinet,
nāch der ich vil dicke hān geweinet:
hüet dīs lībes vor mir
10 an dem werde an sunnentage vor ir.
dīn schulde ist daz ir hulde gegen mir kleinet.'

II   63 C

Si swigen dar zuo,
daz manz verre vernam in kurzer stunde.
dar kam dörper vil mit grōzem schalle.
15 Ruodolf malch sīn chuo
und ruofte dien dien er guotes gunde:
'trinkint und sint mir bī hiute alle.
helf man im, sō helfent mir ouch sēre,
daz ich vor Ellen bejage hiute ēre.
20 ich wil Chuonzen slān
daz hunde in in mugen zem herzen gān:
ern gewirbt umb Ellen niemer mēre.'

III   64 C

'Wir sunz understān',
sprāchen zwēne der wægsten und der meier:
25 'bittent Chuonzen daz er Ellen abe lāze.'
'des mac niht ergān,
ich gab ir ein geiz und hundert eier
unde bin ir holt recht āne māze.'
'da vür sol dich Ruodolf vil wol mieten.'

164. 9–10 'Defend yourself against me in her presence in the meadow on Sunday.'
21 'so that dogs may get at his heart'.
29 *mieten* 'repay'.

30 'nu lānt hœren, waz wil er mir bieten?'
'zwō geize und ein huon.'
Chuonze sprach 'daz wil ich gerne tuon:
ich tete ie daz biderbe liute mir rieten.'

165

I   83 C (Bartsch XXVII, 20)

Herbst wil aber sīn lop niuwen:
er wil briuwen   manigen rāt,
wan daz stāt   dien sīnen ēren wol.
er wil manic her berāten
5   veizer brāten   unde wil
trachten vil   dar zuo si machen vol:
des sīn lop sich üeben sol.
niuwen wīn
trinkent si, derz hirne rüeret
10   und ouch vüeret   ir muot hō:
des si frō   danne alle müezen sīn.

II   84 C

Würste und hammen, guot geslechte
ouch in rechte   herbest birt.
dar zuo wirt   in noch sīs rātes mē:
15   ingwant bletze, term und magen
und ouch kragen   zuo der gluot.
herbest tuot   in baz danne sumer ē.
man slecht nū sō manig vē:
des vint man
20   guotiu krœse, houbt und vüeze
und ouch süeze   hirn und die.
herbst was ie   sīns rātes lobesan.

III   85 C

Nū sol ein wirt sīnen gesten
gebens besten,   des uns gīt
25   herbstes zīt   (sō hāt er wol getān):

165. 2 *briuwen*: here 'produce'.
4–5 'He will provide a great company with fat roasts . . .'.
21 *die* 'legs'.
24 *gebens* = *geben des*.

dess von rāte ūf müezen glosten.
swaz daz kosten   danne sül,
wirt, sō vül   si, daz si vollen hān.
ān klobwürste solt dus niht lān:
30   mangen buoc
gib in, dar zuo guote grieben;
des in lieben   herbest muoz.
wirt, nū tuoz: sō hānt si danne genuoc.

IV   86 C

Doch klage ich des sumers schœnc
35   und die dœne   wunnenclīch,
der sō rīch   ē was vil manic lant,
die die wilden vogel sungen,
daz si klungen,   daz der schal
suoze hal: des was uns fröide erkant.
40   die went œsen winters bant,
diu sō kalt
sint, daz heide und ouwe velwent
und ouch selwent   tage clār.
daz tuot bar   uns fröiden manicvalt.

V   87 C

45   Noch klage ich mīn meisten swære,
daz mich lære   trōstes ie
mīn frowe lie,   swie wē mir nāch ir was,
und si mich lāt sus verderben
unde werben   in der nōt,
50   daz der tōt   mir tæte līchte baz,
wan ez næme schiere ende daz.
sus lāt si
mich in langem ungemüete,
ald ir güete   wende ez noch,
55   wan ir doch   mīn triuwe wonet bī.

26 *dess = des si: des* C.
42 *daz = daz si.*
54 *ald*: here 'unless'.

166

I   99 C (Bartsch XXVII, 24)

Ir sult iuwer swenzel
(ēst erne zīt) krispen, dirne guot,
krenzel   machen ouch ūf die vīrtage.
swiem arbeit in erne
5   hāt, doch hāt man dā frœlīchen muot:
gerne   pfligt man dā sō lōser sage;
wan dar kumt sō   manig stolziu dirn und knappe
des man dō   wirt frō.
ir singet dan sō vil süezeclīche hō:
10   ouch ist [in] erne recht fröide ūf dem strō.

II   100 C

Heinlīchi mag enden
vil, der die zīnr frowen wol hān mac:
wenden   tuot sim des līcht senden pīn:
der aber frowen minnen
15   gert, der huote pfligt nacht unde tac,
gewinnen   wirt im dō līchte niemer schīn.
des bin ich bar   fröiden und vol sorgen,
wiez gevar,   wan dar
minne ouch ich dā mich huote frömdet gar:
20   frömde friunds nam ie sō kleine war.

III   101 C

Minne, dīn süez twingen
hāt betwungen mich in sūren pīn:
ringen   tuost du mich mit sender nōt.
du gīst mir ze herzen
25   süez ein wīp, der ich muoz frömde sīn:
smerzen   muoz mich daz unz ūf den tōt.
ir wunne gāt   sō suoze mir ze herzen,
ez verstāt   die getāt
sō wol, daz si sō mange wunne hāt:
30   des Minne mich von ir niht scheiden lāt.

166. 2 *ēst erne zīt* after *guot* C.
4 *swiem* = *swie man.*
12 *vil dˢ die han mag zinr frowen wol* C.
zīnr = *ze sinr.*
16 'will then perhaps never catch a glimpse of them'.
20 *frömde: frȫmdes* C.
22 *pīn: strit* C.

HEINRICH VON MEISSEN, VROUWENLOP

(FRAUENLOB)

HEINRICH VON MEISSEN was probably born about 1260 and died in 1318. The name *Vrouwenlop* may have been given him either on account of his *Leich* in praise of the Virgin, or for his championship of *vrouwe* against *wip* as in **168**. References in his work indicate that he was in the army of Rudolf of Habsburg in 1278, and that he was present at the ceremony in Prague in 1286, at which Wenceslas II became a knight. He spent some time in Carinthia and at North German courts. Legend has it that he founded the first school of *Meistersinger* in Mainz, but there is no direct evidence of this; he was in any case revered by the *Meistersinger* as one of their twelve masters.

His poetry abounds in metaphor and his style is richly ornamented, often in eccentric fashion. The metrical forms show a similar complication, with *Stollen* of six lines in **167** and **168**, and of seven in **169**.

167

J fol. 103 (Ettmüller 140)

Zwār wīp, sīt du der hōhsten wünne ein garte bist,
darin mit list
diu Minne ūz blicken touwet,
[unt dar in man schouwet]
5   der bluomen lust (ich hœr si sīn maget und doch gevrouwet),
durch vollen wunsch iu ist geworht ein kranz in wībes güete,
dā des gedanken snelle wirt gevangen mit.
wer kan den schrit
ūz herz in herzen arke?
10   jā du, Minne starke,
du blüemest wol der vrouwen sit ūz dem rīchen sarke,
dā prīs, dā lop nie wart volzalt in werender ēren vlüete.
ich muoz ein lieplich strāfen zern
dir, Minne, und doch kein wandel nern:
15   du soldest wern

167. 3 'Love looks forth from their glances with dewy freshness.'
13–14 'I must administer a gentle rebuke to you, Love, and yet not countenance what is reprehensible.'

dā wīp verhern
ir vriunt und leit durch liep beschern,
ir vīenden doch niht arges swern:
jā Minne, sprich: dā līt ein wē, daz gīt ein rīch gemüete.

168

38 C, J fol. 104 (Ettmüller 151)

Lob ich diu wīp, dannoch sint vrouwen ungelobet,
dā bī vürobet
der vrouwen prīs die beide
mit des lobes kleide.
5 sint vrouwen wīp, wīp vrouwen nicht? jā durch liep durch leide!
wīp ist ein name, der al ir art mit eime namen decket.
seht unwīp under wīben ouch! daz prüeve ein man;
wer merken kan,
der volge mīner witze.
10 nāch des rechtes spitze,
ē daz ein wīp mit berender wē vrouwen stuol besitze,
wie solde ir name geheizen sīn ob sich ir wandel wecket?
man sinne ez ūz, man sinne ez īn,
kein vrouwe mac sie nicht gesīn;
15 ir nemelich pīn
muoz in den schrīn
dā sich der vrouwen wanc unfīn
ouch birget nach dem künden mīn:
in beiden wirt ein wandelname 'unwīp' dar ūf gestecket.

169

J fol. 110 (Ettmüller 313)

Gefīolierte blüete kunst,
dīnes brunnen dunst
unde dīn gerœset flammenrīche brunst

---

168. Text according to J unless noted.
  4 Cf. **130** and **151.** 24.
  6 *wīp* with C: *vrouwe* J. *namen: nennen* J.
  7 As C: *vnwib sint vnder vrouwen ouch* J.
  10 'in strict accordance with right'.
   11 *mit berender wē*: 'with pangs of childbirth'; this refers to the previous poem in the same cycle in which the poet characterizes *maget* as virgin, *wīp* as married woman, *vrouwe* as one who has borne a child.

die hete wurzelhaftez obez;
5 gewidemet in dem boume künste rīches lobes
hielt wipfels gunst
sīn list, durchliljet kurc.

durchsternet was sīnes sinnes himel,
glanz als ein vimel,
10 durchkernet lūter golt nach wunsches stimel
was al sīn blüete, geveimet ūf lob,
gevult ūf margarīten nicht ze kleine unde grob;
sīnes silbers schimel
gab gimmen velsenschurc.

15 ach kunst ist tōt! nu klage, armōnīe,
planēten tirmen klage nicht verzīe,
pōlus, jāmers drīe.

gnāde im süeze trinitāt,
maget reine, entfāt,
20 ich meine Conrāt
den helt von Wirzeburc.

169. 4 *wurzelhaftez*: *wortelhaftez* J.
  6 *hielt*: *hielt er* J.
  15 *myt myr* after *klage* J.

Translation: 'Blossoming of art, violet-flowered, the gushing forth of your
fountain, and your rosy flaming ardour bore soundly-rooted fruit; endowed in
the tree of art with rich praise, his skill, ornamented with choice lilies, retained the
favour of the tree-top. The heaven of his thought was set with stars, shining with
radiance; all his blossom was as solid gold to the core as the heart could desire,
refined to win acclaim, filled with pearls neither too small or coarse; the brilliance of
his silver gave rock-hardness to his gems. Alas, art is dead! now lament harmony,
creation of the planets, and heaven, do not cease to bewail the three-fold grief. Have
mercy on him blessed Trinity, pure Maiden, receive him; Konrad I mean, the renowned poet of Würzburg.'

NOTES

Metrical Abbreviations

In the schematic metrical patterns in the Notes, the abbreviations *mv*, *wv*, *k*, *s* are used for the respective cadences (see pp. xx–xxi). A denotes anacrusis, lower-case letters the rhyme, x a rhymeless line. Thus the line

$$\overset{\times}{\text{Ich}} \left| \overset{/}{\text{saz}} \overset{\times}{\text{ūf}} \right| \overset{/}{\text{eime}} \overset{\times}{} \left| \overset{/}{\text{stei}} \overset{\backslash}{\text{ne}} \right.$$

is rendered schematically as: A 4 *k* a.
Exact repetition of a *Stollen* is indicated by the sign : ‖.

ANONYMOUS

I

An early example of the woman's complaint. The German is probably the original and the Latin an imitation, following the rules of German metre and containing awkward phrases (*silva nobilis, antiquus meus amicus*) necessitated by the metrical pattern. The first line is an example of a nature introduction. The initial position of the verb *gruonet* represents an archaic type of word-order, largely superseded even in OHG. Archaic too are the simple paratactical construction, the assonating rhymes in ll. 9 and 10, and the accumulation of unstressed syllables in ll. 8–10.

Metrical form

 line 8 A 4 *mv* (rhymes with preceding Latin line)
   4 *k* a
   4 *k* a
  A 4 *k* b
  A 4 *k* b

2

This poem appears to be an accompaniment to a circular dance (MHG *reige reie*), and if so is the only relic of its kind in German. The lack of anacrusis, the high proportion of strong beats without accompanying unstressed syllables mark the dancing rhythm strongly. The rhyme *umbe* : *megede*, in which the final vowel forms the rhyming link, is of a kind common in twelfth-century works but not found in the *Minnesang*. The free metrical treatment probably indicates an early date.

Metrical form

 4 *k* a
 4 *k* a
 4 *mv* b
 4 *mv* b

3

This poem has been the object of much speculation. The difficulty of interpretation is caused by the MS. reading *chunich*, with *chünegin* above it. Three
interpretations have been suggested for the reading *chunich*:

1. The English King Richard Coeur de Lion, known in Germany because
of his imprisonment at Dürenstein.
2. Oswalt, seventh-century King of Northumbria. The legend is attested
only in versions of the fifteenth and sixteenth centuries. Naumann (*Reallexi-
kon*, III, 256*b*) suggests that this strophe is a survival from a lost Oswalt epic,
written in a similar verse-form to the epic *Salman und Morolf*.
3. Christ, King of Heaven (*Engellant*). This is improbable, chiefly because
the poem is preserved in the MS. amid a group of secular love poems.

Most editors since Lachmann have preferred to adopt the reading *chünegin*,
taking it to refer to Eleanor of Poitou who became Queen of England in 1154
and who was famous for her beauty and her patronage of the arts. She is
referred to in a Latin poem of the *Carmina Burana* (no. 78) in which the
author praises his lady's beauty even above hers. It is therefore likely that
she should be the subject of the German poem.

The basic formula of the poem ('I would give all the world in exchange for
her love') is found in many varying forms in the courtly poetry of France and
Germany, and elsewhere.

Metrical form

    4 *mv* a
    4 *mv* a
    4 *k* b
    4 *mv* x
    4 *k* b

Signs of early date are the rhyme *darben*: *arme*, and the lack of anacrusis.

The strophe form of *Salman und Morolf* is similar, except that normally
ll. 3 and 5 are *mv*, and line 4 is 4 *k* x.

4

This poem, ascribed in the MSS. to two poets of doubtful authenticity, is an
early example of the woman's complaint. *Rōse*, *vogellīn*, and *walt* are part of
the stylized picture of nature, which is usually closely associated with emotion,
as in this example, in which *rōse* (a frequent symbol of love) is linked with
minne, and *sumerwunne* is virtually identical with the joys of love. The use
of *geselle* and *man* for 'lover' is an archaic feature (cf. **1**, **2**, **5**, and **7**), as are
also the assonating rhymes.

Metrical form (similar to Der von Kürenberc **10**)

A 4 *k*+4 *s* a
4 *k*+4 *s* a
4 *s* x
A 4 *k*+4 *s* b
A 4 *k*+4 *mv* b

5 and 6

These two poems, similar in content and form, and therefore probably by the same poet, are included by MS. C among the poems ascribed to Dietmar. They are, however, much more archaic than the rest of Dietmar, and the MS. tradition also suggests that they are wrongly ascribed to him. MSS. B and C have an otherwise identical run of sixteen strophes ascribed to Dietmar, within which MS. C inserts these two poems. C also adds to the common tradition a further run of strophes which are undoubtedly not by Dietmar. The fact that these two poems are an insertion in the tradition common to B and C and that they are archaic in character, suggest that they have been falsely ascribed to Dietmar. They are therefore best placed among the anonymous poems.

Both these poems are typical examples of the *Frauenklage*: in the first the woman complains in a general way of envious rivals, in the second she addresses her lover directly, exhorting him to renounce other women. In both the central idea is reinforced by a comparison with external nature which reflects the speaker's feelings. In **6** this takes the form of a nature introduction. In **5** the falcon's untrammelled flight is compared to the lady's free choice of a lover, in **6** the desolation of the declining year forms a parallel to the lady's grief and the dimming of her eyes with tears. In both the comparison is explicitly stated (**5**. 9; **6**. 4). A stylistic feature common to both poems is repetition, either verbal as in *warte* in ll. 2 and 3 of **5**, or the repetition of the same thought, varied by the use of a synonym: in **5** *erkiusest, erkōs* beside *erwelton*, in **6** *sich gelouben* beside *mīden*. Both poems have the rhyme *getān: man*.

The image of the falcon is elsewhere associated with the idea of love (cf. **15**). The theme of envious rivals is closely paralleled in **33**.

Metrical form

5			6	
A 4 *k* a	A 4 *k* f		A 4 *k* a	A 4 *mv* f
A 4 *k* a	A 4 *k* f		A 4 *k* a	A 4 *mv* f
A 4 *k* b	A 4 *mv* g		A 4 *mv* b	
A 4 *k* b	A 5 *mv* g		4 *mv* b	
A 4 *mv* c			4 *k* c	
A 4 *mv* c			A 4 *k* c	
A 4 *k* d			A 4 *k* d	
A 4 *k* d			A 4 *k* d	
4 *mv* e			A 4 *k* e	
A 4 *mv* e			A 4 *k* e	

The virtually exclusive use of assonating rhymes is unlike Dietmar. The longer last line of **5** serves to mark the end with greater finality.

7

This poem, ascribed in A to Walther von Mezze, is similar to **6** but is probably of later date. In both poems the desolation of winter reflects the speaker's mood, but here the comparison is not explicitly made. A new theme is introduced, that of the lover's youthful inexperience, which makes him a prey to faithless women.

Metrical form

A 4 *k*+4 *mv* a
A 4 *k*+4 *mv* a
A 4 *k*+4 *mv* b
A 4 *k*+4 *mv* b
A 4 *k*+4 *mv* c
A 4 *k*+4 *mv* c (MFU: A 4 *k*+5 *mv* c)

8

Preserved in the text of a Latin love letter, purporting to be by a girl, among a collection of model letters composed by Werinher von Tegernsee, in a MS. formerly in the monastery of Tegernsee. The thought of the poem is already implicit in the letter, e.g. 'ad te . . . quem teneo medullis cordis inclusum' and 'tu cordis mei intima fortiter penetrasti' (for the complete Latin text, cf. MF, p. 318). The two central motifs, that of the opening formula and the image of the key of the heart, are of such wide currency in the *Volkslied* and elsewhere that it is not necessary to search for exact parallels; they could well be spontaneous creations.

Metrical form

2 *mv* a+2 *mv* a
4 *mv* a
4 *k* b
4 *k* b
A 4 *mv* a
A 4 *mv* a

The strophe is skilfully constructed. Each pair of lines corresponds to a division in the thought. Lines 3 and 4 correspond exactly to each other by having two strong stresses together at the beginning of the line (*du bíst* and *ín mínem*).

9

This is (apart from one strophe in the *Carmina Burana*) probably the earliest extant example of the dawn song in Germany. Preserved only in MS. C among a run of strophes ascribed to Dietmar, it is unlike those poems which can be ascribed to him with relative certainty. One of the most marked features of genuine Dietmar is the loose connexion between related strophes; they are variations on a theme rather than a closely integrated whole. They are centrifugal, whereas here the construction is progressive and the parts are clearly subordinated to the whole which is of predominant importance.

This poem contains the basic elements of the dawn song in simple and concise form: the natural setting, the warning of dawn's approach in the song of the bird, the sorrowful parting of the lovers. The motif of the watchman who wakes the lovers and the refrain, which are a sign of Romance influence, are absent.

The technical structure is skilful and shows none of the archaic features found in Dietmar. The three strophes correspond to the three phases of the action.

Metrical form

A 4 *k* a (no anacrusis in I)
A 4 *k* a
A 4 *mv* b (no anacrusis in II)
A 5 *mv* b (no anacrusis in II)

There is a similar final lengthening in 5.

DER VON KÜRENBERC

Metre

Each first half of every line is 4 *k* or 4 *mv* (with exception of **17**. 3 which is 4 *s*). In all the *Männerstrophen* the second half of each line is 4 *s* except in the last half-line of the strophe where it is 4 *mv*. This same pattern is also found in the following *Frauenstrophen*: **14** and the first strophes of **10** and **15**.

In all the other *Frauenstrophen* the second and fourth half-lines are 4 *k*, and the last half-line of each strophe is 4 *mv* except in **11** where it appears to be 4 *s*. The metrical pattern of **10** is similar to that of Anonymous **4**.

10

These two strophes appear in MS. C at the beginning of the sequence of *Frauenstrophen*, and must therefore have been understood as such. Had the second strophe been taken as spoken by a man, as is almost certainly the case, it would no doubt have been placed at the end among the other *Männerstrophen*. Such a misunderstanding is undoubtedly due to the corrupt text of this poem, which therefore served to preserve the original connexion between the two strophes intact.

Some editors have in fact preferred to interpret both strophes as spoken by a woman, but this gives a much less satisfactory sense. Kraus, for instance (MF³⁰), reverses the order of the two strophes, taking that beginning with l. 10 to contain the woman's part of the conversation between the lovers referred to in ll. 8–9. It is, however, much more likely that the MS. preserves the original order and that the poem is an example of the *Wechsel*, in the particular form which contains an address to a messenger.

I begins with a general dictum which announces the theme of the whole poem (cf. also **11** and **20**). The lady then addresses her admonition to her lover through the messenger. II is the man's reply, rejecting thoughts of parting. The two strophes are clearly linked by the fact that the second is an answer to the first, by the verbal echoes (*man, manst*, probably also *scheiden*), and by the metrical form. They are not, however, closely integrated in other respects, and represent an early stage in the development from the single strophe to a more complex whole.

11, 13, 14, 16

These single *Frauenstrophen* are best taken together since there are marked similarities between them. They are also closely related to **10** and **15** which are here treated separately because of the particular problems they present. All the *Frauenstrophen* of Der von Kürenberc apart from **12**, can in fact be regarded as examples of the woman's complaint. In them the poet treats the theme of the sorrowful aspects of love from slightly differing points of view.

In the early anonymous poems the woman complains of her lover's infidelity (**1**), or of jealous rivals who have robbed her of his love (**5, 6, 7**). Here, in **11** and **16**, a new but related theme is introduced, that of the slandering ill-wishers who destroy the relationship between the lovers: in **11** the *merker*, in **16** the *lugenære*. They correspond to the *lauzengiers* of the Provençal poets.

No. **11** begins with a general dictum announcing the theme and is in this respect like **10** and **20**. In **13** and **16** the sorrows of love are seen rather from within, without reference to external causes. No. **13** is a delicate portrayal of the woman's state of mind, induced by the thought of the knight; **14** is a veiled, indirect expression of hopeless love.

12

These two strophes are separated in the MS. but they undoubtedly belong together as a loosely connected dialogue, the second strophe replying to the theme of the first. Their disruption can be explained by the separation of *Frauenstrophen* and *Männerstrophen* in the MS. The first strophe is probably addressed to a messenger. The poet's indirect reference to himself in l. 5 is paralleled by similar instances in other poets, e.g. Neidhart who frequently mentions himself in the third person (cf. **122–5**).

Both speakers are imperious in the expression of their sentiments. The lady's dominant role is unlike that in the early *Minnesang*, and is probably explained by the knight's indirect praise of himself: his rejection of the lady's commands, however imperious, is a sign of his superiority. The poet is described as singing his verses to music, as was customary in the *Minnesang*, though few of the tunes have survived.

13, 14. See note on **11.**

15

This is the most famous of Der von Kürenberc's poems, and one for which many widely differing interpretations have been proposed. Discussion has turned chiefly on the following points: is the poem to be interpreted literally (the loss of a real falcon) or symbolically (the falcon as symbol of the lover)? Is the speaker the same in both strophes, or is the poem an example of a dialogue, the first strophe being spoken by the man, the second by the woman (since only the second has formally the characteristics of a *Frauenstrophe*)? Thirdly, do the *sīdīne riemen* of the second strophe and the description of the bird's plumage as *alrōt guldīn* indicate new additions to the bird's adornment since he flew away? If they are interpreted as such, the further assumption has been made (e.g. by Kraus, MFU, p. 27) that they are the signs of a new amorous bondage.

The most convincing is undoubtedly the symbolic interpretation which is supported by the woman's plea in the last line: may God unite those who love each other. This would be entirely out of place if the poem were intended literally. There are ample parallels for the symbol of the falcon representing the lover in the poetry of different languages, for instance in Kriemhild's dream in the *Nibelungenlied* (strophe XIII) or in the words of Juliet in Shakespeare's *Romeo and Juliet*, II. ii (tassel = terzel, male falcon):

> O' for a falconer's voice,
> To lure this tassel-gentle back again.

Once the symbolic interpretation is accepted, it is clear that the speaker must be the same in both strophes. The woman is lamenting the loss of her lover: in the first strophe she describes how after she has tamed the falcon to her liking, he flies away; in the second she sees him flying free beyond her reach and utters the wish that lovers may be united.

The best analysis of the poem is that of Wapnewski (*Euphorion*, 53, 1959, pp. 1–20). He examines the poem afresh in the light of technical terms of falconry and is able by this means to prove conclusively the correctness of the symbolic interpretation of the poem as two *Frauenstrophen*. Thus *floug in anderiu lant* is a technical expression, denoting the return to a wild state and the escape from captivity (here applied to the man leaving the service of the lady). The *sīdīne riemen* of l. 12 can only denote the jesses which were attached to the legs of the falcon in the initial stages of training and remained there permanently, whether the bird was at rest or in flight. This disposes of the suggestion that they are the signs of a new amorous bondage. They are simply mentioned, together with the golden sheen of the plumage, as a proof that the lady recognizes the falcon as the one she had herself tamed and adorned.

That this interpretation is the correct one is borne out by the strict parallelism in the construction of the two strophes, a statement in I being balanced by a similar or contrasting statement in the same position in II. Thus to ll. 2–3 describing the taming of the falcon, corresponds the mention of the jesses as the sign of that taming in ll. 11–12; to the description of the adornment of the plumage in ll. 5–6 corresponds the statement of ll. 13–14: *und was im sīn gevidere alrōt guldīn.* There is a parallelism by use of contrast in the first and last long lines of each strophe: in ll. 1–2 the falcon is tame, in ll. 9–10 he is flying free; in ll. 7–8 the speaker describes how the falcon flies away, and in ll. 15–16, she expresses the veiled wish that they may be reunited.

17–20

The single *Männerstrophen* depict a range of feeling. Just as there are two different types of woman in the *Frauenstrophen*, so here there are two differing attitudes on the part of the man: the proud assertion of **20** contrasts with the submissive note of **19**. Nos. **18** and **19** imply the presence of hostile onlookers (more expressly referred to in **11** and **16**): thus **18** is an injunction to secrecy, so that no one will discover the relationship between the lovers, and in **19** the man is only able to address his suit to the lady through the messenger, lest he should injure her reputation. For the first time, in Der von Kürenberc, the love relationship is set against a social background.

There are further instances of Der von Kürenberc's characteristic indirect mode of expression: in **17** the subtly veiled praise of the knight and the lady, in **20** the disguised reference to the poet himself as the *ritter*.

DIETMAR VON AIST

21

These three strophes clearly belong together thematically although they do not constitute an integrated poem in the modern sense. They represent a type characteristic of Dietmar in which two of the three strophes (here I and II) form a more closely related unit, and the third is more loosely connected with them. All the strophes treat the theme of the unhappiness of love: the first is spoken by the woman and is an example of the *Frauenklage*; the second is a dialogue between the lovers which takes up the theme of the first; the third is spoken by the man.

Metrical form

I   4 *mv*+4 *mv* a
     4 *wv*+4 *mv* a
     4 *wv* b+4 *wv* b+2 *wv* c
     4 *mv*+2 *wv* c

II A 4 *wv*+4 *mv* a
     4 *wv*+4 *mv* a
     4 *wv* b+4 *wv* b+2 *wv* c
     4 *mv*+2 *wv* c

III A 4 *mv*+4 *mv* a
    A 4 *wv*+4 *mv* a
     4 *mv* b+4 *mv* b+2 *wv* c
    A 4 *mv*+2 *wv* c

The last half line of each strophe and the preceding short line which corresponds to it are analysed differently as follows: Rathke, 2 stresses (*in mīnem*
muote); Kraus (MFU), 3 *k* plus a rest equivalent to one foot (*in mīnem*
muote ∧); Heusler, 4 *k* (*in mīnem muote*). In each strophe the rhymes are
differentiated as follows: in I and II pure rhyme at the end of the line is combined with an impure internal rhyme in the third line (*schœne:kœme*;
geliebe:schieden); in III impure end rhyme is combined with a pure internal
rhyme in l. 3.

22

As in **21** the first two strophes are more closely connected, the second being
a reply to the first. Like **10** they are an example of a *Wechsel*, here in the form
of an address through a messenger. All three strophes are concerned with the
same central theme—the sufferings of love. I is the man's address to the
messenger, II the lady's reply, III her reflection on the difficulties of her
position. The lovers' enforced separation suggests the familiar motif of ill-
wishers; this is made clear in III in which the lady's complaint implies hostile
criticism from without.

Metrical form

```
 I    4 k+4 k a
     A 4 mv+4 k a
       4 k b
     A 4 k b
     A 4 mv c
       5 mv c

II   A 4 k+4 k a
     A 4 mv+4 k a
       4 mv b
     A 4 mv b
     A 4 mv c
     A 5 mv c

III    4 mv+4 k a
     A 4 mv   4 k a
       4 mv b
     A 4 mv b
     A 4 mv c
       5 mv c
```

As in **21** the rhymes are skilfully disposed: I has two pairs of assonating
rhymes, followed by a pair of pure rhymes; II has three pairs of pure rhymes,
and in III there is a pair of assonating rhymes, followed by two pairs of pure
rhymes. For the lengthening of the final line to five beats cf. **5**.

23

It is not certain whether both strophes are spoken by the man, or whether the first is to be ascribed to the lady, making the poem an example of the *Wechsel*. The first strophe begins with a nature description of a conventional kind, which has symbolic significance. The awakening of nature in spring brings hope. Strophe II contains an indirect plea to the lady to fulfil the man's desires, since his long service of her has made him more worthy to be rewarded. If she grants his request, she will have acted well—the plea is thus reinforced by subtle flattery of the lady. The metrical pattern is much more straightforward than that of **21** or **22**. Each half-line is 4 *mv*, and all the rhymes are pure. There is anacrusis in each line except the last.

24

These two strophes form a *Wechsel*: they are both concerned with the same theme from the point of view of the man and woman respectively. The first strophe, like the corresponding one of **23**, begins with a three-line natural description. The bird singing in the lime tree at the forest edge recalls memories of a former happy encounter in a similar setting, and the flowers at their meeting-place remind the lover of the lady. As in **23** the fourth line connects the natural description with the emotion of the speaker.

The second strophe expresses the lady's longing for the man. Here again natural objects have symbolic significance: the flowers and birds of ll. 15–16 are closely linked to joy in love and separation from them is synonymous with grief. The metrical scheme is the same as that of **23**, except that here there is anacrusis only in the last two long lines of I and the first of II.

MEINLOH VON SEVELINGEN

Metrical Form

As in Der von Kürenberc and Dietmar, the basic unit remains the eight-beat Germanic long line, divided into two halves, and the strophic structure is uncomplicated. There is thus apparently no Romance influence on the form. There are three strophe patterns: the simplest is that of **30** (six long lines); there is secondly that of **26** (eight long lines with a half-line *Waise* inserted between the two last), and thirdly that of the remaining strophes (six long lines with a half-line *Waise* inserted between the two last).

In all, the basic pattern of the long line is the same: 4 *k* in the first half, 4 *mv* in the second half. There are occasional examples of *Kadenzentausch* (Heusler's term), i.e. a substitution of different cadences, and a sign of early date. Thus in **29**, the third long line is 4 *k* in the first half, 4 *s* in the second half, and in **25**, **26**, and **28** the first half of the third long line is 4 *mv*. Anacrusis is present, except in **25**. 1; **26**. 9, 16; **27**. 12; **28**. 5; **29**. 12; **30**. 5; **31**. 11; **32**. 11; **33**. 9, **34**. 3, 11.

25, 26, 27, 29, 31, 34

These single *Männerstrophen* are similar in content and style. They show the new courtly conception of *minne*, already hinted at to some extent in Der von Kürenberc and Dietmar, but only here fully expressed for the first time. The lady is the pattern of courtly perfection; this idea is expressed in a variety of epithets of a conventional nature: *edel, liep, schœne, biderbe, guot, in rehter mâze gemeit, der besten eine*, or descriptive phrases such as the following: *ich gesach mit mînen ougen nie baz gebâren ein wîp, an ir ist anders wandels niht, si ist sælic zallen êren, der besten tugende pfliget ir lîp*. Her fame has spread abroad and has determined the lover to seek her out. His attitude is one of humble submission, expressed in the concept of service (*dienen, dienest*). The lady has absolute sway over him (**26.** 15–17). There is an instance of the hyperbole characteristic of the topoi of courtly love in **31**: were he to die in her service, he would serve her again in another life. The bestowal of her love would confer a unique distinction (**25.** 7). Love has an all-powerful effect, possessing the senses completely (**27.** 9–10). It brings sorrow, which only the lady can avert (**29.** 3–6). All these common motifs of courtly love can be paralleled in the poetry of the troubadours; some, for instance the effects of love, are found in Ovid.

In contrast with these courtly motifs is the unambiguous reference to the reward expected by the lover: *nâhe bî geligen* (**26**, cf. also **30.** 9 and **34.** 12–13). **27** and **34** are examples of the *Botenlied*. Only one of the poems begins with a nature introduction (**34**): as is usual, summer symbolizes joy.

28

This poem is one of three gnomic strophes grouped together as nos. 4, 5, and 6 in BC (4 and 5 are omitted here). All three deal with the rules of behaviour to be observed in the service of love: strophe 4 describes the conduct appropriate to win the favour of good women, strophe 5 the necessity for secrecy, strophe 6 treats the theme of the *merkære*, the watchful critics intent on hindering the relationship between the lovers. Speedy action and deception are the necessary counter-measures.

30, 32, 33

The *Frauenstrophen* are in certain respects more akin to those of the early period than the more courtly *Männerstrophen*. In none of them is the lady the unattainable figure of the later poets, but is submissive to the man. In all three strophes she clearly expresses her devotion to the lover, and her determination to be faithful to him, in spite of the watchers and her rivals. **33** has a certain similarity to the early *Frauenklagen* which lament the loss of love through the fault of jealous rivals (see Anonymous **5**, **6**, and **7**). There is even close verbal similarity between the opening of **33** and ll. 10–12 of **5**. The tone of the poem is, however, different. Whereas the earlier poems are all instances of the tragic lament at the loss of love, here there is a triumphant assertion of superiority over the rivals, who have failed to win the man's love.

There is an admixture of courtly elements in the vocabulary: *mīn muot sol aber hōhe stān, trūren, mīnes herzen leit*, and in the idea that the excellent qualities of the man necessarily inspire love (cf. the same motif applied to the woman in **25**).

KAISER HEINRICH

35

This poem is skilfully constructed, both in subject-matter and form. The first strophe forms an introduction, with the theme of enforced separation in the first four lines, and that of the indirect greeting to the lady through poetry in the last three lines. The next three strophes all express the contrast between the emptiness of worldly power, and the happiness of love. In each case the poet appears to speak as one with expectations of the highest power, rather than as one already in possession of it: thus it is as if vast dominions were his, when he is with the lady (ll. 8–9); he would rather renounce his claim to the crown than renounce his love (l. 21), and could enjoy happiness in love, even were the crown never to be his (ll. 22–24). *Diu rīch und diu lant* (l. 8) is an apt description of the imperial domains, and *krōne* probably refers to the imperial crown. This perhaps indicates that the poem was composed before 1191, when Heinrich was crowned Emperor (he had been crowned king of Germany in 1169). The phrase *ze āhte und ze banne* is also appropriate to the idea of power which underlies the poem.

The poem contains several of the recurring ideas of the *Minnesang*: the poet hints that he is separated from the lady against his will, no doubt by the conventions of society, but he has no intention of renouncing her (*vermīden*), and vows devotion to his life's end. Love causes *senden kumber* (this or similar designations for the pains of love are very common). His poetry brings joy to others (this is the significance of l. 27) and with the loss of her his art, which is his greatest comfort, would be lost too. With the expression of this idea the poem returns to the theme of *gesanc* with which it begins.

Metrical form (the first instance of a tripartite structure)

```
 I  A 4 wv a ⎞
    A 4 mv b ⎠ :‖
    A 4 mv c
    A 4 mv c
    A 5 mv c

II  A 4 mv a ⎞
    A 4 mv b ⎠ :‖
    A 4 mv c
    A 4 mv c
    A 5 mv c
```

III and IV A 4 *wv* a ⎱ :‖
 A 4 *mv* b ⎰

A 4 *wv* c
A 4 *wv* c
A 5 *wv* c

There are feet with two unstressed syllables (e.g. ge|sange die | süezen), or even with three (*daz ich* | *si von* | *munde rehte* | *mohte* | *grüezen*). Kraus (MF[30]) removes all accumulations of three unstressed syllables by transpositions, contractions, and omissions, but it is preferable not to tamper with the text for metrical reasons. All the rhymes are pure, with the exception of *undertān*: *man*. The rhyme *enmac*:*tac* in I beside *tac*:*mac* in IV is probably a deliberate device to bind the beginning and the end of the poem together.

36

This poem is a *Wechsel*, with the first strophe giving the man's reflections on his love, the second the lady's. The strophes are linked only by the metrical form and the similar sentiments in each: the fulfilment of love (ll. 3–5 and l. 14); the man's devotion (ll. 7–10) is paralleled by the lady's assertion in ll. 19–20. There is the additional motif of jealous rivals (cf. **5** and **33**), and that of the opening formula, which has similarities to **35**. II and IV.

Metrical form

A 4 *k* a+4 *s* b:‖

A 4 *k* c+4 *s* d
A 4 *k* +4 *k* c
A 4 *k* +4 *s* d

The basic unit is the eight-beat Germanic long line throughout, but none the less the *Abgesang* is differentiated from the *Aufgesang* by the following means: a different total of lines, the substitution of a different cadence in l. 8, and the different disposition of rhyme. There is a balance between the long line with end-rhyme, and that with internal rhyme, showing the relative independence of the half-line.

37

These two strophes, bound together by the same metrical form and the similarity of sentiment in each, are somewhat problematical. The difficulty arises from the use of *geselle* in l. 10. Except in rare instances, this word is used only of the man, and this might mean that the lady is speaking in both strophes. It is, however, more likely that the poem is a *Wechsel*, with the lady speaking in I and the man in II. There is little other internal evidence; the phrase *daz ich ie bī dir gelac* could be spoken by either man or woman, and *holt* could refer to either, but the phrase *du zierest mīne sinne* is more likely to refer to the refining influence of the lady on the man.

Metrical form

> 4 *k* a+4 *s* b
> A 4 *k* a+4 *s* b

> (A) 4 *k* +4 *s* c (no anacrusis in I)
> A 4 *k* d
> A 4 *k* d+4 *s* c

The rhyme cddc in the *Abgesang* is the first instance of an enclosing rhyme.

HEINRICH VON VELDEKE

38, 39

These two poems, closely connected in theme and expression, present the same situation from the point of view of the man and lady respectively, and are, as it were, an extension of the *Wechsel*. In **38** the poet speaks directly in the first person, in **39** the lady is presented as expressing her thoughts as if in a monologue. Both poems begin with a reference to the reawakening of spring, with a significant difference which sets the tone of each: in **38** the poet contrasts his own unhappy state with that of nature, whereas in **39** the lady affirms her joy in spring, which is not to be shaken by the injurious behaviour of another (*deheinen bōsen cranc*). The central point at issue is the standard of courtly behaviour expected of a lover, of which the man, by his own confession and the lady's indictment, has fallen short. This infringement of the code is expressed by the use of the terms *dump* (**38.** 7, 30; **39.** 17), *dumpheit* (**38.** 14, 24; **39.** 18), *dorperlīke* (**39.** 22), and the phrase *ūter māten* (**38.** 31). The positive ideal is contained in the words *hovesch* (the opposite of *dorperlīk*) and *wīsheit* (**38.** 25), which is contrasted with *dumpheit*. Other ideas common in the courtly lyric are the praise of the lady as a paragon of beauty and virtue, the conception of love as a service (**39.** 10), love as dispossessing a man of his senses (**38.** 19-20). These two poems show clearly the sovereign position of the lady in the courtly lyric, and her role as guardian of standards of behaviour. The concluding lines of **39**, with their proverbial ring, are similar to the aphoristic opening lines of Der von Kürenberc **10**, **11**, and **20**.

Metrical form

> **38. I** 4 *wv* a ⎫
> 4 *wv* a ⎬ :‖
> 4 *mv* b ⎭

> A 4 *mv* b
> 4 *wv* a
> 4 *mv* a

The other strophes are identical except in the different placing of anacrusis.

39. I 4 *mv* a ⎫
      4 *mv* b ⎭ :‖

  A 4 *mv* b
  A 4 *mv* a
  A 4 *mv* b
  A 4 *mv* a

In II, III, IV, and V anacrusis is differently placed, and ll. 1, 3, 6, and 8 are *wv*.

40

This poem shows that the Tristan story was so well known that a reference to it would be immediately intelligible. The poet uses the comparison with Tristan to stress his unparalleled love: Tristan's love was induced by the love potion, whereas the poet's love is not only voluntary, but greater, and therefore deserves a response. The idea that the love potion compels involuntary love is probably an original feature of the story, since it is found in the versions of Béroul (*The Romance of Tristan*, ed. Ewert, ll. 1384 and 1412 ff.), and in those of Eilhart and Gottfried.

In Eilhart's poem, probably composed about 1170, but only preserved in complete form in a fifteenth-century version, Marke learns after the lovers' death of the force of the potion:

> daz hēte gemachit ein trang,
> daz sie sich āne iren dang
> minnetin alsō sēre.
> (Eilhart von Oberge, ed. F. Lichtenstein, 9470 ff.)

Gottfried's description is similar:

> mit sweme sin ieman getranc,
> den muoser ane sinen danc
> vor allen dingen meinen
> und er da wider in einen.
> (*Tristan und Isold*, ed. F. Ranke, 11439 ff.)

There is a strophe in an Old French poem usually ascribed to Chrétien de Troyes (Frank no. 5*b*), which makes a comparison between the poet's love and that of Tristan, and which formed a model for a German poem by Bernger von Horheim (MF 112, 1). It is possible that Heinrich von Veldeke knew the Old French poem, since both refer in similar terms to the love potion, but it is not necessary to posit a direct source, since analogies with Tristan or other famous lovers are common.

Metrical form

4 *mv* a ⎫
4 *wv* b ⎭ :‖

4 *mv* a
4 *mv* a
4 *wv* b
4 *mv* c
2 *wv* d+2 *wv* d
4 *s* c
4 *s* c

41

This poem serves as it were as an epilogue to **38** and **39**. Here the poet relates the happy outcome of his sufferings when the lady finally grants him her favour. There are many verbal echoes of **38** and **39**, firstly in the details of the natural description in the first strophe, the repetition of *umbevān* in l. 15 (cf. **38**. 33; **39**. 23), and of *blītscap* in l. 22 (cf. **39**. 8 and *blīde* **38**. 5, 12). The mention of the blackbird is an unusually precise feature in the *Minnesang* of the classical period, and is paralleled only once in a poem of Uolrich von Guotenburc (MF 77, 36).

Metrical form

4 *wv* a ⎫
4 *mv* b ⎬ :‖
4 *wv* a ⎭

4 *mv* b
4 *wv* c (rhymes only with the corresponding line in the other strophes)
4 *mv* b

42

This panegyric of love, with its element of greater abstraction in the near-personification of *minne* in the first strophe (something not found in the earlier lyric), is a clear example of the courtly cult of love, influenced by Romance models. The idea that love is the source of all good is a common one. There is great virtuosity in the repetition of the key word *minne*.

Metrical form

A 4 *mv* a ⎫
A 4 *mv* b ⎬ :‖

A 4 *mv* a
A 4 *mv* a
A 4 *mv* b

43

This poem is unusual in that the natural description extends over two strophes. The reference to *būken* shows the same precision as that to *merelāre* in **41**.

Strophe III is an indirect plea for the lady's favour: his fault (*sculde*) is excess of love, and he will perish unless the lady deigns to accept a lesser penance than death. This indirect plea is reinforced by veiled flattery of the lady, in the poet's wish that he might only entreat her favour in a way fitting to her.

Metrical form

> 4 *k* a+4 *k* b
> (A) 4 *k* c+4 *k* d
> (A) 4 *k* a+4 *k* b
> (A) 4 *k* c+4 *k* d
>
> 4 *s* e+4 *mv* e
> (A) 4 *s* e+6 *k* a

The b rhyme of I is repeated in a different position in II. The e rhyme of I recurs in III, and in related form in II. Rhyme d of I is repeated in a different position in III.

FRIEDRICH VON HAUSEN

44

The idea of lifelong devotion is paralleled in **50**. The poem ends with a subtle tribute to the lady: his constancy is only proportionate to her excellence. The poem of Folquet de Marseille which has influenced **52** contains a similar idea of the heart as the lady's dwelling.

Metrical form

> I A 4 *mv* a
> 4 *mv* b
> A 4 *mv* b
> A 4 *mv* x+4 *mv* a
> A 2 *mv* a
> A 4 *mv* c
> A 4 *mv* x+4 *mv* c

The other strophes only differ in the placing of anacrusis. The rhyme *lip*:*wip* is repeated in all three strophes, *pflegen* in l. 13 recurs in l. 26, and *bekomen*: *genomen* of II is echoed by *gefromen*:*komen* in III.

45

This poem expresses the hopelessness of serving the lady in terms which are a reversal of the usual complaint of the *huote*. Paradoxically, the poet wishes he might experience the distress of being the victim of envious ill-wishers, because this would mean the lady had granted him her favour.

Metrical form

In the absence of the corroborative evidence of another MS., it is difficult to obtain a satisfactory text of this poem. For instance, l. 6 is longer in strophe I than in II and III, and this is probably due to scribal additions. There has been no agreement among editors (for a review of the various suggestions see Kraus, MFU, pp. 132–5). It seems most probable that the lines were originally intended as four-stress throughout, but in the present state of the text it seems preferable not to attempt a metrical analysis. Kraus for instance can only reduce it to a satisfactory scheme by introducing eighteen alterations in twenty-four lines (MF[30]).

46

This poem appears to be written from abroad, perhaps from Italy, the *berge* of l. 18 being no doubt the Alps. The poet laments his real separation from the lady and contrasts this with his former imagined unhappiness at home.

Metrical form

I A 4 *mv* a ⎫
  A 4 *wv* b ⎭ :‖

   4 *mv* a
   4 *mv* a
  A 4 *wv* b
  A 4 *mv* c
  A 4 *mv* c

II differs from I by a different distribution of anacrusis, and by having exclusively pure rhymes.

47

These four strophes in the same *Ton* are transmitted in two pairs in the MSS., the first pair in C only, the second pair at a later place in C, and also in B. The somewhat loose connexion between them and the fact that strophe IV is not bound by rhyme to the other three has prompted different decisions by editors. Some print I and II together, and III and IV together as two separate poems; Brinkmann rejects IV and rearranges the rest in the order I, III, IV. It is on the whole most satisfactory to take the four strophes as belonging together: they all circle round the same theme in a manner reminiscent of the earlier poets, they are all formally connected. Rhymes in *-uote(n)* link I and II, in *-ēre(n)* II and III, in *-funde* II and III. IV is bound more loosely to the rest by verbal echoes of I in the words *minne, nōt, betwungenlīche*. The theme of the poem is conventional in the likening of love to madness (5) and the accusations directed against the person of Love instead of the lady.

Metrical form

I   6 *k* a ⎫
    6 *k* b ⎭ : ‖

```
        3 mv c+3 mv c
A   3 mv c+3 k d
    6 k d
```

The other strophes have different placing of anacrusis, and l. 13 is defective (see note).

48

This poem is a *Wechsel*, in which both halves treat the theme of interfering ill-wishers. In the first strophe the man curses them for intervening between himself and the lady, in the second strophe the lady announces her determination to withstand their envy. The phrase *die valschen diet* is reminiscent of similar designations with *fals* in the Romance lyric. As Bartsch was the first to point out, the poem has the same form as *Pois prejatz mi, seignor* of Bernart de Ventadour, though there is no similarity in content.

Metrical form

```
(A) 3 mv a ⎫
 A  3 mv b ⎭ :‖

 A  3 mv a (defective in I)
 A  3 mv b
 A  3 mv a
 A  3 mv b
 A    mv b
```

49

The near personification of *herze* in this poem is reminiscent of 53. There is a similar formal pattern in the anonymous trouvère poem *Mult m'a demore* (Frank 2*b*), and one possible textual parallel to ll. 5–8: if the lady delivers him from his suffering, no *empereres de France* will have experienced such joy. This may, however, be a coincidence, as such phrases are commonplaces.

Metrical form

```
I (A) 3 mv a ⎫
  (A) 4 wv b ⎭ :‖

  A  4 wv b
     3 mv a
  A  3 mv a
  A  4 wv b
```

Kraus (MFU, p. 118) takes the longer lines as 5 *k*+rest = 6 beats in all, and is not convinced of the formal similarity with the Old French poem. The other strophes have different placing of anacrusis.

50

This poem contains several common themes: the praise of the lady's beauty as an example of divine workmanship, the acceptance of suffering as the necessary accompaniment of love (5–7), devotion to the lady since youth, the interpretation of the love relationship in feudal terms (17).

Metrical form

All the lines are four-stress, in the following arrangement:

Aufgesang   A 4 *mv* a ⎫ :‖
             A 4 *wv* b ⎭

Abgesang   A 4 *wv* b
             A 4 *mv* a (no anacrusis in II)
             A 4 *wv* b
             A 4 *mv* a
             A 4 *mv* c
             A 4 *mv* c

Rhyme a is also repeated in the second strophe. This is the first poem attested with a refrain.

51

This poem shows an ambivalent attitude towards the *huote*. It has the advantage of preventing the approach of undesired rivals (5–7), on the other hand it also attempts to hinder true love (30). The thought expressed in ll. 15–16 is frequently found elsewhere, e.g. Der von Kürenberc **18**.

The metrical pattern is the same as that of *Pensis d'Amors voil retraire* by Gace Brulé (*vide* Frank 3*b*).

Metrical form

I A 4 *wv* a ⎫ :‖
   A 4 *wv* b ⎭

   A 4 *wv* a
   A 4 *wv* b
     4 *wv* c
   A 4 *wv* c

The other strophes have different placing of anacrusis. The use of echoing rhymes (*Responsionen*) serves to bind the strophes closely together: thus *güete, gemüete,* and *hüete* in I are paralleled by *huote, muote,* and *guoten* in IV; *mîde, nîde,* and *wîben* in II are balanced by *wîben, lîde,* and *mîden* in III; *wære, enbære,* and *merkære* in II are echoed by *swære* and *wære* in III and *mêre* and *unêre* in IV, and *sinne, minne,* and *willen* in I by *wille, sinne,* and *minne* in IV.

52

This poem deals with the conflict between love for the lady and love of God: the service of God is placed higher, but the service of love is not rejected altogether. It is an example of the transference of feudal terminology to these relationships (e.g. 15 *dienen*, 16 *holt*, 31 *undertān*, 32 *lōn, dienst*, 50 *ein holdez herze*). Lines 31–32 and 40 are the clearest expression of the idea of a feudal contract, in which service has a right to reward. The conception of the lady's beauty as the handiwork of God is paralleled in **50**.

As was first pointed out by Bartsch, this poem is influenced in subject-matter and form by *En chantan m'aven a membrar* by Folquet de Marseille (Frank 11*b*). The main point of contact in subject-matter is between strophe I of Friedrich von Hausen and III of Folquet de Marseille, in which the poet describes his distracted state as such that he does not hear what is said to him.

Metrical form

I A 4 *mv* a
A 4 *mv* a
A 5 *mv* b
A 2 *mv* b
A 4 *mv* c
A 5 *mv* c
A 2 *mv* d
A 4 *mv* d
A 5 *mv* e
A 5 *mv* e

There is great virtuosity in the use of *Responsionen* (fully listed by Kraus, MFU, p. 142). Strophe I is bound in this way to all the others, and all the rhymes in III are paralleled in other strophes.

53

Strophes I and III are transmitted in the MSS. together, and II at a later point followed by another strophe in the same *Ton* — *Nieman darf mir wenden daz ze unstæte* (25 B, 28 C), which in spite of the arguments of Kraus (MFU, pp. 153–4) does not appear to belong to the same poem. Most editors arrange the strophes in the order I, II, III, but neither this order nor that of the MSS. is entirely satisfactory. It is probable that another genuine strophe is missing.

In this poem, as in **52**, the poet examines the particular dilemma of the Crusader but from a different point of view. Here the conflict is that between *līp* (the physical person) and *herze* (the seat of thoughts and emotions). This is a further development of the conception of the heart as the embodiment of the sentient being, almost as a distinct personality, which is seen in **49**.

The poem is apparently modelled on the first strophe of a crusading poem by Conon de Béthune, *Ahi, Amors, com dure departie* (Frank 6*b*) in which the same dichotomy occurs:

> șe li cors va servir Nostre Signor,
> li cuers remaint del tot en sa baillie.

There are other similar instances of the conflict between body and heart in the Romance and German courtly lyric (e.g. Reinmar **85**. 19 f.) and Hartmann von Aue's *Büchlein* is a theoretical disputation between *lip* and *herze* on the nature of love.

Metrical form

A 5 *wv* a ⎫
A 5 *mv* b ⎭ :‖

A 5 *mv* b
A 5 *wv* a
A 5 *wv* a
A 5 *mv* b

Heusler and Kraus (MFU) take ll. 1, 3, 6, and 7 as 6 *k*, and ll. 2, 4, 5, and 8 as 6 *s*.

ALBREHT VON JOHANSDORF

54-56

These four strophes are in the same *Ton*. A has I, II, and III, in that order, but ascribed to Niune, B and C have the order I, IV, III, and at a later point C has II separately. I and II clearly belong together thematically and probably make up a complete poem. III is tenuously linked to I and II by the opening phrase, which probably refers to a Crusading journey. III and IV are connected only by the parallel closing formula: *Ich meine . . .*, and the criticism of falsehood in both (*valsche ræte* III; *valschen muot* IV), but in the first instance this is a general complaint, in the second specifically directed against false lovers. They are better treated separately, although some editors consider all four strophes as making up one whole.

54 treats of the Crusader's dilemma (cf. Friedrich von Hausen **52** and **53**). The lady thinks him faithless because he leaves her, whereas he asserts in a typical paradox, that although he departs, his constancy is greater than hers. The second strophe is a prayer for the lady's well-being.

55 and **56** are of a general didactic nature. The first is a lament on the mutability of earthly things, and an exhortation to live justly to avoid divine wrath. **56** is a disquisition on the conduct appropriate to true love. For the idea that love is not to be accounted a sin, cf. Friedrich von Hausen **52**. 19.

Metrical form

54. I   4 *mv* a
            3 *mv* b
        A 5 *mv* a
        A 3 *mv* b

A 4 *mv* c
A 3 *mv* d
A 5 *mv* c
A 3 *mv* d
A 6 *mv* e
A 4 *mv* e
A 5 *mv* f
A 3 *wv* g
A 5 *wv* g
A 6 *mv* f

The other strophes differ only in the placing of anacrusis. This is the first instance in the collection in which the two parts of the *Aufgesang* are differentiated by rhyme.

57

In the first strophe the poet laments his fruitless service of the lady in his songs, in the second he threatens indirectly to transfer his love elsewhere. The epigrammatic last line is probably a pronouncement of the lady's, in which— again in a veiled manner—she rejects the idea of divided loyalty. Kraus argues (MFU p. 224) that it is more logical if the question is addressed to the lady, and he thus emends *herre* to *vrouwe*.

Metrical form

(A) 3 *wv* a ⎫
(A) 6 *mv* b ⎬ :‖
　　　　　　 ⎭
    7 *mv* c
A 7 *mv* c

58

The first two strophes argue the case in favour of partaking in the Crusades, whereas the third has a more particular application to the Crusader's problems. The arguments of the first two strophes are not altogether clearly expressed. Lines 7–9 counter the objection that God Himself could intervene without man's help: God is not obliged to do so, just as He had no need to suffer death on the Cross. He was, however, moved by pity for fallen mankind. Lines 10–17 state the corollary: whoever will not take pity on Him in return cannot hope for mercy. Lines 19–20 advance a doctrinal reason: the heathen refuse to assent to the Virgin Birth.

In the third strophe the poet asks how he himself can deserve God's mercy, should he remain at home. He can renounce all sins but cannot abandon his love. The prayer that it may not be accounted a sin is reminiscent of 56.

Metrical form

A 4 *mv* a ⎫
A 6 *wv* b ⎬ :‖
A 4 *mv* c ⎭

A 6 *mv* d
A 6 *mv* d
A 5 *mv* x
A 6 *wv* e
A 4 *wv* e

In some lines, e.g. l. 3, there is no anacrusis.

59

This poem combines the theme of unrewarded service with unremitting praise of the lady. If the lady grants her favour, she will be supreme among women (l. 4); even if she does not, however, she is still wholly virtuous (l. 7). The poet expresses a doubtful hope of reward reinforced by the refrain, which contains the association of *sumer* with *vröide* found in the stylized *Natureingang* of earlier poets. The change of song from *wē* to *wol* is reminiscent of Walther 110.

Metrical form

(A) 4 *wv* a ⎫
   5 *mv* b ⎭ :‖

   3 *wv* c
   3 *wv* c
(A) 5 *mv* d
   5 *mv* d

60

Of these four strophes, only two are preserved in B; in C other strophes intervene between the pairs I and II and III and IV (recorded in reverse order). The usual ordering here adopted was first suggested by Wilmanns. The poem is clearly a *Wechsel*, but the attribution of the strophes to the man and the woman respectively has been the subject of dispute. Kraus (MFU, p. 229) takes I, II, and III as *Frauenstrophen*, and IV as spoken by the man, but this would be unusual in its lack of balance. Angermann is undoubtedly right in taking both I and IV as *Männerstrophen*, because there are clear links between them, as there are between III and IV. In I the man asks whether he is to experience joy: this uncertain attitude is in keeping with IV, in which he places all his hopes in the lady's favour. Line 23 also suggests that the man has spoken earlier, and refers back to his indirect plea for a reward in I. In II and III the lady replies obliquely to the man's remarks. The reference to *scheiden* in l. 10 is prompted by the man's wish in l. 5. In ll. 15–16 the lady hints that true love is of slow growth, and in ll. 20–21 the injunction to the man to be constant is couched in a generalized form.

Metrical form

5 *mv* a ⎫
5 *mv* b ⎭ :‖

5 *mv* c
3 *mv* c
5 *mv* c

Some lines have anacrusis, e.g. l. 13.

61

This is perhaps the classic formulation of the idea that the service of love is its own reward. The man seizes a moment when the lady is alone to press his claims. He has served her and sung in her honour (cf. **57**). Although the lady shows signs of relenting, addressing him as *vil lieber man* (l. 18) and admitting that his words have affected her (l. 30), she yet takes the attitude that to give in would be to bring dishonour on herself (cf. Reinmar **90**).

There is irony in the last verse. The lady appears after all to promise a reward (l. 40), but it turns out that this is to consist in the improving nature of the service itself, enhancing the lover's worth and giving him joy. There are many reminiscences of Reinmar and Walther in the diction (fully listed by Kraus, MFU, pp. 234–5).

The poem shows close affinities to a Provençal *tenson* (debate) between a man and a lady, usually attributed, but with some uncertainty, to the Italian Marquis de Montferrat, attested between 1183 and 1207 (cf. Frank 13*b*). Similar features are the following: the lady, though expressing affection for the man, repels his too eager advances, reminding him that favour can only be won through patience and suffering. The Provençal poem is also composed of seven six-line strophes (but of different structure), and the speeches are similarly arranged in the pattern 2 lines+2, 1+1.

Metrical form

3 *wv* a ⎫
5 *mv* b ⎭ :‖

4 *mv* c
7 *mv* c

There is considerable use of *Responsionen*, e.g. *stān:gegān* of I is echoed in VII by *vervān:bestān*.

62

These loosely connected strophes circle round the Crusading theme. The first two are concerned with the man, the second with the lady. I is a general exhortation to earn a divine reward, renouncing this life in exchange for external bliss (the use of the word *solt* is reminiscent of Walther **110**). In II the Crusader asks Love to set him free until he returns, but if this is impossible, may the lady share his reward. III is spoken by the lady and is very similar to the old *Frauenklage*, expressing grief at desertion by the lover, but here set in the new context of the Crusader's departure. IV begins with praise of the lady for her virtue, which causes the Crusader to carry her with him in his heart. The last line, expressing renunciation of the world, returns again to the theme of the first strophe.

Metrical form

I   3 *mv* a ⎫
    A 6 *mv* b ⎬ :‖
    A 4 *mv* c ⎭

    6 *mv* d
    5 *mv* d
    A 5 *mv* e
    A 3 *mv*+4 *mv* e

HEINRICH VON MORUNGEN

63

This poem praises the lady as the pattern of perfection, both in beauty and goodness. It is characteristic of the courtly ideal that moderation is stressed, both in behaviour (*mit zühten gemeit*) and appearance (*smal wol ze māze*). The sun and moon images are typical of Morungen's individual usage and revitalize related words used in close proximity with them—thus *lūter* (l. 14) and *überliuhtet* (l. 23) are by no means stereotyped dead metaphors. A supplementary strophe, 3 BC, has been omitted, as certainly a later imitation.

Metrical form

The metre is dactylic.

    4 *mv* a ⎫
    4 *mv* b ⎬ :‖
    4 *mv* c ⎭

    4 *wv* d
    3 *mv* c
    3 *wv* d

64

The presentation of love as a magic power in the opening lines is reinforced by the use of similes drawn from the elements of fire and water in III, and the ascription of supernatural powers to the lady's gaze in IV. The first strophe contains an arresting paradox: if the lady wishes to avenge herself, she could not do better than grant his request—the extreme of joy would kill him. The second strophe makes use of antithesis. The central idea is the vasselage of love; in the opening lines it is the lady who commands. In the following lines the poet reverses the conventional idea in the wish that she might, instead, be subject to him. This use of paradox and antithesis also serves, like the images, to intensify the effect of the emotion portrayed.

Metrical form

$$6\ mv\ \text{a} \brace 5\ mv\ \text{b}\ :\|$$

3 *mv* b+4 *mv* c

6 *mv* c

5 *mv* b

There is considerable use of *Responsionen*; thus for instance strophe IV is bound to all the others in this way.

65

In MS. A there are only two strophes, the *Aufgesang* of II being followed by the *Abgesang* of III—no doubt an error in copying. All the key ideas of this poem are expressed by means of images. The lady dwells in the poet's heart where she entered *sunder tür*: this idea of the eyes as gateway to the heart is frequently found in medieval poetry. The second strophe expresses the poet's fruitless service in an image which combines two proverbial ideas: that of calling into the forest as useless labour, cf. pseudo-Neidhart *swaz ich hān gesungen, deist gerüefet in den walt* (H/W, p. 189), and that of the echoing response, cf. Freidank *swie man ze walde rüefet, daz selbe er wider güefet* (124. 3). The word *schal* in l. 11, appropriate to the image, links it with the poet's songs which resound in the lady's ears—and yet she pays no heed. In the third strophe the lady's hard-heartedness is further stressed in the image of the talking bird which would by now have learnt to respond. The final hopelessness is summed up in the last visual image which again has a semi-proverbial ring; there is a play on the double meaning of *geneigen*, literally 'to fell', figuratively 'to incline, dispose', thus: 'I could more easily fell a tree by my pleas without an axe than incline the lady towards me.'

Metrical form

$$6\ mv\ \text{a} \brace \text{A}\ 2{+}4\ k\ \text{b}\ :\|$$

2+4 *k* x

4 *k* c

6 *mv* a *or* x

5 *k* c (probably with final pause = 6 beats in all)

66

This poem is a *Wechsel* in which the speakers alternate. There is a strict parallelism between I and II, and III and IV respectively. I and II are concerned solely with the emotions of the speakers themselves: in I the choice of the lady from among all others is a common topos; II is the lady's complaint at parting, mixed with joy at the man's devotion. III and IV turn outwards: in III the man curses those slandering ill-wishers who interfere with their relationship, and in IV the lady complains of those who calumniate the man. The assertion that he always speaks well of women is a common motif—cf. for instance Reinmar **89. 7**. Lines 31–32 have a proverbial ring (for similar types of expression, see **65**). Similar instances are found in other poets, e.g. Gottfried's *Tristan* 11362: *si triben in mit spotte umbe und umbe als einen bal*. The refrain of I and III has similarities with that of **70**, but it is characteristic of Morungen that it is here used, as are other light images, not as an element of external characterization but as a means of expressing emotion.

Metrical form

I   4 *mv* a ⎫ :‖
     4 *mv* b ⎭

     4 *mv* c
     4 *mv* d
     4 *mv* c
A 4 *mv* d

The other strophes differ in the placing of anacrusis. Kraus (WU, p. 442) takes the dialect rhymes of II and IV (*bat:nat* and *wal:bal*) as a deliberate device to characterize the inferior poetic technique of the woman.

67

This complaint of hopeless service and the lady's indifference introduces once again the image of the talking bird, as in **65**. The mention of the nightingale gains added point from the fact that *nahtegal* is a frequent designation of the lyric poet. Strophe III contains the familiar topos of the heart as the lady's dwelling-place, here given the additional associations of siege and occupation by the use of the terms *besitzen* and *bestān*.

Metrical form

5 *mv* a ⎫ :‖
7 *mv* b ⎭

7 *mv* b
5 *mv* a
3 *mv* a
5 *mv* b

68

This poem contains a combination of traditional topoi and individual images. Into the first category fall the service *an hōher stat*, devotion since childhood, and the related idea that the poet was born only to serve the lady. The association of the lady with the sun in the second strophe forms a transition to the images of III in which she is identified directly with the morning-star and the sun. Not only radiance but also remoteness is suggested, and this translates into pictorial form the idea of l. 2. Similarly, the wish for evening and sunset is closely linked with the theme of *genāde* in the two preceding strophes.

Metrical form

Different schemes have been proposed, either: three beats in all the first half-lines + four beats in all the second half-lines (either *klingend* as in l. 1, or *voll* as in l. 2), or (Kraus, MFU) a mixture of six-beat and eight-beat lines, i.e. 2+4 *k* in ll. 1, 3, 5, and 3+4 *v* + final pause in the other lines. The strophe falls into three parts, the first two of two lines, the third of three lines, with a consequent variation in the arrangement of the rhymes. The b rhyme of each strophe is repeated also at the end of the first half of the last line.

69

These three strophes make up a *Wechsel*. In I the man praises a lady and swears constancy. The comparison of the first line is a variation on one commonly found, cf. **35, 36, 41.** II refers obliquely to I: the lady's disapproval of the man's choice is disguised in the form of a general admonition, and even the more specific reproach of ll. 13–14 is indirectly expressed. In III the complaint is made explicit, and the strophe has affinities with the earlier *Frauenklage*.

Metrical form

$$\text{I} \quad \left.\begin{array}{l} 4\ wv\ \text{a} \\ 5\ mv\ \text{b} \end{array}\right\} :\| \qquad\qquad \text{II, III} \quad \left.\begin{array}{l} 4\ wv\ \text{a} \\ 5\ mv\ \text{b} \end{array}\right\} :\|$$

$$\begin{array}{l} \text{A } 4\ mv\ \text{b} \\ \text{A } 4\ mv\ \text{x} \\ \text{A } 5\ mv\ \text{b} \end{array} \qquad\qquad\qquad \begin{array}{l} \text{A } 4\ mv\ \text{c} \\ \text{A } 4\ mv\ \text{x} \\ \text{A } 5\ mv\ \text{c} \end{array}$$

The c rhyme of II is the same as the b rhyme of I.

70

This poem is both a dawn song and a *Wechsel*, with alternating strophes spoken by the man and the lady respectively (cf. **66**, a *Wechsel* which has affinities with the dawn song). Strophe I contains an image characteristic of Morungen: the radiance emanating from the lady is mistaken for the moonlight. Similar refrains are found in Romance dawn songs, e.g. *Reis glorios, verais lums e clartatz*, by Guiraut de Bornelh, which has the refrain *et ades sera l'alba*.

Metrical form

Kraus (MFU) takes the first line of each strophe to be four-beat, the other lines to be three-beat + final pause. The refrain is either two- or three-beat. All the cadences are of the same type, with a disyllabic variant in ll. 10 and 12. There are two *Stollen* rhyming ab, ab, and an *Abgesang* rhyming ccc + refrain.

71

This complex poem, of which only the first strophe is preserved in C and the rest in the late MS. E, among the additions (e), ascribed to Reinmar, combines two images with varying associations, that of the mirror or reflection (*glas* in I, *brunnen* in III) and that of the dream. In medieval poetry these two images are sometimes found together as symbols of the transitory or the illusory, for instance in the prologue to Wolfram's *Parzival* (ll. 20–24), or in the following lines of Walther:

> Ein meister las, troum unde spiegelglas (L/K 122. 24)
> daz si zem winde bî der stæte sîn gezalt.

Here the mirror has also the added significance of the fatal attraction of love. Heinrich von Morungen has in this poem made use of the different associations of these images, and merged them into a loosely connected whole, but their significance would have been more readily apparent to a medieval audience.

The mirror image is frequently used in courtly poetry to describe the lady's eyes, into which the lover gazes and is lost. This is then associated with Narcissus who fell in love with his own reflection. Both these ideas are combined in a poem by Bernart de Ventadour (*The Songs of Bernart de Ventadorn*, ed. Stephen G. Nichols, Jr., *et al.*, Chapel Hill, 1962, p. 167). Heinrich von Morungen does not explicitly mention the mirror of the lady's eyes, but it is hinted at in lines 7 and 21; the comparison with Narcissus occurs in ll. 22–24. The opening lines of the poem contain a different idea, that of the intangible reflection. When the child snatches at it, the mirror breaks and joy turns to sorrow. This provides a link with the dream image which similarly illustrates the illusory nature of joy.

In the dream the poet is contemplating his happiness: *und ersach sich an der besten wunne sîn* (once more a visual image). It is clear from what follows that this happiness consists in the fulfilment of love (cf. particularly ll. 29–30). Love introduces the figure of the lady herself, perfect as in reality, but with signs of sorrow in her face. The sorrow aroused in the poet by this sight is explicitly referred to the hopeless love of Narcissus—the image of mirror and dream is thus combined. The dream-motif has a two-fold significance: it is firstly prophetic of sorrow, as is very frequent in medieval literature; secondly, it contains the contrast between fulfilment in the dream and the reality of waking, a common theme in courtly and folk poetry alike (cf. for instance Walther **103**). This explains ll. 29–32—the *wunne* was only a wish-fulfilment, and in reality the lovers are parted by circumstance.

As Bartsch first pointed out, there is an anonymous troubadour poem which is an exact parallel in its combination of the motif of the broken mirror and that of Narcissus (cf. Frank 17*b*).

As in Morungen, it is through the eyes that sorrow enters. The striking verbal parallels and the use of a similar form make it likely that the troubadour poem served as a model.

Metrical form

The strophes have the same number of lines and the same rhyme scheme as the Provençal poem.

6 *k* a } :‖
6 *mv* b }

6 *mv* b
6 *k* a
6 *k* a
6 *mv* b

72

The association of death with love is frequent, usually in a figurative sense, or more literally, as here. The poet protests that his love will transcend death, and the feudal conception of subjection and service is transferred to the next world. The description of the lady as a gentle murderess is a typical example of oxymoron, one of the stylistic figures most frequently found in the love lyric.

Metrical form

  6 *k* a
A 5 *mv* b (probably 6 *s*, including rest) } :‖

  6 *k* c ? (this line is defective)
  6 *k* d
A 6 *k* c
A 6 *k* d
  4 *mv* e
A 4 *k* f
A 4 *mv* e
A 4 *mv*+4 *k* f

HARTMANN VON AUE

73-74

The first two strophes appear in sequence in BC. Although the third strophe is numbered 11 in C, there is a sign in the MS. to indicate that it should follow after 2 C. The strophe numbered 3 in C, although in the same metrical form, introduces a new theme of grief at the lord's death, combined with the sorrows of love, and is given separately as **74**, as probably not belonging to the same poem. If it is omitted and 4 C follows next, a close logical sequence is obtained.

73. The mention of summer and winter in the opening lines is reminiscent of the convention of the *Natureingang*. Hartmann contrasts summer with his unhappiness, and winter symbolizes his continuing grief. The poet blames only himself for his lack of success: he has been rewarded according to his deserts. The conclusion is summed up, as is frequent, in a general dictum, here in a metaphor taken from the sphere of knighthood, which occurs also in *Iwein* 3224.

Metrical form

A 5 *mv* a ⎫
A 5 *mv* b ⎭ :‖

A 5 *mv* b
A 5 *mv* c
A 5 *mv* c
A 5 *mv* c
A 5 *mv* c

Heusler posits a rest at the end of each line, and counts six beats. For the fourfold repetition of the same rhyme in the *Abgesang*, cf. **80**.

75

The poem affirms untiring devotion and humble submission in spite of the hopeless nature of the service. Since the poet cannot approach the lady directly, he sends his song as a messenger 'whom she will hear but not see'.

Metrical form

A 4 *mv* a ⎫
A 3 *mv* b ⎬ :‖
A 3 *mv* c ⎭

A 2 *mv* d
A 4 *mv* d
A 5 *mv* e
A 3 *mv* e

76

This apparently contradictory poem explores the theme of hopeless service. It shows the progression from despair and outright rejection in I to the mood of complete submission of the final strophe. The poet begins by revoking his pledges of eternal devotion and abandoning his part in the warfare of love (*strît* 7, *kriec* 10). The strophe ends with the categorical affirmation that he will serve another.

In the second strophe he begins to express scruples: the opening line condemns faithlessness, and although it would bring him greater advantage (ll. 15–18), he now speaks of it only as a hypothesis: *und wolte ich ungetriuwe sîn*. The concluding lines of II already suggest that he has rejected it: rather than speak ill of the lady or grieve her, he would prefer to bear the blame as well as the injury she inflicts on him. III elaborates this idea: if she does not reward him, it is because he is unworthy. The only 'revenge' he desires is to wish her well (IV). Even if he can expect no reward, he is content, like many another, to live on hope alone (V). The last strophe roundly condemns the faithless lover, and reaffirms humble submission: the *niemer* of the last line echoes the *iemer* of l. 1, and thus emphasizes the return to the point of departure.

Metrical form

A 4 *mv* a ⎫
A 4 *mv* b ⎭ :‖

A 3 *mv* c ⎫
A 3 *mv* c ⎪
A 2 *mv* d ⎬ :‖ (In the repetition the c rhyme is replaced by a new rhyme).
A 4 *mv* e ⎭

77

In this poem the theme of hopeless service is treated in terms of the warfare of love (*ranc* 3, *strīt* 7, *vīent* 11). To the same complex of ideas belongs the comparison of ll. 14–16: the lady's power surpasses even that of the emperor. In the last line a different but related terminology is introduced, that of feudal tribute and bondage. This links the conclusion to *dienst* in l. 1.

Metrical form

A 4 *mv* a ⎫
A 3 *wv* b (*or* 4 *k*) ⎭ :‖

A 2 *mv* c+2 *mv* c
A 3 *mv* d
A 3 *mv* d
A 4 *mv* e
A 7 *mv* e

78

In this poem Hartmann is concerned not merely with outward allegiance to the Crusading ideal, but with the inner qualities which it demands. The second strophe contains the familiar idea of a divine reward, here combined with earthly renown (l. 24). The use of *zinsen* in l. 13 suggests the paying of a feudal tribute. In strophe III the world appears as a deceptively alluring figure, as is common in medieval literature and art (cf. Walther **109**). Her close associate is the devil, lying in wait (l. 34). In strophe IV the poet declares his willingness to renounce the world, since his lord's death has bereft him of earthly joy. The last lines introduce an idea similar to that found in **62**, that half the reward may be granted to the dead lord.

Metrical form

The structure is unusual in that the *Aufgesang* is doubled:

A 4 *mv* a ⎫
A 2 *mv* b ⎭ :‖

A 4 *mv* c
A 2 *mv* d } :‖

A 3 *mv* e
A 3 *mv* e
A 3 *mv* f
A 3 *mv* f

79

The poem begins with a general dictum: he who does not rejoice in good fortune can derive no benefit from misfortune. The poet, on the other hand, can turn misfortune to good account. The second and third strophes repeat the key word *stæte*: this implies not only outward constancy in behaviour towards others, but inner constancy and the ability to remain true to one's self. The poet has failed in this respect and thus forfeited the lady's favour, but he has learnt the appropriate lesson, and in future no one shall surpass him in *stæte*.

Metrical form

A 4 *mv* a
A 7 *mv* b } :‖

   5 *mv* c
(A) 2 *mv* d+2 *mv* d
A 5 *mv* c

80

The poet mocks at the admiration conventionally accorded to courtly ladies and spurns them for their haughtiness. There are striking similarities between the thought and expression of the second strophe and the poem of Walther's (**101**), in which he likewise distinguishes between *wîp* and *frouwe*.

Metrical form

The two *Stollen* do not exactly correspond to each other, as is usual:

I   4 *mv* a
A 4 *mv* a
    4 *k* b
    4 *k* b

A 4 *mv* c
A 4 *mv* c
A 4 *mv* c
A 4 *mv* c

The other strophes have different placing of anacrusis.

81

This Crusading poem gains much of its point from the play on the word *minne*, used in the double sense of secular and divine love. The poet does not state clearly in which sense he is using the word in each particular instance, but only lets it be inferred from the poem as a whole. The first strophe is couched in general terms: Love has captured him and set him free upon oath. It is not clear that the journey referred to is necessarily a Crusading journey; indeed the use of terminology usually associated with the conception of love as warfare suggests rather that the obligation is one imposed on him by secular love. This is deliberate ambiguity.

Strophe II begins by chiding those who merely boast of their love in empty words: thus *Minne* of l. 9 is worldly love, whereas l. 13 refers to a higher kind of love. The use of *sich ellenden* makes it clear that a Crusading journey must be meant. Strophe III contrasts the illusions and false hopes of those who sing of worldly love, with the twofold bond of divine love, which is a mutual contract.

Lines 15–16 have provoked much discussion. There have been two main interpretations: (1) (without a comma after *her*) 'If my lord Saladin and all his host were alive, they would never move me a foot from Germany'. This does not seem to make good sense in the context when the poet has already announced his firm intention of departing. The singular verb *lebte* would have to refer to both subjects and it would imply that the whole of Saladin's army was also dead. (2) 'If my lord were alive, Saladin and all his host would never move me a foot from Germany.' This would be in accordance with **78** in which Hartmann similarly attributes his resolve to go on a Crusade to his lord's death, which had turned him away from worldly joy. The lines would then mean: had my lord still been alive, I too would have been preoccupied with earthly pleasures, and nothing would have induced me to go on a Crusade.

A further point at issue is the date of the Crusade to which the poem refers. Saladin died in 1193. According to the first interpretation, he was already dead when the poem was written: this would point to the Crusade of 1197/8. On the other hand, if the second, more probable interpretation is preferred, Hartmann appears to speak as if Saladin were still alive: this would point to the Crusade of 1189/90. This is the date usually favoured, but the evidence is not strictly compulsive: Hartmann could be using the reference to the might of Saladin to emphasize his resolve, irrespective of whether he was alive or dead.

Some critics have taken this poem to represent Hartmann's renunciation of the worldly *Minnesang*, and have therefore assumed that his poems were all written before the Crusade in which he took part: i.e. probably that of 1189/90. The evidence is, however, insufficient, and it is unwise to place too great a reliance on the work of medieval poets for biographical purposes.

Metrical form

A 6 *wv* a
(A) 5 *mv* b } :‖

A 7 *mv* c
A 7 *mv* d
A 6 *mv* d
A 6 *mv* c

It is possible, as Plenio suggests, that the lines of each *Stollen* are intended as 7 *k* and 6 *s* respectively (the pause occurring appropriately at the end of the *Stollen*). This would make them similar to the lines of the *Abgesang*.

REINMAR

82

These three strophes are given here in the order attested by C, and to some extent by B. Although A is an older and usually more reliable MS. and although it is frequent for a poem to begin with a general dictum such as that in line 10, the order of C gives a much better logical sense, particularly since l. 19 takes up again the theme of *nîden* expressed in the preceding strophe in l. 16.

The poem is a reply to the critics. I announces the poet's intention of persisting in his love. II is couched in general terms, but refers indirectly to the particular situation, as the return to the first person in the last line makes clear. The man who strives to attain high honour (that is through the service of his lady) is by virtue of that alone made fortunate and gains the esteem of others. Any envy aroused by this is therefore easy to bear. III is a rebuke to those who accuse the poet of folly, which is a sign that they do not share his laudable aims. The last lines give the poet's final self-justification in aphoristic form. It is characteristic once more that as in II the poet's feelings are expressed at one remove.

Metrical form

A 4 *mv* a ⎱
A 4 *mv* b ⎰ :‖

A 6 *k* c
A 6 *k* c
A 4 *k* d
A 4 *mv* x
A 6 *k* d

83

The strophes are arranged in the MSS. in the order I, IV, II, III. Some editors print I and IV, and II and III as two separate poems, but it is more in keeping with the usual pattern of the *Wechsel*, if Kraus's rearrangement is adopted, as here (cf. MFU, p. 341). Definite links can be shown between all four strophes: I is the woman's complaint of envious interference and her longing for the man's presence. II expresses the man's hope of reward after long service. I and II are alike in implying that the lovers are separated.

III is clearly a reply to II, marked by the repetition of the key-word *genâde* in the same position. IV is the man's response to the granting of the lady's favour; the words *frô* and *hôchgemüete* echo the promise in ll. 20–21.

Metrical form

$$\left.\begin{array}{l} \text{A 4 } mv \text{ a} \\ \text{A 4 } mv \text{ b} \end{array}\right\} :\|$$

A 4 *mv* c
A 4 *k* d
A 4 *mv* c
A 6 *k* d

84

This poem affirms unswerving devotion in the face of hopeless odds. In I the poet compares himself with the man favoured with good fortune in love. This leads in II to a reply to his detractors: how can he sing of joy without experiencing it ? Lines 17–18 hint at the familiar motif of the interference of the same ill-wishers. III and IV express unchanging devotion, and the poem ends on a resigned note, which echoes the closing lines of I.

Metrical form

$$\left.\begin{array}{l} \text{A 4 } mv \text{ a} \\ \text{A 6 } mv \text{ b} \end{array}\right\} :\|$$

A 6 *mv* c
A 4 *mv*+2 *mv* c
A 4 *mv* d
A 4 *mv* e
A 4 *mv* d
A 4 *mv* e

There is skilful use of *Responsionen*: thus the rhyme *tac:lac* of IV echoes *tac:mac* in I; in addition the last word of the first half of l. 6 in each strophe echoes an end-rhyme elsewhere:

I. *man*, IV. *began:an.*
II. *nôt*, III. *tôt:nôt.*
III. *tac*, I. *tac:mac*, IV. *tac:lac.*
IV. *sîn*, III. *sîn:mîn.*

85

The theme is that of untiring devotion in spite of the lady's indifference (the use of *genâde* in l. 31 suggests, not that she has rewarded him, but that the 'favour' consists in being allowed to serve her). He was born to serve her, and even though the ignoble promptings of *lîp* suggest that he should serve another, his heart remains faithful (a new variation on the familiar *lip–herze* antithesis). The motif of the theft of a kiss is found also in the troubadours. Wolfram rejects Reinmar's excessive praise of the lady in *Parzival* 115. 5:

> Sîn lop hinket ame spat,
> swer allen frouwen sprichet mat
> durch sîn eines frouwen.

A poem of Walther's (*Ein man verbiutet âne pfliht*, L/K 111, 22), whose corrupt text, however, makes interpretation difficult, seems likewise to criticize extravagant praise and concludes with the lines:

> bezzer wære mîner frouwen sanfter gruoz
> deist mates buoz. }

In the second strophe of the same poem the lady refers to the theft of a kiss and rejects the idea of receiving it back.

Metrical form

A 4 *mv* a }
A 6 *mv* b } :‖

A 5 *mv* c
A 5 *mv* c
A 4 *mv* d
A 6 *mv* d
A 2 *mv* d

In strophe V the a rhyme is repeated in the *Abgesang* instead of rhyme d.

86

The six strophes in the same *Ton* given here together have been differently treated by editors. Thus Haupt took the first three strophes and the last three as two separate poems, and Brinkmann prints strophes I and II as separate from the rest, whereas Kraus takes them all together (*Die Lieder Reinmars des Alten*, I, 35 f.). The main difficulty arises from the MSS. tradition which is as follows:

A has only the first three strophes in the order I, II, III.
b has three strophes in the order IV, I, III.
C has all the strophes in the order IV, II, I, III, and at a later position in the MS., V, VI.
E has all the strophes together in the order I, III, II, VI, V, IV.
i has only II.

If all the strophes are taken together, the order suggested by Kraus and adopted here gives the best sense.
The arguments in favour of considering all the strophes as belonging

together are the following: one MS. transmits all the strophes together, and in the other MSS. it is not always the same group of strophes which is preserved, but rather different sections of a larger unit. All the strophes circle round the theme of unrewarded service. The metrical pattern seems to be the same throughout, although it has been argued that the second and fourth lines of I and II only are six-beat, as opposed to five-beat in the other strophes. This partly depends, however, on which MS. reading is preferred: thus the A reading of l. 4 adopted here is five-beat, whereas that of C is six-beat:

und si der wāren schulde ouch deheine hāt.

All the strophes appear to be connected by *Responsionen*; thus the rhyme *rāt*: *hāt* of I is repeated in VI and the rhyme *leit*: *kündekeit* of II is echoed in *leit*: *unbereit* of IV. III, IV, V, VI, all are bound by rhymes in -*ē*.

Against the connexion of all the strophes it may be argued that the theme of 'testing' only occurs in I and II and that these are the only strophes which have no -*ē* rhymes. If ll. 2 and 4 of I and II were originally six-beat, then their metrical pattern is slightly different.

On the whole, however, the arguments in favour of unity seem stronger. The poem begins, as is frequent, with a general dictum: it is not prudent to put a woman to the test by endeavouring to ascertain the truth of accusations against her. II applies this to the poet's own case: he has never attempted to test the lady and has never been untrue, and yet she inflicts suffering instead of joy. No wonder then that he is sometimes roused somewhat to anger (a typically discreet expression of annoyance). Constancy, which is praised as a virtue, has robbed him of all joy. In addition women seem to favour those who act extravagantly and not that man (i.e. the poet himself) who cannot (III). IV continues the theme of unhappiness: he knows *minne* only in the guise of sorrow. He can only hope to excel in the patience with which he bears his suffering (V). This leads to the concluding thought in VI: only such patience may perhaps finally hope for a reward.

There is a close parallel to strophe I, with similar turns of phrase, in a poem attributed to Gace Brulé (cf. Frank 19*b*).

Metrical form

A 4 *mv* a ⎫
A 5 *mv* b ⎭ :‖

A 4+3 *mv* c
A 3+4 *mv* c
A 4 *mv* d
A 4 *mv* x
A 5 *mv* d

Line 2 has apparently six beats, but as all the MSS. agree in the length of the line, it has not been changed. Kraus interprets the five-beat lines as six-beat, with the addition of a pause, and ll. 5 and 6 as 4+4. (*Die Lieder Reinmars des Alten*, I, 46.)

87

The strophes are given in the order attested by B, C, and E. The first two strophes are a reply to adverse criticism. To those weary of his complaints, the poet affirms his inability to rejoice so long as his love goes unrewarded. Strophe II counters the accusation that his love is not so great as he protests. III is in praise of women in general, but with the particular lady in mind as exemplifying the highest virtues of her sex, as the transition to the poet's own desires in l. 26 shows. Walther refers directly to this praise of womanhood in his elegy on Reinmar's death (**106**), and indirectly in his own lines on the same subject (cf. **101**. 40 f.). IV poses a dilemma: if he were to be admitted to her favour, his unworthiness would detract from her high worth; on the other hand, if she is to remain inaccessible, he continues to suffer. The last strophe sums up the themes of the whole: his devotion in the face of the lady's indifference, the inevitability and the sincerity of his complaints.

Metrical form

A 4 *mv* a ⎱
A 6 *mv* b ⎰ :‖

  6 *mv* c
A 7 *mv* c
A 3 *mv* d
  5 *mv* x
A 5 *mv* d

88

The six strophes are given in the order attested by C, and confirmed in part by A and E: thus A has the first three strophes in the same order, and VI as the last strophe, and E has the same order as C, except that VI is in second position. Vogt (MF³) excludes IV and V as not belonging to the rest, but in fact all the strophes refer to the same situation. Kraus rearranges them in the order I, IV, II, V, III, VI (cf. MFU, p. 355), but this is not necessary.

The theme is the poet's devoted service and his hope of a remedy. The opening line expresses his attitude to his suffering: it is sweet, because associated with the lady, and he does not complain in spite of it (l. 4). In II he appeals for advice how this suffering may be converted to joy, but no one is able to suggest a remedy, and his devotion earns him nothing but mockery. III begs the lady to moderate her anger and expresses the determination to persist in her service. IV takes up the complaint of II that others are unable to help him and laments the fact that women seem to prefer unworthy suitors. V refers explicitly to one taunt which forms part of the general mockery, in order to introduce the plea for a reward: the aspersions about the lady's age may induce her to grant him her favour before it is too late. VI concludes with the proposal that she should act as if he were dear to her and give him a fair trial.

Metrical form

A 4 *mv* a $\Big\}$:‖
A 6 *wv* b

A 4 *mv* c
A 4+3 *mv* c (Kraus, MFU: 4+4, with final pause)
A 6 *k* d
A 4 *mv* x
A 6 *k* d

89

The poet protests that he cannot speak ill of women, that he does not complain (for ll. 3–7 cf. **88**. 3–4), that the lady is not to blame if he has chosen her without her consent. Yet his very insistence is an indirect complaint, and the emphasis on his own *stætekeit* as the cause of all his ills is discreet self-praise.

Metrical form

(A) 6 *mv* a $\Big\}$:‖
A 5 *mv* b

A 4 *mv* c
A 4 *mv* x
A 6 *mv* c

The five-beat lines are perhaps six-beat, including a pause, appropriate at the end of the *Stollen*.

90

The strophes are arranged, as is usual, in the order suggested by Haupt. The poem is a *Botenlied*, addressed to the messenger by the lady, who is shown as revealing her inmost thoughts: on the one hand her affection for the man which she intends to keep secret, on the other her determination to guard her reputation. Such a presentation of the lady's attitude is indirectly flattering to the poet.

Metrical form

4 *mv* a $\Big\}$:‖
4 *mv* b

4 *mv* c
A 4 *mv* x
4 *mv* c

WALTHER VON DER VOGELWEIDE

91

These three strophes, of which MS. A undoubtedly preserves the correct order, are linked in theme and expression, and are better treated together although III was probably written later than the other two.

The events referred to are those of 1198–1201. In 1197 the Emperor Heinrich VI had died, having previously secured the election of his infant son Friedrich (later the Emperor Friedrich II) as his successor. Heinrich's brother, Philip of Swabia, first attempted to protect the interests of his nephew, but was soon persuaded to claim the throne for himself. In this he was opposed by the rival candidate, Otto of Brunswick, who was supported by Richard Cœur de Lion. Otto was crowned king by his supporters in Aachen in July 1198, and Philip in Mainz in August or September of the same year. Walther's poem laments the confusion and strife engendered by the electoral contest.

In I the poet depicts himself in the symbolic attitude of meditation, that in which he is shown in the MSS. illustrations, and one frequently found in medieval literature and art. He reflects on the goal of existence for the individual, the attainment of the typically medieval combination of worldly prosperity and esteem with divine grace. This ideal is unrealizable amidst the present anarchy. The use of the phrase *fride und reht*, which forms part of the coronation formula, is an indirect plea for an ordered rule, which is made explicit in II. There is a strong visual element—the physical attitude of meditation, the image of the heart as a casket enshrining the highest values of life, the graphic personification of abstractions in the last lines.

II reinforces the plea for the restoration of order with a moral lesson drawn from the animal kingdom. The poet surveys the whole of the natural world and its creatures, divided, as is traditional, into creeping, walking, and flying things, and fishes. All animals, like man, are at strife with each other. The poet then associates with the class of flying creatures (*vogel* 35, *mugge* 43) a familiar commonplace usually attached to the bees, which belong to the same group. All the details which Walther here mentions—the firm rule, the choice of king and laws, the distribution of duties—are features of this commonplace which goes back to Vergil, and which is frequently used as here to point a moral. Shakespeare similarly makes use of the political application in *Henry V*, I. ii. 183:

> for so work the honey-bees,
> Creatures that by a rule in nature teach
> The act of order to a peopled kingdom.
> They have a king and officers of sorts;
> Where some, like magistrates, correct at home,
> Others, like merchants, venture trade abroad,
> Others, like soldiers, armed in their stings,
> Make boot upon the summer's velvet buds; . . . .

Walther has here extended the commonplace to the whole of the animal kingdom, but its particular connexion with the class of flying creatures and the fact that it is the fly (*mugge*) which is credited with a king, makes it clear that it is the commonplace of the bees of which he is thinking. (For other examples see MLR, LII, 3, July 1957, pp. 397–402.) The last lines refer to specific dangers within and without which make it imperative to recognize Philip's claims, thus restoring law and order. The *cirkel* of l. 46 are probably the factious princes who support Otto, whereas *die armen künege* of l. 47 are those foreign monarchs, lesser by comparison with the Holy Roman Emperor, whose interference was feared, in particular Richard Cœur de Lion, who actively supported Otto, and Philip Augustus of France. The exhortation in the last line to place the crown on Philip's head gains point from the fact that the imperial insignia were in Philip's possession.

The poet turns in III to the disordered state of the Church. The repetition of the words *sach* and *hôrte* forms a link with II, and stresses the poet's visionary ability to penetrate the meaning of events. This section refers to the year 1201, when the Pope finally declared openly in favour of Otto by excommunicating Philip and his followers (l. 65), whereas according to Walther he should have excommunicated Otto (66). There had been indecisive fighting between the two rival parties of Otto and Philip, here identified as *pfaffen* and *leien* respectively, since Walther interprets the contest as one between Church and State. He chides the papal party for resorting to spiritual power to decide the issue, when temporal power is insufficient (63–64). Walther cautiously expresses his particular complaint of the Pope indirectly in the mouth of the hermit, who is probably intended to represent the true Christian spirit, by comparison with the Pope who is misusing spiritual power. He further minimizes the harshness of the criticism by alleging the Pope's youth (he was thirty-seven at the time of his election), but the tenor of the whole is unmistakably hostile to the Papacy.

Metrical form

There are regularly alternating pairs of lines which are 4 *k* and 4 *mv* respectively. The conclusion of each section is marked by the introduction of a four-beat *Waise* before the final rhyming line. Anacrusis is usual, except in emphatic lines, e.g. 48.

92

The poem is a sequel to the central section of **91**. Philip is now described as wearing the imperial crown, which miraculously fits him as if made for him. This further emphasizes the indubitability of Philip's claims, now confirmed by the conferring of the rightful insignia, which possessed symbolic significance. The last lines are aimed at the supporters of Otto, who had been crowned, as was prescribed, in Aachen by the Archbishop of Cologne, but without the correct insignia, which were in Philip's possession.

There are four other strophes in this form, the so-called *Erster Philippston*, three of them related fairly closely in subject to this one.

Metrical form

A 6 *mv* a
A 6 *mv* a
A 6 *mv* b

A 6 *mv* c
A 6 *mv* c
A 6 *mv* b

A 4 *mv* d
A 6 *mv* d
A 6 *k* e

A 4 *mv* f
A 6 *mv* f
A 6 *k* e

Both *Aufgesang* and *Abgesang* are thus divided into two equal, but not identical halves.

93

After the death of Philip in 1208 Walther supported Otto until the latter's fortunes began to decline and Friedrich II was crowned German king in 1212. These two strophes show Walther in the act of transferring his loyalties to Friedrich, and were probably written about 1213–14. They express a sharply worded criticism of Otto's meanness, illustrated by a visual image in II: Walther applies two standards of measurement, that of stature and that of inner worth, which gain point from the fact that Otto was tall but Friedrich short. When Otto is measured outwardly, his height far exceeds his generosity; when he is measured according to his good qualities, he shrinks to dwarf-like proportions, whereas Friedrich far outgrows him.

Metrical form: the so-called *König Friedrichs-Ton*

A 6 *wv* a
A 6 *wv* a
A 8 *k* a

A 6 *wv* b
A 8 *s* c

A 6 *mv* c
A 8 *k* b

A 6 *mv* d
A 6 *mv* d
A 8 *s* d

There is no anacrusis in the emphatic line 16.
The melody is partially preserved in MS. Z; cf. Maurer[1], pp. 71 and 76.

94

This plea addressed to Friedrich II was probably written about 1220. In another poem Walther similarly contrasts *wirt* and *gast*:

'Sīt willekomen, her wirt', dem gruoze muoz ich swīgen:
'sīt willekomen, her gast', sō muoz ich sprechen oder nīgen.

(L/K 31, 23)

Lines 4 ff. allude to the themes of the *Minnesang*. The last line probably refers to the Emperor's difficulties in attempting to secure the election of his son as king of Germany and his delay in carrying out the promised Crusade, which caused his excommunication in 1227.

Metrical form as **93**, without anacrusis in l. 3.

95

The granting of the fief appears to be in direct response to the request of the previous poem. The *bœse hërren* of l. 3 is probably aimed chiefly at Otto, whom Walther castigates elsewhere for his meanness, and *schelten* (9) refers particularly to the type of song criticizing a reluctant patron. The last line takes up again the theme of ll. 4–9 of the previous poem.

Metrical form: the same as **93**.

96

This poem is usually thought to have been written in Vienna in 1203, the year in which Walther is attested in the retinue of Bishop Wolfger of Passau, and when he probably returned to Vienna for the wedding of Leopold VI in the summer of 1203. The opening formula suggests that the poet is returning after a period of absence, and the phrase *her wider* (the reading of A, corroborated by *wider her* of E) appears to indicate that Walther is in Austria. Kraus takes the poem as a deliberate counterpart to Reinmar **87**. The praise of Germany and its inhabitants may have been prompted as a reply to certain aspersions cast on the uncourtly Germans in the poems of the troubadour Peire Vidal, who also wrote a poem praising his native Provence, which Walther may have known. The opening strophe is quoted in the *Frauendienst* of Ulrich von Liechtenstein. The final line probably contains a discreetly worded plea for a place at the Viennese court. MS. C alone appends a sixth strophe expressing hopeless service of a lady, which is here omitted as out of keeping with the rest and probably not authentic.

Metrical form

This has been variously interpreted.

Aufgesang: 4 *mv* a
5 *mv* b (taken by some editors as six-beat with a pause) } :‖

Abgesang: 4 *k* c
3 *mv* d (or 4 with final pause)
6 *mv* d
4 *mv* c

As Schirmer points out, if ll. 2 and 4 are taken as five-beat and l. 6 as four-beat, there are eighteen stresses in both parts of the strophe.

97

The poet pleads with Moderation, a frequently prized courtly virtue, to guard him from the two extremes of love, which both cause suffering (8–10). The lower extreme is the striving after an unworthy love, whose pangs are discreditable; the loftier extreme awakens the aspiration towards higher worth (the contrast between *unlobelīche* and *wirde* expresses the familiar idea that love confers worthiness and esteem). The poet sees himself on the brink of this second kind of love, and is aware that *māze* delays (17), since it is immoderate, but the emotion of love (*herzeliebe* 18) carries him away notwithstanding. The whole is thus a vain plea for moderation, which is essentially incompatible with *minne*.

Metrical form

$$\left.\begin{array}{l} 6\ k\ \text{a} \\ 6\ k\ \text{b} \\ \text{A}\ 6\ s\ \text{c} \end{array}\right\} :\|$$

A 4 *wv* d
6 *wv* d
A 4 *mv* e
A 4 *mv* x+4 *mv* e

98

This poem is given in the order attested by EF (with the exclusion of an unauthentic penultimate strophe). The poet rejects the idea of a one-sided love which brings pain, in favour of a shared relationship, and in the last strophe declines to praise the lady in vain and accept suffering in exchange for happiness. The outspoken temerity of the criticism is softened by the final *revocatio*: love has robbed him of his senses. Walther thus skilfully makes use of a conventional idea for a special purpose.

Metrical form

$$\left.\begin{array}{l} 4\ wv\ \text{a} \\ 6\ mv\ \text{b} \end{array}\right\} :\|$$

4 *mv* c
6 *wv* x
6 *mv* c

99

As in **101** Walther opposes inner and outer qualities. To those who criticize him for addressing his songs to a lowly object, he replies that love cannot be regulated according to wealth and beauty. Inner qualities are more important.

This idea is one common in proverbial wisdom (e.g. 'handsome is as handsome does') and in courtly poetry, e.g. Heinrich von Rugge:

> Nach vrouwen schœne nieman sol
> ze vil gevrāgen, sint si guot . . . .

(MF 107, 27)

Strophe III contains the central idea of the whole poem: mere physical beauty may hide a disagreeable personality, whereas a lovable nature is able to confer beauty on its possessor. As in **101** Walther makes use of a play on words to reinforce his point: thus in strophe II *liebe* is synonymous with *minne*, but in III it is the quality of being *liep*, which arouses love. The two following strophes are a particular application to the poet's own situation: the lady possesses beauty and a sufficiency of worldly goods (21) and thus satisfies the superficial criteria of society. In addition, however, as in **98**, the poet demands from the lady an active response to his love, and this is the main condition which he imposes.

Metrical form

Aufgesang: 4 *mv* a ⎫ :‖
            4 *mv* b ⎭

Abgesang: 4 *mv* c
    A 8 *mv* c

100

Like **98** the poem is a plea for shared love. The poet complains of the lady's coldness, but is willing to excuse her if it is a deliberate feint. For a similar motif cf. Der von Kürenberc **18**. As in **99** there is the suggestion that the lady is of lesser social standing, with the contrast between outer and inner attributes (l. 24).

The metrical form has been variously interpreted:

Kraus (WU)	Plenio, Schirmer
4 *k* a ⎫ :‖	3 *wv* a ⎫ :‖
6 *s* b ⎭	5 *mv* b ⎭
4 *k* c	3 *wv* c
4 *k* c	3 *wv* c
6 *s* d	5 *s* d
6 *s* d	5 *mv* d

As Schirmer points out, if the second scheme is accepted, the number of beats in the strophe corresponds to the number of lines in the whole poem (i.e. thirty-two), which is probably deliberate.

101

The strophes are given in the order suggested by Lachmann and substantiated in part by the different MSS. In the first strophe the poet speaks of his ability to adapt himself to the mood of others. II applies this particularly to his poetry: his songs were formerly joyful, but since joy and *minne* have disappeared from society, he can no longer sing in courtly fashion. III gives the reason for the loss of joy (cf. particularly l. 30): women make no distinction between different kinds of men. Line 32 points forward to the corresponding distinction which can be made among women, and which is elaborated in IV. Walther here uses the different meanings associated with the words *wîp* and *frowe* to make his point. It must be borne in mind that *frowe* was socially superior to *wîp* and that this gives added significance to Walther's use of *wîp* as a term of the highest praise. *Wîp* is here used meaning (1) a member of the female sex in general, e.g. *wîbe* in 40; (2) the possessor of the highest qualities in the female sex, true womanliness. Similarly *frowe* has here the double sense of (1) a lady of high birth; (2) a person with the attributes expected of high birth, as in 49 (cf. English 'lady' in this transferred sense). This praise of *wîp* is reminiscent of Reinmar **87**. 19 ff.

V follows on from the distinction made in IV: the poet formerly addressed his songs to *frowen* in exchange for a mere salutation, but since they are now reluctant to grant him even this, he will leave another to sing their praises, and turn instead to *wîp* who know how to thank him. There are similarities to the second strophe of **96**, where Walther had disclaimed any reward beyond a greeting, and to Hartmann **80**.

Metrical form

```
A  6 mv a ⎫ :‖
A  6 k  b ⎭

   4 mv c ⎫ :‖
   4 wv d ⎭

   4 mv e
   4 mv e
   4 k f
   4 k x
(A) 4 wv f
```

There is no anacrusis in the emphatic l. 40.

102

MS. C alone appends a further strophe, whose text is corrupt, and which is therefore best omitted.

Metrical form

```
A  4 mv a ⎫ :‖
A  4 wv b ⎭

(A) 6 mv c (line 5 is defective)
 A  5 mv d (or A 6 s d)
 A  6 mv d
 A  6 mv c
```

103

The order here adopted is that proposed by Kraus (WU) which is the most satisfactory. Strophes I–II depict the offering and acceptance of a garland, which the lady is to wear while partaking in a dance, possibly at the May festival. Strophes III–IV repeat the same sequence in the heightened form of a dream (which is, however, not made clear until ll. 30–32). The transition from reality to dream is abrupt, but a link is provided by l. 16, in which the poet hints at a possible further reward. This leads on to the common poetic motif of wish-fulfilment in a dream. The poet again offers to give the lady a garland and invites her to accompany him to a distant spot to pluck flowers —undoubtedly a symbolic expression of the enjoyment of love. In the midst of happiness, the poet is recalled to a harsh reality in which he is bereft of joy—again a common poetic motif. Strophe V is concerned once more with reality: the poet searches for the lady, hoping to find her among the dancers wearing a garland. As Wilmanns/Michel point out, there is a widely current folk song in which a dancer searches for his former partner and demands the reward of a kiss.

Metrical form

Differing schemes have been proposed. The most likely is as follows:

A   3 *mv* a ⎫
    6 *mv* b ⎭ :‖

A   4 *wv* c
(A) 4 *k* d
    4 *k* d
(A) 4 *wv* c

Kraus (WU) takes the first line of each *Stollen* as 4 *s*, Hatto the first and the last line of the *Abgesang* as five-beat (*German Life and Letters*, III, 2, 1950, p. 144).

104

This poem has certain affinities with the genre of the *pastourelle* found in Romance poetry, in which a knight recounts his wooing of a village girl, with the dialogue between them. Walther's poem is unusual in that the events are related from the point of view of the girl.

The metrical form has been much disputed. MS. C has full stops after *linden* and *vinden* and the corresponding words in the other strophes, which usually indicates the end of a line but sometimes only marks a rhyme word. Most editors take *Under der linden / an der heide* as two separate lines, but the scansion of these short lines is disputed. It is more satisfactory to take these two units as making up a regular four-beat line, with internal rhyme at the caesura. Another difficulty is the scansion of the refrain. It is probably: *tándáradéi* + rest.

(A) 2 *wv* a+2 *wv* b ⎱ :‖
(A) 4 *mv* c   ⎰

    4 *mv* d
    4 *s* x
    4 *mv* d

105

This lament for the silencing of courtly poetry by uncourtly strains is un-doubtedly aimed at the 'village' poetry of Neidhart. Walther gives sharp point to his strictures by the use of the expressive proverbial phrase in 20 ff. and the satirical comparison of the frogs. The nightingale of l. 31 is the courtly lyric poet (cf. Gottfried's *Tristan* 4749).

Metrical form

  Aufgesang: 4 *wv* a ⎱ :‖
                4 *wv* b ⎰

  Abgesang: A 5 *mv* c
          (A) 5 *mv* d
              5 *mv* d
              4 *mv* c (or more probably 5 with rest, to bring it into line
                              with the rest of the *Abgesang*)

Some editors take the four first lines to be 5 *k*, so that if a rest is posited in the last line, all the lines would be five-beat.

106

The poem combines a moving lament for Reinmar's art with a characteristic outspokenness, which introduces an original element into an otherwise con-ventional genre. Walther's admission that he does not regret Reinmar as a man, and that Reinmar would mourn him less were he dead, points to the rivalry which certainly existed between them and which is manifested also in Walther's parodies of Reinmar. The elegy is a testimony to the fame of Reinmar's poems and of his untiring praise of women. Apart from the line which Walther quotes, there are other reminiscences of the same poem; thus ll. 11–13 are similar to Reinmar **87**. 23, and l. 21 is an indirect quotation of **87**. 22. In addition there are other reminiscences of Reinmar's work, showing that Walther knew it well (cf. particularly **89**. 7, 12, and 19–20).

Metrical form

    4 *mv* a
    4 *mv* a
    6 *k* b

    4 *mv* c
    4 *mv* c
    6 *k* b

6 *k* d
6 *k* d
7 *mv* e (or 8 *s* e)
6 *k* f
6 *k* f
7 *mv* e (or 8 *s* e)
7 *mv* e (or 8 *s* e)
Most lines have anacrusis.

107

An extract from Walther's *Leich*. The poem begins with an invocation of the Trinity, and is a prayer to God to redeem sinful man and restore the true spirit of Christianity. The Virgin is addressed in this passage in her capacity as mediator between God and man.

The *Leich* is a development of the liturgical sequence, sung between Gradual and Gospel, consisting originally of prose sections of varying length, but, apart from introduction and conclusion, in exactly corresponding pairs, since the parts were intended to be sung in antiphony. At a later stage, rhyme was introduced on the pattern of hymns. In the Roman Missal five sequences survive for particular Feasts, e.g. the *Victimae paschali* at Easter. The form was later also used for secular subjects, e.g. by Uolrich von Guotenburc in his *Minneleich* (MF 69, 1).

Walther's poem has certain features characteristic of the original type of sequence, in that it treats a religious subject, and has sections of differing length and structure. Section III falls into two exactly equal halves, in keeping with the original antiphonal character of the sequence. In addition, each of the four sections has a counterpart in the second half of the *Leich*, but except in the case of III, the correspondence is approximate, not identical. Sections I, II, and IV depart from the original pattern, in that they are tripartite in form.

The extract here chosen is couched in phraseology characteristic of the Middle Ages. The elements of which it is made up are three-fold: firstly, there is the interpretation of Old Testament events and personages as a prefiguration of Christian history (typology)—thus Aaron's rod, Ezekiel's gate, and the burning bush symbolize the Virgin Birth, and Solomon is the type of Christ; secondly, there is the application of other Scriptural passages to the Virgin (*balsamīte, ūf gēnder morgenrōt*); thirdly there is the use of extra-biblical analogies, such as that of the sun shining through glass, derived from patristic literature. The mysteries of the Christian religion are clothed in paradox: thus *maget und muoter*, the bush burning yet untouched, the conquest of death by death.

Metrical form

I 4 *k*+4 *s* a	II A 2 *mv* a+2 *mv* a
A 4 *k*+4 *s* a	A 4 *mv* b
A 4 *k*+4 *s* b	2 *mv* c+2 *mv* c
A 4 *k*+4 *s* b	A 4 *mv* b
A 4 *k*+4 *s* c	A 2 *wv* d+2 *wv* d
A 4 *mv*+4 *s* c	4 *mv* b

III	4 *mv* a	IV	2 *wv* a+2 *wv* a
	A 4 *mv* a		8 *k* b
	A 4 *mv* a		2 *wv* c+2 *wv* c
	A 2 *mv* a		A 8 *k* b
	A 4 *k* b		2 *wv* d+2 *wv* d
	A 4 *mv* c		A 2 *wv* e+2 *wv* e+4 *k* b
	A 4 *mv* c		
	A 4 *mv* c		
	A 2 *mv* c		
	A 4 *k* b		

It is fairly common in the *Leich* that syntactical and metrical divisions do not correspond, thus l. 13 carries on from the preceding section.

108

The order here adopted is that of BC, with the inversion of the last two strophes as suggested by Kraus (WU). Some editors have taken the first two strophes and the last three as two separate poems, but there is a strong connecting link between them, quite apart from the bond of metrical form.

In I the poet claims from courtly society honour and kindly treatment as his due, since he has served it well for forty years with his songs. He himself is now turning away from his art and can profit from it no longer, but society will continue to benefit, and in exchange he demands its good graces. This first strophe thus already foreshadows the rejection of the world in the last three strophes.

In II the poet substantiates his claim to be considered a member of courtly society, even were he to be reduced to a state of penury. There can be no higher ideal of life than the courtly, if it is directed towards thoughts of the end of life—this again points forward to the final strophes.

III is a rejection of the world and its snares, similar to **109**. The world now has the poet at its mercy, but he prophesies its ultimate destruction. IV turns to a different aspect of mortality, not the world, but the flesh. The *schœnez bilde* is the body. The poet imagines it decaying in death, when the soul (*wunder* 41) has left it. In 45 the poet returns to the present, begging the body to set him free from its corruption, in the expectation that body and soul will be reunited at the Day of Judgement. V is concerned with the fate of the soul, which enjoins the body to renounce earthly in favour of heavenly love. The final strophe is thus closely connected with the turning away from poetry in the first strophe.

Metrical form

The so-called *gespaltene Weise*, in which the *Abgesang* is placed between the two *Stollen*. All the cadences are *männlich voll*.

A 4 a
A 4 b
A 4 b (no anacrusis in l. 3)
A 4 a

A c 6 d   The initial word of ll. 5 and 7 rhymes with the end rhyme of the
A 4 c   following line. The *Abgesang* falls into two symmetrical halves.
A e 6 d
A 4 e

A 4 f
A 4 g
A 4 g
A 4 f

109

This dialogue introduces the common allegorical figure of the world (cf. W. Stammler, *Frau Welt*, Freiburg/Schweiz, 1959). There is a sculptured figure, corresponding to Walther's description in ll. 21–24, on the south façade of Worms Cathedral—a woman fair in front, but foul behind, crawling with serpents and toads. The *wirt* of l. 1 is the devil, who frequently appears in close association with the world, as, e.g., in the Litany: 'the deceits of the world, the flesh and the devil'. There are many different metaphorical conceptions attaching in medieval thought to the devil and the world, whose roles frequently overlap: the devil is 'the prince of this world' (John xii. 31), the world is a house of which he is master, he is a usurer to whom man is in debt through sin (a debt which Christ cancels out by his death on the Cross); the world is the devil's handmaiden, his wife, or a harlot who entices men into his service.

It seems that Walther here draws chiefly on the idea of the world as a house with the devil as its master (*wirt* thus means 'master', 'host'), and that of the devil as a usurer driving a hard bargain. *Frô Welt* is his associate, and at the same time she is depicted as the mother of the world's children (l. 17). The poet's assertion that he has paid his debt in full indicates that he has renounced the temptations of the world and the devil and repented of past sins.

Metrical form

A 4 *mv* a ⎫
A 4 *mv* b ⎭ :‖

A 4 *wv* c
A 4 *wv* x + 4 *wv* c
A 4 *mv* d
A 4 *mv* x + 4 *mv* d

In strophe I the cadences of the first four lines are all disyllabic; in II and IV they are monosyllabic, whereas in III disyllabic alternates with monosyllabic.

110

The text of this poem, only preserved complete in C, with part of the first strophe in E, and part of the third strophe in w^x, is corrupt in many places. Since it was first pointed out that the basic metrical pattern seems to be the long line of the *Nibelungenstrophe*, divided by a caesura into 4 *k* + 4 *s*, and rhyming in couplets, most editors have rearranged the text accordingly. For the majority of lines the received text fits this metrical pattern, as, e.g., in l. 1, where the caesura falls after *verswunden*, and the metrical division corresponds to a syntactic one. The text is, however, so corrupt that in at least thirteen lines (roughly a quarter of the whole), considerable emendation and transposition is necessary in order to 'restore' the metrical pattern. In addition the text suggested by editors sometimes has awkwardly placed caesuras which do not coincide with a syntactical division, e.g. in l. 7:

> *liut unde lant dar inn ich |* (Kraus, Brinkmann, Wapnewski)

It has therefore been thought preferable to leave the text as it is, emending only when the MS. does not make sense. The metrical pattern is not perfect, but this seems the lesser evil.

The poem, usually known as Walther's elegy, is thought to be his last. It refers to events of 1227. In it the poet contrasts the transitoriness of earthly things and the delusory joys of the world with the permanence of a divine reward. The first strophe expresses the mutability of human existence in the familiar image of life as a dream. The poet sees around him nothing but change and decay which are a reflection of his own mortality. In the second strophe he turns to the joyless state of society in general, lamenting particularly the loss of courtly manners and fashions which symbolizes the disappearance of the courtly spirit within. The *unsenfte brieve* of 26 are the papal encyclicals of October 1227, announcing the excommunication of Friedrich II for his delay in carrying out the promised crusading expedition. The last lines introduce the contrast between earthly and heavenly joy, expanded in the last strophe, which characteristically expresses the illusory nature of worldly joy in a series of pictorial images, including that of the world itself as a figure fair without and foul within, reminiscent of *Frô Welt* of **109**.

GOTTFRIED VON STRASSBURG

III

This poem has as its chief theme the evils of covetousness (*gîte*), which is one of the Seven Deadly Sins. It is classed by Walther among the sins barring the way to heaven (L/K 26, 21), and by Freidank as the source of all evil-doing (cf. Vulgate, 1 Tim. vi. 10.):

> swer gîtekeit und erge hat
> deist gruntvest aller missetât.
>
> (91. 2)

Were it not for covetousness, there would be harmony in the world (1). It has grown rampant since the Fall (8) and no man is free from its taint (9). The last three lines introduce the related theme of falsehood, inseparable from *gîte*: men show only falsehood and fickleness (*anderunge*) in word and deed, because they pursue selfish ends. The possible meanings of the cryptic last line are as follows: (1) moral teaching and practice are nothing but hypocrisy, because they conflict with the real state of the world and are merely a cloak for universal selfishness; (2) moral teaching and practice are corrupted by the sinful nature of man. Those who should set an example are no better than the rest. This complaint is found in Freidank (69. 21) with a similar emphasis on the corruption of both teaching and practice:

> Die uns guot bilde solten geben,
> die velschent gnuoge ir selber leben;
> die hœhsten tragent uns lēre vor,
> die manegen leitent in daz hor.
> Swes leben ist wandelbære,
> des lēre ist lihte unmære.

In a poem of Walther's (L/K 34, 27) a similar complaint is directed specifically against priests.

112

This poem is concerned with the familiar theme of the vicissitudes of Fortune. Fortuna, as a personified figure, goes back to Roman art and literature, where she was portrayed as standing either on a wheel or on a sphere, as a sign of her instability. From this there develops the two-fold tradition of the Middle Ages. Most commonly Fortune turns a wheel to which her victims are attached, thus changing their fate with each revolution (l. 1 may derive from this conception). The fact that fortune is here stated to be of glass symbolizes the fragile nature of her blessings. The association of glass with fortune (*vitrea Fortuna*) is found in one of the *Sententiæ* of Publilius Syrus, a common source of medieval proverbial wisdom from which Gottfried may well have derived the idea. All the other characteristics here ascribed to Fortune are commonplaces.

111 and **112** *Metrical form* (similar to that of Walther **92**, with the division of both parts of the strophe into equal halves)

6 *mv* a
6 *mv* a
6 *k* b

6 *mv* c
6 *mv* c
6 *k* b

4 *k* d
8 *k* d
6 *k* e

4 *k* f
8 *k* f
6 *k* e

All lines have anacrusis except **111.** 1, 10, 12 and **112.** 7, 10.

WOLFRAM VON ESCHENBACH

113

The poem begins with what is at first sight a disguised request to be allowed to behold the lady. Like the falcon, the poet's eyes wish to soar towards her (the image also suggests the lady's inaccessibility). It is then made clear in the last two lines that like the owl seeing in the dark, he perceives her only with the eyes of the heart (a common topos). The apparent request of the first lines thus merely suggests the lady's remoteness.

The second strophe expresses the faint hope that one day she may reward him for his faithful service, but the ironical remark of the last line leaves a note of doubt.

The last strophe is obscure, and some editors have denied its connexion with the foregoing. The poet begins by protesting that he causes no injury to women. Although the lady has wronged him, he makes no complaint, and is mindful of his good breeding. This cryptic last line undoubtedly means that he will not speak ill of her; for a similar idea see Reinmar **89.** 6–14 and Hartmann **76.** 19–28. It is a typical example of a disguised complaint, couched in a protestation to the contrary. The whole poem can be thus shown to be made up of traditional elements—the inapproachable and hard-hearted lady, hopeless service, but yet no complaint. It is individualized, however, by the striking images.

Kraus, on the other hand, takes the view that the poem is concerned with two women, that of I–II, whom the poet now serves, and that of III, who formerly ill-treated the poet, but whom he will not now accuse (KLD II, p. 671 f.). He refers the lines to the passage at the end of Book II of *Parzival* where Wolfram rails at one woman for her falsehood, but protests his allegiance to the female sex in general. There is another reference in similar terms at the end of Book VI, where he asks women to admit that he knows how to speak well of them, in spite of his former complaint of one woman. Kraus refers l. 15 to *Parzival* 114. 19 where the poet states that his criticism of one woman has brought upon him the wrath of the whole sex, and ll. 16–18 to *Parzival* 114. 4–18: in contrast to his former outspokenness in *Parzival*, he will now exercise restraint. Kraus thus takes the poem to have been written after the relevant section of *Parzival*. It is, however, much more satisfactory to assume that the poem deals with one unified theme which can be explained without reference to anything outside it.

Metrical form

Aufgesang:　A 4 *mv* a ⎫
　　　　　　 A 4 *mv* b ⎬ :‖
　　　　　　　　　　　 ⎭

Abgesang:　A 4 *mv* c (no anacrusis in l. 17)
　　　　　　 A 4 *mv* c

In strophes II and III *Aufgesang* and *Abgesang* are joined syntactically.

114

The two opening strophes contain the traditional elements of the *Naturein-gang*—summer, flowers, foliage, birdsong—but expressed with a freshness and individuality characteristic of Wolfram. The unconventional features are the vocabulary—*urbort, waltsinger, biclīch, glesten, des touwes anehanc, erliuternt*—and the arresting syntax of the first line (the traditional natural description takes the form of a verbal clause, cf. the opening lines of **1, 7, 23, 34, 38, 43**).

In the two first strophes the description of nature is intimately linked with the poet himself; thus in I the poet compares himself with the birds who sing their familiar song only in summer, whereas he can sing a new song even when frost lies on the ground, in the hope of winning the lady's favour. There is thus already a hint of the plea for a reward which forms the climax of the poem. There is a similar close connexion in II, once more pointing forward to what is to follow. As the flowers and the bird-song are aroused by spring, so he too awakes to a new song.

The last three strophes express the poet's plea for a reward and his endur-ing loyalty. Their coherence of theme is marked by a similar direct address to the lady in each (*güetlich wīp, guot wīp, werdez wīp*) and the repetition of the keyword *helfen* or its derivatives in each of them.

Metrical form

$$
\begin{array}{ll}
\textit{Aufgesang}: & \text{4 } wv \text{ a} \\
& \text{7 } mv \text{ b (probably+rest } = 8 \text{ } s) \\
\textit{Abgesang}: & \text{4 } mv \text{ c} \\
& \text{A 6 } mv \text{ c}
\end{array}
$$

115–118

These poems are examples of the *tageliet*, in which the coming of dawn brings about the lovers' parting. In two of the poems the opening lines describe how the lady perceives the signs of day: in **115** this is related in narrative form, in **118** in direct speech. In **116** and **117** it is the watchman who announces the approach of day; in **117** he refrains from singing his dawn song until he has warned the lovers.

The coming of day is an object of dread. This is graphically suggested in the image of day as a bird of prey whose claws rend apart the clouds (**116**). The day brings sorrow (**115.** 7–8; **118.** 3) and is cursed by the lovers (**118.** 28). Another common feature is the refusal to recognize the signs of day (**116.** 27–30; for the same motif cf. *Romeo and Juliet*, III. v), or the attempt to shut it out (**115.** 12–14).

In all but **118** (since it is unlikely that ll. 1–4 are spoken by the watchman or that the speech is addressed to him), the watchman appears—a figure probably introduced into the German *tageliet* from the Romance lyric. There are earlier examples of the genre in which there is no watchman and the lovers are awakened by bird song, e.g. Anonymous **9**. In **116** and **117** the watchman is depicted as the sympathetic and faithful friend of the lovers, who safeguards their interests and offers good advice.

A central feature of the dawn song is the lovers' complaint. In **115** and **116** it is only the lady who speaks; in **117** the complaint is put into the mouth of the man, and in **118** there are parallel expressions of grief in strophes I and II.

The situation which the *tageliet* describes is fraught with danger because of its secrecy (*tougen* **115**. 2; *verholne* **116**. 19; *tougenlîche* **117**. 4). Frequent mention is made of the perils attendant on the man's departure and safe return (**116**. 6–8, 17–22; **117**. 26; **118**. 11) and there is the risk of betrayal (**117**. 21). None the less the knight disregards the watchman's warning in the final leave-taking (**116**. 36–37; **117**. 31 ff.).

The motif of *urloup* occurs in all the poems. The sorrows of parting prompt renewed enjoyment of love. This is described now with a discreet hint (**116**. 39–40), now in considerable detail, as in **115**, **117**, and **118**. The actual leave-taking is accompanied by a farewell to joy in **117**. 29–30 and **118**. 42. (For this same motif, cf. **9**. 12.) The bond between the lovers transcends physical absence (**115**. 18–20; **116**. 31–32). These last two examples are variations on the familiar theme of the heart as dwelling-place (as, e.g., in **8**).

115 *Metrical form*

I *Aufgesang*: 　A 5 *mv* a　⎫
　　　　　　　　A 4 *k* b　⎬ :‖
　　　　　　　　　5 *mv* c　⎭

　Abgesang: 　　4 *mv* d
　　　　　　　　A 5 *k* x
　　　　　　　　A 4 *s* e
　　　　　　　　A 5 *mv* e
　　　　　　　　A 4 *mv* d

In each strophe the first *Stollen* is clearly marked off by a syntactical pause, whereas the second merges syntactically into the *Abgesang*. There are variations in the placing of anacrusis in strophes II and III.

116 *Metrical form*

I *Aufgesang*: 　(A) 2 *wv* a+4 *mv* b　⎫
　　　　　　　　A 4 *mv* c (Hatto: 5 *s*)　⎬ :‖

　Abgesang: 　A 4 *mv* d
　　　　　　　　A 4 *mv* e (Hatto: 5 *s*)
　　　　　　　　A 4 *mv* d
　　　　　　　　　6 *mv* e (Hatto: 5 *mv*)

Line 6 is metrically unsatisfactory, KLD therefore deletes *bi naht*.
In strophes I, IV, and V *Aufgesang* and *Abgesang* are not divided syntactically.

117 *Metrical form*

　Aufgesang: 　3 *k* a
　　　　　　　　4 *wv* b+2 *mv* c (Kraus, KLD II, p. 686: 4+3 *s* = 7)　⎫ :‖

Abgesang: A 3 *k* d
A 3 *k* d
A 3 *k* d (Hatto: 2 *wv*)
A 3 *s* e (Hatto: 2 *mv*)

A 3 *k* f
A 3 *k* f
A 3 *k* f (Hatto: 2 *wv*)
A 3 *s* e (Hatto: 2 *mv*)
4 *mv* e

In strophe I there is no syntactical division between *Aufgesang* and *Abgesang*.

118 *Metrical form*

I A 2 *mv* a+2 *mv* a+2 *mv* x
A 4 *s* b

A 2 *mv* c+2 *mv* c+2 *mv* x
A 4 *s* b

4 *mv* d
A 4 *mv* d
A 4 *mv* x
A 6 *k* x
5 *k* x+pause = 6 *s* x
A 4 *k* e
A 4 *mv* x
A 4 *mv* x
A 4 *k* e

The high proportion of unrhymed lines is a deliberate curiosity. As Kraus has shown (KLD II, p. 693), many of them are echoed in rhymes of other strophes, e.g. *mir* (3): *ir*: *mir* (41, 43). The last strophe is distinguished from the rest by the lack of syntactical division between *Aufgesang* and *Abgesang*.

119

This poem takes its significance from the references to the conventions of the dawn song, particularly as they appear in **114–18**. The first strophe is addressed to the watchman and only the second strophe makes it clear that the poem is not itself a *tageliet*, but that it contrasts the settled joys of marriage with the painful delights of the illicit love portrayed in the preceding poems. All the details mentioned can be paralleled in the dawn songs proper: the love is secret; the watchman's song brings grief after joy, as in **116**. 9–10; the watchman gives good advice, as in **116** and **117**; the morning star heralds the dawn, as in **116**. 28; the knight's escape is perilous. By contrast love in marriage needs no concealment and fears no betrayal (13, 19).

Metrical form

The structure is unusual in that the *Aufgesang* is placed in the centre of the strophe. Syntactical divisions do not coincide with the divisions into *Aufgesang* and *Abgesang*, except at the end of the second strophe, where the distinction gives prominence to the final lines.

Abgesang:	A 3 *mv* a (Hatto: 4 *s*)
	A 3 *mv* a (Hatto: 4 *s*)
Aufgesang:	A 4 *k* b
	A 4 *k* b
	A 2 *mv* c
	A 4 *k* d
	A 4 *k* d
	A 2 *mv* c
Abgesang:	A 4 *mv* x
	A 4 *s* c

NEIDHART VON REUENTAL

120

This poem is a dialogue between two girls. Some editors have taken the first two strophes to be separate from the dialogue, but it is more likely that they form part of the first speech, particularly on account of the use of the first person in l. 2 and the fact that *wol dan* of l. 12 refers back to what has been said already. The same pattern, with a first speech of three strophes, including the *Natureingang* is found in **123**. The first two strophes are not mere description, but are closely linked with the emotions of the speaker in ll. 2-3 and in l. 10 which is echoed in the closing line of the poem. In the third strophe the girl addresses her companion, inviting her to accompany her to the lime tree, the scene of the village festivities, and the symbolic tree of love. In IV the companion agrees, urging the other to secrecy since, as l. 20 hints, she intends to meet her lover.

Metrical form (bipartite)

2 a
6 a

4 b
6 b
4 b

All the cadences are of the same type (*mv*). Only the first line of each strophe has anacrusis. Lines 16 and 21 are corrupt and Wiessner's emendations, here adopted, bring them into line with the other first lines.

121

The poem is given in the order of R, except that in R, VIII precedes VII. In MS. c it bears the superscription *enhalb mers gesungen*, and is a Crusader's lament for home. The poem refers to the expedition of Leopold VII of Austria to Syria and Damietta (1217–19), in which many Bavarians took part. The Crusaders suffered from pestilence (l. 54) and the overbearing behaviour of Italians and Burgundians (ll. 41–42). The reference to *ougest* in l. 73 is probably an allusion to the exhortations of the papal legate who promised indulgences to those who stayed until the autumn of 1219.

The poem begins with the customary natural description. The bird song of the second strophe provides a transition to the poet's own situation—he would gladly earn the gratitude of those at home with his song, since it is disregarded by the Italians and French. In strophes III–VII the poet imagines himself sending a messenger, assuring the lady of his constancy and informing those at home of the Crusaders' plight. In VIII the wish to act as messenger himself arouses further thoughts of the lady. Success in love would be beneficial to his poetry and would thus gladden others (IX). In X the poet imagines those at home dancing, with himself taking part. This recalls him abruptly to reality, and the last strophe sums up the weariness and longing for home, pregnantly expressed in the closing line. As in other poems, there is a mixture of courtly vocabulary (e.g. *sendiu arebeite*) and colloquial expressions (*geswanzen, narre*).

Metrical form

    I A 4 *k* a
       A 4 *mv* b
       A 2 *mv* b
         4 *k* a
       A 4 *mv* c
       A 2 *mv* c
         8 *k* a

There is some variation in the position of anacrusis in other strophes.

122

The first three strophes are spoken by the poet, who describes the beauty of the season and exhorts the girls to prepare for the dance. The last four strophes are spoken alternately by a girl and her companion. The first one answers the poet with a complaint of men's fickleness, to which the second replies that there are still men who know how to serve women, her suitor among them. The first girl then offers the present of a belt in exchange for the revelation of the suitor's identity, which is given in the final verse.

There is deliberate irony in the contrast between the village setting and the vocabulary of courtly poetry applied to it: *höfesch, wolgetān, minneclīch, tump, vreude und ēre, getiuwert, dienen, lōnen, trūren, holt*. Similarly, there is a pointed contrast between the courtly word *zieren* and its uncourtly equivalent *zäfen*. Side by side with the conventional diction of courtly love there is a greater precision of concrete detail, lacking in the earlier poets: *Beier, Swäbe, Vranken; ir brīset iuwer hemde wīz mit sīden wol zen lanken; gürtel, nōne.* In keeping with this semblance of greater realism is the mention of the poet's name in the last verse.

Metrical form

  Aufgesang: (A) 4 *k* a
            A 2 *mv* b } :‖

  Abgesang: 6 *k* c
           A 4 *k* c
           A 4 *mv* x+4 *k* c

For the tune, given in MS. c, cf. Hatto/Taylor no. 1, and Rohloff no. 11.

123

The first three strophes are spoken by a girl, as ll. 10 and 14–15 make clear. They contain the customary description of the summer season and the invitation to a companion to prepare for the dance. Strophes IV and V are an exchange between the girl and her mother. The mother taunts the girl with duplicity and attempts to prevent her departure, to which the girl replies with insolence. VI and VII relate the breaking open of the chest and the fulfilment of the girl's intentions, with the revelation of the lover's identity in the last strophe as in **122**. There is a contrast between the stylized vocabulary of the nature description and the speech of mother and daughter, with such forceful expressions as *kradem*.

Metrical form

  (A) 6 *k* a
  A 6 *k* a

  A 4 *mv* b
  A 4 *mv* b
     6 *mv* b

124

Strophe I is a nature introduction. Neidhart varies his customary assertion that the beauty of the season is unsurpassed, by the humorous exaggeration of the phrase *sīt künc Karels zīten*. In II Wendelmuot contrasts her own sorrows with the joys of spring—she has been punished by the locking away of her finery. Her companion Rīchilt demands an explanation, and in strophes III to V Wendelmuot describes her scornful refusal of a peasant suitor, in favour of Riuwental, named, as is customary, in the last strophe.

Metrical form

    6 *k* a
    6 *k* a
  A 2 *mv* b
    4 *mv* b
    3 *k* c
  A 4 *k* c

125

The first two strophes of natural description are unusual in that ll. 13–16 introduce the sadness of the narrator in contrast to the joys of the season. Strophes III–VI consist of a dialogue between two girls. The use of the word *besunder* in l. 20 indicates that they both speak. The most satisfactory arrangement is to take ll. 22–24 as spoken by the first speaker, and ll. 25–40 by the second. Thus *leit und ungemüete* of l. 25 is a response to l. 22, whereas it would be merely a feeble repetition if the speaker were the same in both cases. In VI the first speaker reveals the object of her affections as the knight of Riuwental.

The unconnected last strophe is once more spoken by the poet, expressing his wish for a permanent home—no doubt a request to a patron. It is paralleled to some extent by the introduction of his own emotions in II. It is not unusual in the Romance lyric for the poet to turn at the end of a poem to his own affairs.

Metrical form (tripartite)

  I A 4 *k* a ⎞ :‖
    A 2 *mv* b ⎠
      2 *mv* c
    A 4 *mv* c
    A 6 *k* d
    A 4 *k* d

The placing of anacrusis varies slightly in the other strophes.

126

Strophe I describes the depredations of winter, II the proposal for an indoor dance. In III the invitations are issued, with a rich display of names, as in V. In IV the poet pleads against the prevailing fashion in headdresses. In V there is a change to the past tense in the description of a brawl between the peasants. In VI the poet turns to his own poverty: formerly he had a fine head of curls (this idea is probably suggested by the thought of some peasant dandy) but now his only care must be the provision of food for his family. The diatribe against the man responsible is probably only a piece of humorous self-mockery. For a similar final strophe, cf. **125**. Again it can be taken as a plea for reward, here indirectly expressed.

For the tune, see Hatto/Taylor no. 3, and Rohloff no. 35.

Metrical form

6 *mv* a
4 *mv* b
7 *mv* c (Hatto/Taylor: 8 *s*)
6 *mv* a
4 *mv* b
7 *mv* c

6 *mv* d
4 *mv* e
4 *mv* e
3 *mv* d (Hatto/Taylor: 4 *s*)

127

The poem begins, as is customary, with a nature introduction, but the first strophe is equally concerned with the poet's suffering, in harmony with the desolation of the season. The stock situation of rejected service is given a comic turn at the end of the second strophe by the introduction of the peasant rival Hildebolt. Strophes III and IV are a diatribe against upstart peasant wooers, and V a detailed inventory of their fashionable clothes. Strophe VI is a description of a brawl at the dance similar to that of **126**.

In the last two verses the poet turns to the outer circumstances of his life. He has been driven from Riuwental by the intrigues of his enemies, but has found shelter in Melk, where the prince (Duke Frederick of Austria) has taken him in. MS. c alone inserts a further verse between these last two describing in more detail the poet's banishment from Bavaria. The popularity of this poem is shown by its survival in so many MSS. For the tune, see Hatto/Taylor no. 10, and Rohloff no. 49.

Metrical form

8 *k* a
7 *mv* b
8 *k* a
7 *mv* b
8 *mv* c
11 *mv* c

128

The first strophe combines a lament for winter with that for the poet's own sufferings. The lady is hard-hearted, but he will none the less continue to serve her. A further cause of grief is his persecution by the peasant Adeltir, on account of his song. A deliberately comic note is struck at the end of III by the incongruous simile, which is, however, appropriate to the peasant opponent. IV is an account of an episode at the dance, when Lanze roughly wrests kerchief and garland from the poet's mistress (though her identity is not made clear until ll. 68–70). The incident arouses memories of all the past injuries suffered at the hands of boorish peasants and the desire for revenge. In the last strophe the poet gets the better of his rival by ridiculing his would-be courtly clothes and affected manner of speech. For the tune, see Hatto/Taylor no. 12, and Rohloff no. 28.

Metrical form

> 4 *k* a ⎫
> 4 *k* b ⎪
> 4 *mv* c ⎬ :‖
> 7 *mv* d ⎭   (Hatto/Taylor: 8 *s*)
> 4 *mv* e
> 4 *k* f
> 4 *mv* e
> 4 *k* f

REINMAR VON ZWETER

129

It is in keeping with the didactic nature of Reinmar's poetry that he should portray love as a school of virtue, teaching social graces, inner excellence, and inspiring knightly deeds.

Metrical form

Aufgesang: (A) 4 *mv* a
          (A) 4 *k*+4 *mv* a
          A 4 *k*+5 b (probably with a pause marking the end of the
                   Stollen = 4 *k*+6 *s* b)

          A 4 *mv* c
          (A) 4 *k*+4 *mv* c
          (A) 4 *k*+5 b (probably with pause = 4 *k*+6 *s* b)

Abgesang: A 6 *k* d
          A 6 *k* d
          A 5 *k* e
          A 4 *mv* f
          A 4 *mv* f
          A 2+4 *k* e

130

Such allegorical interpretation of clothing or armour in terms of virtues or vices is common in medieval poetry.

Metrical form: as **129** and **130** except that the first half of l. 5 has only three beats, a variant found also in other poems of the same *Ton*.

131

The metaphor of life or the world as a storm-tossed sea of sin, in which man is shipwrecked without divine aid, is of wide currency in theological literature (cf. for instance *Ezzos Gesang* 395 f.). To the same metaphorical complex belongs the image of priests who instead of being fishers of men, fish only for money and let the soul perish. There is a similar criticism in Freidank 152, 16 ff.:

> Daz netze kam ze Rōme nie,
> dā mite sant Pēter vische vie;
> daz netze ist nu versmāhet.
> rœmesch netze vāhet
> silber, golt, bürge und lant;
> daz was sant Pēter unbekant.

Metrical form as **129**.

ULRICH VON SINGENBERG

132

The first two strophes spoken by the poet and the third by the lady are bound together by a refrain, varied to suit the change of speaker. The refrain expresses the continuing reality of unrewarded service; in I and II it deliberately negates the effect of the preceding lines which are seen as merely wish-fulfilment.

Metrical form

A 4 *mv* a ⎫
A 6 *mv* b ⎭ :‖
A 6 *mv* c
A 7 *mv* c
A 5 *mv* d
A 7 *mv* d

133

The first four strophes refer to the situation of the dawn song, as the refrain makes clear. The speaker describes the joys experienced by lovers, whose only sorrow is the enforced parting at dawn, contrasting with them in III his own unhappiness. The last strophe is set directly in the context of the dawn song. It is apparently an exhortation by the watchman to the knight to depart. The motif of the exchange of hearts is very common in the dawn song. The variation of the refrain in the last verse with the introduction of a new speaker is similar to **132**.

Metrical form

A 4 *mv* a ⎫
A 8 *mv* b ⎭ :‖
A 8 *mv* c
A 8 *mv* c

BURKHARD VON HOHENFELS

134

This invitation to an indoor winter dance has a strongly marked rhythm appropriate to the subject. The images of the last lines (*lüedert, lucket, klobe,* and l. 18) are derived from bird-snaring and falconry. Winterstetten applies a similar metaphor to *Minne* in **148**. 39–40.

Metrical form

2 *wv* a+2 *wv* b
2 *wv* a+2 *wv* b
2 *mv* c
2 *wv* d+2 *wv* d+2 *mv* c

135

The poet makes use of animal similes in each strophe, applying them in I to the lady, in the rest to himself. In III–V the similes are derived from traditional animal lore. The use of eagle and falcon metaphorically is common, cf., e.g., Reinmar (MF 156, 12):

> ze fröiden swinget sich mîn muot,
> als der valke enfluge tuot
> und der are ensweime.

The image of the fish caught in a net, or more often on a hook, is common in both secular and religious poetry, typifying either the heart caught in the toils of love, or the soul captured by Christ. The ape simile is derived from Aesop, that of the bees obeying their ruler from a tradition going back to Virgil (see note on **91**). The final image of the unicorn tamed by a pure virgin is derived from the *Physiologus*, a collection of allegorical interpretations of animals, widely current in the Middle Ages. In it the unicorn typifies Christ, the pure maiden the Virgin, but like the fish image above, the simile is also found in secular contexts.

Metrical form

4 *wv* a ⎫
4 *mv* b ⎭ :‖

1 *mv* c+3 *wv* d
1 *wv* d+3 *mv* c

The regular alternation of the two types of cadence and the rhyming of the first word of l. 5 with the last of l. 6, and of the last word of l. 5 with the first of l. 6 is extremely skilful.

136

This dialogue between two girls, in which one complains that her clothes have been locked away, preventing her from going to the dance, is similar to those of Neidhart. There is, however, a new element in the introduction of the idea of social inequality between the girls, the one envying the freedom of the other and determining to avenge herself by taking a suitor of inferior rank. The refrain serves to emphasize the desire of both girls to be free of all restraint, in that the straw garland symbolizes the wish to remain single and is also the traditional punishment for free love, whereas the rose garland here symbolizes, as often, virginity, being the traditional adornment of the bride (cf. Grimm, *Deutsches Wörterbuch* under 'Kranz').

Metrical form

2 *wv* a ⎫
4 *mv* b ⎭ :‖

4 *wv* c ⎫
2 *mv* d ⎭ :‖

6 *mv* e
6 *mv* e

137

The imagery of this poem is extremely varied: the predominant metaphor is that of the chase (I, II, and V); IV contains the related metaphor of bird-snaring, III that of sea-faring, whereas III and V have variations of the idea that Love delineates an image in the lover's heart. In addition I–III each introduce a traditional animal simile.

In the first strophe *herze* sends *sin* and *muot* to pursue the quarry. These three keywords are paralleled by *sin . . . muot . . . gedenken* (referring this time to the lady), which are swift to escape pursuit, and could only be out-witted by the fox's cunning. Strophe II develops this theme further, with varied repetition of the three keywords, as in I. The lady's strength, which binds the poet in bonds of love, is compared to the lion's. In III the metaphor changes: the anchor of grief is contrasted with the sails of joy. Lines 26–28 combine two common ideas, the image delineated in the heart, and that irremovably locked in the breast. For the first, cf. the Shakespeare sonnet beginning: Mine eye hath play'd the painter and hath stell'd / Thy beauty's form in table of my heart, for the second, Anonymous 8. The reference to the griffin's fabled strength is in keeping with the animal similes of the two preceding strophes.

Strophe IV prepares the return to the metaphor of the hunt with the image of the lady as the bird-snarer, as in **138**: *werfen, vâhen, stric, swingen, gevangen* are all appropriate to the image. In V Minne is the huntress, seeking out and assisting the lover who practises *triuwe*, and flattering all his desires. Lines 47–50 are related to 26–28, with the difference that now Love is expressly stated to be the painter.

The three-fold arrangement of keywords, repeated in I and II, is also present in the other verses: *hôher muot, fröiden segel, werder trôst* in III, *blic, gruoz, schœne* and *fröiden, sælde, êre* in IV, *fröiden, wunsch, gedanken* in V. The verses are also linked together by the use of similar or grammatical rhymes, e.g. *enbor:vor* beside *spor:vor*; *gewunnen* beside *gewinne* and *gewan*.

Metrical form

$$
\left.
\begin{array}{l}
4 \; mv \; \text{a} \\
4 \; mv \; \text{b} \\
4 \; wv \; \text{c}
\end{array}
\right\} :\|
$$

5 *mv* d
4 *wv* e
4 *wv* e
5 *mv* d

138

The first strophe praises the lady in terms of the image of the sun outshining the stars, which is found elsewhere, for instance in Walther, who describes the lady appearing among others *alsam der sunne gegen den sternen stât* (L/K 46, 15). The metaphor is continued with *zünden* in l. 8. Into the second and third strophes are interwoven metaphors of bird-snaring and falconry (cf. also **135** and Wolfram **113**, which may have influenced the poet) with the difference that in II these are implicitly expressed, in III explicitly stated. In II *wilder muot* attempts to fly free, but is riveted by a glance from the lady's eyes, bound and caught in the snare. In III the metaphor is made explicit with a simile: like a falcon his heart tries to escape but cannot. The emphasis now changes: fearing that the lady, like the quarry, will elude it, it swoops back to her. The metaphorical associations are thus extremely intricate: both the lady and the lover are compared, directly or indirectly, now with the falcon, now with the quarry. The words *wild, strîchen, bant, stric, fluht, swingen, vliegen, valke, gir,* and *wenken* (used similarly in **135.** 3 and **137.** 9, 17) are appropriate to the metaphorical complex. Similarly, the description of the lady's gaze in ll. 13 and 18–20 suggests, in addition to the literal meaning, the keen-eyed hawk paralysing its victim.

Metrical form

$$
\left.
\begin{array}{l}
4 \; wv \; \text{a} \\
4 \; mv \; \text{b}
\end{array}
\right\} :\|
$$

4 *mv* c
4 *mv* d
4 *mv* c
4 *wv* e
4 *wv* e
4 *mv* d

ULRICH VON LIECHTENSTEIN

139

The poem, designated as *sancwîse*, is chiefly in praise of *merken* and *huote,* the watch and guard imposed upon conduct. The poet rebukes their detractor (ll. 1–4), commending them if they are prompted by worthy motives, since they are the protectors of virtue in women. Strophe IV turns to the poet's own lady, who guards herself from reproach, save in one particular: she fails to recognize his suffering and his constancy. The praise of *huote* thus leads to a complaint of unrewarded service. The transition is achieved by the use of *huote* and *merken* in a double sense: the former designates both the watchfulness of the *merkære* and the guard the lady imposes upon herself; the latter has in addition to its specialized meaning when connected with *merkære* (as in l. 3), the ordinary sense of 'perceive' (as in ll. 5–7, 26, 29, 33).

Metrical form

A 4 *mv* a ⎫
A 4 *mv* b ⎬ :‖
A 4 *mv* c
A 4 *mv* c
A 4 *mv* c

There are frequent echoing rhymes, e.g. *gehaz*:*baz* (I); *haz*:*daz*:*baz* (II).

140

This dialogue, designated as *tanzwīse*, formulates some of the classic conventions of *minne*, particularly in strophes I and III. The man offers constant service and praise of the lady in hope of reward. The lady replies by declaring that the joy engendered by service is itself a gain (for a similar idea of service as its own reward, cf. **61**). She rejects his extravagant praises as a mockery.

Metrical form

All the lines are four-beat with the same type of cadence and without anacrusis. The speakers are differentiated by the rhyme scheme as follows: in I and III the same rhyme is repeated throughout the strophe, and in the first four lines of the last strophe; in II each line rhymes with the corresponding line in IV, and lines 33–35 repeat the rhymes in the last three lines of II and IV.

141

This poem, designated as *ūzreise*, is in the spirit of the *Frauendienst*, in which the poet recounts his fantastic exploits under arms in service of the lady. The first five strophes are a general exhortation: chivalrous deeds are a means of winning both honour and renown and the lady's favour. The close connexion between knighthood and *minne* is shown in V, in which pusillanimity is equated with treachery towards women. In the last two strophes the poet affirms his determination to conquer the lady's love by feats of arms.

Metrical form

6 *k* a
6 *k* a
A 4 *k* b
2 *mv* c+2 *mv* c
A 4 *k* b

There are echoing rhymes, e.g., *schouwen*:*frouwen* in I and VI, and grammatical rhyme in III: *grüezen*:*süezen*; *grüezet*:*gesüezet*.

GOTTFRIED VON NEIFEN

142

The poem begins with a nature introduction: the desolation of winter is paralleled by the poet's sorrow. The lady's eyes have pierced through to his heart and wounded him. This idea and that of love as a sickness in l. 16, are both common topoi. Since she alone is the cause of his suffering, the poet asks *Minne* to assist him in winning the lady's love, the only cure for his disease.

Metrical form

```
1 mv a+3 wv b
6 mv c
4 wv b
6 mv c

6 k d
4 k d
6 k d
6 mv a
```

Rhyme a, binding the first word of the strophe to the last, is an identical rhyme, but variety is introduced either by the addition of a further element as in *bant*:*gebant*, or by the semantic contrast between homophones as in *wer* (interr. pron.): *wer* (3rd pers. pres. subj.).

143

The second and third strophes of the MS. have been transposed, as is usual, on account of the sense. The opening lines express a contrast between the joys of spring and the poet's sorrows. Praise of the lady is mingled with a complaint of her indifference. The last line alludes once more, as in **142**, to the idea of love as a sickness which only the lady can cure.

Metrical form

```
2 wv a+5 mv b (Kraus, KLD II, p. 106: 2+6 s)
2 wv a+5 mv b (ibid.: 2+6 s)
4 mv c
A 1 wv d+2 wv d+4 mv c (ibid: 1+2+5 s)
```

The pattern is varied in the last line of the last strophe as follows: 2 *mv* d+ 2 *mv* d+3 *mv* c. There are several echoing rhymes, e.g., *zīt*:*gīt*; *strīt*:*enzīt*.

144

This poem contains the usual elements: the nature introduction, the complaint of unrequited love, the request to *Minne* to reward constancy. Love is described in conventional terms as a wound (l. 12), as bondage (32 and 43), and as a flame (33–36). There is remarkable skill in the use of the so-called *Pausenreim*: the poet manages to repeat two pairs of these rhymes in each strophe, without violating syntax or sense. The first pair of rhymes in each

Stollen are identical rhymes, but differentiated from each other by the same means as in **142**. In addition, the first internal rhyme in the first line rhymes with the last line of the strophe, and there are several instances of echoing rhymes, e.g., *haz:baz* beside *daz:baz*.

Metrical form

3 *mv* a+1 *mv* b
1 *mv* b+3 *wv* c
1 *wv* c+5 *mv* d
4 *mv* b
1 *mv* b+3 *wv* c
1 *wv* c+5 *mv* d
6 *k* e
6 *k* e
7 *mv* a (probably 8 with final rest)

WAHSMUOT VON KUNZICH

145

This poem combines a gracefully turned complaint of the lady's indifference with malediction of the *merkære*, in a polished verse form. There is effective use of contrast: *vor allen wīben*: *vor einem man*; *lieben*: *leiden*; *herzeliep*: *herzeleit*.

Metrical form

6 *wv* a
5 *mv* b (probably 6 *s*, with pause marking end of *Stollen*) } :||

6 *wv* c
4 *mv* d
6 *wv* c
5 *mv* d (probably 6 *s*, with pause marking end)

146

The first strophe alludes indirectly to the dawn song, in particular by implication to the lovers' complaint at parting, with which the poet contrasts his own situation: although he has not experienced happiness such as theirs, yet he remains joyful. He has served constantly, and if the lady finds his service wanting, the will must serve for the deed.

Metrical form

4 *mv* a
4 *mv* b } :||

A 6 *k* c
3 *mv* d (Kraus, KLD II, p. 602: 4 *s* with rest)
6 *k* c
A 5 *mv* d (ibid.: 6 *s* with rest)

147

The nature introduction is at once a lament for the passing of summer and for its failure to bring joy. The second strophe expresses the common idea of the wound inflicted through the eyes to the heart, here combined with that of love's darts. Only the lady has the physic to cure this wound.

Metrical form

6 *k* a }
4 *mv* b } :‖

4 *mv* c
6 *k* a
4 *mv* c

The unusual enjambement in ll. 13–14 is no doubt a deliberate attempt to break the even flow of the lines, thus avoiding monotony and marking the conclusion more forcibly.

ULRICH VON WINTERSTETTEN

148

The poem begins with a nature introduction, unusual in that it presents the manifestations of summer, with a certain ironic detachment, as suitable material for the poet. The refrain provides the only link with the main subject of the poem, although there is also present an implicit contrast between the joys of summer and the pains of love. The elaboration of the *hort* image permits the poet to give an original twist to the old ideas of the heart as dwelling place (15–16) and the heart remaining with the beloved (13–14). The reference to Cupid is unusual in the *Minnesang*, in which only the personification of *Minne* is customary, as in the last strophe. The sovereign power of love is illustrated by the image of the bird-snarer.

Metrical form

4 *wv* a
3 *mv* b (Kraus, KLD II, p. 584: 4 *s*) } :‖
5 *mv* c (ibid.: 6 *s*)
2 *wv* d+2 *wv* d+2 *mv* c
5 *mv* c (ibid.: 6 *s*)
Refrain   4 *mv* e
5 *mv* e (ibid.: 6 *s*)

149

The poem is chiefly remarkable for its form, which is used to express traditional ideas of the pains of love, now as bondage (l. 6), now as wound (l. 14), for which the only remedy is the lady's kiss.

Metrical form

4 *k* a+2 *k* a+2 *mv* b
4 *k* c+2 *k* c+2 *s* b
4 *k* d+2 *k* d+2 *mv* e
4 *k* f+2 *k* f+2 *s* e
4 *wv* g+4 *mv* h
4 *wv* g+4 *mv* h
4 *k* i+2 *k* i+1 *wv* j+1 *mv* k
4 *k* j+4 *s* k

150

The poem contains familiar elements of the dawn song: the secret relationship, the watchman's song announcing day, the lovers' lament, renewed love-making before parting, the exchange of hearts. It shows signs of Wolfram's influence.

Metrical form

A 2 *mv* a+4 *k* b ⎫
A 4 *s* a   ⎬ :‖

A 4 *mv* c
A 4 *mv* c
A 4 *mv* d
A 4 *mv* x
A 4 *mv* d

KONRAD VON WÜRZBURG

151

This poem combines the topoi of love as a flame and a wound with extravagant praise of the lady, concluding with the allegorical idea of the clothing of virtue, as in Reinmar von Zweter, 130.

Metrical form

2 *mv* a   ⎫
2 *wv* b+2 *mv* c ⎬ :‖

2 *wv* b   ⎫
2 *wv* b+2 *mv* c ⎬ :‖

3 *mv* c
4 *mv* c
4 *mv* c
4 *mv* c

The eightfold repetition of rhyme c in each strophe and the subtle variation in the two groups of paired lines show great technical skill.

T

152

This extreme example of technical virtuosity is remarkable in that syntax and sense hardly suffer from the intricate rhyme scheme, except in the unusual construction *weinen trīben*. The poem is a complaint of day as bringer of sorrow to those who have enjoyed love's delights secretly, and is thus related to the *tageliet*, of which two examples by the same poet are extant.

Metrical form

The outline metrical form is as follows:

6 *k* a
7 *mv* b } :‖

6 *k* c
6 *k* d } :‖

In addition each single word or prefix rhymes with another word in the corresponding line in the same half of the strophe; thus the words in the first line of the first *Stollen* (l. 1) rhyme with those in the first line of the second *Stollen* (l. 3).

153

The lady's heart is described as an ambush where love lies in wait to despoil the lover. The image is that of highway robbery, as ll. 7–8 make clear. If, however, he is able to surprise her in her hiding-place, she can be made to return what she has stolen. The transition from the return of what has been stolen to the exchange of embraces between the lovers is not altogether happily effected in l. 12, and the whole metaphor gives the impression of being artificially contrived.

Metrical form (there are twenty-five poems written in the same form, mostly of a religious or didactic nature)

A 8 *k* a
A 8 *k* a
  4 *k* a
A 4 *mv* b

A 8 *k* c
A 8 *k* c
  4 *k* c
A 4 *mv* b

A 7 *mv* d
A 4 *mv* d
A 4 *k* e
A 8 *k* e
A 8 *k* e
  4 *k* e
A 4 *mv* b

154

This poem views earthly things in typical medieval fashion as symbolic: sleep is the image of death, the shadow of the brevity of life, heat of the flames of hell, flowers of the vanity of pleasures, the mirror of fleshly corruption. The picture of the charnel house, with its insistence on physical decay, common in the treatment of such themes, introduces a forcible admonition to avoid sin and the torments of hell.

Metrical form as **153**.

155

This poem follows naturally upon the preceding one: it is a reminder that time is the one commodity whose loss can never be repaired.

Metrical form as **153**.

STEINMAR

156

Into the extravagant praise of the lady (couched in conventional terms) are introduced two original similes, that of the falcon in ll. 6–7, and that of the last strophe, in which the lady is compared to an angel, freeing the soul from purgatory.

Metrical form

$$
\left.
\begin{array}{l}
4 \ wv \ a \\
4 \ mv \ b
\end{array}
\right\} :\|
$$

4 *mv* c
4 *wv* x
4 *mv* c

157

The first two strophes depict the frequent contrast between summer and the poet's mood. The refrain, subtly varied in each verse, expresses the dominant theme of unrewarded love. Strophe III describes how the radiance of the lady's beauty penetrates through the eyes to the heart: the poet appears to combine the topos of the wound of love (as in **142**. 10–14 and **147**. 8–9) with that of the sun shining through objects without infringing their wholeness, an image usually applied to the Virgin Birth, as in Walther's *Leich*, **107**. Up to this point the poem is in the traditional vein. Strophe IV breaks the illusion by introducing the deliberately ludicrous images of the pig and the dragon, suggesting at once self-mockery and mockery of the conventions. In strophe V the poet's well-wishers, to whom his complaint is addressed, remind him of the lady's virtues. He replies by begging them to wish him success with the lady, but the down-to-earth expression *dur ganzen kern* concludes the poem on an ironic note.

Metrical form

$$
\left.
\begin{array}{l}
4\ wv\ \text{a} \\
4\ mv\ \text{b}
\end{array}
\right\} :\|
$$

$$
\begin{array}{l}
4\ mv\ \text{c} \\
4\ wv\ \text{x} \\
4\ mv\ \text{c}
\end{array}
$$

Refrain
$$
\begin{array}{l}
4\ mv\ \text{d} \\
4\ wv\ \text{x} \\
4\ mv\ \text{d}
\end{array}
$$

158

In this summer song there is a comic contrast between the conventional phraseology of the *Minnesang* and the object to which it is applied, as in the juxtaposition of *mīnes herzen frouwen* and *eine dirne diu nāch krūte gāt*. The situation, with preparations for the dance and stolen meetings against the wishes of a tyrannical mother, is reminiscent of Neidhart.

Metrical form

$$
\left.
\begin{array}{l}
4\ mv\ \text{a} \\
4\ k\ \text{b}
\end{array}
\right\} :\|
$$

$$
\begin{array}{l}
4\ wv\ \text{c} \\
4\ wv\ \text{c} \\
2\ mv\ \text{d} \\
4\ mv\ \text{d}
\end{array}
$$

Refrain
$$
\begin{array}{l}
3\ mv\ \text{e} \\
6\ mv\ \text{e}
\end{array}
$$

159

This parody of the *tageliet* contains several motifs common in the genre: secrecy, the announcing of daybreak (here by the shepherd instead of the watchman) renewed love-making before parting.

Metrical form

$$
\left.
\begin{array}{l}
\text{A}\ 4\ k\ \text{a} \\
\text{A}\ 4\ s\ \text{b}
\end{array}
\right\} :\|
$$

$$
\begin{array}{l}
\text{A}\ 4\ s\ \text{c} \\
4\ k\ \text{x}{+}4\ s\ \text{c}
\end{array}
$$

DER WILDE ALEXANDER

160

The poem is allegorical, as the last strophe shows. The depiction of childish pleasures serves to illustrate the transitoriness of life and the passage of time (*alsus gēt diu zīt von hin*), and the loss of innocence. The strawberry and the violet are sometimes used in Christian iconography as emblems of righteousness and humility respectively, and they probably have this function here. The forest represents the world, and the snake the temptation of sin. The words of the *waltwīser* and the shepherd are exhortations to flee evil. The allusion to the parable of the foolish virgins makes the moral import clear. The last lines probably signify the final loss of vain earthly pleasures.

For the tune, see Holz/Saran/Bernouilli II, p. 13.

Metrical form

4 *wv* a
4 *wv* a
4 *mv* b
4 *mv* b
4 *k* c
3 *k* c
4 *mv* b

HADLAUB

161

The first two strophes are a lament for summer and the joy of admiring ladies in their summer attire. Only he can rejoice in winter who is fortunate in love. The last two strophes are a malediction of the *merker*, who guard the lady too closely.

Metrical form

6 *mv* a
A 2 *mv* a+2 *mv* b
6 *mv* c
A 2 *mv* c+2 *mv* b

A 5 *mv* d
6 *mv* e
A 2 *mv* e+2 *mv* d

162

The first three strophes are an eloquent complaint of domestic care and the difficulty of providing for a family. In the last two strophes the poet describes the sorrows inflicted by the lady as even more painful.

Metrical form

6 *mv* a
A 2 *mv* a+3 *mv* b
6 *mv* c
A 2 *mv* c+3 *mv* b
A 4 *mv* d
6 *mv* e
A 2 *mv* e+3 *mv* d

163

This dawn song is unusual in that it is spoken entirely by the watchman, expressing fears for the safety of the lovers and his own, if they do not heed his warning of the approach of day.

Metrical form

A 4 *k* a
A 4 *k* a
A 4 *mv* b
A 4 *k* c
A 4 *k* c
A 4 *mv* b

A 4 *mv* b
A 4 *k* d
A 4 *k* d
A 4 *mv* b

164

This peasant quarrel is reminiscent of similar scenes in Neidhart. It is depicted with vigour and humour, particularly in the unexpected conclusion, when two goats and a hen suffice to buy off the rival lover. The dialect words *stetschen* and *getschen* and the phrase of 21 are appropriate to the milieu.

Metrical form

3 *mv* a ⎫
6 *k* b ⎬ :‖
6 *k* b ⎭
6 *k* d
6 *k* d
3 *mv* e
5 *mv* e
6 *k* d

165

Steinmar had already written a poem in similar vein, praising the abundance of food and drink brought by autumn; to this realistic enumeration Hadlaub appends two strophes in conventional style, lamenting the passing of summer and the lady's hard-heartedness.

Metrical form

4 *wv* a
2 *wv* a+2 *mv* b
2 *mv* b+3 *mv* c
4 *wv* d
2 *wv* d+2 *mv* e
2 *mv* e+3 *mv* c

4 *mv* c
2 *mv* f
4 *wv* g
2 *wv* g+2 *mv* h
2 *mv* h+3 *mv* f

166

The first strophe is an invitation to the village girls to prepare for the harvest festivities; it has similarities to Neidhart **122**. The mention of the free enjoyment of love in l. 10 leads the poet in the second strophe to contrast with it his own unhappy situation: the guard imposed on the lady prevents access to her. The last strophe elaborates further the theme of sorrowful yet inescapable love.

Metrical form

4 *k* a
5 *mv* b
2 *k* a+4 *mv* c
4 *k* d
5 *mv* b
2 *k* d+4 *mv* c

2 *mv* e+4 *k* x (4 *k* d in III)
2 *mv* e+2 *mv* e
5 *mv* e
5 *mv* e

FRAUENLOB

167

This poem contains a rich accumulation of metaphors. Womanhood is a garden of delight, in which the individual women are flowers. Love resides in their glances like dew on a flower. The garland of womanly virtue can capture swift thought (6–7). Love can enter the shrine of the heart (8–10). In ll. 11–12 Love is described as dispensing a never-ending abundance of blessings on women from an over-flowing coffer. The use of *blüemen* in the sense of 'adorn' is a link with the garden metaphor above. A further metaphorical idea, that of a boundless sea, is introduced with *vlüete*.

With the beginning of the *Abgesang*, the theme changes; Love is reproached for permitting women to grieve their friends and not repulse their enemies. The paradoxical reply imputed to Love is in keeping with the complication of the whole: love's pains bring a rich reward.

The manner of expression is complex: nouns replace adjectives, as in *der bluomen lust, des gedanken snelle*; verbs are replaced by periphrastic verbal constructions such as *ein lieplich sträfen zern,* and nouns and verbs occur in unusual combinations such as *wandel nern.*

Metrical form

A 6 *mv* a	A 6 *mv* d	A 4 *mv* f
A 2 *mv* a	A 2 *mv* d	A 4 *mv* f
A 4 *k* b	A 4 *k* e	A 2 *mv* f
4 *k* b	4 *k* e	A 2 *mv* f
A 8 *k* b	A 8 *k* e	A 4 *mv* f
A 8 *k* c	A 8 *k* c	A 4 *mv* f
		A 8 *k* c

168

This poem forms part of the cycle in which Frauenlob disputes with rival poets on the theme of *wîp* versus *vrouwe.* In it he takes the opposite view to Walther (**101**) in preferring *vrouwe* as a term of the highest praise. As with Walther the thought is complicated by the use of *wîp* and *vrouwe* in more than one sense as (*a*) social classifications, (*b*) terms of praise. The chief ideas, which are tortuously expressed, are as follows: *vrouwe* is supreme (1–4); *wîp* is a generic term for the whole sex (5–6), which may also include imperfect women (*unwîp*); a woman cannot be accounted a *vrouwe* if she has faults (11–14); both *wîp* and *vrouwe* (now used in a social sense) can be *unwîp* if imperfect. In keeping with the polemical nature of the poem, there are few metaphors: the garment of praise (4), *vrouwen stuol,* and the shrine enclosing womanly faults (16–18).

Metrical form as **167.**

169

There is an extraordinary accumulation of metaphors in this extravagant panegyric of Konrad von Würzburg: flower and tree metaphors (*gefioliert, blüete, geræset, obez, boum, durchliljet*); the fountain of inspiration (2); fire (3); the heavens: precious metals and gems. The last group is particularly appropriate to Konrad von Würzburg in that they are of the type he uses in his poem in praise of the Virgin. As in **167,** a new theme begins with the *Abgesang:* the appeal to the planets and heaven to lament.

Metrical form

A 4 *mv* a	A 4 *mv* d	A 6 *k* f
3 *mv* a	3 *mv* d	A 6 *k* f
A 5 *mv* a	A 5 *mv* d	4 *k* f
A 4 *mv* b	A 4 *mv* e	4 *mv* g
A 6 *mv* b	A 6 *mv* e	3 *m* *vg*
3 *mv* a	3 *mv* d	A 3 *mv* g
A 3 *mv* c	A 3 *mv* c	A 3 *mv* c

GLOSSARY

ABBREVIATIONS

HG = High German
LG = Low German
MHG = Middle High German
NHG = New High German

OHG = Old High German
pret.-pres. vb. = *preterite-present verb*
st. = *strong*
wk. = *weak*

ph = pf; f = v; verbs with ge- prefix will usually be found under root, e.g. gemerken under merken.
Asterisk denotes Limburg forms found in Veldeke.

A

abe, *ave prep.+dat.* from 105. 35.
adv. down 35. 13. *dar ave therefrom 39. 37
abent *st. m.* evening 68. 19
aber *adv.* again 24. 4; however 44. 4.
conj. but aver 115. 6
ach *interj.+gen.* alas 35. 4. *st. n.* pain 48. 9
ader *conj.* or 65. 17
ænic *adj.+gen.* without 45. 17
affe *wk. m.* ape 135. 13
ahî *interj. expressing either pain or pleasure* oh, alas 23. 1
âht *st. f.* outlawry. ze âhte und ze banne outlawed and banished 35. 28
ahten *wk. vb.+gen. or* ûf pay attention to 121. 14
al *adj.* all. *adv.* completely, quite 7. 12; 12. 6. *allet neut. sing. nom.* 42. 5.
alliu, elliu *neut. pl., fem. sing. nom.*
allez *neut. sing. acc. used adverbially* quite, completely 65. 15; 126. 46. aller-, alre- *gen. pl. preceding superlative adj. or adv.* 52. 13; 112. 11
alde, alder *conj.* or 12. 8; 108. 39; unless 165. 54
algelîch *adj.* each, all 32. 7
al(l)eine *adv.* alone 5. 1
allenthalben *adv.* on all sides 1. 9
alrêrst(e) *adv.* for the first time 46. 12
alrôt *adj.* completely red 15. 14
alsam *adv., conj.* as, like 45. 4
alsô, als(e) *adv.* so, thus, as 1. 10; 5. 9; 18. 3; 21. 5. *conj.* as, when 10. 7; 15. 4; 19. 3; 35. 14; as if 77. 18; 86. 24
alsus *adv.* thus 94. 2

alten *wk. vb. intrans.* grow old 121. 57. *trans.* make old 73. 23
alterseine *adj., adv.* quite alone 73. 18
alumbe *prep.+acc., adv.* around 126. 19
alze *adv.* all too 75. 24
ampt *st. n.* office, calling 141. 18
*an see *unnen
an(e) *prep.+acc., dat.* to, up to, in, at, on 3. 2; 3. 5; 12. 2; 14. 1; 18. 6; 19. 3. an dîn lôn to win your reward 114. 4. *adv.* up 112. 1
ande *adj., adv.* painful 58. 5
ander *adj.* second, other. anderre *gen. pl.* 6. 7
anders *adv.* in other respects 73. 8
anderswâ *adv.* elsewhere 61. 36
anderunge *st. f.* change, inconstancy 111. 11
âne, ân *prep.+acc., gen.* without 2. 3
anehanc *st. m.* covering, dew 114. 8
ânen *refl. wk. vb.+gen.* renounce, do without 127. 1
ange *adv.* closely, anxiously 91. 6
anger *st. m.* meadow 142. 1
angest *st. f.* anxiety 71. 17
angstlîch *adj.* anxious 45. 10
ankern *wk. vb.* cast anchor 137. 22
antheiz *st. m.* promise, oath 76. 5
antlüt *st. n.* countenance 161. 10
antwürten *wk. vb.* answer 65. 10
anvallen *st. vb.* assail, besiege 162. 3
*aprille *wk. m.* April 43. 1
ar *wk. m.* eagle 135. 1
ar(e)beit *st. f.* pains, toil, distress 84. 35; 89. 11; 90. 39

arc *adj., st. n.* evil, ill 66. 18; 76. 25
arke *st. f.* ark, coffer 167. 9
arm *st. m.* arm 3. 5; 34. 12
arm, arn, *adj.* poor 21. 26. +*gen.* 58.
  11. die armen künege the vassal
  kings 91. 47
armen *wk. vb.* be poor 94. 2
armōnïe *st. f.* harmony 169. 15
art *st. f.* kind, nature 107. 12
asche *wk. f.* ash 154. 9
ātem *st. m.* breath 95. 9
*ave see abe
aver *see* aber

B

babest *st. m.* pope 91. 72
bach *st. m.* stream 155. 3
badestube *wk. f.* bath-house 154. 6
bal *st. m.* ball 66. 31
balde *adv.* swiftly 12. 9
balsamīte *st. f.* balsam, balm 107.
  25
ban *st. m.* banishment 35. 28
banen *wk. vb.* prepare way 142. 24
bannen *st. vb.* banish, excommunicate.
  pret. bienen 91. 65
bant *st. n.* bond 135. 6
bar *adj.*+*gen.* bare 142. 16
baz *adv.* better, more 36. 20; 116. 39.
  baz tuon+*dat.* be more pleasing, advantageous to 45. 23; 99. 15. *bat 39.
  15
bedenken *wk. vb.* consider 83. 4; provide for 107. 17. *refl. wk. vb.* consider,
  resolve 73. 22
*bedriegen *see* betriegen
bedürfen *pret.-pres. vb.*+*gen.* need 60.
  26; 62. 28; 68. 8
begān, begēn *st. vb.*+*gen.* do, accomplish, commit 66. 12; 86. 42; 139. 25;
  provide for 162. 4
begiezen *st. vb.* wet 115. 16
begin *st. m., n.* beginning 71. 31
beginnen *st., wk. vb.*+*gen.* begin 71.
  19; 84. 37. *st. pret.* began 44. 12.
  wk. pret. begunde 9. 9; bigonde
  164. 3
behaben *wk. vb.* hold, retain 112. 2
behagen *wk. vb.*+*dat.* be pleasing to
  66. 20
behalten *st.vb.* keep 10. 3. behalten *pp.*
  stored up 62. 5
Bēheim Bohemia

behüeten *wk. vb.* guard, prevent 89. 28.
  refl. wk. vb. be on one's guard 22. 10.
behuot *pp.* guarded, watched 136. 10;
  139. 16. behuot vor protected against
  67. 18
behūsen *wk. vb.* house 127. 47
beide *num.* both. beide und both and
  35. 28
Beier *st. m.* Bavarian 122. 19
bein *st. n.* leg 91. 22
beiten *wk. vb.*+*gen.* wait for 88. 22
bejagen *wk. vb.* win 110. 48; retrieve
  155. 15
bejehen *st. vb.*+*gen.* declare, confess
  80. 22
bekennen *wk. vb.* get to know, know
  49. 4; 110. 13. bekant *pp.* 125. 26
bekēren *wk. vb.* change, convert. *refl.*
  repent 91. 45
bekerkelt *pp.* imprisoned 108. 45
bekleiden *wk. vb.* dress, clothe.
  bekleit *pp.* 148. 6
bekomen *st. vb.* come 44. 16; 105. 40
belangen *impers. vb.*+*acc. pers. and
  nāch long for 144. 8
belīben *st. vb.* stay, remain 50. 7; 58.
  27; 63. 16. belīben an cling to 82. 6
benemen *st. vb.*+*dat. pers., acc. thing
  take away from, rob of 7. 5; 11. 5;
  27. 5; 62. 13
benennen *wk. vb.* name 63. 25
bern, gebern *st. vb.* bear 68. 13; 142. 9
bēr(e) *st., wk. m.* net 135. 7
berāten *st. vb.* provide for 95. 4. +*gen.*
  provide with 165. 4
berc *st. m.* mountain 46. 18
bereit *adj.* prepared, ready, available,
  attainable 67. 22; 78. 17; 141. 19. +
  gen. provided with 130. 6. +*gen. thing,
  dat. pers.* 137. 7. *adv.* readily, quickly
  121. 22
bereiten *wk. vb.* prepare. bereitet *pp.*
  tilled, cultivated 110. 10. *refl. wk. vb.*
  +*gen.* provide oneself with 126. 1
bergen *st. vb.* hide 118. 8. *refl.* 18. 2;
  137. 15
berihten *wk. vb.* inform 98. 4. +*gen.*
  provide with 137. 46
berouben *wk. vb.*+*acc. pers., gen. thing
  rob someone of 44. 9
beschāchen *wk. vb.* rob 153. 4
bescheiden *st. vb.* explain, interpret
  130. 2

bescheidenlĭch *adj.* discriminating, sensible, discreet **73.** 20; **86.** 50; **101.** 3

bescheinen *wk. vb.* show **49.** 13

beschern *wk. vb.* appoint, grant **62.** 22; **78.** 21

beschouwen *wk. vb.* see, contemplate **46.** 2; **72.** 6

besehen *st. vb.* be prudent, wary **90.** 17

besem *st. m.* birch, rod **129.** 4

besengen *wk. vb.* singe **107.** 8

besitzen *st. vb.* take possession of, possess **67.** 21; **93.** 13; **168.** 11

besliezen *st. vb.* shut, lock (away), enclose **8.** 3; **107.** 28; **115.** 13; **139.** 17. **vor besliezen**+*dat.* lock away from **136.** 23

besorgen *wk. vb.* care for **112.** 3; **126.** 53

best *adj.* **beste** *adv.* best **44.** 11

bestān, bestēn *st. vb. trans. and intrans.* remain **61.** 40; **115.** 10; **121.** 72; take possession of **67.** 24. +*dat.* appertain to **86.** 39. +**an** cling to, cleave to **50.** 18; **71.** 28. *used impers.*+*acc. pers., gen. thing* concern. **die sīn doch niht bestāt** which concerns them not at all **48.** 11. **er bestāt sīn buoze** he will pay for it **128.** 68

bestaten *wk. vb.* make good use of **23.** 11

besunder *adv.* separately **125.** 20; especially **143.** 12; **149.** 14

beswæren *wk. vb.* oppress, grieve, importune **74.** 5; **90.** 27; **112.** 4; **128.** 44

betagen *wk. vb. intrans.* dawn. *trans.* dawn upon, shine upon **133.** 13; await morning **70.** 10

bete *st. f.* request **61.** 34

betiuten *wk. vb.* explain **149.** 1; signify **154.** 2

betrāgen *wk. vb. used impers.*+*acc. pers., gen. thing.* **mich betrāget des** I grow weary of that **76.** 68; **109.** 29; **121.** 42

betriegen *st. vb.* deceive **96.** 35. **be-driegen* **38.** 30

betrüeben *wk. vb.* sadden **110.** 30

bette *st. n.* bed **104.** 2

bettespil *st. n.* game of love **159.** 17

bettestat *st. f.* bed **104.** 16

betwingen *st. vb.* subjugate, constrain. +*gen. or* **ūf** compel **12.** 13; **21.** 4; **45.** 19; **47.** 2; **61.** 18

betwungenlĭche *adv.* in a state of subjection **47.** 28

bevangen *pp.* covered **125.** 3

bevinden *st. vb.* find **104.** 25

bevor(n), bivor *adv.* before. **hie bevor(n)** formerly **33.** 10; **68.** 11. **hī* **bevoren 38.** 12

bewarn *wk. vb.* guard, preserve +*gen.* **163.** 20. +**vor** (against) **54.** 7; **60.** 5. *refl.*+**vor 109.** 31. *refl.* guard against false behaviour **56.** 9; **62.** 29; preserve oneself from harm **108.** 52

bewegen *refl. st. vb.*+*gen.* renounce **62.** 40; resolve, agree **118.** 31

bewenden *wk. vb.* apply. **ez wær bewendet wol** it would serve a useful purpose **144.** 30

bewinden *st. vb.* wind round **15.** 6

bezeichenen *wk. vb.* signify **154.** 4

bezzer *comp. adj.* better **47.** 11

bī *prep.*+*dat., acc.* with, beside **35.** 9; **36.** 4; around **103.** 28. *adv.* near

*bidden see **biten**

biderbe *adj.* worthy, estimable **23.** 10; **26.** 1; **108.** 20

bīe *wk. f.* bee **135.** 19

biegen *st. vb.* bend **91.** 30

bienen *see* **bannen**

bieten *st. vb.* offer, bid **35.** 20; **69.** 18; **52.** 6. *refl.*+**ze** expose oneself to **71.** 20. **an bieten** offer **108.** 4

bilde *st. n.* image **71.** 2; **108.** 37

bilden *wk. vb.* portray **137.** 26

binden *st. vb.* bind, tie up **123.** 14; **137.** 19

binnen *adv.* within **38.** 22

bisen *wk. vb.* run (of cattle stung by gadfly; *cf. Engl.* breeze 'gadfly') **160.** 7

*bit see **mit**

biten *st. vb.* ask, request, pray **38.** 32; **53.** 19. +*gen.* pray for **106.** 13. **bidden* **39.** 22

bīten *st. vb.* wait **106.** 24

bitter *adj.* bitter **60.** 6

bivor *see* **bevor**

biz *prep., conj.* until. **biz daz 71.** 4

bīzen *st. vb.* bite **160.** 32

blanc *adj.* white, shining **115.** 28; **116.** 32

blat *st. n.* leaf **43.** 15

blecken *wk. vb. intrans.* be visible **130.** 8. *trans.* show **141.** 23

bleich *adj.* pale **86.** 36
blenden *wk. vb.* dazzle **98.** 28
bletz *st. m.* piece of offal **165.** 15
blic *st. m.* shine, radiance, glance **138.** 20
bliclïch *adj.* brilliant **114.** 7
*blïde *adj.* joyful, happy (*cf. Engl.* blithe) **38.** 5; **39.** 1
*blïtscap *st. f.* joy **38.** 12
bliuwen *st. vb.* strike **47.** 14
blôz *adj.* bare, naked. +*gen.* lacking in **7.** 2; **70.** 29; **89.** 24; **108.** 27
blüemen *wk. vb.* adorn **167.** 11
blüen *wk. vb.* blossom **107.** 2
blüete *st. f.* blossom **169.** 1
bluome, *blüme *st., wk. f.* flower **23.** 5; **43.** 1
bluomenhuot *st. m.* garland of flowers **128.** 47
bluot *st. m.* blossom **144.** 23
bluot *st. n.* blood **107.** 20; **144.** 22
bœse, *bôse *adj.* inferior, bad, evil, mean **17.** 7; **39.** 7; **56.** 5; **66.** 32; **69.** 10; **83.** 15; **93.** 7, 8, 9; **95.** 3
boln *wk. vb.* throw, aim **61.** 28
bône *st., wk. f.* bean **93.** 4
borgen *wk. vb.* borrow **101.** 8; +ze borrow from **109.** 6; lend **112.** 6
bosch *st. m.* bush **107.** 7
bote *wk. m.* messenger **19.** 4; **22.** 1; **34.** 1; **90.** 1
boum *st. m.* tree **5.** 8
brâ *st., wk. f.* brow **126.** 30
brâte *wk. m.* roast **165.** 5
brechen *st. vb. intrans. and trans.* break, pluck **48.** 8; **103.** 24; **112.** 12; be false to **81.** 8. *breken break off **39.** 40. gebrechen **65.** 3. abe brechen rob, deprive of **86.** 22
breit *adj.* broad, wide **23.** 3; **63.** 5; **107.** 9
breite *st. f.* breadth **121.** 28
breiten *refl. wk. vb.* increase **118.** 10
*brengen *see* bringen
brennen *st. vb. intrans.* burn **107.** 7; shine **138.** 3. *wk. vb. trans.* burn **108.** 36
bresten *st. vb., impers.+dat. pers., gen. thing* lack **134.** 6
brief *st. m.* letter, missive **110.** 26; promissory bond (*Schuldbrief*) **109.** 4
bringen *wk. vb.* bring **12.** 9. brâht *pp.* **32.** 4; **118.** 3. *brengen **39.** 38
brïsen *st., wk. vb.* lace **122.** 21

briuwen *wk. vb.* brew, produce **111.** 3; **165.** 2
brôt *st. n.* bread **162.** 10
brüeven *see* prüeven
brunne *wk. m.* well, fountain **71.** 23
brunst *st. f.* ardour **169.** 3
brust *st. f.* breast **115.** 28. brüstelïn *st. n. dimin.* **116.** 36
büezen *wk. vb.* remedy, make amends. gebüezen **142.** 19
buoc *st. m.* hock **165.** 30
buoche, *büke *wk. f.* beech tree **43.** 2; **160.** 16
buosemblech *st. n.* breastplate; plastron **128.** 79
buoz *st. m.+dat. pers., gen. thing as in* sô ist mir sorgen buoz thus I shall be freed from distress **88.** 15; **103.** 36
buoze *st. f.* penance **110.** 40; reparation **128. 68.** *büte **43.** 34
burc *st. f.* castle **105.** 35
bürtic *adj.* native **128.** 34
butze *wk. m.* scarecrow **95.** 7

C *see* **K** *or* **Z**

D

dâ(r) *adv. and conj.* there, where **43.** 8; **46.** 11. *pleonastic use with rel. pronoun* **49.** 12. *in combination with other advs.* dar inne therein **8.** 6; **96.** 40. dâ . . . inne **108.** 41. dâ . . . bï thereby, therein **92.** 2. dâ her from there, hither **124.** 19; from that time on **76.** 61. dâ her von kinde from childhood on **68.** 12. dâ hin away, departed. der fröide mïn den besten teil hât er dâ hin he has taken the best part of my joy with him **78.** 42. dâ nâch afterwards **52.** 50; **142.** 13. dar umbe, drumbe for that reason **22.** 21; **41.** 19; in exchange **35.** 19. darunder meanwhile **76.** 28; **87.** 14. dâ von by means of which, as a result of which **138.** 14. dâ vor formerly **138.** 3. dar zuo in addition **37.** 15
*dach *see* tac
dagen *wk. vb.+gen.* be silent. gedagen **86.** 7; **140.** 21
dan, dannen *adv.* thence **35.** 10; **105.** 40
danc *st. m.* thought, intention, thanks. âne sïnen danc against his will **40.** 1; *cf.* **89.** 31. danc haben be thanked

56. 7; 84. 20. danc sagen (*seggen)
+*dat. pers.*, *gen. thing* thank 39. 5;
42. 12; 121. 12. danc wizzen+*dat.*
pers., *gen. thing* be grateful to . . . for
57. 2
danken *wk. vb.* thank 101. 64
danne, denne *adv.* then, than 15. 2;
22. 6; 35. 26; 85. 16
dannoch *adv.* still, besides, nevertheless
117. 38
dar *adv.* thither; further, in future
108. 11
darben *wk. vb.*+*gen.* lack 12. 16. *refl.*
renounce 3. 3
daz *conj.* that, so that (+*subj. to express
purpose*) 3. 4; 7. 8; 10. 6; 14. 3. *dat
38. 2
decken *wk. vb.* cover. *pret.* dahte 91. 1
dehein, dekein *pron. adj. positive* any
22. 18. *neg.* no 32. 13
denken *wk. vb.* think 71. 6. gedenken
+*gen.* or an think, wish 13. 3; 20. 7;
32. 2; 79. 4; 99. 3; 105. 11
der, diu, daz *demonstr. pron.*; *def. art.*;
rel. pron. *dē, dī, dat. des gen. sing.
neut. used adverbially* therefore 80. 22.
dien *Alemannic dat. pl.* 165. 3
dernider *adv.* down 91. 63
dēst *contraction of* daz ist 4. 7; 47. 12;
135. 18 = des ist 135. 10
deste *adv.* all the more 61. 42; 88. 39;
138. 6
dēswār *contraction of* daz ist wār indeed 76. 43
deweder *pron.* one of two, neither of
two 92. 6
dicke *adv.* often 14. 2
die *st. f.* leg 165. 21
dienen *wk. vb.* serve 30. 12; 47. 13;
52. 15, 40; 57. 4; 60. 22; 68. 6; 72. 12;
deserve, earn 33. 5; 62. 4. *dienen
39. 10. gedienen serve 73. 17; repay
132. 19
dien(e)st *st. m.* service 27. 1; 45. 3; 52.
32; 61. 14, 38; 67. 20; 68. 2, 6; 69. 18
diet *st. f.* people 48. 5
diezen *st. vb.* resound, roar 91. 25
dīhen *st. vb.* flourish. in den kumber
sint gedigen have got into this state
of distress 131. 5
dīn *gen. of pron.* du. *2nd pers. sing.
possess. adj.* 169. 2
dinc *st. n.* thing, affair 87. 28; 110. 41

dingelīn *st. n. dimin.* household affairs
124. 26
dingen *wk. vb.* hope 86. 54
dirne *st. f.* girl 158. 5
diser, dirre *demonstr. pron.* this 34. 10;
of this world 110. 33
diutsch, tiu(t)sch *adj.* German 63. 25:
96. 33; 121. 14
dō *adv.* then 6. 10. *conj.* when 6. 9
doch *adv.* yet, however 115. 32. *conj.*
although 76. 63
dol *st. m.* suffering 144. 33
dol(e)n *wk. vb.* suffer 41. 27; 128. 20
dōn *st. m.* song, strain, metrical and
musical pattern 61. 21; 105. 2; 114. 2;
116. 38; 121. 58. dœnen *wk. vb.* sing
149. 9
*dōn *see* tuon
donreslac *st. m.* thunderclap 54. 11
*dore *see* durch
dorf *st. n.* village 121. 18
dorn *st. m.* thorn, briar 13. 6
dörper *st. m.* peasant, boor 127. 24
dörperlīch, dörpellīch *adj.* boorish
110. 25. *dorperlīke *adv.* 39. 22
dort *adv.* there; in the next world 72. 12
*dōt *see* tōt
*dragen *see* tragen
drāte *adv.* swiftly 155. 4
drī, *neut.* driu, *card. num.* three 91. 9
drīen *wk. vb.* make threefold 169. 17
dringen *st. vb.* penetrate, thrust, jostle
44. 22; 115. 12; 127. 19. gedringen
127. 15
drischelstap *st. m.* handle of threshing
flail 126. 42
dritte *ord. num.* third 91. 13
drōn *wk. vb.* threaten 126. 46
druc *st. m.* pressure 150. 12
drucken *wk. vb.* press 116. 24. *pret.*
druhte 118. 18
du *2nd pers. sing. pron.*
*dū *conj.* when 38. 21
dulden *wk. vb.* suffer 128. 65
*dump *see* tump
dunken, dünken *wk. vb.*+*acc. pers.*
seem 4. 1; 24. 9; 69. 14. dūhte *pret.
indic.* 6. 10; 73. 20; *pret. subj.* 46. 8.
diuhte *pret. subj.* 22. 19
dunst *st. m.* spray 169. 2
durch, dur *prep.*+*acc.* through, for the
sake of, on account of 25. 3; 27. 11. dur
daz because 73. 30. *dore 38. 36

durchkernet *pp.* filled to the core **169.**
10

durchliljet *pp.* lily-adorned **169.** 7

durchsternet *pp.* set with stars **169.** 8

durfen, dürfen *pret.-pres. vb.* may,
need **86.** 17; **119.** 17

dürre *adj.* dry **64.** 16

dwingen *see* twingen

E

ē *adv.* rather **35.** 21; **86.** 25; formerly
91. 56; **123.** 5. *prep.+gen., dat.* before
76. 6; **112.** 4. *conj.* before **35.** 21. ē daz
60. 16. ē *(conj.)* . . . ē *(adv.)* instead
of . . . **112.** 8, 9

ē *st. f.* marriage. **162.** 5. ēlīch *adj.*
married **162.** 1

ebene *adv.* evenly, fittingly **92.** 3; **97.** 7

edel *adj.* noble, precious **22.** 9; **26.** 2;
37. 17; **106.** 19; **127.** 47

ēhaft *adj.* legal, valid **58.** 16

eht, et *intensifying adv.* indeed, just
43. 35; **82.** 8; **85.** 6, 34; **86.** 43; **116.** 17;
139. 16

ei *st. n.* egg **126.** 44

eide *wk. f.* mother **124.** 11

eigen *st. n.* property **127.** 41

eigen *adj.* own; subject to (feudal overlord). sich für eigen jehen+*dat.*
declare allegiance to **57.** 10. sich vür
eigen neigen+*dat.* incline in allegiance before **135.** 11. *adj. used as
noun* thrall **77.** 18

ein *card. num.* one. *indef. art.; pl.*
148. 12. *weakened form* en **133.** 4.
eine *wk. m. sing.* alone **21.** 20; +*gen.*
free from **148.** 15. einen *wk. m.
sing. acc.* **9.** 10; **162.** 4. eines *gen.
sing. used adverbially* at one moment
127. 36

einander *indecl.* one another **21.** 15

einhürn(e) *wk. m.* unicorn **135.** 25

eischen *st. vb.* ask for **39.** 14. *pret.*
*isch **39.** 31, 33

eit *st. m.* oath **81.** 8

Elbe *st. f.* Elbe **96.** 25

elbe *st. f.* elf **64.** 1

ellen *st. n.* prowess **116.** 37

ellenboge *st., wk. m.* elbow **91.** 3

ellende *adj.* banished, wretched **162.** 27

ellenden *refl. wk. vb.* go into exile
81. 13

en *see* ne *or* ein

en(t)bern *st. vb.+gen.* lack, do without
51. 12; **61.** 11; **76.** 37. *entbāre *pret.
subj.* **39.** 32

enbieten *st. vb.* send message, offer,
command **27.** 1; **34.** 4; **81.** 6

enbinden *st. vb.* loosen **156.** 11

enbor *adv.* upwards **133.** 20

*ende *part. and conj.* and **38.** 10; **39.** 2;
40. 7

ende *st. n.* end, direction **111.** 6; **147.**
10. ein ende geben+*dat.* put an end
to **59.** 12. ende haben be finished **120.**
25. ein ende hān+*gen.* achieve
fulfilment of **71.** 29. an ein ende
komen+*gen.* bring to a conclusion
21. 6; get to the bottom of, fathom
86. 5. ende nemen finish **60.** 2. nimt
sīn ende comes to the end of his life
76. 56. an dem ende finally **7.** 1;
53. 16. ze ende finally **128.** 7

endecken *wk. vb.* uncover **70.** 27

ende(c)līche(n) *adv.* finally, once and
for all **81.** 7; **98.** 18; **121.** 43; **84.** 31;
88. 22

endelōs *adj.* unceasing **132.** 8

enden *wk. vb.* end **47.** 25

Ēnēas Aeneas **44.** 3

enein *adv.* in agreement. enein wer-
den+*gen.* agree upon **126.** 21

enge *adj.* narrow **127.** 25

engegen *prep.+dat., adv.* towards

engel *st. m.* angel **96.** 34

Engellant *st. n.* England **3.** 4

engelten, engelden, enkelten *st. vb.*
+*gen.* pay penalty for, suffer for, from;
be punished for **22.** 13; **45.** 8; **120.** 4;
124. 15

engēn *st. vb.* vanish **70.** 11

enklingen *st. vb.* resound **114.** 6

enpfallen *st. vb.* fall away **110.** 16

enpfān, enphān, entvāhen *st. vb.* receive **49.** 11; **65.** 8; **68.** 6; **160.** 22

enplanden *st. vb.* make difficult. der
sol ez dem lībe wol enplanden he
should exert himself **141.** 17

enthalten *st. vb.* contain **98.** 13

entnücken *wk. vb.* nod, doze **154.** 1

entpfrömden *wk. vb.+dat.* make alien
to **51.** 30

entriuwen *adv.* in truth **89.** 22

entsagen *refl. wk. vb.+dat.* set oneself
free from **78.** 35

*entseggen *wk. vb.* refuse **39.** 15

entsehen, entsēn *st. vb.* bewitch (by glance) **64.** 1

entsitzen *st. vb.* fear, dread **73.** 24

entslāfen *st. vb.* fall asleep **21.** 20

entspringen *st. vb.* spring up **103.** 22

entstān *st. vb.* understand **10.** 16

entwer *adv.* hither and thither **127.** 16

entwerfen *st. vb.* depict **115.** 29; **137.** 47

entwīchen *st. vb.* escape **77.** 16

entwonen *wk. vb.* wean oneself **109.** 18

envor *adv.* hie envor formerly **126.** 51; **127.** 39

enwec *adv.* away **155.** 2

enzīt *adv.* in time **142.** 21

en(t)zünden *wk. vb.* kindle **64.** 15; **144.** 34

enzwei *adv.* in two **65.** 3

en(t)zwischen *adv.* in between **64.** 24

er *3rd pers. sing. pron. masc.*

erarnen *wk. vb.* pay penalty for **163.** 25

erbarmen *wk. vb.* move to pity; be moved to pity **58.** 9, 10; **94.** 1

erbeiten *wk. vb.+gen.* wait for, await **87.** 16; **119.** 16

erben *wk. vb.* be handed on **106.** 3

erbern *st. vb.* bear **158.** 8

erbluon *refl. wk. vb.* blush **13.** 5

erbunnen *anom. vb.* grudge **157.** 13

erde *st., wk. f.* **91.** 30

erdenken *wk. vb.* imagine **133.** 22

ēre *conj.* before **39.** 40

ēre *st. f.* honour **41.** 10; **61.** 24; **63.** 1; **66.** 27; **73.** 26. nāch ēren in accordance with honour, in honourable fashion **76.** 41, 65

ērebære *adj.* full of honour **156.** 3

ēren *wk. vb.* honour **29.** 11; adorn **134.** 8

ergān, ergēn, irgān *st. vb.* happen, turn out, be fulfilled, proceed **7.** 12; **23.** 14; **28.** 10; **48.** 17; **50.** 8; **54.** 28; **118.** 30; **139.** 11; **161.** 20. *refl.* walk about **161.** 3

ergeben *st. vb.* give, submit, subject **117.** 8

erholn *wk. vb.* attain, procure **144.** 40

erkennen *wk. vb.* know, recognize, understand **21.** 3; **25.** 2; **63.** 1; **73.** 28; **84.** 30; **87.** 20. *refl.* examine oneself **55.** 11

erkiesen *st. vb.* choose, perceive **5.** 7, 10; **38.** 16; **51.** 13; **66.** 2; **68.** 9; **115.** 1

erkomen *st. vb.* be alarmed **22.** 14

erkrachen *wk. vb.* crack, be broken **141.** 33

erkuolen *wk. vb.* grow cold **66.** 16

erlachen *wk. vb.* break into laughter **159.** 13

erlān *st. vb.+acc. pers., gen. thing* dispense from, fail to grant **73.** 21

erlangen *wk. vb. used impers.* mich erlanget nāch I long for **147.** 6

erlīden *st. vb.* suffer **54.** 3

erliutern *wk. vb.* brighten **114.** 8

erlœsen *wk. vb.* set free, redeem, relieve **114.** 18

erlouben *wk. vb.* permit **57.** 12. *refl. +gen.* renounce **69.** 20

ermanen *wk. vb.+gen.* remind **154.** 6

ermel *st. m.* sleeve **128.** 81

erne *st. f.* harvest **166.** 2

ernenden *wk. vb.+an* make bold, venture upon **53.** 22

erniuwen *wk. vb.* renew **75.** 23. **ernouwen* **41.** 4

ernœten *wk. vb.+gen.* oblige, compel **72.** 7

erschamen *refl. wk. vb.* be ashamed **103.** 13

erschīnen *st. vb.* appear **113.** 10; **115.** 25

erschricken *st. vb. intrans.* start, be startled **116.** 27, 35

ersehen *st. vb.* perceive **71.** 23. *3rd pers. sing. *ersīt* **39.** 39. *refl.* be rapt in contemplation **70.** 26. *refl.+an* feast one's gaze on **71.** 12

erslīchen *st. vb.* take by surprise **153.** 6

ērst *superl. adj., adv.* **49.** 4. von ērste first of all **73.** 29; **126.** 56

ersterben *st. vb.* die **106.** 3

erstürzen *refl. wk. vb.* plunge **155.** 7

ertber *wk. f.* strawberry **160.** 23

ervarn *st. vb.* find out **144.** 28

ervinden *st. vb.* find out, experience **47.** 18; **88.** 29; **114.** 19

ervürhten *wk. vb.* fear **45.** 18

erwachen *wk. vb. intrans.* wake **54.** 23

erwarmen *wk. vb.* grow warm, warm oneself **94.** 3

erweln *wk. vb.* choose **5.** 11; **53.** 4

erwenden *wk. vb.* avert, remove, prevent **29.** 4; **45.** 5; **53.** 17; **116.** 5

erwerben *st. vb.* win, attain, earn **84.** 17; **88.** 12. **erwerven* **43.** 25

erwinden *st. vb.* desist **118.** 23

erzeigen *wk. vb.* show 65. 22. *refl.*
84. 32

erziehen *st. vb.* bring up 110. 7; maltreat 126. 7

ēst *contracted form of* ez ist 148. 8

et *see* eht

eteslīch *adj.* some 27. 8; 64. 12; 81. 11;
121. 58

eteswār *adv.* somewhere 77. 15

eteswenne *adv.* sometimes 65. 10

ēweclīche(n) *adv.* eternally 54. 26

ez *3rd pers. sing. pron. neut.; pleonastic
use with another subject,* e.g. ez stuont
ein frouwe alleine 5. 1

F *see* V

G

gābe *st. f.* gift 62. 2

gāch, *gen.* gāhes, gæhes *adj.* swift.
mir ist gāch I hasten 78. 32; 121. 44;
155. 6. gāhen *wk. vb.* hasten 28. 7

gadem *st. n.* closet, chest 123. 25

galle *st., wk. f.* gall 56. 13

gampelspil *st. n.* sport 108. 31

gan *see* gunnen

gān, gēn *st. vb.* go, proceed 2. 1, 4;
16. 1; 19. 2; 54. 18; 103. 37. imperative
ginc 126. 24. hine gān pass (*of time*)
84. 2; 89.25. gegān 61. 4.ūf gān, gēn
rise 68. 16; 107. 2. umbe gān, gēn circulate 63. 3; +mit associate with 82. 12

ganc *st. m.* way 158. 13; gait 161. 32

gans *st. f.* goose. gense *dat. sing.* 128.
36

ganz *adj., adv.* perfect, complete, whole
27. 12; 65. 5; 107. 5, 9

gar *adv.* completely 35. 6

garte *wk. m.* garden 158. 22

gast *st. m.* guest 94. 8; 117. 26; stranger
138. 7

gebærde, gebērde *st. f.* bearing, behaviour 63. 2; 88. 27; 153. 4

gebāren *wk. vb. intrans. or refl.* behave, conduct oneself 62. 25; 83. 30;
87. 11. alse si mir vor gebāret as she
pretends 88. 20

gebe *st. f.* gift 131. 11

gebeine *st. n.* bones 154. 11

geben *st.vb.* give 16. 6. *contracted forms*
gīst 108. 26; gīt 123. 4; gent=gebent
161. 26. gegeben 91. 8. gegīt 112. 5.
refl. entrust oneself 116. 21

gebende *st. n.* 1. headdress in general;
2. headdress of married woman;
wimple 110. 24; 128. 53

gebieten *st. vb.* command 9. 8; 26. 16;
47. 26; 63. 17

gebieterinne *st. f.* mistress 107. 24

gebite *st. f.* waiting 86. 51

gebot *st. n.* command, sovereignty
54. 22; 84. 34; 114. 20

gebræmet *pp.* trimmed 128. 82

gebrech *st. n.* (?) tearing off 128. 75

gebūre, gebūwer *st., wk. m.* peasant
105. 39; 124. 23

gedanc *st. m.* thought 24. 7; 27. 6;
54. 14

gedanke *wk. m.* thought 167. 7

gedenken *st. n.* thought 137. 8

gedinge *st. f., wk. m.* hope 76. 60;
138. 18; 139. 34

gedranc *st. m., n.* throng, crowd, press
134. 5

*gedrinken *st. vb.* drink 40. 6

gedult *st. f.* patience. *gedolt composure 39. 29

gedultec *adj.* patient

gedulteclīchen *adv.* patiently 86. 52

*gedwanc *st. n* constraint 39. 4

gefioliert *pp.* violet-flowered 169. 1

gegen, gein, gēn *prep.+dat.* towards,
at the approach of 34. 10; 44. 26; 121.
8; 122. 22; 157. 2

gehaben *refl. wk. vb.* fare 90. 8; 121. 37.
+an turn to 52. 28

geharre *st. n.* tarrying 121. 74

gehaz *adj.* inimical 69. 21

gehiure *adj.* pleasing 101. 47

geil *adj.+gen.* glad 108. 9; 121. 61

geiz *st. f.* she-goat 164. 27

geladen *pp.* laden 100. 8

gelāz *st. m., n.* behaviour 96. 30; 114.
23

geleite *st. n.* safe conduct 91. 24

gelenke *st. n.* waist 134. 12

gelīch *adj.* like, equal 67. 11. ez ist
den liuten gelīch it bears a human
likeness 14. 8. gelīche *adv.* 88. 49

gelīchen *wk. vb.* liken, treat alike 101.
28; 133. 3. *refl.* resemble 131. 1

gelieb, geliep *adj.* fond of each other
15. 16. *subst.* lover 21. 14

gelingen *st. vb. used impers.* turn out,
succeed 28. 12; 61. 39; 76. 33; 85. 17

geloube *wk. m.* belief 58. 12

gelouben *wk. vb.* believe **21.** 12; **35.** 22; **73. 25.** *refl.+gen.* take leave of, renounce **6.** 6

geloubet *pp.* in leaf **122.** 13

gelt *st. m., n.* price, reward **84.** 23

gelten *st. vb.* be worth, be valid **78.** 23; **84.** 20; repay **153.** 13

gelücke, gelucke *st. n.* fate, lot, fortune **45.** 16; **79.** 1; **112.** 1, 9

gelust *st. m., f.* desire **157.** 37

gemach *st. m., n.* rest, peace, comfort **80.** 5

gemäzen *wk. vb.* moderate **118.** 51

gemeine *adj.* common, shared **100.** 30. *adv.* with one accord **86.** 40

gemeit *adj.+gen.* happy, gay **16.** 8

gemellīche(n) *adv.* gladly **79.** 2

gemüete *st. n.* mind, heart **34.** 9; **47.** 2; **51.** 3; **84.** 12; **125.** 10

gemuot *adj.* disposed. wol gemuot, grōz gemuot happy **36.** 14; **109.** 16; **114.** 30; **143.** 16

genāde *st., wk. f.* favour, mercy **45.** 1; **63.** 16; **67.** 20; **68.** 7, 8; peace **111.** 1. ūf (*ūp) genāde in expectation of favour **43.** 34; **52.** 38

genāden *wk. vb.* have mercy on

genædic *adj.* merciful. genædeclīchen *adv.* **84.** 2

genesen *st. vb.* recover, be cured **52.** 36

genieten *refl. wk. vb.+gen.* enjoy possession of **12.** 8

geniezen *st. vb.+gen.* enjoy benefit, use of **7.** 4; **47.** 4; **54.** 13; **83.** 13

genōz, *genōt *st. m.* companion, equal **43.** 9; **93.** 20

genōzen *wk. vb.* compare **135.** 27

genuoc, gnuoc *adj.* enough; *pl.* many **21.** 10; **28.** 12; **88.** 24

geplätze *st. n.* chatter **127.** 38

geræte *st. n.* household goods, riches, instrument **159.** 18

gerich *st. m.* vengeance **135.** 30

gerihte *st. n.* rule **91.** 38

ger(e)n *wk. vb.+gen.* desire;(*technical term of falconry*) be eager to fly, bate **38.** 19; **45.** 11; **61.** 36; **71.** 32; **73.** 14; **113.** 3. *st. n.* **114.** 22

gerne *adv.* gladly, willingly **15.** 16; **19.** 5; **21.** 3; **50.** 6; **68.** 19

gerœset *pp.* rosy **169.** 3

gerte *st., wk. f.* rod **107.** 2

gesamnen *refl. wk. vb.* unite **60.** 16

gesanc *st. m., n.* song **35.** 1; **65.** 14; **114.** 10

geschehen, geschēn happen **47.** 20; **64.** 28. *geschīt 3rd pers. sing. pres. indic. (infin.* geschīn) **38.** 9

geselle *wk. m.* companion, lover **1.** 8, 10; **4.** 8; **7.** 3; **16.** 3; **37.** 10; **116.** 16; **123.** 10

geselleclīche *adv.* united **115.** 30

gesellen *refl. wk. vb.* associate oneself **58.** 22

geselleschaft *st. f.* company **106.** 25; **116.** 4; fashion **131.** 3

geslaht *adj.* formed, fashioned. wol geslaht beautiful **70.** 4

geslechte *st. n.* offal **165.** 12

gespil(e) *st., wk. m., f.* companion **110** 9; **122.** 30; **125.** 17

gestalt *pp.* fashioned. wie gestalt of what kind **140.** 11. baz gestalt more beautiful **122.** 2

gesteine *st. n.* jewels **37.** 17; **103.** 5

*gesüken *wk. vb.* request, entreat **43.** 27

gesunt *adj.* well, whole, cured **55.** 5; **142.** 36

geswanzen *wk. vb.* prance **121.** 67

geswinde *adv.* swift **155.** 8

getāt *st. f.* matter **166.** 28

getelinc *st. m.* peasant, fellow **127.** 13

*getemen *see* zemen

getouwet *pp.* covered with dew **123.** 9

getriuwe *adj.* true, trusty **88.** 10; **104.** 28

getschen *wk. vb.* shout **164.** 6

getwerc *st. n.* dwarf **93.** 16

gevallen *st. vb.* please **5.** 8; **19.** 7; **36.** 19

gevar *adj.* coloured **63.** 20

gevater *st. m.* godfather, friend **127.** 34

geveimet *pp.* refined **169.** 11

gevider(e) *st. n.* wings, plumage **15.** 5, 13; **134.** 18

gefriunden *wk. vb.* win friendship of **60.** 8; **85.** 21

gevrouwet *pp.* wedded **167.** 5

gevüege *adj.* fitting, tolerable **82.** 17; well-behaved **96.** 15

gewalt *st. m., f.* power, violence **35.** 11. +gen. **62.** 3

gewaltic *adj.+gen.* having power over **64.** 10

gewalticlīchen *adv.* violently **128.** 57

gewant *st. n.* clothing, garment 120. 22

gewar *adj.+gen.* aware; gewar werden perceive 109. 24

*gewerven *st. vb.* solicit, entreat 39.
16

gewerft *st. n.* activity, profession 121.
63

gewin *st. m.* gain, profit, advantage
47. 6

gewinnen *st. vb.* win, acquire, experience 11. 4; 13. 7; 14. 5; 37. 4; 45. 20;
46. 7; 71. 17; 87. 18. an gewinnen
+*dat. pers., acc. thing* take from 116.
24

gewis *adj.+gen.* certain 8. 2

geworht *pp. of* würken fashioned
107. 5

gewürme *st. n.* reptiles, creeping
things 91. 33

gickelvêch *adj.* variegated, brightly
coloured 123. 35

giht *see* jehen

gimme *st. f.* gem 169. 14

gir, gier *st. f.* desire 134. 5; 138. 22.
die gir verhaben (*falconry*) restrain
desire to fly 113. 3–4 (*see* gern)

gît *see* geben

gîte *st. f.* covetousness 111. 7

glanz *st. m.* lustre, splendour 107. 9

glanz *adj.* bright 128. 40

glas *st. n.* glass, mirror 71. 2; 107. 5;
window 116. 33. glesîn *adj.* glass 99.
24; 112. 9

glast *st. m.* shine, radiance 117. 25;
138. 5. glesten *wk. vb.* shine 114. 7

glatz *st. m.* bald pate 126. 49

glitze *st. f.* brightness 154. 7

glosten *wk. vb.* glow. ûf glosten begin
to glow 165. 26

gluot *st. f.* fire 64. 18; 165. 16

gofenanz *st. m.* indoor dance 126. 16

golt *st. n.* gold 14. 7

golze *wk. m.* boot 124. 10

got *st. m.* God 7. 7

grâ *adj.* grey 127. 22. grâwen *wk. vb.*
grow grey, dawn 116. 3

gram *adj.* sad 76. 48; angry 128. 59

grap *st. n.* grave 35. 14

gras *st. n.* grass 91. 28

grât *st. m.* fishbone 108. 60

griebe *st. f.* cracklings (cf. Eng.
greaves) 165. 31

grîfe *wk. m.* griffin 137. 30

grifen *st. vb.* seize. +nâch snatch at
71. 3. +zuo resort to 91. 64

grimme *adj.* grim 58. 7

grîs *adj.* grey 126. 4

grîse *st. f.* greyness 123. 11

grop, grob *adj.* coarse 169. 12

grôz *adj.* great 21. 10. *grôt 41. 15

grüene *adj.* green 110. 37

grüezen, gruozen *wk. vb.* greet 35. 1;
52. 10; 66. 29. *st. n.* 119. 4; 141. 11

grunt *st. m.* bottom 137. 22

gruonen *wk. vb.* grow green 1. 9; 23. 3;
121. 1. *grünen 43. 4

gruoz *st. m.* greeting, salutation 47. 9;
79. 11; 113. 7; 137. 33; 141. 29

güete *st. f.* goodness 44. 27; 47. 4;
60. 25; 63. 7

güet(e)lîch *adj., adv.* kind, gracious 45.
21; 114. 14; 139. 5

güet(e)lîche(n) *adv.* 25. 13; 34. 13; 36. 3

guldîn *adj.* golden 15. 14

gülte *st. f.* debt 109. 3

gunnen *pret.-pres. vb.+dat. pers., gen.
thing* grant, allow, wish 17. 8; 47. 9;
49. 15; 66. 27; 76. 45; 164. 16

gunterfeit *st. n.* counterfeit 151. 23

guot *adj.* good 20. 6. *gût 38. 1; 39.
29

guot *st. n.* good, blessing, wealth, property 22. 23; 78. 16; 91. 11; 99. 12;
122. 47; 144. 20. *gût 42. 5. ze guote
vervâhen account as good 58. 33. ze
guote with good intent 82. 2; 100. 11.
für guot nemen take in good part
85. 6

gürtel *st. m.* belt 122. 38

gfeterlîn *st. n.* companion 160. 32

H

habe *st. f.* possession 35. 12

habedanc *st. m.* thanks 94. 6

haben, hân *wk. vb.* have 5. 9; 11. 5;
14. 1, 4; 15. 4; 17. 5. hân für consider
as 47. 12; 142. 20. hân baz consider
more highly 108. 20. diu ir lîp schö-
ner künde hân who could conduct
herself better 26. 14

hac *st. m.* enclosure 155. 4

hacche *wk. f.* harlot 78. 29

hæl *adj.* secret, furtive 161. 32

haft *st. m.* support 78. 5

halm *st. m.* straw 102. 9

halp *adj.* half 62. 20

halten, halden *st. vb.* keep, retain. den
strīt halden continue the struggle 54. 4
hamme *st., wk. f.* ham 165. 12
hant *st. f.* hand 110. 6
hār *st. n.* hair 67. 23
harpfen *wk. vb.* harp 105. 24
harte *adv.* very 10. 16. *comp.* harter
more 106. 15
haz *st. m.* hatred, enmity 36. 16; 45. 22;
61. 17; 85. 16; hateful qualities 99.
13. haz tragen+*dat.* feel hatred for
139. 12
hazzen *wk. vb.* hate 73. 10
*hē, her *3rd pers. sing. pron. masc.*
39. 22; 41. 7. heme *acc., dat. sing.*
39. 11, 19, 23
*hebben *wk. vb.* have 38. 15. hevet
3rd pers. sing. pres. indic. 41. 8, 11.
hadde *pret. indic.* 38. 16, 34
heben, heven *st. vb.* raise, begin 43. 5,
19. *refl.* raise oneself, arise, begin 15.
7; 24. 4; 49. 22; 60. 1; 91. 55; 122. 14
hei, hey *interj.* oh 64. 10
heide *st. f.* heath, moor 5. 2; 23. 6
heide *wk. m.* heathen 53. 3; 58. 19
heil *st. n.* good fortune 23. 14; 49. 15;
84. 32; 121. 62
heil *adj.* whole 144. 12
heilen *wk. vb. intrans.* heal 160. 33.
geheilen *trans.* 147. 13
heim *st. n.* home. heim *advbl. acc.* homewards 121. 49. heime *advbl. dat.* at
home 62. 36; 83. 2. *advbl. subst.* a home
(cf. NHG ein Daheim) 125. 50
heimlīch, heinlīch *adj.* familiar, intimate 67. 11; 117. 36
heinlīchi *st. f.* intimacy 166. 11
heizen *st. vb. intrans.* be called 44. 3.
trans. bid, call 27. 3; 47. 15; 66. 14.
geheizen *intrans.* be called 102. 5.
trans. promise 73. 32
hel *adj.* loud, clear 114. 9. hellen *st.
vb.* resound 161. 2
helfe *st. f.* help 58. 3
helfelīch *adj.* helpful 113. 7
helfen *st. vb.* help 45. 3
helle *st. f.* hell 48. 8; 54. 7
helm *st. m.* helmet 110. 42
hel(e)n *wk. vb.* conceal 85. 40; 125. 39;
153. 9
helsen *wk. vb.* embrace 153. 12
helt *st. m.* hero, lord, person of renown
6. 8; 169. 21

hem(e)de *st. n.* shift, smock 13. 2;
122. 21; 130. 2
her *adv.* hither 9. 11; 12. 9; 65. 5; up to
now 58. 25; 65. 15; 121. 60. her nāch
later 116. 19
her *st. n.* host, army 81. 15; 121. 54
hēr(e) *adj.* lofty, superior, proud 64. 9;
89. 14; 96. 14; 104. 10
herberge *st. f.* lodging, shelter, haven
109. 32
herb(e)st *st. m.* autumn 165. 1, 13
*here *3rd pers. sing. pron. fem. acc.,
dat.* 38. 32; 43. 28. *3rd pers. possess.
adj. fem. sing., masc., fem., neut. pl.*
38. 15, 18; 41. 5; 43. 6
hērlīche *adv.* magnificently 107. 4
hērre, herre, hēre, her *wk. m.* lord,
sir 41. 15; 54. 27; 57. 11
hērsch *adj.* proud 101. 59
hert *st. f.* flock 159. 5
herte *adj.* hard 110. 42
herwider *adv.* back again 153. 12
herze *wk. n.* heart 4. 7. *herte 38. 7, 23
herzeclīch *adj.* heartfelt, beloved 86. 6;
133. 2; 145. 23
herzeclīche(n) *adv.* heartily, from the
heart 35. 15; 68. 1
herzeleit *st. n.* heartfelt suffering,
pains of love 99. 27; 145. 24
herzeliebe *st. f.* love 97. 18
herzeliep *adj.* beloved 88. 2; 99. 1
herzeliep *st. n.* heartfelt joy, beloved
60. 4, 8; 87. 8; 137. 49; 145. 19
herzensenede *pres. part. as adj.* heartfelt, grievous 125. 19
herzesēr *st. n.*, herzesēre *st. f.* heartfelt suffering 47. 20; 89. 12
*het *3rd pers. sing. pron. neut.* it 38. 1
hī *interj.* oh 136. 16
hie, hī *adv.* here 2. 1; in this life 72. 9.
hie bevor(n), hie vor *see* bevor *and*
vor
himel *st. m.* heaven 71. 26
himelrīche *st. n.* heaven 156. 15
hin(e) *adv.* towards, away. hin ze 24. 8.
wā . . . hin whither 68. 15. bī mir hin
past me 100. 4
hinder *prep.*+*dat.* behind. hinder sich
back 91. 48. *adv.* backwards. hin
hinder 128. 6
hinden *adv.* behind 126. 34
hinne(n) *adv.* hence 1. 11; 37. 1; 58. 1.
hinne vür henceforward 121. 33

hīnt *adv.* last night **122.** 42
hirne(e) *st. n.* brain **165.** 9
hirte *wk. m.* shepherd **159.** 4
hitze *st. f.* heat **95.** 5
hiufelbant *st. n.* hip-belt **128.** 80
hiure, hiuwer, hiwer *adv.* this year
  128. 37; **155.** 12
hiuselīn *st. n. dimin.* house **125.** 52
hiute *adv.* today **67.** 5
hōch *adj.* high. hōher muot elevation
  of spirit, joy **64.** 19; **69.** 12; **87.** 26;
  100. 23; **122.** 7
hōchgemüete *st. n.* joy **83.** 28
hōchgemuot *adj.* joyful, proud **61.** 42;
  62. 26; **87.** 10; **126.** 33
hōhe, hō *adv.* high **15.** 7; **30.** 2; **43.** 21;
  67. 4; **84.** 12.· *hōge **38.** 19
hœhen *wk. vb.* elevate, gladden **34.** 9;
  83. 20
hœnen *wk. vb.* mock **101.** 50. gehœnen
  105. 4
hœren *wk. vb.* hear **12.** 3; **24.** 14; **51.** 7.
  +zuo belong **102.** 16. gehœren **87.** 4;
  overhear **123.** 16. +*dat. or* zuo belong
  60. 15
hof *st. m.* court **97.** 5; **105.** 37
hovelīch *adj.* courtly **105.** 1; **128.** 76
hōfesch, hovesch, hübesch *adj.*
  courtly **11.** 3; **39.** 25; **101.** 21; **122.** 14
hōi *st. n.* hay **159.** 11
hol *st. n.* cave **153.** 8
holn *wk. vb.* fetch **62.** 1
holt *adj.*+*dat.* kindly disposed towards,
  fond, devoted, submissive **4.** 8; **10.** 6;
  12. 14; **31.** 1; **37.** 15; **51.** 28; **52.** 16, 50;
  61. 26; **90.** 12; **99.** 6, 23; **127.** 11.
  holdez herze tragen+*dat.* be well
  disposed towards **90.** 16; **126.** 33
honec, honic *st. m.* honey **110.** 36
hor *st. n.* mud
horn *st. n.* horn **163.** 30
hornunc *st. m.* February **95.** 2
hort *st. m.* treasure **148.** 9. horden *wk.*
  vb. hoard **148.** 19
hosen *wk. f. pl.* hose **127.** 26
houbet *st. n.* head **35.** 24
houbetsünde *st. f.* capital sin **154.** 13
hübesch *see* hōfesch
hüetel *st. n.* kerchief **123.** 19
hüeten *wk. vb.*+*gen.* guard, watch
  48. 10; **139.** 22; **117.** 13. *st. n.* **139.** 13
hulde *st. f.* favour, mercy **43.** 26;
  45. 5

hunt *st. m.* dog **164.** 21
huobe *st., wk. f.* (*land measure*) holding
  110. 46
huon *st. n.* hen **164.** 31
huot *st. m.* hat, headgear, kerchief **103.**
  39; **124.** 10; **127.** 26
huote *st. f.* watch, guard, *collective*
  watchers **21.** 7; **45.** 2; **61.** 1; **100.** 9;
  134. 14; **139.** 12; **145.** 16; **161.** 24;
  cover(t) **137.** 6
hūs *st. n.* house **126.** 53. gotes hūs
  church **91.** 67
hūssorge *st. f.* domestic care **162.** 22
hūt *st. f.* skin **161.** 11

I

ich *1st pers. sing. pron. gen.* mīn
icht, iht *st. n.* anything. *adv.* at all
  44. 25; **57.** 11; **109.** 5. *īt **41.** 20
ie *adv.* ever **25.** 4. ie der man each man
  134. 10
iedoch *adv.* however **44.** 8
ieg(e)līch, ieclīch *pronom. adj.* each
  51. 6; **55.** 11
ieman, iemen *pron. m. subst.* anyone;
  neg. no one. *īman **38.** 17
iemer, immer *adv.* always **8.** 6; **12.** 16.
  neg. never **111.** 6
iender, inder(t) *adv.* anywhere, somewhere **46.** 15; **128.** 15; **125.** 49
iesā *adv.* straight away **108.** 42
ieze *adv.* now **93.** 20
īlen *wk. vb.* hurry **80.** 6
i'me = ich ime **7.** 8
in(e) = ich ne **4.** 9; **19.** 7
in *prep.*+*acc., dat.* in **4.** 6; **164.** 21
īn, in *adv.* within, in **39.** 38; **107.** 4
inder(t) *see* iender
ingesinde *st. n.* retinue, servant, vassal
  50. 17; **125.** 16
ingewer *st. m.* ginger **127.** 29
ingwant *st. n.* innards, entrails **165.**
  15
inne *adv., prep.*+*gen.* within **97.** 4;
  121. 19
inne bringen, *brengen *st. vb.*+*gen.*
  make to realize **39.** 38; **141.** 31
inne werden *st. vb.*+*gen.* realize, perceive **38.** 26; **50.** 15; **60.** 3; **88.** 18
innen, innān *adv.* within **110.** 38; **128.**
  83
inneclīche(n) *adv.* inwardly, heartily
  104. 17; **109.** 14; **110.** 28; **132.** 22

ir *3rd pers. pron. gen., dat. sing. fem.*;
gen. pl. all genders; *3rd pers. possess.*
adj. fem. sing., pl. all genders
irgān *see* ergān
irre *adj., adv.* astray **92.** 10
irren *wk. vb.* prevent; harry, trouble
64. 24; **111.** 9. *pret.* *irde **41.** 13
īs *st. n.* ice **126.** 1
*isch *see* eischen
īsengewant *st. n.* armour **12.** 10
*īt *see* icht
iuwelenslaht *adj.* owl-like **113.** 5
iuwer *2nd pers. pl. pron. gen.*; *2nd pers.*
pl. possess. adj. iuwerre *dat. sing. f.*
possess. adj. **72.** 12

J

jā *interj.* indeed **61.** 3
jæmerlīch *adj.* miserable, wretched
110. 23
jæmerlīche *adv.* **110.** 18
jagen *wk. vb.* chase, hunt **115.** 11
jāmer *st. m.* grief **67.** 4
jāmerbære *adj.* grievous, grief-stricken
150. 19
jāmern *wk. vb. used impers.*+*acc. pers.*
move to pity **55.** 1
jāmerschric *st. m.* pang of grief **149.** 5
jāmertac *st. m.* day of sorrow **108.**
34
jār *st. n.* year **15.** 2. *pl.* life **76.** 8
jārlanc *adv.* at this time of the year;
for the rest of the year **6.** 4; **7.** 2
jehen *st. vb.*+*acc. or gen.* say **21.** 10.
giht *3rd pers. sing.* **102.** 10; **108.** 54.
+*dat. pers. and gen. thing* say sth. of
someone; ascribe, assign sth. to some-
one **63.** 8; **78.** 47; **113.** 11; **129.** 3. ir
(*gen.*) ze vrowen jehen claim her as
my lady **76.** 55. gejehen **125.** 14
jenenther *adv.* from there **126.** 46
jener *pron.* that **103.** 21; of the next
world **110.** 33
joch, jō *interj., adv., conj.* indeed **5.** 14;
19. 5. jone *neg.* **14.** 7
jude *wk. m.* Jew **109.** 6
jugent *st. f.* youth **7.** 11
junc *adj.* young
juncvrouwe *wk. f.* maiden **160.** 43
junger *st. m.* pupil **129.** 2
jungest *adv.* recently **34.** 8; **70.** 15;
90. 25. ze jungest recently **10.** 9;
finally **55.** 14

C, K

kæse *st. m.* cheese **162.** 10
kal *adj.* bare, bald **126.** 47
kāle *st. f.* torment **21.** 27
karc *adj.* shrewd **139.** 2
caritāte *wk. f.* mercy **38.** 32
karkelvar *adj.* ashen **108.** 43
katze *st. f.* cat **161.** 33
kein *neg. pron. adj.* no **86.** 4
keiser *st. m.* emperor **49.** 5
keiserlīch *adj.* imperial **92.** 4
kel(e) *st., wk. f.* throat **161.** 10
kēre *st. f.* movement **154.** 3
kēren *wk. vb.* turn, apply +an *or* ze
33. 7; **41.** 12; **71.** 11; **87.** 22; **98.** 25.
refl.+an apply oneself to **79.** 17.
gekēren divert **48.** 15
kerenter *st. m.* charnel house **154.** 10
kern *st. m.* kernel **157.** 48
chünegin *see* küneginne
chunich *see* künec
kielbrüstic *adj.* shipwrecked **131.** 8
kiesen *st. vb.* choose, perceive **91.** 39;
101. 43; **122.** 5
kinne *st. n.* chin **38.** 22; **91.** 5
kint *st. n.* child, youth, maiden **9.** 6;
126. 1, 13. von kinde from childhood
on **50.** 13; **59.** 1. kindelīn *st. n. dimin.*
71. 1. kindesch *adj.* young **7.** 10
kiste *st., wk. f.* chest **123.** 29
kīt *3rd pers. sing. of* keden, queden
say **101.** 61
kiusche *adj.* pure **78.** 2
kiusche *st. f.* purity **135.** 26
klā(we) *st., wk. f.* claw **116.** 1; **137.** 30
klage *st. f.* complaint **35.** 18; **58.** 4;
114. 18; cause for lament **119.** 1
klagen *wk. vb.* complain, lament **22.** 16.
st. n. **73.** 1
klār(e) *adj.* clear, beautiful **41.** 3; **63.** 21
klē *st. m., n.* clover **94.** 9
klein *adj.* small **23.** 2; precious **107.**
28
kleinen *adv.* little **163.** 15
kleinen *wk. vb.* decrease **164.** 11
kleit *st. n.* garment **130.** 1; **161.** 5. klei-
den *wk. vb.* clothe **127.** 24
klenke *pl. of* klanc *st. m.* (?) (*usually*
klenge) derogatory designation of the
poet's song **128.** 18
klingen *st. vb.* resound **165.** 38
klobe *wk. m.* cleft stick used as bird-
trap **134.** 20; **148.** 40

klobwurst *st. f.* **165.** 29; *either* (1) sausage hanging on cleft stick **(klobe)**, *or* (2) sausage in fat-gut **(klobdarm)**.

klōse, klūse *st., wk. f.* hermit's cell **44.** 19; **153.** 1

klōsenære *st. m.* hermit **91.** 70

knappe *wk. m.* lad **128.** 42

kneht *st. m.* servant, farm-labourer **91.** 40; **159.** 1

collier *st. n.* collar, neck-piece of armour **126.** 36

komen *st. vb.* come **4.** 8. **kum(e)t** *3rd pers. sing. pres. indic.* **21.** 21; **22.** 22; **79.** 6. **kom** (**36.** 7), **kam** (**46.** 18) *pret. indic.* **kæme** (**35.** 24), **kœme** (**21.** 6) *pret. subj.* **komen** *pp.* **30.** 3. bī **komen** approach **62.** 14

***koninginne** *see* **küneginne**

korn *st. n.* corn **126.** 54

kōsen *wk. vb.* speak **153.** 2. **gekōsen 158.** 18

kosten *wk. vb.* cost **141.** 20

koufen *wk. vb.* buy **126.** 54

***cracht** *st. f.* power (cf. Dutch kracht) **40.** 4

kradem *st. m.* noise **123.** 24

kraft *st. f.* force **115.** 12

krage *wk. m.* neck **126.** 36

kranc *st. m.* fault, imperfection, injury **39.** 7; **56.** 5

kranc *adj.* inferior, small, faulty, imperfect **57.** 4; **58.** 24; **135.** 10; **143.** 4.

krenken *wk. vb.* weaken, shake, pain, injure **61.** 22; **64.** 17; **101.** 39

kranz *st. m.* garland **103.** 1. **krenzelīn** *st. n. dimin.* **128.** 40. **kränzel 128.** 55. **krenzel 166.** 3

kriec *st. m.* war, conflict **76.** 10; **111.** 6.

kriegen *wk. vb.* struggle **146.** 17

kriechen *st. vb.* crawl **91.** 29

krispen *wk. vb.* goffer **166.** 2

cristen *adj., st. m.* Christian **110.** 23

kristenheit *st. f.* Christendom **91.** 72

criuze, kriuze *st. n.* cross **53.** 10; **58.** 10

krōne *st. f.* crown **35.** 21

krœnen *wk. vb.* crown **101.** 52

krœse *st. n.* small intestine **165.** 20

krump *adj.* crooked, squinting **47.** 24

krūt *st. n.* plant, plant undergrowth **160.** 29; cabbage **158.** 5

küele *adj.* cool **123.** 1

küene *adj.* bold **141.** 7

kumber *st. m.* distress **35.** 12; **45.** 6; **60.** 7; **61.** 7; **65.** 13; **88.** 1; **118.** 10

kumberlīch *adj.* distressing **44.** 17

kūme *adv.* with difficulty, hardly **81.** 8; **121.** 53

künde *st. f.* knowledge **11.** 4

kündekeit *st. f.* cunning **86.** 12; **137.** 10

künden *wk. vb.* make known, proclaim **138.** 9; **163.** 30

kündic *adj.* known **110.** 6

künec, chunich *st. m.* king

kunft *st. f.* coming **117.** 17

küniginne, küneginne, chünegin *st. f.* queen **3.** 4; **61.** 13; **82.** 27. ***koninginne** *wk. f.* **40.** 2

kunnen *pret.-pres. vb.* know how to, be able **7.** 9; **26.** 14; **42.** 2; **43.** 27

kunst *st. f.* skill, art **94.** 2; **106.** 6, 19; **137.** 9

künsterīch *adj.* knowledgeable, skilled **129.** 3

kunt *adj.* known **55.** 7

kuo, chuo *st. f.* cow **164.** 15

kurc *adj.* choice **169.** 7

kurz *adj.* short **24.** 15

küssen *wk. vb.* kiss **49.** 6; **70.** 17. *st. n.* **85.** 38

kützeln *wk. vb.* tickle **134.** 12

L

lachen *wk. vb.* laugh, smile. *st. n.* **84.** 19. an **lachen** laugh at, smile at **78.** 25

laden *st. vb.* load **113.** 15

lære *adj.* empty

lāge *st. f.* snare, ambush **109.** 30; **153.** 8

lamp *st. n.* lamb **107.** 27

lān *see* **lāzen**

lanc *adj.* long, tall **41.** 2; **93.** 13

lange *adv.* 1. 10. **langer** *comp. adv.* **83.** 26

langen *wk. vb.* grow long **123.** 2

lanke *st., wk. f.* hip **122.** 21

lant *st. n.* land **12.** 7. ze **lande** homewards, home **30.** 3

last *st. f.* burden **117.** 21

laster *st. n.* shame, discredit **87.** 35

lāzen, *contracted* **lān** *st. vb.* let, leave, abandon, omit **5.** 13; **10.** 15; **18.** 5; **47.** 1; **48.** 5; **66.** 13. lie *pret.* **21.** 26; **47.** 2; **66.** 10. *refl.* entrust oneself **68.** 7. abe **lāzen** abandon, give up **88.** 21; **164.** 25. ***lāten 38.** 29; *pret.* **līt 41.** 27

leben *wk. vb.* live **29.** 1. geleben **62.**
27; experience **35.** 23; **46.** 1; **68.** 19;
84. 38
leben *st. n.* life **17.** 5
lebendic *adj.* alive **53.** 13
lebetac *st. m.* life **155.** 8
ledic, lidic *adj.* free, **53.** 9; **84.** 21; **98.**
19; unmarried **162.** 3
legen *wk. vb.* lay, place. *refl.* lie down.
pret. leiten **91.** 63. gelegen cause to
lie down **30.** 9; **83.** 23. für legen submit
87. 28. hin legen put down, off **85.**
45; **161.** 5
lēhen *st. n.* fief, entitlement **95.** 1;
123. 21
leide *adv.* harmfully, grievously. leide
tuon wrong **73.** 10. *comp.* leider **123.**
28; unfortunately **9.** 2; **125.** 14
leiden *wk. vb.*+*dat.*,*intrans.* be painful,
displeasing to **88.** 11; **145.** 7. *trans.*
make displeasing, hateful **32.** 5
leie *wk. m.* layman **91.** 58
leim *st. m.* mud **125.** 52
leisten *wk. vb.* perform, carry out **9.** 8;
73. 32; **116.** 8; **120.** 18. geselleschaft
leisten keep company **106.** 25
leit *adj.* unpleasant. mir ist leit I regret **45.** 20; **84.** 36
leit *st. n.* suffering, unhappiness **10.** 10;
16. 6; **17.** 3. ach leides alas **35.** 4. mir
ze leide to my distress, to grieve me
leite *see* legen
leiten *wk. vb.* lead. geleiten lead
safely **118.** 13
leitesterne *wk. m.* guiding star, lode-
star **92.** 12
leitlīch *adj.* grievous **71.** 5
lenge *st. f.* length, stature **93.** 11. die
lenge for any length of time **131.** 7
lengen *refl. wk. vb.* be protracted
147. 7
lerche *wk. f.* lark **135.** 4
lēre *st. f.* teaching **97.** 3; **111.** 12; **135.** 9
lēren *wk. vb.* teach **97.** 7
lernen *wk. vb.* learn **44.** 12. gelernen
59. 14
leschen *wk. vb.* extinguish fire **144.**
36
lesen *st. vb.* gather **123.** 10
leuwe *wk. m.* lion **137.** 15
*lïchten *wk. vb.* grow bright **39.** 2
līden *st. vb.* suffer **41.** 21; **45.** 12
lieb *see* liep

liebe *st. f.* pleasure, happiness **28.**
7; **86.** 29; love **64.** 2; **67.** 24; **99.** 10,
11; **100.** 7; **115.** 32; **121.** 21; **142.** 40;
charm (*quality of being* liep) **99.** 15,
16, 17. durch ir liebe for her sake
35. 14
lieben *wk. vb.* be pleasing **88.** 11. *refl.*
make oneself agreeable
lieber *comp. adv.* rather **22.** 5
liegen *st. vb.* lie **111.** 12
lieht *st. n.* light **116.** 30
lieht *adj.* bright, resplendent **63.** 5;
120. 9; bare **7.** 2
liep *st. n.* lover, object of love **5.** 3, 13;
10. 11; **22.** 21; **24.** 10; **82.** 1; **84.** 9; happiness (*opp.* leit) **11.** 2; **17.** 3; **73.** 5.
swer iu iht ze liebe tuot if anyone
does you a kindness **132.** 22
liep, lieb *adj.* dear, pleasing, charming
5. 6; **6.** 12; **10.** 1; **17.** 6; **19.** 4, 8;
21. 2; **99.** 18. *līf *adj.* **41.** 6
liet *st. n.* strophe, poem, song **35.** 5. diu
liet verses
ligen *st. vb.* lie **3.** 5; **24.** 10; **26.** 8. *3rd
pers. sing.* līt *from* liget **36.** 4; **46.** 3;
62. 5. geligen **34.** 13; **37.** 10; lie low
105. 5
līht *adj.* light, slight **85.** 33; **132.** 4
līhte *adv.* easily, perhaps **20.** 2; **44.** 23.
vil līhte perhaps **62.** 18. *used substantivally*+*gen.* a small amount **54.** 11
līhter *comp. adv.* **112.** 2
lilje *wk. f.* lily **94.** 7
liljerōsevarwe *st. f.* white and red
colour **108.** 43
linde *st., wk. f.* lime-tree **6.** 3
lint *adj.* soft **161.** 11
līp *st. m.* body, life, person **27.** 2; **44.** 20;
78. 16; **83.** 11; **87.** 13; **88.** 31. *in para-
phrase for pers. pron., e.g.,* ir līp she
31. 10
list *st. m., f.* knowledge, skill, device,
cunning **56.** 11; **79.** 3; **107.** 15
līt *see* ligen *and* lāten
liuhten *wk. vb.* shine **63.** 5; **116.** 30.
geliuhten **70.** 2; **118.** 35. an liuhten
shine on **92.** 7
liut *st. m.* (*usually pl.*) people **10.** 15;
14. 8; **52.** 6; **81.** 2; **82.** 12
liuten *wk. vb.* sound, ring **122.** 49
lobelīch *adj.* praiseworthy **10.** 4
loben *wk. vb.* praise **25.** 1. geloben
86. 23

lobesam *adj.* praiseworthy 4. 2. lobesan 165. 22
loc *st. m.* lock of hair 144. 6
loch *st. n.* cave 153. 11
lōch *st. m., n.* bush 125. 11
lōn *st. m.* reward 49. 11; 52. 32; 57. 4;
61. 40; 108. 25
lōnen *wk. vb.* reward 52. 40; 73. 35;
76. 20
lop *st. n.* praise, repute 54. 25; 63. 3;
73. 27
lōs *adj.* free; charming, pleasing 142. 25;
153. 3. lōse *adv.* 148.
louf *st. m.* course 155. 6
loufen, *st. vb.* run 78. 30
lougen *st. n.* denial 109. 22; 123. 17
lougen(en) *wk. vb.* deny 125. 40
loup *st. n.* foliage 6. 3; 114. 1
*louven *wk. vb.* put forth leaves 43. 3
lucken *wk. vb.* lure 134. 16
lūde *see* lūt
lüedern *wk. vb.* lure 134. 16
luft *st. m., f.* air 95. 5
lüge *st. f.* lie 86. 5
lugenære *st. m.* liar 16. 6
lust *st. f.* pleasure
lusten, lüsten *wk. vb. used impers.+
acc. pers., gen. thing* mich lustet I desire. *pret.* luste for lustete 118. 27.
gelusten 14. 3
lūt *adj.* audible, loud 24. 3. *lūde adv.*
43. 20
lūter *adj.* clear, pure. lūter vor free of
63. 14
lützel *adj.* little, few. *adv.* hardly, not
45. 8; 98. 21. *neut. subst. used adverbially* 71. 15
lūzen *wk. vb.* lie in wait 153. 2

M

mac *st. m.* kinsman 81. 1; 121. 36
*mach *see* mugen
machen *wk. vb.* make, cause 11. 1;
16. 5. *maken 42. 6. gemachen 62.
32
mære *adj.* pleasing, of interest, dear
100. 26; 125. 17
mære *st. f., n.* news, tidings 30. 1;
46. 16; 76. 2. *māre *st. f.* 38. 1
magen *st. m.* stomach 165. 15
maget, meit *st. f.* unmarried girl, maid
2. 2; 58. 20; 107. 1; 120. 22

maht *st. f.* power 64. 13
māl *st. n.* instance, time. ze einem māl
on occasion 125. 42. zeinem māle
once 142. 26
man *st. m.* man 7. 10; 10. 18; 18. 6;
20. 4; lover 2. 3; 4. 4; vassal 101. 59.
indef. pron. one 9. 2. *indef. pron.*
*men 38. 3
māne *wk. m.* moon 63. 4
manec, manic, menic *adj.* many a 4. 7
manen *wk. vb.+acc. pers., gen. thing*
remind, admonish 6. 12; 10. 8, 10; 24.
7; 60. 21
manicvalt, manecvalt, manechfalt
adj. manifold, various 43. 17
manlīch *adj.* manly 141. 21
manneglīch *adj.* everyone 127. 33
mantel *st. m.* cloak 130. 7
margarīte *wk. f.* pearl 107. 25; 169.
12
marter *st. f.* sacrifice, martyrdom 58. 8
māse *wk. f.* spot 160. 22
mat *st. m., adj.* checkmate 85. 9
*māte *see* māze
materje *st., wk. f.* material 148. 4
māze *st. f.* moderation, measure 26. 12.
*māte 38. 31. āne māze immeasur-
ably 22. 3. ze māze moderately 63. 15;
not at all 80. 2. ze māze sīn, komen
suit 83. 32; 124. 30; 128. 74. in solher
māze of such a kind 80. 23. der māze
daz of such a kind that 126. 32.
gelīcher māze in the same way,
exactly 87. 13
mē *see* mēr
megetīn *st. f.* maiden 19. 2
meie, meige *wk. m.* May 63. 21; 114. 2;
136. 3; 143. 1
meier *st. m.* farmer 164. 24
meinen *wk. vb.* mean, intend, love
49. 12; 56. 13; 61. 41; 82. 22; 90. 19;
164. 7. +an apply to, refer to 69. 2
meist *superl. adj.* most 89. 6
meister *st. m.* master 79. 21; 86. 38;
farmer 126. 43; doctor 147. 13; husband 162. 12
meisterinne *st. f.* mistress 121. 29
meisterschaft *st. f.* mastery, skill 78. 7;
129. 3
meit *see* maget
melde *st. m. (?) or contracted from* mel-
dennes *st. n. subst. infin.* betrayal
117. 21

melden *wk. vb.* betray **75.** 20
melken *wk. vb.* milk **164.** 15
*men *see* man
menigī *wk. f.* throng **12.** 6
menneschlīch *adj.* human **107.** 15
mer *st. n.* sea **54.** 9; Mediterranean **3.** 2
mēr, mē *comp. adj.* more **45.** 11
mēre, mē *comp. adv.* more **15.** 2; **40.** 4; ever **91.** 18; **129.** 6; in future **127.** 10
mēren *wk. vb.* increase **71.** 9; **106.** 20. *intrans.* **125.** 31
*merelār *st. f.* blackbird **41.** 5
merkære, merker *st. m.* watcher, slanderer, ill-wisher **11.** 6; **32.** 1; **45.** 7; **119.** 13; **139.** 2; **145.** 9; **161.** 24
merken *wk. vb.* notice, observe **37.** 16; **55.** 10; **87.** 44; **139.** 7, 26, 29. *st. n.* spying, watching **139.** 3, 6, 8, 10, 11. gemerken **139.** 6
mez *st. n.* measure **93.** 18
mezzen *st. vb.* measure **93.** 11
michel *adj.* great **93.** 19
michels *adv.* much **106.** 15
mīden *st. vb.* avoid, shun **6.** 8; **22.** 4; **73.** 25
miete *st. f.* reward **96.** 5
mieten *wk. vb.* reward, repay **164.** 29
mīle *st. f.* mile **144.** 30
milte, milde *adj.* generous **93.** 13, 16
milte *st. f.* generosity **93.** 11
minne *st., wk. f.* love **4.** 4; **10.** 14; **12.** 15; **98.** 28
minneclīch *adj.* lovable, beautiful **35.** 9; **61.** 2; **66.** 3
minneclīche *adv.* graciously **67.** 6
minne(n)diep *st. m.* thief of love **152.** 4
minnen *wk. vb.* love **1.** 12; **10.** 5; **17.** 7; **35.** 15
minnesanc *st. m.* poetry of love **108.** 11
minnesinger *st. m.* poet of love **81.** 17
minner, minre *comp. adj., adv.* less **87.** 31
minnist *superl. adj.* least **10.** 17
*misdōn *see* missetuon
misselingen *st. vb. used impers.* fail **81.** 17
missereden *wk. vb.* speak ill **89.** 13
missesagen *wk. vb.* speak wrongly **79.** 8
missetāt *st. f.* misdeed **85.** 42
missetuon *st. vb.* do wrong **83.** 16. *misdōn **39.** 20
mit *prep.+dat.* with. *bit **38.** 27

mitewist *st. f.* participation **107.** 14
mitte *adj.* middle, mid **68.** 18
mitten *adv.* mitten in in the midst of **110.** 36
morgen *st. m.* morning. morgens in the morning **116.** 12
morgenblic *st. m.* morning light **115.** 1
morgenlīch *adj.* of the morning **118.** 4
morgenrōt *st. m.* dawn **107.** 2
morgensterne *wk. m.* morning star **68.** 15; **116.** 28; **119.** 9
mort *adj.* dead **121.** 54
müede *adj.* weary **80.** 8
müejen, müen *wk. vb.* trouble, annoy **51.** 18; **53.** 5; **66.** 28; **82.** 9; **108.** 19
müemel *st. f.* aunt, female relation **136.** 22
müezen *pret.-pres. vb.* must, may **7.** 12; **8.** 6; **10.** 13; **96.** 40. *pres. indic.* *mūt **38.** 8. *pret. indic.* *mūste **40.** 1. muose **71.** 24. *pret. subj.* müese **45.** 12
mugen *pret.-pres. vb.* be able **14.** 4; **21.** 12; **102.** 5. *3rd pers. sing.* *mach **40.** 8
mugge *st. f.* fly **91.** 43
mül *st. f.* mill **105.** 21
munt *st. m.* mouth **49.** 7. von munde by word of mouth **35.** 2. mündelīn, mündel *st. n. dimin.* **71.** 16; **144.** 6
muochen (*obscure*) fancies **128.** 73
muos *st. n.* food **162.** 6
muot *st. m.* mind, purpose, intention, inclination, mood **13.** 8; **37.** 12; **84.** 22; **132.** 21. mir ist ze muote I feel **103.** 26. hōher muot *see* hōch
muoter *st. f.* mother **58.** 20
mūs *st. f.* mouse **161.** 33
*mūt *see* müezen

N

nac *st. m.* back of neck **92.** 11. näckelīn, nekil *st. n. dimin.* **126.** 35; **161.** 10
nāch *prep.+dat., adv.* to, towards, in pursuit of, after, near **137.** 3; (longing) for **1.** 8; **88.** 29; in imitation of **67.** 10; in accordance with **85.** 4; **99.** 12. vil nāch almost **27.** 9; **109.** 19. *nā **41.** 24
nāch gēn *st. vb.+dat.* be inferior to **99.** 16
nāch loufen *st. vb.+dat.* run after **78.** 30
nagen *wk. vb.* gnaw **154.** 12

nähe *adv.* near, nearly 26. 8; 36. 10;
46. 11. nähe gie affected nearly 52. 23.
nähe sprechen affect with words
86. 27. nār *comp. adv.* 63. 26
nähen *wk. vb.* approach 62. 30
nähgebūre *wk. m.* neighbour 95. 6
naht *st. f.* 37. 13. des nahtes by night
63. 5
nahtegal *st. f.* nightingale 104. 7;
114. 11
name *wk. m.* name 87. 19
narre *wk. m.* fool 121. 71
naz *adj.* wet. nat 66. 15
nazzen *wk. vb.* grow wet 115. 6
ne, en *neg. part.*; *attached to verbal
forms, e.g.* 5. 14; 52. 2. +*subj.* unless
e.g. 4. 8; 91. 24; but that, without 36. 9
*nedere *see* nidere
*negein *pronom. adj.* no 39. 7; 43. 36
nehtint *adv.* at night 12. 1
neigen *wk. vb.* incline 135. 12. geneigen 65. 24
nein *neg.* no
neinā intensified form of nein 61. 13
nemelīch *adj.* pertaining to name 168.
15
nemen *st. vb.* take, accept 44. 18; 101.
54. genemen 93. 2. ūz nemen except
63. 13. sich (*acc.*) an nemen+*acc.*
take on 140. 12
nennen *wk. vb.* name 87. 20
nern *wk. vb.* save, cure, nourish; countenance 167. 14
nicht, niht, niet, nit *adv.* not. *st. n.*+
partitive gen. nothing 14. 4; 21. 20; 148.
39; 161. 28. *nīt 38. 6
nīden *st. vb.* envy 5. 12; 36. 15; 41. 19;
st. n. 48. 12
nider *adj.* low, base 97. 11; lowly 108.
17
nider(e) *adv.* low, down 68. 20; 97. 8, 9.
nider sich down 70. 20. *nedere 43.
21
nie *adv.* never 19. 8
nieman, niemen *pronom. subst.* no one
29. 2; 36. 20
niemer, nimmer *adv.* never 35. 24;
42. 11
niender, ninder, nindert *adv.* nowhere
71. 26; 139. 20; not at all 116. 28, 30
niene *adv.* not, not at all 27. 6; 75. 19;
82. 19. *nīne 38. 29
niewan *see* niuwan

nīgen *st. vb.* bow 103. 14; 148. 41
nīt *st. m.* envy 45. 2; 139. 11, 12. mir
ze nīde to annoy me 51. 11
niuwan, niewan, niwan *adv., conj.*
nothing but, only, except 7. 9; 58. 30;
89. 7; 109. 29
niuwe *adj.* new 71. 19; 87. 1; 114. 3.
*nouwe 38. 1
niuwen *wk. vb.* renew 165. 1
*niwet *adv.* not, not at all 39. 12
noch *adv.* nor, still 4. 2; 19. 2; *conj.*
nor 14. 5. *noch dan moreover 38. 18
nōne *st. f.* ninth hour from 6 a.m.,
nones 122. 9
nōt *st. f.* need, necessity, distress 44. 17;
84. 16; impediment 58. 16. *dore nōt
of necessity 43. 34. mir ist nōt I need
cf. 58. 8. nōt *used adjectivally* 58. 3
(*comp.* nœter)
nōtic *adj.* needy 110. 45
*nouwe *see* niuwe
nu, nuo *adv.* now 7. 2; 17. 2; 118. 5.
conj. now that 45. 8

O

ob(e) *prep.*+*dat., adv.* above 92. 11;
148. 38
ob(e) *conj.* if 33. 5; 35. 24. *of 42.
10
obedach *st. n.* shelter 125. 55
obene *adv.* above 24. 1
obez *st. n.* fruit 169. 4
œdelich *adj.* hateful. *adv.* œdelīchen
127. 21
œsen *wk. vb.* loosen 165. 40
Oesterrīche, Ōsterrīche *st. n.* Austria
121. 70
*of *see* ob(e) *conj.*
offenbār *adj.* obvious 123. 18. *openbāre *adv.* 38. 2
offenlīche *adv.* openly, obviously 111.
12
ofte *adv.* often 22. 13
*ofte *conj.* or 38. 17
ordenunge *st. f.* order 91. 42
ōre *st., wk. n.* ear 114. 6
ōrenlōs *adj.* deaf 98. 27
ouch, och *adv., conj.* also 5. 9; 6. 4;
24. 16; 87. 27
ouge *wk. n.* eye 5. 11
ougen *wk. vb.* show 79. 12
ougenweide *st. f.* feast for eyes 92. 9
ougest *st. m.* August 121. 72

ouwe *st. f.* water meadow, meadow 104. 8

owī, owē *interj.* alas 1. 12

P

palas *st. m.* palace, hall 107. 28

phaffe *wk. m.* priest 91. 58

pharre *st. f.* parish 121. 77

pfat *st. m., n.* path 104. 18

Pfāt *st. m.* Po 48. 15

pfeffer *st. m.* pepper 162. 17

phellerīn *adj.* silken 127. 28

pfīfe *wk. f.* pipe 134. 6

phlanze *st. f.* plant 121. 70

phlegen, pflegen *st. vb.+gen.* exercise, cultivate, do, care for 87. 24; 125. 47; be accustomed 44. 13; 70. 14; 113. 18; 119. 11. *pret.* *plāgen *from* plegen 43. 18. gepflegen 119. 11

pfleger *st. m.* custodian 161. 34

pflihten *wk. vb.+zuo* associate oneself with 137. 43

phose *wk. m.* pouch 127. 28

pilgerīn *st. m.* pilgrim 121. 40

pīment *st. n.* spiced wine 40. 7

pīn *st. m.* punishment, torment, pain 41. 27; 148. 14

pīneclīch *adj.* tormenting, irritating 128. 75

***plāgen** *see* **phlegen**

plān *st. m.* meadow 161. 18

planēt(e) *wk. m., f.* planet 169. 16

poisūn *st. m.* potion, love potion 40. 3

pōlus *st. m.* pole, heaven 169. 17

porte *st., wk. f.* gate 107. 3

primāte *wk. m.* archbishop, bishop 131. 10

prīs *st. m.* renown, good repute, worth 78. 18; 117. 4, 39; 118. 33

prüeven, brüeven *wk. vb.* consider, examine, test, arrange 126. 20; 148. 3; 168. 7

Pülle Apulia 94. 1

Q

***quam** *pret. of* **quemen** *st. vb.* come 39. 17

***quāt** *adj.* evil, bad 38. 28

queln *st. vb.* suffer torments 154. 15

R

rat *st. n.* wheel 105. 23

rāt *st. m.* counsel, help, remedy 22. 22; 27. 8; 45. 3; 55. 13; 61. 33. des wirt rāt there is a remedy for 79. 18. *dat. sing.* *rāde 39. 17

rāten *st. vb.* advise 32. 12; guess, find out 98. 8. *pret.* *rīt 39. 36

rechen *wk. vb.* avenge 47. 22; 58. 6; 124. 18. *refl.* 64. 5

rede *st. f.* speech, words, matter 60. 12; 65. 20; 87. 23; gossip (*cf.* NHG Nachrede) 32. 4; argument 58. 19; poem 106. 11

reden *wk. vb.* speak 10. 8; 21. 5; 26. 5. wol redend eloquent 106. 22. gereden 26. 7

reht *st. n.* right, law; duty, obligation 91. 39; 108. 5; 140. 9. reht hān have a right to, be right 47. 25; 74. 1. ze rehte rightly, by rights 56. 9; 92. 5

reht, recht *adj.* true, right 26. 10; 41. 8; 44. 25; 67. 24

rehte *adv.* truly, properly 35. 3; 52. 20. rehte tuon+*dat.* do justice to 108. 24

reie, reige *wk. m.* round dance

reien, reigen *wk. vb.* dance in circle 121. 64; 122. 7; 124. 7; 136. 1

rein *adj.* excellent, perfect, pure 42. 6; 56. 6; 63. 19

reine *adv.* excellently 85. 23

reise *st. f.* journey 81. 4

reit *adj.* curly 144. 6

reizen *wk. vb.* stimulate, entice 97. 14; 134. 20

rennen *wk. vb.* run, ride swiftly 144. 30

respen *wk. vb.* pull in, hitch up 134. 7

rīch *st. n.* kingdom 35. 8; 54. 27; 63. 3; emperor 77. 14

rīch(e) *adj.* powerful, rich 36. 1; 47. 27. *rīke 41. 15

rīchen *wk. vb.* enrich 93. 1

rīchheit *st. f.* riches 45. 11

rīchtuom *st. m.* riches 35. 11

rieme *wk. m.* jess (of falcon) 15. 12; band 123. 33

rīfe *st. m.* hoar frost 114. 4

Rīn *st. m.* Rhine 3. 2

rinc *st. m.* ring; of chain mail 110. 42; of dancers 128. 67

ringe *adj., adv.* slight

ringen *wk. vb.* lessen 143. 14. geringen 128. 9

ringen *st. vb.* struggle 52. 22; 59. 9. +

nāch strive after 45. 14; 77. 3; 84. 18; 143. 14

rinkeloht *adj.* buckled 127. 26

rinnen *st. vb.* run 126. 50

rint *st. n.* ox, cow. *pl.* cattle 160. 7

rīs *st. n.* branch 160. 20

rise *wk. m.* giant 93. 20

rīse *st., wk. f.* veil, kerchief 124. 10; 128. 45

*rīt *see* rāten

rīten *st. vb.* ride 1. 11; 37. 1; 118. 36

riter, ritter *st. m.* knight 11. 3; 12. 3; 13. 4; 20. 5; 22. 9; 116. 37

ritterlīch *adj., adv.* knightly, courtly 80. 4; 129. 12

riuschen *wk. vb.* roar 105. 22

riutel *st. f.* rod, stick 126. 43

riuwe *st. f.* grief 73. 1

riuwen *wk. vb.* grieve, cause repentance, regret 88. 4; 106. 14; 106. 22; 135. 30

roc *st. m.* tunic 127. 25; gown 130. 4

röckel *st. n. dimin.* gown, kirtle 123. 31

Rōde *wk. m.* Rhône 38. 11

rōr *st. n.* reed 91. 28

ros *st. n.* horse 12. 10

rōse *st., wk. f.* rose 4. 3

rœseleht *adj.* rosy 143. 19

rōsenkranz *st. m.* rose garland 136. 10

rōserōt *adj.* rose-red 158. 23

rōt *adj.* red 34. 2

roup *st. m.* theft 153. 9

*rouwe *wk. m.* grief 38. 13; 46. 7

rucken *wk. vb.* push, pull, press 103. 39; 117. 35; 126. 34; 133. 20; 134. 8

rüemen *refl. wk. vb.* boast 81. 9

rüeren *wk. vb.* affect 165. 9

rūm *st. m.* room 121. 56

rūmen *wk. vb.* leave 12. 7; 12. 12

rūnen *wk. vb.* whisper 32. 6. gerūnen 127. 12

ruochen *wk. vb.* care, deign 52. 18; 61. 32; 84. 26. geruochen 76. 39. +*gen.* take note of 114. 15. *gerūken 43. 31

ruofen, rüefen *st. vb.* (*also wk.*) call 9. 6. geruofen 65. 9

ruote *st., wk. f.* rod 47. 14

ruowe *st. f.* rest 21. 19

ruowen *wk. vb.* rest. geruowet lān leave alone 58. 18; 128. 71

S

sā *adv.* straightway 85. 16

sache *st. f.* thing, matter 105. 28

*sachte *see* sanfte

sælde *st. f.* good fortune, bliss 26. 6; 58. 11; 73. 16; 85. 37; 118. 24

sældehaft *adj.* fortunate, blessed 62. 5; 73. 15

sælden *wk. vb.* make joyful 132. 13

sælderīch *adj.* joyful 157. 11

sælec, sælic *adj.* fortunate 31. 9; 45. 18; 62. 31. *sālech 42. 4

sage *st. f.* talk

sagen *wk. vb.* say, tell 22. 2. *contracted forms* seit, seite, geseit. gesagen 66. 18

*sal *see* soln

salz *st. n.* salt 126. 54

sam, sem *adv., conj.* as 96. 31

sam *prep.*+*dat.* together with, like 17. 2

sament, sant *prep.*+*dat.* together with 9. 12; 17. 4; 136. 34

sanc *st. m.* song 23. 2; 73. 3; 115. 1; 117. 2

sanfte *adj., adv.*, senfte *adj.* soft, gentle, pleasing 9. 5; 72. 1; 86. 43; 87. 20. sanfte tuon be pleasing 69. 4. *sachte *adv.* 41. 21

sant *see* sament

sarc *st. m.* shrine 167. 11

sāt *st. f.* crop 113. 13

sāze *st. f.* ambush 91. 21

schaben *wk. vb.* erase 109. 4

schade *wk. m.* harm, injury 19. 6; 52. 43; 76. 24; 82. 17. *scade 38. 27.

schedelīch *adj.* harmful, injurious 10. 2; 14. 6; 128. 52

schaden *wk. vb.* injure 66. 21

schaffen *st., wk. vb.* create, cause, do, procure 69. 5, 16; 78. 43; 91. 38; 127. 31

schal *st. m.* sound, noise, echo 65. 11; 116. 27; 124. 3; 164. 14

schallen *wk. vb.* make noise 105. 25

scham(e) *st. f.* shame 140. 32

schamelop *st. n.* shaming praise 140. 26

schamen *refl. wk. vb.*+*gen.* be ashamed 97. 5

schande *st., wk. f.* shame, disgrace 109. 23; 135. 3

schanze *st. f.* throw at dice, stake 139. 35

schapel *st. n.* garland, chaplet 103. 18; 128. 40

schaperūn *st. m.* short cloak 127. 25.

schar *st. f.* company, crowd **123**. 20

schar *st. f.* punishment **77**. 16

scharpf *adj.* sharp **161**. 26

schate *wk. m.* shadow, reflection **71**. 23

schedelīch *see* schade

scheiden *st. vb. intrans.* part, depart **21**. 15; **22**. 7; **34**. 8; **62**. 17. *refl.* **16**. 4. *st. n.* **10**. 1, 12; **50**. 10; **60**. 5; **66**. 9. *trans.* part, discriminate, settle **53**. 8; **101**. 31. gescheiden *intr.* **35**. 10. *tr.* **126**. 43

schelten *st. vb.* reproach **95**. 9

schiere *adv.* quickly, soon **9**. 2; **37**. 5; **59**. 12

schiezen *st. vb.* shoot. ūf schiezen shoot up **93**. 18

schilt *st. m.* shield **78**. 17. under schilde under arms **129**. 12; **141**. 6

schiltær(e) *st. m.* painter **115**. 29

schimel *st. m.* brilliance **169**. 13

schimpf *st. m.* game, pastime **118**. 30

schīn *st. m.* brightness **23**. 6; **63**. 6; reflection **71**. 3; **135**. 14; appearance **160**. 11; **161**. 7; sight **166**. 16. schīn tuon show **46**. 14; **117**. 12. schīn werden become manifest **44**. 24; **73**. 13

schīnen *st. vb.* shine **107**. 5; **112**. 11

schōne *adj., adv.*, schœne *adj.* beautiful, handsome **5**. 12; **15**. 10; **17**. 1; **18**. 3; **20**. 5; **35**. 20. *scōne **38**. 10

schœne *st. f.* beauty **50**. 2; **61**. 19

schoph *st. m.* forelock **127**. 22

schouwen *wk. vb.* look at **36**. 18; **65**. 4; distinguish **96**. 29. *scouwen **38**. 17. *st. n.* appearance **109**. 22

schōz *st. m., n.* lap **135**. 25

schrage *wk. m.* trestle **126**. 19

schreien *wk. vb.* cause to shout **124**. 7

schrīen *st. vb.* call, scream, croak **105**. 30. ūf schrīen exclaim **157**. 23

schrīn *st. m.* casket, shrine, chest **91**. 15; **123**. 26; **168**. 16

schrit *st. m.* step **121**. 65

schulde, schult *st. f.* debt, obligation, fault, guilt, cause, reason **24**. 11; **58**. 29; **73**. 14; **107**. 22; **125**. 38. *sculde **43**. 30. *scolt **39**. 28. von schulden rightly, by rights **25**. 10; **44**. 1; **69**. 21; **100**. 18; through her own fault **33**. 11

schuldic *adj.* indebted **109**. 6; guilty **73**. 18

schuldehaft *adj.* under obligation, guilty **113**. 16

schuoch *st. m.* shoe **127**. 26

schuole *st. f.* school **129**. 1

schürzen *wk. vb.* shorten, restrict **155**. 6

schütze *wk. m.* marksman **148**. 33

sē *st. m.* sea, lake **62**. 33; **105**. 29; **121**. 23

segel *st. m.* sail **137**. 24

segen *st. m.* blessing **54**. 23

segenen *wk. vb.* bless **146**. 8

*seggen *wk. vb.* say **39**. 5

sehen, sēn, *sīn *st. vb.* see **6**. 9; **15**. 9; **18**. 4; **23**. 5; **64**. 23. *3rd pers. sing.* *sīt **38**. 3; **41**. 25. gesehen perceive **5**. 4; **26**. 13; **78**. 48; **88**. 5. *pret.* *gesāgen **43**. 14. an(e) sehen, gesehen, look at **29**. 13; **66**. 7; **68**. 11; **90**. 26

seine *adv.* slowly, not at all **144**. 21

seit *see* sagen

selp *pronom. adj.* self, same **5**. 10; **19**. 5; **28**. 13

selde *st. f.* dwelling **107**. 24

selderīn *st. f.* cottager, peasant **158**. 3

sēle *st. f.* soul **62**. 9, 10; **72**. 8

selh *see* solh

selten *adv.* seldom, never **21**. 8; **49**. 13

selwen *wk. vb.* make dull **165**. 43

sem *see* sam

senden *wk. vb.* send **15**. 15; **120**. 14. gesenden **19**. 3. ūz senden send out **137**. 2

senelīch *adj.* yearning, pertaining to pains of love **128**. 4

senen *wk. vb.* long, yearn *refl.* **89**. 10. *pres. part.* senende, senede, sende **22**. 1; **35**. 12; **61**. 7; **66**. 10; **67**. 16; **69**. 16; **73**. 4; **84**. 3, 30; **88**. 34; **121**. 6, 19; **125**. 15, 31, 35

senfte *see* sanfte

sēre *adv.* sorely, exceedingly **41**. 13; **47**. 14

sēren *wk. vb.* afflict **125**. 32

setzen *wk. vb.* set, place, appoint **63**. 12; **91**. 3, 40; plant **121**. 70

sich, sih *3rd pers. refl. pron. acc.*

sicher *adj.+gen.* sure **44**. 4

sicherheit *st. f.* oath of submission **81**. 5; promise **126**. 26

sicherlīchen *adv.* certainly **121**. 46

sīde *st., wk. f.* silk **122**. 21

sīdīn *adj.* silken **15**. 12

sie, si *3rd pers. pron.* she, they

siech *adj.* sick **49**. 2

sige *st. m.* conquest **133**. 14

sigen *wk. vb.* conquer 105. 8. **gesigen an** get the better of 58. 19

sigenunft *st. f.* victory 110. 44

sīgen *st. vb.* fall 159. 14

silber *st. n.* silver 14. 7

sin *st. m.* mind, sense, senses, good sense 7. 5; 21. 18; 35. 17; 37. 3; 47, 5; 61. 15; 73. 15; 82. 10, 25; 91. 36

sīn *anom. vb.* be. *3rd pers. sing. pres. indic.* *is 38. 1. *3rd sing. pret. subj.* *wāre 38. 5. bī sīn+*dat.* associate (oneself) with 88. 42; 101. 3

singen *st. vb.* sing 4. 6; 12. 4; 24. 2; 35. 5. singen unde sagen formula expressing lyric and narrative aspects of poetic art 87. 42. *st. n.* song, poetry 43. 6; 61. 37; 105. 1; 114. 3. gesingen 57. 1; 127. 12

sinnen *st. vb.* think 168. 13

sīt *adv.* since, later. *conj.* since (*temporal and causal*) 11. 8; 15. 9; 21. 13; 24. 13, 15. *sint 38. 27; 39. 1

site *st. m., f.* custom, mode of behaviour 10. 5; 75. 4; 86. 50

sitich *st. m.* parrot 65. 17

sitzen *st. vb.* sit 91. 1

siuftebernd *adj.* grieving, afflicted 150. 15

siuren *wk. vb.* turn sour 98. 22

slac *st. m.* blow 110. 16

slāfen *st. vb.* sleep 9. 1; 65. 15

slāhen, slān *st. vb.* strike, slay, slaughter 73. 36; 116. 1; 164. 20; 165. 18. ze tōde slāhen kill 107. 19. umbe slān toss about 66. 32. abe slāhen cancel 109. 3

slaht *st. f.* kind, sort 22. 18; 84. 3

slange *wk. m., st. f.* snake 160. 28

sleht *adj.* smooth 115. 24

slīchen *st. vb.* creep 134. 18

sliezen *st. vb.* lock. ūf sliezen unlock 123. 25

slite *wk. m.* sledge 126. 1

slōz *st. n.* lock, bolt 115. 13

slüzzel *st. m.* key 123. 25. sluzzelīn *st. n. dimin.* 8. 5

smac *st. m.* fragrance 108. 44

smal *adj.* slim, small 63. 15; 126. 58; 127. 41

smalz *st. n.* fat, lard 162. 16

smēhen *wk. vb.* scorn 148. 31

smerze *wk. m.* pain 112. 7

smerzen *wk. vb.* pain 166. 26

smiegen *st. vb.* press, rest 91. 4

smieren *wk. vb.* smile 134. 4

smit *st. m.* goldsmith 92. 3

smuc *st. m.* embrace 150. 10

smucken *wk. vb.* press close 117. 36; be elusive 134. 16. sich gesmücken press close 153. 14

snē *st. m.* snow 70. 3

snel *adj.* swift 118. 20

snelle *st. f.* swiftness 167. 7

snīden *st. vb.* cut 130. 4; make clothes 136. 35

snit *st. m.* harvest 121. 70

sō *adv.* thus, as, so, then 4. 1; 7. 5; 18. 5; 106. 25; in that case 98. 26. *conj.* when 18. 4; whereas 45. 11. *replacing rel. pron.* 114. 8

soldener *st. m.* hired soldier 110. 48

solh, selh *pronom. adj.* such 47. 3; 75. 27. *sulic 40. 7

soln, suln *pret.-pres. vb.* owe, ought, shall 1. 12; 21. 24; 73. 33; 109. 5. solte was destined 79. 5. *sal 40. 5. *1st, 3rd pers. pl. pres. indic.* sun, sün 106. 10; 134. 1; 149. 17

solt *st. m.* wages, reward 62. 4; 110. 45

sorclīch *adj.* grievous 134. 17

sorge *st., wk. f.* care, sorrow, grief 7. 12; 11. 1; 44. 13; 55. 4

sorgen *wk. vb.* be sorrowful 101. 6; 109. 5. +umbe be concerned about 84. 27

Souwe *wk. f.* Save (a tributary of the Danube) 38. 11

spān *st. m.* fringe of curls 126. 52

sparn *wk. vb.* spare, omit

spāte *adv.* late 12. 1. *spāde 39. 19

spehen *wk. vb.* espy, choose, discern, discriminate 80. 23; 98. 26. *st. n.* spying 139. 2

sper *st. m., n.* spear 110. 48

spiegel *st. m.* mirror 71. 4

spil *st. n.* sport, delight 80. 15

spiln *wk. vb.* play, be active 137. 14; 139. 32; flash 112. 11; 138. 19. vor spiln dazzle with visions 137. 45

spinnen *st. vb.* spin 123. 23

spitze *st. f.* point 168. 10

spor *st. m., n.* trace, track 137. 42

spot *st. m.* mockery 58. 4; 61. 24; 73. 23; 87. 5. ze spotte in pretence 87. 41

spotten *wk. vb.*+*gen.* mock 84. 12

sprechen *st. vb.* speak 44. 6. guot, wol
sprechen+*dat.* speak well of 75. 2;
76. 21; 106. 9; 132. 17. *pret.* *sprac
39. 3 (*infin.* *spreken). gesprechen
66. 26; 85. 4; 87. 45
springen *st. vb.* spring, spring up 43. 1.
gespringen 128. 67
spruch *st. m.* saying 93. 5; 129. 8; poem
101. 15
spüren *wk. vb.* perceive 154. 8
staete, stēte *adj.*, *adv.* constant 36. 9;
61. 22, 31; 69. 6. *städe 40. 2
staete *st. f.* constancy 44. 25
staeteclīche *adv.* constantly 89. 15
staetekeit *st. f.* constancy 99. 25
staetelōs *adj.* inconstant 79. 13
staffel *st.*, *wk. m.* foot of piece of furni-
ture 123. 27
stān, stēn *st. vb.* stand, be fitting, suit
5. 1; 12. 1; 13. 1; 20. 8; 50. 10; 54. 22;
61. 2; strive 122. 42. *3rd pers. sing.*
*steit 42. 13. wol stēn be in good con-
dition, beautiful 6. 5; 38. 22. stān an
depend on, reside in 45. 1; 75. 1. wiez
umbe uns ... stē how we fare 121. 40.
gestēn 54. 25. gestān 69. 3; 78. 39.
an stēn+*dat.* suit 130. 1. abe gestān
+*gen.* desist 140. 6
stap *st. m.* staff 108. 13; hobby-horse
74. 9. krumber stap crozier 131. 10
star *st. m.* starling 65. 17
starc *adj.* strong, violent; firm 54. 9;
126. 26
stat *st. m.*, *f.* place 24. 5; 53. 20; 67. 22;
68. 2; 75. 7
stechen *st. vb.* pierce. ūz stechen, ūz
gestechen pierce out 32. 11; 47. 24
stecken *wk. vb.* fix
stein *st. m.* stone 91. 1; millstone 105. 22
steln *st. vb.* steal. abe gesteln+*dat.*
steal from 153. 10
sterben *st. vb.* die 31. 11. *sterven
43. 36
sterne *wk. m.* star 18. 1
stetschen *wk. vb.* stutter 164. 3
stīc *st. m.* path 91. 20
stīgen *st. vb.* rise, climb 35. 13; 116. 2
stille *adj.*, *adv.* still, quiet 43. 12
stimel *st. m.* stimulus 169. 10
stimme *st. f.* voice 125. 6
stinken *st. vb.* smell 95. 9
stiure *st. f.* assistance, financial contri-
bution 155. 14

stiuren *wk. vb.* help 157. 1
stoc *st. m.* stick, stocks, prison
stocwarte *wk. m.* jailer 160. 47
stœren *wk. vb.* destroy, interrupt, dis-
turb 91. 7; 105. 17; dislodge 134. 13
stōle *st. f.* stole 91. 64
stolz *adj.* proud, splendid 110. 25;
137. 11. stolzlīche *adv.* 29. 1
storch *st. m.* stork 113. 13
stōzen *st. vb.* push, thrust, drive 105. 35
sträfen *wk. vb.* reproach 157. 21. *st. n.*
rebuke 167. 13
sträle *wk. f.* dart 147. 8
sträze *st. f.* road, street, path 91. 22.
*sträte 38. 35
streben *wk. vb.* strive 76. 66
strenge *adj.* severe 118. 51
stric *st. m.* snare 137. 34; 149. 6
strich *st. m.* track 137. 41
strīchen *st. vb.* go 121. 49; 136. 17
strīt *st. m.* conflict, struggle, dispute
52. 11; 54. 4; 75. 27
strīten *st. vb.* fight, dispute, contend
54. 1; 87. 29; 91. 34, 61; 96. 23
strō, strou *st. n.* straw 102. 11; 136. 9
stube *wk. f.* room, parlour 126. 14
stücke *st. n.* piece, fragment 112. 12
stunde, stunt *st.*, *wk. f.* hour, time
47. 16. zeiner stunt once 49. 6. *te
einen stunden, zeinen stunden formerly 39. 9; 148. 12
stuol *st. m.* chair 168. 11
sturm *st. m.* battle 91. 34
süberlīch *adj.* clean, pretty 120. 22
süeze *adj.* sweet, pleasing, dear 35. 1;
61. 21; 72. 1. *süte 38. 24
süeze *st. f.* sweetness, pleasure
süezen *wk. vb. intrans.* be sweet. *trans.*
make sweet 141. 15. *refl.* be pleasing
141. 12
sūgen *st. vb.* suck 109. 17
*sūken *see* suochen
*sulic *see* solh
sūmen *wk. vb.* delay 116. 17. *refl.*
121. 50
sumelīch *adj.* some, many a one, all
88. 36; 100. 22
sumer *st. m.* summer 2. 4; 22. 23
sumerwunne *st. f.* summer's joy 4. 9;
6. 1
sumerzīt *st. f.* summer-time 34. 10
sun *st. m.* son 93. 6
sun, sün *see* soln

sünde *st. f.* fault, sin **52.** 19; **56.** 3; **58.** 31

sünden *wk. vb.* err, sin **35.** 22. *refl.*+ an sin against **144.** 35

sunder *prep.*+*acc.* without **24.** 11; **39.** 3

sunne *st., wk. f., m.* sun **63.** 19

sunnentac *st. m.* Sunday **164.** 10

suochen *wk. vb.* seek **20.** 4. **süken* **43.** 8

sūr *adj.* sour **119.** 3

sūren *wk. vb. intrans.* turn sour, be embittered **160.** 35

sus *adv.* thus **35.** 13; **47.** 10; as it is **94.** 8; in that case **98.** 7; in other respects **136.** 38

*sūte *see* süeze

swā *conj.* wheresoever, where, if **37.** 18; **87.** 22

swach *adj.* inferior, poor, worthless, small **22.** 22; **136.** 47

swachen *wk. vb.* be discreditable, dishonourable, detract from **92.** 6; **97.** 11; **108.** 19

swære, swēre *adj., adv.* heavy, sorrowful **46.** 9; **69.** 15; **98.** 15. **swāre* **38.** 8

swære, swēre *st. f.* distress, pain **45.** 14; **71.** 20; **112.** 8; **125.** 19

swalwe *st., wk. f.* swallow **125.** 51

swanne, swenne *conj.* whenever, if ever, when **13.** 1; **35.** 9, 10; **59.** 14; **67.** 24

swanz *st. m.* train of dress **134.** 7. swenzel *st. n. dimin.* **166.** 1

Swāp *st. m.* Swabian **122.** 20

swar *conj.* whithersoever **5.** 6

swarz *adj.* black **110.** 38

swaz *rel. pron.* whatsoever **2.** 1

sweben *wk. vb.* float **131.** 9

*swegen *see* swīgen

sweim *st. m.*, ze sweime gān roam, make oneself scarce **127.** 18

sweimen *wk. vb.* hover, range **135.** 2

swelh *interr. pron.* whosoever, whichever **33.** 9; **115.** 29

swer *indef. rel. pron.* whosoever **10.** 3

swern *st. vb.*+*gen.* swear **54.** 20

swert *st. n.* sword **73.** 36

swie *adv. and conj.* however, although **44.** 23; **65.** 12

swīgen *st. vb.* be silent **65.** 16. *pret.* *swegen **43.** 12. geswīgen fall silent **108.** 42.

swin *st. n.* pig **157.** 31

swinden *st. vb.* decrease, vanish **6.** 2; **114.** 21; **125.** 15

swingen *st. vb.* swing, soar **97.** 15; **113.** 4; **134.** 18; **137.** 38; **138.** 19

T

tac *st. m.* day **24.** 12. **dach* **39.** 1

tägelīch *adj.* day-like **116.** 3

tagewīse *st. f.* dawn song **117.** 2

tagen *wk. vb.* dawn **66.** 8

tal *st. n.* valley. hin ze tal down **70.** 19; **126.** 34

tandaradei refrain of **104**: imitation of bird song?

tanne *wk. f.* fir **160.** 16

tanz *st. m.* dance **103.** 37; **122.** 14; **126.** 19; **127.** 30

tanzen *wk. vb.* dance **110.** 22; **121.** 64

tarm *st. m.* intestine **165.** 15

tāt *st. f.* deed **67.** 18

*te *see* ze

tehtier *st. n.* helmet **126.** 36

teil *st. m., n.* part, lot, portion **108.** 12; **114.** 6; **121.** 35. ein teil *acc. used adverbially* a little **68.** 17; **84.** 4

teilen *wk. vb.* share **17.** 4

Tīdō Dido **44.** 5

tievel *st. m.* devil **126.** 45

tihten *wk. vb.* compose verse **148.** 3

tirme *wk. f.* creation **169.** 16

*tīt *see* zīt

tiure *adj.* costly, precious, rare **101.** 45

tiuren, tiuwern *wk. vb.* make worthy, estimable, enhance worth of, praise **23.** 12; **56.** 4; **98.** 24; **101.** 41; **122.** 28. *intrans.* be rare **157.** 3

tiu(t)sch *see* diutsch

toben *wk. vb.* rage **54.** 9

tolde *st., wk. f.* tree-top **126.** 4

tōre *wk. m.* fool **139.** 1

tōrheit *st. f.* folly **80.** 17

tœren *wk. vb.* fool, beguile **134.** 14; **137.** 20. *refl.* be foolish **82.** 22

*toren *see* zorn

tōt *st. m.* death **45.** 12. **dōt* **43.** 33

tōten *wk. vb.* kill **72.** 2

tōterinne *st. f.* murderess **72.** 1

tou *st. m., n.* dew **114.** 8. touwen *wk. vb.* be dewy **167.** 3

toufen *wk. vb.* baptize **131.** 5

tougen *adj., adv.* secret **51.** 16; **91.** 50; **115.** 2; **125.** 15

tougenlîch *adj.* secret **122.** 41. tougenlîche *adv.* **57.** 11; **85.** 40

toup *adj.* deaf, insensitive **65.** 9; **139.** 4

trachten *wk. vb.* strive **165.** 6

tracke *wk. m.* dragon **157.** 33

træge *adj.*, trâge *adv.* slow **110.** 9, 13

tragen *st. vb.* bear, wear **35.** 16; **45.** 6;
73. 1; **122.** 39. *contracted form* treit
56. 1; **113.** 7; **120.** 24. getragen **86.**
41; **107.** 18. *dragen **38.** 9

trahen *st. m.* tear **66.** 15

tratz *st. m.* spite, defiance **126.** 48. ûf
mînen tratz to spite me **127.** 21

treffen *st. vb.* strike, catch **134.** 12.
getreffen **99.** 11

treit *see* tragen

treten *st. vb.* step. getreten **85.** 8

trîben *st. vb.* drive. umbe trîben toss
about **111.** 5

triegen *st. vb.* deceive, betray **7.** 9;
28. 11; **70.** 5; **78.** 25

trinitât *st. f.* Trinity **169.** 18

trit *st. m.* step **139.** 20

triuteleht *adj.* dear **144.** 27

triuten *wk. vb.* caress **152.** 3

triuwe, triwe *st. f.* faith, loyalty, promise, assurance **46.** 14; **56.** 7; **93.** 1

triuwen *wk. vb.* think, expect, trust
80. 7. trouwen **49.** 24. getriuwen
83. 19

trôn *st. m.* throne **107.** 23

trôst *st. m.* comfort, consolation, hope
35. 28; **68.** 20; **73.** 2. trœstelîn *st.
n. dimin.* **102.** 6

trôsten, trœsten *wk. vb.* comfort, console **23.** 8; **67.** 16. *refl.* **148.** 29. sich
getrôsten, getrœsten+*gen.* console
oneself for the loss of, renounce **44.** 23;
48. 17

troum *st. m.* dream **71.** 10

troumen *wk. vb.* dream **110.** 2

trouwen *see* triuwen

trüebe *adj.* dim, dark **63.** 20

trüeben *wk. vb. trans.* distress **74.** 6

truoben *wk. vb. intrans.* grow dim **6.** 4

trügelîchen *adv.* treacherously **93.** 2

trürec, trüric *adj.* sad **13.** 8; **22.** 8

trüreclîche(n) *adv.* sadly **45.** 10

trüren *wk. vb.* sorrow, grieve **44.** 13.
st. n. grief, sorrowful longing **21.** 1;
27. 13; **114.** 21; **122.** 35. getrüren
46. 7; **67.** 3

trût *st. n.* sweetheart, lover **5.** 14; **6.** 6

trütgespil *wk. m.,f.* companion **120.** 12

truz *st. m.* enmity **158.** 35

*tû, tût *see* zuo

tücken *wk. vb.* snatch **153.** 11

tugen *pret.-pres. vb.* be of use, avail
35. 27; **78.** 11. *most used forms: 3rd
pers. sing. pres.* touc, *pret.* tohte

tugent *st. f.* excellent quality, virtue
25. 3; **36.** 5; **63.** 19; **67.** 17; **71.** 13, 25

tugentlîch *adj.* excellent, virtuous
56. 8

tumben *wk. vb.* render foolish **112.** 6

tump *adj.* foolish, inexperienced **49.** 3;
53. 14; **58.** 4; **61.** 9; **68.** 3; **69.** 11;
73. 34; **89.** 29; **122.** 24. *dump **38.** 7;
42. 14. *dumpheit *st. f.* inexperience,
folly **38.** 24

tunkel *adj.* dark. *st. f.* morning twi-
light **18.** 1

tuon *anom. vb.* do **5.** 9; **13.** 6; **66.** 9.
*dôn **42.** 3. sô getân of such a kind
90. 39. minneclîch, wol getân beauti-
ful **6.** 11; **9.** 3; **23.** 5. wale gedân **40.**
9. baz getân more handsome **95.** 6.
wiez under uns zwein ist getân how
things stand between us **18.** 8. getuon
22. 17; **52.** 46; **88.** 53. ûf tuon open
107. 3

tür *st. f.* door **65.** 6

turren *pret.-pres. vb.* dare **146.** 10.
geturren **83.** 29

turst *st. m.* thirst, drought **162.** 20

*tuschen *prep.*+*dat.* between **38.** 11

tûsent *card. num.* thousand **24.** 9

tûsentstunt *adv.* a thousand times
104. 12

tûsentvalt *adj., adv.* a thousand-fold
140. 25

twahen *st. vb.* wash **107.** 20

twerh *adj.* sideways **127.** 17

twerhes *adv.* askance **80.** 21

twingen, dwingen *st. vb.* compel,
constrain, press, oppress **74.** 2; **75.**
16; **115.** 15; **121.** 4. *st. n.* compulsion
166. 21

U

übel *adj.* evil **64.** 21; **145.** 9. *adv.* ill
32. 2; **58.** 17. *st. n.* **96.** 19

übellîchen *adv.* nastily, spitefully
126. 48

uber, über *prep.*+*dat.*, *adv.* over,
above **5.** 2

übergulde *st. f.* der zweier übergulde of more worth than these two
91. 14

überhēr *adj.* too high-born, over-proud
101. 65

überhœren *wk. vb.* fail to hear, disregard 86. 33

überliuhten *wk. vb.* outshine 63. 23

übersehen *st. vb.* overlook, neglect,
omit 58. 17

überwinden *st. vb.* overcome 68. 10;
137. 18

üeben *wk. vb.* exercise, display 23. 6.
refl. 165. 7

ūf *prep.+acc., dat.* upon; because of
73. 26; in pursuit of 78. 18; 113. 9;
140. 9; in anticipation of 166. 3; at the
risk of 119. 18. *adv.* up 15. 7; 35. 13;
68. 16; 85. 44; 142. 3. ūffe on your
head 103. 4. *up 43. 34

umbe *prep.+acc., adv.* around, about,
for, for the sake of, in exchange for, con-
cerning 20. 6; 45. 23; 63. 3; 66. 32;
98. 23; 101. 48; 111. 5; 122. 39; 128. 40.
umbe daz for that reason 26. 5. umbe
waz wherefore 31. 2. umbe niht in
vain 57. 2. dar umbe, drumbe *see*
dā(r)

umbeslīfen *st. vb.* turn 134. 5

umbevān, ummevān *st. vb.* embrace
38. 33; 70. 23; 71. 26; 118. 14

umbevanc *st. m.* embrace 150. 11

unbekant *pp.* unknown 60. 19

unberāten *pp.* unprovided for 126. 60

unbereit *adj.* inaccessible 86. 31

unbesungen *pp.* devoid of song 126. 5

unbetwungen *see* betwingen

*unblīde *adj.* unhappy 41. 24

undanc *st. m.* des habe ich undanc
I am to blame 76. 34. des haben
undanc a curse on them 99. 10

unde, und *conj.* and 4. 4; 99. 21; since
47. 16

*unde *see* *unnen

ünde *st., wk. f.* wave 54. 9

ünden *wk. vb.* surge 131. 2

under *prep.+dat., adv.* under, among,
between 10. 18; 18. 8. under diu
ougen before one's gaze 112. 11

understān *st. vb.* prevent 164. 23

undertān *pp.* subject, submissive 35. 8;
52. 31; 75. 3; 85. 30

undertænic *adj.* subject 149. 5

underwīlen(t) *adv.* sometimes 35. 18;
52. 9; 83. 1; 86. 18

underwinden *refl. st. vb.+gen.* take
on 142. 15

unēre *st. f.* dishonour, discredit 47. 8

unēren *wk. vb.* dishonour 87. 12

unerlōst *pp.* not relieved 21. 13

ungebære *st. f.* distress 91. 69

ungedulde *st. f.* impatience

ungelīche *adv.* incomparably 105. 18

ungelücke *st. n.* misfortune 73. 13;
89. 3

ungemach *st. m., n.* distress 48. 4;
66. 28; 67. 1; 86. 34; 125. 22; 150.
22

ungemüete *st. f.* sadness, distress 22.
12; 82. 14; 125. 25

ungemuot *pp.* untroubled 51. 18

ungenāde *st. f.* lack of mercy, misfortune, unpleasantness 126. 6

ungenæme *adj.* displeasing 128. 80

ungereiet *pp.* not participating in the
dance 124. 8

Ungerlant Hungary 96. 26

ungerne *adv.* unwillingly 51. 7

ungescheiden *pp.* united 115. 19

ungetriuwe *adj.* faithless 76. 14

ungevüege *adj.* unseemly, uncourtly,
rough 101. 1; 105. 2; 128. 56

ungefuoc *st. m.* evil, disgrace 107. 21

ungewent *pp.* unaccustomed 44. 14

ungewin *st. m.* misfortune 71. 27; 135.
18

ungewis *adj.* uncertain 77. 2

ungewon *adj.+gen.* unaccustomed 90.
38

unguot *adj.* unkind 49. 23

unheil *st. n.* misfortune 144. 15

unkunt *adj.* unfamiliar, foreign 38. 25

unlobelīch *adj.* discreditable 97. 13

unmære, unmēre *adj.* of no account,
object of indifference 53. 15; 59. 6;
69. 17; 85. 11. *unmāre 39. 30

unmæren *wk. vb.* be an object of indifference 88. 8

unmāze *st. f.* lack of moderation 97. 10

unmāzen *adv.* immoderately, im-
measurably 86. 32

unminne *st. f.* lack of love, false love
90. 34

unminneclīche *adv.* in a manner inap-
propriate to minne 101. 17

unnæher *adv.* more distant 57. 5

*unnen *pret.-pres. vb.+dat. pers., gen.
thing* grant. *pres.* an 39. 12. *pret.* unde
39. 11
unnōt *st. f.* lack of necessity 58. 8;
81. 3. mir ist des unnōt I have no
need of that
unnütze *adj.* of no avail 148. 33
unprīs *st. m.* discredit 140. 35
unreht *st. n.* wrong. *te unrechte
wrongfully 38. 36
unrehte *adv.* wrongly 73. 28
unriuweclīch *adj.* joyful 110. 19
*unsachte *adj., adv.* unpleasing, grievous 38. 8
unsælikeit, unsēlikeit *st. f.* misfortune, malice 66. 17
unsanfte *adv.* sadly, unwillingly 52. 11;
85. 31; 121. 7. unsanfte tuon be unpleasing, painful 60. 17
unsenfte *adj.* displeasing, sad 110.
26
unsenftreclīche *adv.* sadly, reluctantly
35. 6
unsin *st. m.* foolishness 73. 16
unstæte *adj.* inconstant 22. 24; 55. 12;
57. 9
unstæte *st. f.* inconstancy 85. 20
unstate *st. f.* inopportune occasion. ze
unstaten stēn be inimical to 64. 5
untriuwe *st. f.* faithlessness 76. 13.
*untrouwe 38. 14
untūwer *adj.* worthless 124. 24
unvalschlīch *adj.* well-intentioned 139.
8
unverborgen *pp.* unconcealed 119. 13
unverdienet *pp.* undeserved 87. 6
unverschart *pp.* unharmed 107. 10
unversunnen *pp.* mindless 71. 22
unverzaget *pp.* undaunted 108. 15
unfīn *adj.* unpleasing 168. 17
unfrō *adj.* sad 44. 1
unvrœlīchen *adv.* unhappily 33. 13
unvrömed(e) *adj.* intimate 117. 35
unvrowelīch *adj.* unwomanly 67. 18
unfruot *adj.* foolish 139. 7
unfuoge *st. f.* unseemliness, uncourtli-
ness 101. 20; 105. 8, 33
unwæge *adj.* unfitting 117. 18
unwendic *adj.* inevitable 62. 18
unwert *adj.* unworthy, not esteemed
88. 19; 139. 11
unwīp *st. n.* unwomanly woman 101.
44

unwīse *st. f.* disharmony, discordant
noise 105. 23
unze *prep., adv.* unze an+acc. until,
up to 3. 2; 86. 29. *conj.* until, while,
as long as 17. 5; 25. 4; 83. 26
*up *see* ūf
üppiclīch *adj.* proud, showy, luxurious
127. 24
urborn *wk. vb.* exact tribute 114. 2
urloup, urlop *st. m., n.* leave, farewell
115. 23; 116. 39; 117. 39
ursprinc *st. m.* springing up 114. 1
ūz *prep.+dat.* out of, from 12. 6;
50. 2. *adv.* out 107. 4; 114. 1; 161. 35;
finished 162. 19. *ūt 38. 20
ūzen *adv.* outside 128. 83
ūzer *prep.+dat.* out of, beyond 142. 39.
*ūter 38. 31
ūzerwelt *pp.* choice, supreme 118. 47
ūzreise *st. f.* song to accompany
knightly expedition, march

F, V

vadem *st. m.* thread 123. 23
vāhen *st. vb.* capture 81. 5; 137. 35, 40.
in daz hār vāhen+acc. attack 162.
20. gevāhen 148. 40. vāhen ze have
recourse to 134. 6
val *adj.* dun coloured 126. 8
valde *see* valte
valke *wk. m.* falcon 5. 4, 5; 15. 1, 9;
135. 4; 138. 22
vallen *st. vb.* fall, die 56. 12. +an touch
58. 21
valsch *adj.* false 48. 5; 55. 13. valsch-
līch 139. 19
valsch *st. m.* falsehood 50. 15; 63. 14;
111. 11
valt *st. m.* pleat 144. 5
valte, valde *st. f.* fold, pleat 123. 32
*van *see* von
varn *st. vb.* go, depart, behave, fare
17. 2; 25. 4; 52. 15; 55. 1; 91. 22. lā
varn never mind 79. 5. gevarn 78. 22;
106. 26
varend *pres. part.* transient, of this
world 74. 6; 91. 11
vart *st. f.* journey, Crusading journey
58. 6; 78. 46
vāren *wk. vb.+gen.* lie in wait 78. 34
varwe *st. f.* colour, complexion 13. 5;
86. 36
vaste *see* veste

vē *st. n.* cattle **165.** 18

vederspil *st. n.* falcon, (*collective*) falcons **20.** 1

vēhen, vēn *wk. vb.* hate, spurn **64.** 4; **85.** 42

vehten *st. vb.* fight, struggle **53.** 3; **157.** 34

veiz(t) *adj.* fat **128.** 36; **165.** 5

vel *st. n.* skin **115.** 24

*vele *see* vil

vels *st. m.* rock **155.** 4

velsenschurc *st. m.* rock-like hardness **169.** 14

velschen *wk. vb.* pronounce to be false **76.** 28

velt *st. n.* field **91.** 28

velwen *wk. vb.* cause to fade (*see* val) **127.** 5; **165.** 42

vēn *st. vb.*, *variant form of* vāhen. umbe vēn embrace **63.** 6

venster *st. n.* window **115.** 12

verban *see* verbunnen

verbergen *st. vb.* hide, remove **124.** 5; **148.** 28

verbern *st. vb.* forbear, avoid, spare **53.** 14; **60.** 11; **76.** 51; **88.** 53; **90.** 24; **117.** 2

verbunde *see* verbunnen

verblīchen *st. vb.* grow pale **71.** 18

verborgenlīchen *adv.* secretly **153.** 9

verbrennen *wk. vb.* burn **107.** 8

verbunnen *anom. vb.+dat. pers.*, *gen. thing* forbid, grudge. *st. pret.* verban **53.** 12. *wk. pret.* verbunde **144.** 14

verdagen *wk. vb. intrans.* be silent. *trans.* silence **132.** 8

verdāht *pp.+*an, nāch thinking of, intent on **52.** 8; **84.** 7

verderben *st. vb. intrans.* perish **67.** 20. *trans.* destroy **77.** 12; **90.** 30; **125.** 23. *verderven 43.** 29

verdienen *wk. vb.* deserve, earn **45.** 22; **110.** 45

verdriezen *st. vb.* used *impers.+acc. pers.*, *gen. thing* irk, annoy, weary **61.** 27; **70.** 31; **87.** 3; **106.** 8. *pret.* *verdrōt **43.** 11. *pp.* verdrozzen annoying **136.** 21

verdringen *st. vb.* supplant **105.** 3

vereinen *refl. wk. vb.* isolate oneself, be alone **128.** 13. +*gen.* agree on **101.** 2

verenden *wk. vb. intrans. and trans.* finish **36.** 13

vergeben *st. vb.+dat.* forgive **52.** 18; dispense from **90.** 11. +*dat.* poison **110.** 35

vergebene *adv.* in vain **101.** 55

vergelten *st. vb.* give back, repay **37.** 8; **109.** 2

vergēn *st. vb.* pass over **87.** 36

vergezzen *st. vb.+gen.* forget **21.** 8; **50.** 4. *refl.+*an be mistaken in **93.** 12

verhaben *wk. vb.* cover, restrain **113.** 4

verhel(e)n *wk. vb.* conceal **82.** 20

verhern *wk. vb.* ravage, vanquish. +*gen.* deprive of **115.** 21

verholne *adv.* secretly **34.** 5; **116.** 19

verjehen *st. vb.+gen.* say, assert **61.** 6; **72.** 11; **90.** 15; **133.** 14

verkapfen *refl. wk. vb.* stare fixedly **68.** 21

verkēren *wk. vb.* change, convert **47.** 10; **128.** 22. *refl.* change **55.** 3; turn **64.** 22

verkiesen *st. vb.* renounce, sacrifice **121.** 35; **128.** 55

verklagen *wk. vb.* cease to lament **161.** 15

verkrenken *wk. vb.* weaken, violate **117.** 14

verlāzen, verlān *st. vb.* let, leave, abandon **59.** 7; **76.** 10. +*an entrust to **49.** 10. *refl.+*an entrust oneself to, trust in **52.** 37; **69.** 11

verleiten *wk. vb.* lead astray **97.** 18; **110.** 39

verliesen *st. vb.* lose **8.** 5; **10.** 14; **33.** 11; **128.** 51

verlīhen *st. vb.* lend, grant **51.** 2

verloben *wk. vb.* renounce **54.** 10

vermezzen *refl. st. vb.+gen.* lay claim to **35.** 25

vermīden *st. vb.* shun, avoid **35.** 2

vern(e) *adv.* last year **157.** 10

verne, verre *adj.*, *adv.* far **36.** 7; **63.** 4; **68.** 17. *adv.* very much **52.** 8; **65.** 22

vernemen *st. vb.* hear **30.** 1; **46.** 17

verrāten *st. vb.* betray. *pret.* *verrīt **38.** 7

versagen *wk. vb.* refuse. *contracted form* verseit **67.** 19; **75.** 26; **89.** 16

verschrōten *st. vb.* cut too small, spoil by cutting **93.** 15

versehen *refl. st. vb.+gen.* expect **76.** 58; **79.** 7

versēren *wk. vb.* injure, impair **71.** 15

versigeln *wk. vb.* seal **137.** 27
versinnen *refl. st. vb.+gen.* realize, be aware **52.** 9; **58.** 15; **65.** 20
versmāhen, versmān *wk. vb.* be unpleasing **63.** 10; **68.** 2
versperren *wk. vb.* lock away **123.** 26. +vor *and dat.* lock away from **124.** 12; **158.** 12
versprechen *st. vb.* refuse **124.** 17
verstān, verstēn *st. vb.* understand. +*gen.* be aware of **39.** 21; **52.** 10; **60.** 23; **86.** 33
versteln *st. vb.* steal **85.** 38
verstolne *adv.* secretly **138.** 25
verstōzen *st. vb.* reject, banish **73.** 31; **127.** 43
versūmen *wk. vb.* neglect, waste, hinder **73.** 6; **79.** 16. +*gen.* deprive of **124.** 22. *refl.* delay too long **160.** 44
versuochen *wk. vb.* test **86.** 2
versuonen, versüenen *wk. vb.* reconcile **16.** 7
verswenden *wk. vb.* pass **127.** 8; waste **155.** 13
verswīgen *st. vb.* keep secret **65.** 1; **90.** 14
verswinden *st. vb.* vanish **110.** 1
verswīnen *st. vb.* vanish **152.** 3
vert *adv.* last year **57.** 5; **120.** 14
vertān *pp.* evil **111.** 7
vertragen *st. vb.* bear with, endure **99.** 19. *contracted form* vertreit **128.** 8
vertrīben *st. vb.* drive away, pass (time) **44.** 11; **58.** 24; **80.** 11; **122.** 35; **133.** 6
vertuon *st. vb.* waste **155.** 12
vervāhen, vervān *st. vb.* gain **80.** 7; avail **48.** 13; **61.** 38; **75.** 6; **127.** 9. ze guote vervān account as good **58.** 33
vervluochen *wk. vb.* curse **161.** 31
verwandelōn *refl. wk. vb.* be transformed **121.** 5
verwāzen *st. vb.* destroy, curse **47.** 3; **128.** 50
verwen *wk. vb.* colour **90.** 32
verwīzen *st. vb.* reproach **99.** 7; **126.** 23
verwunden *wk. vb.* wound **149.** 14
verzagen *wk. vb.* despair **105.** 31; **122.** 25
verzern *wk. vb.* expend **155.** 9
verziehen *refl. st. vb.+gen.* renounce **35.** 21
verzinsen *wk. vb.* pay as tribute **74.** 4
vaste *adv.* firmly **103.** 35

veste *adj.* firm, strong **110.** 43. *st. f.* stability **112.** 10
vīent *st. m.* enemy **73.** 11. *used adjectivally* **77.** 11
fier *adj.* splendid, proud **63.** 15
vierzec *card. num.* forty **108.** 7
vil *adj.* (*used substantivally+partitive gen.*), *adv.* much, very **7.** 5; **11.** 2; **17.** 1. *vele **38.** 34
vimel *st. m.* radiance **169.** 9
vinden *st. vb.* find **25.** 4; **47.** 11. *pp.* funden **52.** 39
vingerlīn *st. n.* ring **99.** 24
vinster *adj.* dark **110.** 38
fīol *st. m.* violet **160.** 6
vīr(e)tac *st. m.* holiday **126.** 16
visch *st. m.* fish **91.** 26
viur *st. n.* fire **94.** 3
vlæmen *wk. vb.* speak after the Flemish fashion **128.** 84
flamme *st. f.* flame **107.** 10
flammenrīch *adj.* flaming **169.** 3
vlēhen *wk. vb.+acc. pers., gen. thing* beseech **95.** 3; **123.** 22
vlehten *st. vb.* intertwine **115.** 27
fleisch *st. n.* meat **162.** 17
vliegen *st. vb.* fly **91.** 29
vliehen *st. vb.* flee, shun **69.** 10; **117.** 34
vliezen *st. vb.* flow, swim **91.** 26; **110.** 11
flīz *st. m.* zeal **143.** 12
vlīzen *refl. st. vb.+gen.* practise, strive after **82.** 15
vlīzic *adj.+gen.* intent on **145.** 16
fluht *st. f.* flight, escape **138.** 17
fluochen *wk. vb.* curse **66.** 21; **73.** 8; **118.** 28
vluot *st. f.* wave, flood **167.** 12
vogel *st. m.* bird **38.** 2
vogellīn *st. n. dimin.* **22.** 6
vogelsanc *st. m., n.* bird song **6.** 2
voget *st. m.* ruler, advocate **94.** 1
vol *adj.* full **167.** 6
volenden *wk. vb.* accomplish, finish **62.** 15; **87.** 23
volge *st. f.* compliance with teaching, practice **111.** 12
volgen *wk. vb.* follow **53.** 6. +*gen.* **61.** 33. gevolgen **41.** 24
volle(n) *adv.* fully **49.** 24
volleclīche *adv.* completely **85.** 11
volzeln *wk. vb.* count fully **167.** 12
von *prep.+dat., adv.* from, of, on account of **3.** 2; **99.** 6. *van **38.** 24

vor *prep.+dat.*, *adv.* before, in front of, because of, in preference to **71**. 27; **127**. 22; **145**. I. hie vor formerly **101**. 14. vor ūz *adv.* particularly **149**. 14

forderunge *st. f.* claim **93**. 4

vorne *adv.* in front **126**. 34

frāgen *wk. vb.+gen.* ask **57**. 8; **81**. 3; **82**. 24

Vranke *wk. m.* Franconian **122**. 20

Vranken Franconia, Germany **81**. 16

freischen *st. vb.* learn, experience **46**. 16. gefreischen **51**. 32; **124**. 2

vreise *st. f.* peril **131**. 7

fremede, frömede *adj.* strange, foreign **96**. 22; absent, distant **66**. 22; **125**. 30. frömde *st. f.* distance, absence **46**. 13. fremeden, frömeden *wk. vb.* shun, keep at a distance **24**. 12; **44**. 7; **51**. 15; **71**. 28. *st. n.* **64**. 17

frevellîchen *adv.* shamelessly **105**. 25

vrewen, vreuwen, vröwen *wk. vb.* gladden. *refl. wk. vb.+gen.* rejoice in **88**. 24; **115**. 7. gevreuwen **133**. 11

frî *adj.+gen.* or vor free **36**. 6; **54**. 6; **64**. 14; dispensed from **78**. 10. *vrîlîke adv.* **39**. 4

fride *st., wk. m.* peace **45**. 20; protection **118**. 12

friedel *st. m.* sweetheart **9**. 1; **104**. 9

vrîheistalt *st. m.* unmarried free peasant **124**. 16

vrist *st. f.* span of time **125**. 54; **155**. 2

friundin *st. f.* friend, lover **9**. 8

friunt *st. m.* friend, lover **10**. 1; **45**. 3; **64**. 3

friuntschaft *st. f.* friendship **28**. 5

frô *adj.* joyful **11**. 8. *vrôlîke adv.* **43**. 20

fröide, freude *st. f.* joy **35**. 13; **73**. 2; **160**. 42

fröidebernd *pres. part.* joy-giving **156**. 14

fröidelôs *adj.* joyless **142**. 32

vröidenfrühtic *adj.* rich in joy **135**. 23

frömeden *see* fremeden

frosch *st. m.* frog **105**. 29

frost *st. m.* frost **162**. 20

frouwe *st., wk. f.* lady **56**. 14. vrowelîn *st. n. dimin.* **99**. 1

vrüeten *wk. vb.* be advantageous **111**. 4

vrumen *wk. vb.* be of avail, advantageous. gefrumen **79**. 6; **140**. 24. gefromen **44**. 25

fruo *adv.* early **94**. 8

fruot *adj.* worthy **69**. 5. *vrūt **42**. 1

vüegen *wk. vb.* do, produce, inflict **48**. 9; **86**. 10; **133**. 20; **145**. 11

vüegerinne *st. f.* author, bestower **97**. 1

füeren *wk. vb.* lead, bear **9**. 12; **15**. 11

fuhs *st. m.* fox **137**. 10

vüllen *wk. vb.* fill **169**. 12

vunt *st. m.* find **117**. 30

fuoge *st. f.* propriety, point of good behaviour **57**. 8; **101**. 1, 25

fuoz *st. m.* foot **15**. 11

für *prep.+acc.*, *adv.* in front of, for, as remedy against, instead of, from ... on, in preference to **21**. 1; **28**. 8; **37**. 4; **44**. 9; **54**. 19; **87**. 28; **99**. 24; better than **67**. 13. für dise zit henceforth **76**. 11

vürhten *wk. vb.* fear **60**. 7

vüroben *wk. vb.* surpass **168**. 2

vürspan *st. n.* brooch **130**. 6

vürste *wk. m.* prince **92**. 9

W

wā *adv., conj.* where, when **83**. 15; **87**. 44

wāc *st. m.* wave, sea **121**. 28

wachen *wk. vb. intrans.* wake **114**. 12; **117**. 26

wæge *adj.* well-disposed, worthy **164**. 24

wænen, wēnen *wk. vb.* think **21**. 25; **44**. 16. wæn I think, assuredly **60**. 6; **88**. 14; **89**. 3

wāfen *st. n.* weapon, tool **65**. 24

wāfen, wāfenā *interj.* alas **9**. 6; **47**. 1, 8

wāgen *wk. vb.* endanger, imperil, venture **108**. 30; **158**. 34

wahsen *st. vb.* grow **93**. 20

wahtære, wahter *st. m.* watchman **115**. 1; **150**. 5

*wal(e) *see* wol

walberūn *st. m.* boor **128**. 60

Walhe *st., wk. m.* foreigner, Frenchman, Italian **121**. 14

walt *st. m.* forest **1**. 9

walten *st. vb.+gen.* rule over, enjoy possession of **121**. 63

waltsinger *st. m.* forest songster **114**. 5

waltwîser *st. m.* forester **160**. 19

wambe *st., wk. f.* womb **107**. 27

wan = *indef. pron.* man

wan *adv., conj.* except, but for, nothing but, only **21**. 7; **26**. 9; **35**. 12; **45**. 5; **121**. 28

wan *interr. adv.* why not 5. 13; 84. 17;
if only 144. 9
wande, want, wan *conj.* for, because,
for indeed 6. 8; 12. 11; 17. 7; 40. 3
wān *st. m.* hope, vain hope, fancy, illusion 38. 30; 47. 3; 68. 3, 21
wanc *st. m.* wavering, fickleness,
struggle 134. 15; 135. 8; 168. 17
wandel *st. m.* blemish, imperfection,
fickleness 29. 10; 73. 12; 138. 27
wandelbære *adj.* imperfect, fickle 73.
30; 122. 27
wandelname *wk. m.* term of reproach
168. 19
wandelunge *st. f.* change 121. 8
wange *st. n.* cheek 91. 5. wangel,
wengel *st. n. dimin.* 94. 7; 115. 17
wankel *adj.* fickle 28. 6
wankelmuot *st. m.* fickleness 123. 18
wanne, wenne *interr. adv.* when 9. 11;
87. 27
wāpen *st. n.* armorial bearings 73. 3
war *interr. adv.* whither 58. 22
war zuo for what purpose 126. 36
war *st. f.* heed war nemen. +*gen.* see,
perceive 83. 31; 96. 18; 113. 2
wār *adj.* true 42. 11
wār *st. n.* truth. für wār indeed 54. 16;
76. 29
wārheit *st. f.* truth 7. 7
warnen *wk. vb.* warn, admonish 39. 19.
st. n. warning 116. 34
warten *wk. vb.* look, watch 5. 2; 120. 8.
+*gen.* watch for, gaze at, wait for 5. 3;
64. 26. *pret.* warte 5. 2, 3
warumbe *interr. adv.* why 45. 7
*wat *see* waz
wāt *st. f.* covering, clothing, garment
70. 28; 78. 11; 120. 9, 17
waz *neut. interr. pron., rel. pron.* what.
adv. why 10. 8; 101. 27. *wat 42. 7. *advbl.*
gen. wes why 10. 10; 21. 26; 82. 22
wazzer *st. n.* water, stream 91. 25
*wē *see* wer
wē *adv.*, wē tuon be painful, harm 14. 2;
22. 3; 47. 16; 89. 28; 121. 41. mir ist
wē nāch I yearn for 1. 8; 126. 22.
interj.+*dat.* alas, woe 32. 1; 94. 8
wec *st. m.* way 126. 10
wecken *wk. vb.* wake 9. 2
weder *pron.* which of two, either 46. 6
*weder *see* wider *and* weter
wegen *st. vb.* weigh 57. 3

wegen *wk. vb.* rock 114. 10
wehsel *st. m.* change, exchange 35. 14;
128. 39; 133. 19
weinen *wk. vb.* weep 9. 9. *st. n.* 66. 12.
geweinen weep for, lament
weise *wk. m.* orphan jewel 92. 11; imperial crown 91. 48
*weit, weiz *see* wizzen
weizgot *interj.* God knows 32. 10
wel(e)n *wk. vb.* choose, seek out 25. 4;
85. 23
welh, welch *interr. pron.* which 160. 10
wellen *anom. vb.* wish. *1st pers. sing.*
wil 10. 5. *wille 41. 23. *3rd pers. pl.*
went *for* wellent 165. 40. niene
welle got God forbid 61. 23
wenden *wk. vb.* turn, apply, bestow,
avert 36. 11; 47. 23; 82. 14. +*acc. pers.*,
gen. thing prevent 58. 16; 116. 38.
intrans. be averted 163. 29. gewenden
121. 21
wēnec *adj., adv.* little. *wēnech 38. 35
wenen *wk. vb.*+*acc. pers., gen. thing*
accustom 89. 8
wenken *wk. vb.* vacillate, waver, escape
35. 16; 112. 3; 137. 9, 17
wer *masc. interr. pron.* who 45. 13.
*sō wē whosoever 42. 1
wer *st. f.* defence, hindrance 131. 2
wer *st. f.* granting 135. 6
werben *st. vb.* execute commission, de-
liver message 19. 5; 90. 1; 121. 43; ply
one's trade 105. 21. +umbe strive for,
woo 20. 5; 28. 2; 122. 28
werc *st. n.* work 78. 10
werdecheit, werdekeit *st. f.* worth,
excellence, esteem 64. 19; 67. 17; 85. 4;
87. 30; 97. 1; 108. 14; 136. 46
werdeclīche *adv.* worthily, excellently
65. 8
werden *st. vb.* become 19. 8; 20. 2;
31. 12. *pp.* worden 69. 15. wert *for*
werdet 126. 21
werfen *st. vb.* throw 124. 27. an wer-
fen+*double acc.* throw at 127. 17
werlīchen *adv.* on the defensive 139. 23
werlt, welt *st. f.* world 3. 1; 21. 19. zer
welte in the world 91. 7. wereltlīch,
weltlīch *adj.* 85. 2; 91. 17
wern *wk. vb.* last 62. 8. +*dat. and
acc., acc., or acc. and gen.* grant 61. 24;
73. 33; 114. 20; 117. 4. gewern 61. 12;
144. 13; 145. 12

wern *wk. vb.* prevent, defend. *refl.+ gen.* **139.** 24

werren *st. vb.* harm, injure, deter **25.** 6; **57.** 11. +*dat.* trouble **101.** 12. **gewerren 45.** 2

wert *adj.* worthy, excellent, esteemed **51.** 4; **57.** 6; **61.** 42; **73.** 21; **82.** 11

wert *st. m.* water meadow **164.** 10

wes *see* **waz**

wesen *anom. vb.* be **40.** 10. *pp.* **gewest 68.** 12. *2nd sing. imp.* **wis 40.** 11. **bī wesen** associate with **89.** 20

*****weten** *see* **wizzen**

weter *st. n.* weather; *pl.* **127.** 1. *****weder 41.** 3

wette *st. n.* payment of debt **109.** 8

*****wīc** *st. m.* hesitation **41.** 18

wīchen *st. vb.* depart **144.** 42

widemen *wk. vb.* dedicate **169.** 5

wider *prep.+acc.* towards, to, against, in exchange for **52.** 13; **86.** 15; **101.** 54. *adv.* again **9.** 11. *****weder 41.** 3

widersagen *wk. vb.* refuse, declare enmity against **74.** 7; **109.** 16; **128.** 31

widerteilen *wk. vb.+dat. pers., acc. thing (a legal term)* deprive of **22.** 24

widervarn *st. vb.* befall **99.** 28

widerwegen *st. vb.* repay **150.** 4

wie *adv.* how **60.** 1. **wiez = wie ez 18.** 8; why **44.** 6. *****wi 39.** 21

wigen *refl. wk. vb.+ūf* apply oneself to **132.** 10

wīhen *wk. vb.* consecrate **110.** 43

wilde *adj.* wild **115.** 7; foreign to **141.** 22

wildeclīch *adj.* wild **157.** 33

wilden *wk. vb.* be foreign to **137.** 23

wīle *st. f.* while. **(al) die wīle (unz)** as long as, while **17.** 5; **44.** 20; **60.** 11; **84.** 22. **der wīle daz** while **160.** 18. **wīlen(t)** *adv.* formerly **39.** 9. **ze kurzen wīlen** for a short time **50.** 12

*****wille** *see* **wellen**

wille *wk. m.* will **50.** 8. **dur dīnen willen** for your sake **27.** 11. **drumbe willen** on that account **41.** 19

willeclīch *adj.* willing **121.** 30. **willeclīchen** *adv.* **62.** 7

willekomen *adj.* welcome **62.** 16

wilt *st. n.* wild animal, game, quarry **137.** 2, 6

win *st. m.* wine **165.** 8

winkeldiupe *wk. f.* secret thief **153.** 6

winken *wk. vb.* beckon **78.** 26

wint *st. m.* wind, scent, nothing **96.** 4; **129.** 1; **137.** 13

winter, winder *st. m.* winter **23.** 4; **123.** 1

wīp, wīb *st. n.* woman, wife **6.** 7; **20.** 1; **101.** 40; **124.** 19

wīpheit *st. f.* womanhood, womanliness **101.** 42

wīplich *adj.* womanly **85.** 8

wipfel *st. m.* tree top **169.** 6

wir *1st pers. pl. pron.* we. *gen.* **unser**

wirde *st. f.* excellence, worth **97.** 15; **108.** 21

wirden *wk. vb.* make excellent **132.** 9

wirt *st. m.* master of the house, host, husband, guardian **94.** 9; **109.** 1; **119.** 19; **137.** 43

wis *see* **wesen**

wise *st., wk. f.* meadow **123.** 9

wīse *adj.* wise, experienced, prudent **68.** 5; **86.** 1

wīsheit *st. f.* wisdom, prudence, savoir-faire **38.** 25; **52.** 25; **71.** 22; **73.** 31; **106.** 1

wīse *st. f.* manner, melody **12.** 5; **71.** 10; **95.** 7

wīsen *wk. vb.* guide **86.** 30

wīt *adj.* wide **121.** 65. **wīte(n)** *adv.* **76.** 2; **124.** 1

witte *st. m.* wood **162.** 16

witze *st. f.* insight, understanding **168.** 9

wīz *adj.* white **70.** 3

wīze *st. f.* purgatory **156.** 20

wīzen *st. vb.* reproach **33.** 12; **66.** 25

wizzen *pret.-pres. vb.* know. *1st, 3rd sing. pres.* **weiz 18.** 7. *****weit 42.** 9. *inf.* *****weten 40.** 6

woche *wk. f.* week **77.** 9

wol *adv.* well, very, indeed **7.** 7; **10.** 16; **20.** 8; **47.** 3. **wol ūf** come then **133.** 26. **sō wol+acc.** *or dat.* (1) *in formulas of praise or blessing* **5.** 5; **25.** 11; **30.** 11; **62.** 31; **67.** 21; (2) farewell **6.** 1. **mir ist wol** I am happy **87.** 17. **wol tuon** be pleasing **89.** 16; make happy (*opp.* **wē tuon**) **89.** 28; **98.** 5. *****wal(e) 39.** 10

wolgemuot *adj.* happy **150.** 8

wolgetān *adj.* beautiful **121.** 56

wolken *st. n.* cloud **63.** 20

wonen *wk. vb.* dwell **37.** 12. **bī wonen** accompany **74.** 3

wort *st. n.* word, text of poem **148.**

wortel, wortelīn *st. n. dimin.* word
61. 28; 111. 2

wüeten *wk. vb.* rave, rage, ravage 86.
24; 111. 4

wunder *st. n.* wonder, marvel, abundance 50. 1; 55. 7; 64. 20; 77. 5; 123. 7.
ez nimt mich wunder I am amazed
86. 17

wunderlīch *adj.* marvellous, strange
89. 17. *adv.* 137. 44

wunderlīche(n) *adv.* 89. 25; 109. 30;
112. 1

wunne, wünne *st. f.* joy 11. 2

wunneclīch, wünneclīch, wunnenclīch joyful, beautiful 71. 30; 84. 5;
165. 35

wunsch *st. m.* wish, perfection 133. 22

wünschen *wk. vb.+gen.* wish 48. 7

wunt *adj.* wounded 38. 24

wuofen *wk. vb.* cry, lament 160. 27

würken *wk. vb.* work, effect 50. 2

wurm *st. m.* worm 154. 12

wurst *st. f.* sausage 165. 12

wurze *st.*, *wk. f.* spice 127. 29

wurzelhaft *adj.* soundly-rooted 169. 4

Z

zāfen *refl. wk. vb.* adorn 122. 22

zāhiu *interj.* 94. 4

zam *adj.* tame 20. 2; 115. 7

zamen *wk. vb.* tame 129. 4. gezamen
15. 3

zar *st. m.* action of wresting, *see* zerren
128. 52

zart *st. m.* charm, allure; pleasing treatment 109. 19

ze *prep.+dat.* to, as 23. 14; 89. 23.
adv. too 52. 35. zediu (*instrumental*)
to the end that 50. 7. *te 38. 13

zeglīch *adj.* cowardly 141. 22

zehant *adv.* straightway 136. 12

zēhe *st.*, *wk. f.* toe 95. 2

zeichen *st. n.* token, sign 78. 36

zeigen *wk. vb.* show 122. 36

zeln *wk. vb.* count 35. 12

zemen *st. vb.* be fitting, suitable 26. 4;
78. 1; 84. 19. gezemen 116. 11. *getemen, *getāme *pret. subj.* 43. 28

zerbrechen *st. vb.* shatter 71. 4

zergān, zergēn *st. vb.* pass away,
perish, vanish 23. 4; 64. 7

zern *wk. vb.* consume, use; administer
167. 13

zerren *wk. vb.* pull, wrest, wrench 123.
27; 128. 46

zerstœren *wk. vb.* destroy 51. 8

zerfüeren *wk. vb.* spoil, disrupt, destroy
28. 4

zesamene *adv.* together 15. 15

zewāre *adv.* indeed 6. 10

ziehen *st. vb.* draw, train, move 15. 1;
162. 21. *refl.+ze* associate with 69. 8.
wol gezogen well-bred 96. 33; 141. 7

ziere *adj.* pleasing, dear 9. 1

zieren *wk. vb.* adorn 37. 14

zīhen *st. vb.+gen.* accuse 52. 1. gezīhen 86. 2

zil *st. n.* goal 80. 16; space of time 120. 6

zinne *st.*, *wk. f.* battlement 12. 2; 117. 1

zins *st. m.* tribute 77. 18

zinsen *wk. vb.* pay tribute 78. 13

zirkel, cirkel *st. m.* crown 91. 46

zīt *st. f.* time 23. 1. *tīt 38. 4

zocken *wk. vb.* pull 134. 8

zol *st. m.* toll 137. 40

zorn *st. m.* anger, dissension, annoyance
54. 3; 84. 3. daz ist mir zorn that
angers me 68. 14; 108. 32. *toren 38.
18

zornic *adj.* angry 126. 47

zucken, zücken *wk. vb.* wrest, pull
126. 41; 134. 8; 153. 13. gezücken
127. 30

zuht *st. f.* discipline, (courtly) good
breeding 63. 2; 86. 22; 113. 18

zühtelōs *adj.* discourteous 88. 45

zünden *wk. vb.* kindle 138. 8

zunder *st. m.* tinder 64. 16

zunge *st.*, *wk. f.* tongue, language,
nation 81. 14; 91. 41; 121. 14

zuo *adv.*, *prep.+dat.* to, at 137. 43.
*tū(t) 38. 4; 40. 3

zürnen *wk. vb.* be angry 73. 23

zwei *card. num. neut.* two 16. 7

zweien *refl. wk. vb.* quarrel 91. 57; pair
122. 6

zwēne *card. num. masc.* two

zwī *st. n.* branch 9. 4

zwieren *wk. vb.* wink 134. 4

zwinken *wk. vb.* wink 134. 4

zwiu *interr. adv.* why, to what purpose
128. 75

zwīvel *st. m.* doubt

zwivellīch *adj.* doubtful 102. 1

zwīvellop *st. n.* doubtful praise 101. 50

zwō *card. num. fem.* two 101. 1

ALPHABETICAL INDEX OF FIRST LINES